13.

Health Care
and Information Ethics

PROTECTING FUNDAMENTAL

HUMAN RIGHTS

Audrey R. Chapman, Editor

where studies results
- re differ from expected,
~~CDA~~ raise questions t
if how data might te
used - partie. how we
might respond when
study of data exposes
things we didn't
expect.

"change of paradigm
threatens many entrenched
interests"

like what to do if
data supports that health of pop'n
would be enhanced more by raising the
socioeconomic status of the poor than
by finding ~~the cure for cancer~~? developing advanced treatment
for cancer, genetic disorders

- what is "health"
- re. lower mortality?
~~fewer~~ better quality
while living?

Sheed & Ward
Kansas City

Sheed & Ward™ is a service of The National Catholic Reporter Publishing Company.

Library of Congress Cataloguing-in-Publication Data
Health care and information ethics : protecting fundamental human rights /
   Audrey R. Chapman, editor.
      p. cm.
   Includes bibliographical references and index.
   ISBN 1-55612-922-X (alk. paper)
   1. Medical records--Moral and ethical aspects. 2. Medical records--Access
control. 3. Health services accessibility--Research--Moral and ethical
aspects. I. Chapman, Audrey R.
   R864.H426 1997
   174'.2--dc21   97-772
                                                  CIP

Published by: Sheed & Ward
               115 E. Armour Blvd.
               P.O. Box 419492
               Kansas City, MO 64141-6492

To order, call: (800) 333-7373

Contents

Appendices

Part One

Background

Developing Health Information Systems Consistent with Human Rights Criteria

Audrey R. Chapman

Major changes are currently taking place in this country's health care system. One significant development is the application of computer technology to facilitate storage of and access to medical records. While researchers and policy makers tend to emphasize the advantages of computerization, such as administrative savings and improved quality of care, the establishment of health care information systems also has wider societal implications that have not been adequately discussed. One concern is the significant challenge that computerized health care information systems pose to the protection and promotion of human rights. Realization of four fundamental human rights norms – universality, privacy, nondiscrimination, and consent – may be profoundly affected by the types of health care databases that are instituted, the manner in which access to the data is regulated, and the way the data are used. Fostering human rights objectives and reducing the possibility of human rights abuses in the implementation of these new information systems will require careful design and regulation. These issues are the focus of this volume.

More specifically, this volume explores ways to utilize health care information systems to monitor the status of underserved and disadvantaged communities, while also protecting privacy and nondiscrimination and enabling individuals to have greater control over the uses made of their health care data. In so doing, the study addresses a fundamental dilemma: human rights considerations seemingly impose contradictory requirements for health care information systems. On the one hand, achievement of greater universality in access to basic health care requires careful monitoring of the availability of health care services to the entire population. From a human rights perspective, it is particularly important to track vulnerable, disadvantaged and hitherto excluded or underserved individuals and groups, such as homeless persons, migrant workers and their families, the poor, legal and undocumented immigrants, and ethnic and racial minorities, in order to identify and address problems and obstacles to their receiving health care. To be able to undertake such systematic and ongoing monitoring, researchers need considerable amounts of good quality and appropriate data and the ability to link data sources. On the other hand, rights to privacy and nondiscrimination presume legal and regulatory restrictions on the manner in which data are collected, linked, and applied, as well as strict limitations on access to data. Assuring that data collection and application are consistent with the requirements of the principle of consent also imposes restrictions that can inhibit research.

It is the thesis of this study that electronic health care information systems both offer new opportunities for monitoring access to health care and impose additional challenges for protecting human rights. While computerization of health care data will facilitate many types of research, it will not necessarily confer new capabilities for monitoring the health care status or health care access of vulnerable, disadvantaged, and underserved populations. The first half of this volume will assess the limitations of current data sources and propose new approaches, methodologies, and types of research initiatives. While all health care information systems, paper as well as electronic files, pose risks of the invasion of privacy and the use of data in ways that are harmful to subjects, computerization, particularly in a fragmented and unregulated environment, significantly complicates the situation. The authors in the second half of the volume will consider these problems and propose ways to build human rights protections into the design of health care information systems.

This study is an outgrowth of a previous project sponsored by the Science and Human Rights Program of the American Association for the Advancement of Science (AAAS), with the assistance of the Robert Wood Johnson Foundation, to explore the implications of recognizing access to a basic and adequate standard of health care as a right and to assess the benefits and problems of doing so.[1] That project proposed recognition of a

---

1.   See Audrey R. Chapman, *Exploring a Human Rights Approach to Health Care Reform* (Washington, D.C.: AAAS, 1993). Also see Audrey R. Chapman, ed., *Health Care Reform: A Human Rights Approach* (Washington, D.C.: Georgetown University Press, 1994).

right to a basic and adequate standard of health care consistent with a particular society's level of resources. The human rights approach to health care reform which the project advocated, if adopted, would vest governments with the responsibility to monitor patterns of health care access so as to use these data to undertake appropriate revisions in public policies to achieve greater universality of access. After surveying existing data sources in the United States, however, the project concluded that current data were inadequate for this purpose and that systematic and ongoing monitoring would require new approaches and methodologies.

When this study was begun in early 1994, policy makers at the federal level were considering reform of the health care system, and expansion of access to basic health care seemed likely. A major goal of the project was to contribute to the development of a truly universal health care information system able to monitor the implementation of health care reform across all sectors of the population. To do so, the project sought to identify methodologies for tracking the availability of and access to health care of underserved and disadvantaged populations. The project affirmed the need to assure that all forms of monitoring be consistent with human rights principles, but assumed that there were a variety of approaches that could reconcile a commitment to additional data collection with protections for privacy, nondiscrimination, and consent. It even seemed likely that legislation would be adopted in conjunction with health care reform to set appropriate standards for a national health information system and institute safeguards to diminish the risks of the inappropriate use of health care data.

However, the policy environment changed dramatically during the life of the project, and public support for expanding access to health care declined. The new dynamic was to reduce government budgets, particularly by cutting health and welfare expenditures, eliminating entitlements, and transferring responsibility for health and welfare programs from the federal to the state level. At least in the short term, it seems more likely that the primary use of improved monitoring capabilities will be to assess the impact of significant reductions in Medicaid and Medicare outlays on vulnerable and disadvantaged groups rather than to expand access to health care. Moreover, as will be discussed later in this chapter, the current political context makes it even more difficult to reconcile and balance informational needs with the protection of privacy and nondiscrimination.

Information Revolution in the Health Care Sector

The information revolution in the health care sector is well underway. Medical records, hitherto in paper files, are now being transferred to electronic form in a uniform format and stored in computerized databases, enabling files to be easily expanded, updated, and retrieved for various purposes. Databases maintained by providers and health care institutions are being linked. Health care providers and institutions anticipate significant benefits from computerization. A 1991 Institute of Medicine report on *The Computer-Based Patient Record* argues, for example, that computerization of patient records, development of high-performance health information networks, and adoption of technologies that permit the electronic storage, transmission, and display of medical data will improve the quality of patient care, advance the science of medicine, lower health care costs, and enhance the education of health care professionals.[2]

Health care database organizations are currently being set up that facilitate the collection and maintenance of a greater range of health care information. Some 40 states have already established data organizations, which are agencies mandated to collect and maintain data on individuals' hospital experience. There are also major private sector computerized health care databases. The Medical Information Bureau, supported by 700 U.S. and Canadian life insurance companies, has information on file for about 15 million persons in these two countries. The U.S.-based Physician Computer Network, Inc. operates a national, interactive communications network which links its 2,000 office-based physician members to a variety of health care organizations, including hospitals, clinical laboratories, managed care providers, insurance carriers, and pharmaceutical companies. It also acts as a computer gateway to financial management services.[3] Several proposals for health care reform envision the development of comprehensive, electronic "cradle to grave" medical files on every individual in the United States covered by health insurance.[4]

---

2. Institute of Medicine, *The Computer-Based Patient Record: An Essential Technology for Health Care*, eds. Richard S. Dick and Elaine B. Steen (Washington, D.C.: National Academy Press, 1991), 24.

3. Office of Technology Assessment, *Protecting Privacy in Computerized Medical Information* (Washington, D.C.: U.S. Government Printing Office, 1993), 32-33.

4. Sheri Alpert, "Smart Cards, Smarter Policy: Medical Records, Privacy, and Health Care Reform," *Hastings Center Report 23* (November-December 1993): 14.

The creation of comprehensive, population-based (geographic) health care databases is likely to be the next stage of the health care information revolution. It is anticipated that these inclusive databases will provide health care data for several purposes: to improve the quality of care in a variety of health care settings; to assess the health of the public; to analyze patterns of illness and injury; to document unmet regional health needs; to ascertain patterns of health care expenditures, including those which are inappropriate, wasteful, or potentially harmful; and to identify cost-effective health care providers.[5] According to a 1994 Institute of Medicine study committee, "The more comprehensive or inclusive (or both), the more powerful the information will be at every level and for every potential user and use."[6]

[handwritten: good things]

However, it must be recognized that the potential benefits of inclusive and comprehensive health care databases will depend on the quality and appropriateness of the information they contain. Articles in this volume point out that records created primarily for payment and management purposes cannot always be counted on to give accurate diagnostic information. Moreover, as will be discussed at many points in this volume, current databases do not adequately cover the status of vulnerable, disadvantaged, and underserved groups.

Human Rights Issues

The establishment of computerized health care information systems has significant human rights implications. Decisions currently being made about the types and formats of databases, the manner in which they will be linked, the persons and organizations that will have access to the information, and the uses to which the data may be applied will determine whether the operation and impact of various health care information systems will be consistent with human rights principles. Protection and promotion of four fundamental human rights norms – universality, privacy, nondiscrimination, and consent – will depend upon efforts to address human rights concerns in all stages of the computerization of health care data. Unless

---

5. Committee on Regional Health Data Networks, Institute of Medicine, *Health Data in the Information Age: Use, Disclosure, and Privacy*, eds. Molla S. Donaldson and Kathleen N. Lohr (Washington, D.C.: National Academy Press, 1994), 1.

6. *Ibid.,* 61.

effective human rights safeguards are instituted, it will not be possible to prevent human rights violations or the misuse of the data in ways which are detrimental to data subjects. The possibility of realizing human rights objectives through health care information systems will also require careful design and regulation.

Why does it matter that health care information systems be consistent with human rights principles? There are three reasons, the first of which is the importance accorded to human rights as an expression of human dignity and worth. In the late 20th century, human rights represent the common heritage, aspiration, and standard of achievement for all peoples and all nations. Rights in moral philosophy and political theory are understood as an entitlement a person possesses to some goods, service, or liberty. Human rights are the claims each person has by virtue of her/his common humanity. As such, human rights are viewed as setting the basic norms necessary for a decent human life.

Secondly, the United States has a rights-based political culture. Americans frame their strongest moral claims and expectations in the language of rights. Rights express the ethical and normative foundations of our society. At times the rights orientation in this country, which is far greater than in other Western democracies, can be problematic. As a number of critics have observed, it contributes to an imbalance between rights and responsibilities.[7] Nevertheless, a rights orientation can also make a significant contribution by posing a bulwark to invasions against human dignity and the imposition of new forms of oppression. Although Americans tend to think of rights in terms of protection from intrusion by government or interference by other individuals, in the late 20th century threats to freedom and abuses of human rights may also come from many types of institutions and technologies and affect groups as well as persons.

Thirdly, the United States' government has approved or ratified a number of international human rights instruments, and thereby agreed to abide by their provisions. The United States was among the governments represented in the United Nations General Assembly when it unanimously approved the *Universal Declaration of Human Rights* in December 1948. Subsequently, the U.S. Senate has ratified a series of international human rights instruments based on the *Universal Declaration,* and thereby become a state party. As a state party, this country has an international legal

---

7.   See for example, Mary Ann Glendon, *Rights Talk: The Impoverishment of Political Discourse* (New York: The Free Press, 1991).

obligation to implement four of these conventions: the *International Covenant on Civil and Political Rights;* the International Convention on the Elimination of All Forms of Racial Discrimination; the Convention Against Torture and Other Cruel, Inhuman or Degrading Treatment or Punishment; and the Convention on the Prevention and Punishment of the Crime of Genocide. It should be noted, however, that the United States has not ratified the convention which enumerates a right to health care, the International Covenant on Economic, Social and Cultural Rights. Nor is it likely to do so in the near future.[8]

a. The Universality of Human Rights and Universal Health Care Coverage

Because human rights are predicated on the recognition of the intrinsic value and worth of all human beings, human rights are considered to be universal. Universality means that human rights are vested equally in all persons regardless of their gender, race, nationality, economic status, or social position. Applied to the health sector, the principle of universality underscores that all persons, without regard to their purchasing power, social status, or personal merit, are entitled to basic health care. The achievement of universality of access to health care, or at least significant progress in this direction, was a goal of many of the proposals put forward during the 1993-94 U.S. national debate on health care reform.

Because a human right is a universal entitlement, its implementation is evaluated particularly by the degree it benefits those who hitherto have been the most disadvantaged. The absence of universal health care access in this country confers a special obligation to monitor the status of the groups most affected by the legacy of unequal access to health care.[9] Systematic and ongoing monitoring is a prerequisite to formulating appropriate policies to promote universality. Even in the absence of a commitment to expanding access to health care, a human rights approach requires that all health care policies be evaluated in terms of their impact on vulnerable individuals and groups.

---

8.   Nevertheless, Article 25 of the *Universal Declaration of Human Rights* proclaims every individual's right to a standard of living adequate for the health and well-being of themselves and their families, which includes medical care and necessary social services. *Universal Declaration of Human Rights,* adopted and proclaimed by United Nations General Assembly resolution 217 A (III) on 10 December 1948.

9.   Chapman, *Exploring a Human Rights Approach,* 25-26.

Despite the highest levels of health spending in the world, some 41 million Americans, about one-sixth of the population, do not have basic health insurance coverage. Given the impetus in Congress and many state governments toward reducing expenditures on Medicaid, Medicare and welfare, these figures are likely to continue to rise. In this country, the absence of health insurance frequently translates into an inability to obtain timely and appropriate health care. Moreover, low-income Americans and ethnic minorities, particularly blacks, Hispanics, and native Americans, are far more likely than other groups to be without adequate health insurance.[10] There are also data indicating that the quality of care may vary along racial and economic lines. For example, according to one study, black and poor Medicare patients receive worse care than other acutely ill Medicare patients at some hospitals.[11]

More comprehensive and better quality information collected from health care information systems could enable researchers to better understand current impediments to access to health care and to evaluate the impact of policy changes on specific regions and communities. Assuming that there is a political will to do so, successful design and implementation of reforms to achieve greater universality in the United States' health care system would require careful tracking of health status, use of health care services, and health-related behavior of the population, particularly of disadvantaged and underserved groups.

However, at least in the short term, it will be a higher priority for researchers to track the effects of reductions in health care expenditures and the elimination of entitlements. The shift of responsibility for the provision of health care and welfare to the states has been lauded as a way to encourage innovative and different policy approaches. The Personal Responsibility and Work Opportunity Reconciliation Act of 1996 – welfare reform – makes it even more important to be able to assess the relative strengths and weaknesses of states' health care policies.

Current indicators and statistical data, however, have major limitations that will have to be overcome before it will be possible to undertake systematic and ongoing monitoring for any purpose. A 1993 consultation

---

10. Institute of Medicine, *Access to Health Care in America*, ed. Michael Millman (Washington, D.C.: National Academy Press, 1993), 19.
11. Katherine L. Kahn et al., "Health Care for Black and Poor Hospitalized Medicare Patients," *The Journal of the American Medical Association* 271, no. 15 (1994): 1169-74.

held by AAAS identified the following inadequacies: (1) most indicators cover personal health services; additional population-based health status indicators need to be identified and used; (2) even the largest of the national surveys cannot be disaggregated to small ethnic groups, and none of these surveys can make estimates for the homeless or migratory workers; (3) the current multiple-year time lag between designing surveys, collecting data, and obtaining results makes it difficult to have timely data for purposes of adjusting public policies.[12] Carefully designed research studies utilizing more comprehensive data from health care information systems have the potential to compensate for at least some of these deficiencies and thereby contribute to reforming the United States' health care system to move closer towards universal coverage.

Several of the groups of particular concern to those with a human rights orientation are unlikely to be adequately covered by the medical databases currently maintained by providers and insurers, or by health information systems and proposed databases intended to evaluate the health needs and quality of care received by insured patients. Record systems are likely to cover users of medical care services, not those who do not have access to services. Additionally, as several of the articles in this volume point out, minority and special needs populations who are represented in various health care databases often are not identified accurately in terms of their backgrounds or needs.

Moreover, traditional sources of data for monitoring adequate access to health care in the United States have a limited ability to provide information sufficient to monitor vulnerable population groups. For example, current survey sampling strategies do not provide sufficient sample size to permit estimation of health indicators for many such groups. In most surveys, information identifying individuals as members of underserved groups are either not collected or collected unsystematically. Evaluations of the health status of the homeless, migrant workers, and undocumented aliens are particularly problematic. Almost all surveys of the general population rely on sampling housing units, so the homeless are omitted and migrant workers are not fully covered. Surveys which are conducted over the telephone exclude those too poor to afford telephone service. Undocumented immigrants are likely to be "hidden" from the health information system by misrepresentation of their status or by their exclusion from the sample.

---

12. Chapman, *Exploring a Human Rights Approach*, 51-52.

Thus the establishment of electronic health care information systems will not automatically provide data relevant to understanding the health status of underserved and vulnerable groups and the barriers to their receiving health care coverage. Monitoring these communities on a systematic basis will require more and different types of data than are currently available, and the ability to link various data sets. It will also necessitate developing special databases and research projects that supplement and complement the data that are now collected at the point of treatment or as the by-product of care. Strategies for enumerating and sampling migrant and homeless populations must address both the geographic and definitional mobility of these populations. Assuming that strategies are devised to accurately estimate and sample these populations, several potential problems relating to data quality must also be overcome, including the reluctance that members of some of these groups may have to providing information to persons regarded as official representatives of the government, lack of facility with the English language, and, among the homeless, the high prevalence of mental illness, alcoholism, and illicit drug use.

b. *Threats to Privacy, Nondiscrimination, and Consent*

While a computerized health care information system may facilitate progress toward universality, it also poses risks to the protection of privacy and nondiscrimination, two other fundamental human rights norms. Computerization will increase problems of maintaining the privacy and confidentiality of sensitive personal information contained in medical records and preventing their use for purposes that disadvantage the data subject. The right to protection against arbitrary interference with privacy is enumerated in the *Universal Declaration of Human Rights* and several subsequent international human rights instruments, including the *International Covenant on Civil and Political Rights.*[13] Similarly nondiscrimination, together with equality before the law and equal protection of the law

---

13. The *Universal Declaration of Human Rights* states: "No one shall be subjected to arbitrary interference with his privacy, family, home or correspondence. . . . Everyone has the right to the protection of the law against such interference. . ." *Universal Declaration of Human Rights,* Article 12. Article 17 of the *International Covenant on Civil and Political Rights* contains similar guarantees regarding privacy. *International Covenant on Civil and Political Rights,* adopted and opened for signature, ratification and accession by United Nations General Assembly resolution 2200 A (XXI) on 16 December 1966. Entered into force on 23 March 1976 in accordance with article 49.

without any discrimination, constitutes a basic and general principle central to the realization of human rights.[14]

Privacy considerations are important because medical records contain sensitive information about some of the most intimate aspects of an individual's life. Medical records include details of family and personal history of diseases and treatment, genetic and other types of diagnostic testing, sexual orientation and practices, behavioral patterns, mental state, and patterns of drug use. In addition to objective observations, diagnoses, and test results, medical records may also include subjective inferences made by health care providers, such as impressions of mental abilities and suppositions about lifestyle, including sexual practices and function.

An electronic medical record will also make it possible to link diverse sources so as to have far more extensive data on each patient. Computerization facilitates linking and cross-referencing medical information with other types of records, like financial and credit history, through the use of identifiers, such as name, social security number, and address. Many of the proposals for comprehensive health databases include provisions for establishing a patient identification numbering scheme to easily track encounter data, as well as health cards (similar to credit cards) to access standard items of patient information. Some of the proposals call for the mandatory use of the social security number as the patient identifier. Several recommend the introduction of "smart" cards which would contain a computer chip capable of storing and processing several hundred pages of medical information. Use of a unique patient identifier would enable providers and treatment facilities to integrate data so as to compile a comprehensive longitudinal profile of an individual: a cradle-to-grave view of a patient's health care history.[15] While the availability of these data may facilitate the provision of quality health care delivery and enable researchers to undertake many significant projects, they may also be used for purposes that constitute an invasion of privacy and jeopardize the interests of the person to whom the data relate.

The establishment of computerized health information systems is likely to weaken existing privacy protection and increase risks of the unauthorized

---

14. All individuals are entitled to the rights enumerated in the *Universal Declaration* without distinction of any kind, such as race, color, sex, language, religion, political or other opinion, national or social origin, property, birth or other status. *Universal Declaration of Human Rights,* Article 2.

15. Office of Technology Assessment, *Protecting Privacy,* 8-9.

collection, exchange, and use of information in ways that were not anticipated by the person who provided the data.[16] Although all health care
information systems, both paper and computer, pose privacy and confidentiality problems, electronic storage and computerization raise new issues
and may aggravate existing problems. A 1993 study conducted by the
Office of Technology Assessment on *Protecting Privacy in Computerized
Medical Information* identified the following concerns:

- Because computerization permits the storage of a very large amount
  of data in a small space, an intruder who gains access to electronic
  records can obtain far more data than could be stolen on paper
  records;

- With computerization there is the possibility of "invisible theft,"
  stealing data without taking anything physically, making it difficult
  for patients and providers to detect intrusion;

- Computer systems enable a large number of people to handle or have
  access to information, increasing the potential for surreptitious modification, deletion, copying, or addition of data;

- Computer technology makes possible the linking of data sets that
  were not intended to be collated;

- The computer's ability to transmit large volumes of data instantane-
  ously makes the dissemination of private information easy and inexpensive, thereby spurring increased demands for use of medication
  information by secondary users that employ medical records for
  purposes not directly involved in providing health care, paying for
  it, or assuring its proper delivery.[17]

At the heart of these concerns lies the fact that computerization is
facilitating the access to and application of medical data for non-health
related purposes. Three groups currently have access to medical records.
The first are medical professionals involved in direct patient care. In an era
of specialization and extensive testing, these include doctors' offices,
clinics, hospitals, nursing homes, free-standing surgical centers, and institutional services. The second group are those who pay for medical care,
sometimes referred to as third-party payers, including both private insurance companies and government programs like Medicare and Medicaid, as

---

16. *Ibid.,* 37.

17. *Ibid.,* 15-16, 47.

well as hospitals and outside monitoring agencies that conduct utilization reviews to determine how facilities are being used. The third group are those employing medical data for an extensive range of non-health care related social purposes. One important social or secondary use of these data is medical and social research and public health reporting. Beyond the research community, medical data are also employed for non-health care uses by employers, licensing agencies, credentializing agencies, educational institutions, insurance companies, and rehabilitation and social welfare programs. According to the Office of Technology Assessment, information in medical records is already being used to determine whether people are hired or fired, whether they can secure health and life insurance, whether they are permitted to drive cars, and whether they are placed under police surveillance or labelled as security risks.[18] Moreover, the establishment of comprehensive health information systems is likely to accelerate even further the application of medical information for nonmedical purposes.

Because the United States, unlike other industrialized democracies, does not provide universal health insurance or assure universal access to health care through a national health system, the availability of more extensive health data has quite different implications than it might in those other countries. To cope with financial pressures and, in the case of for-profit health insurance corporations, to maintain profitability, health insurers have decreased the availability of community-rated insurance, under which anyone who applies for coverage is accepted, and instituted experience ratings, under which those deemed high risk for coverage are excluded. These policies have rendered an increasing proportion of the population "medically uninsurable," as insurers deny coverage both for numerous preexisting conditions and for those considered likely to develop such conditions, no matter how minimal the risk. As medical tests identifying genetic predispositions to various diseases and health conditions are further developed, and computerization makes it more difficult to assure privacy of these data, it may become even more difficult to obtain secure and reasonably priced health insurance.[19] Unless and until there are legislative remedies to the insurance crisis, the information revolution is likely to worsen this situation.

---

18. *Ibid.,* 47-48.

19. Chapman, *Exploring a Human Rights Approach,* 4.

Rising health insurance costs have led many large firms to self-insure in order to save the cost of insurance commissions, overhead, and profits, and to obtain the economic benefits gained by investing large reserves for this coverage. Estimates are that 74% or more of employers of 1,000 or more employees manage self-insurance plans.[20] Under the self-insurance model, an employer assumes the risk of health care coverage of employees and usually pays a provider to process claims. The current trend is for employers to evaluate the medical records of applicants and employees to identify higher-risk individuals in order to reduce the costs of medical, disability, and pension claims.[21] Often members of applicants' and employees' families are also screened. Even when claims are being handled by third-party administrators, self-insured employers are frequently given access to patient-identified health claims information. Some third-party administrators provide corporate human resources personnel with dial-in-capability to perform their own analyses of data relating to a firm's employees and dependents.[22]

Moreover, few legal barriers exist to an employer's use of its employees' medical and insurance claims records, particularly for self-insurance plans. Because employers' self-insurance plans fall under the federal Employment Retirement Insurance Security Act (ERISA), they are exempted from state-level insurance laws, confidentiality requirements, and protections. As noted below, applicable federal protections are inadequate.

The increasing availability of medical information has had the effect that more individuals and groups of people are being penalized on medical grounds, often without sufficient medical justification, and frequently without legal recourse. Moreover, unless programs that provide audit trails are instituted, computerization will eliminate a paper trail, potentially making it even more difficult to gather appropriate evidence to show that decisions to hire or fire have been based on medical data. In the case of large companies which self-insure, for example, few of the prospective and current employees who are being screened out to reduce potential risks have

---

20. Committee on Regional Health Data Networks, *Health Data in the Information Age*, 78.

21. H. Jeff Smith, "Medical Data and the Dangerous Triad: Employees, Employers, and Health Insurance," (background paper written for AAAS project on the human rights implications of health care information systems, Washington, D.C., March 1995).

22. Committee on Regional Health Data Networks, *Health Data in the Information Age*, 152, 159.

actual disabilities which inhibit them from fulfilling their job responsibilities. Most of them are asymptomatic or presymptomatic, that is, they merely have a statistically higher probability of having specific health problems. Depriving these individuals of access to insurance or credit, reducing their employability, and using medical records as a basis for surveillance, usually without sufficient warrant, fits most definitions of discrimination.

Because there are few protections in this country to assure that information technologies operate in a manner consistent with human rights principles, problems that preceded computerization are likely to be aggravated by the widespread use of electronic technologies. Reflecting on this situation, the Office of Technology Assessment concluded that:

> Legal and ethical principles currently available to guide the health care industry with respect to obligations to protect the confidentiality of patient information are inadequate to address privacy issues in a computerized environment that allows for intra- and interstate exchange of information for research, insurance and patient care purposes. Lack of legislation in this area will leave the health care industry with little sense as to their responsibilities for maintaining confidentiality. It also allows for a proliferation of private sector computer databases and data exchanges without regulation, statutory guidance, or recourse for persons wronged by abuse of data.[23]

There are few effective legal barriers to private health information being used in ways which disadvantage or discriminate against the persons from whom the data were collected. Under existing law it is legal for health data to be employed for various non-health related applications, such as employment decisions, court surveillance, or insurance evaluations. Even the Americans With Disabilities Act (ADA) of 1990 does not preclude access to and use of medical data for most of these evaluative determinations. The ADA merely bans the use of medical information as the sole basis of employment decisions. It does not prevent employers from utilizing medical information as a factor in decisions related to the hiring, firing, demoting, or not promoting employees. Although the ADA can be interpreted to prohibit discrimination against people with a genetic disorder who are asymptomatic or presymptomatic, the extent of the ADA protection is unclear. In March 1995, the Equal Employment Opportunity Commission

---

23. Office of Technology Assessment, *Protecting Privacy*, 44.

(EEOC) issued a new section to its Compliance Manual (which implements the employment provisions of ADA), concluding that employers may not discriminate against someone in employment decisions solely on the basis of genetic information relating to illness, disease, or other disorders. However, these guidelines do not have the force of law. Nor does the EEOC's interpretation address the question of whether insurance companies may deny providing health insurance to persons with genetic vulnerability to specific diseases. Hence the determination of the scope of the ADA protection against discrimination based on genetic determination will be resolved only after relevant lawsuits are decided by the courts.[24]

c. *Other Rights Challenges in the United States*

Computerization also raises troubling issues about the adequacy of consent and disclosure procedures related to the use of medical information. The principle of consent is implicit in notions of human dignity and individual autonomy at the root of human rights. Informed consent is also one of the most important ethical norms governing medical practice in this country. From an institutional point of view, informed consent is often understood primarily in terms of the obligation to provide patients with sufficient and accurate information to enable them to make genuinely informed and voluntary decisions about their health care.[25] When applied to health care information systems, consent requires that a data subject have meaningful control over the dissemination and applications of their own health care data. At a minimum this means that a patient is familiar with the data contained in her/his record, understands the implications of signing forms that authorize uses of the data, and explicitly agrees to the release of sensitive data for some purposes that may disadvantage the person. It also necessitates a system of notification be put in place to inform individuals about pending uses of their data. None of these criteria are presently being met. Many patients are neither granted access to their medical records nor apprised of which portions are accessible to others and for what applications. Computerization, by increasing the comprehensiveness and ease of access to the medical data stored, is likely to aggravate the problem by making it more difficult for patients to keep track of the full range of their data.

---

24. Joseph S. Alper, "Does the ADA Provide Protection Against Discrimination on the Basis of Genotype?" *Journal of Law, Medicine & Ethics* 23 (1995): 167-172.
25. *Ibid.,* 85-87.

Existing laws in this country offer little real protection against redisclosure of confidential health information without the consent of the data source, and computerization makes it technically more feasible for data to be widely shared. Secondary users rarely have the explicit consent of the source of the data. Typically, patients entering health care facilities are given blanket consent forms to sign, which state that a facility may release medical information concerning the patient to anyone it believes should have it or to named agencies or organizations. In granting blanket advance consent, patients are neither clearly informed about the potential uses of their data nor able to scrutinize, evaluate, or authorize specific applications. Unless there is legal and regulatory reform, even those patients who refuse to sign blanket consent forms will lack the ability to control the uses of their data. Once patients have consented to an initial disclosure of information, for instance to obtain insurance reimbursement, they lose control of further disclosure for unrelated purposes. Moreover, even if laws were strengthened, it would still be difficult to pursue legal remedies. As noted above, the use of electronic technologies makes it difficult for an individual to discover that a particular disclosure has occurred, let alone to prove that the medical data were the source of a decision that has adverse consequences.[26]

While the development of health care information systems poses risks of invasions of privacy and the use of medical data for unauthorized purposes in all countries, it offers particularly difficult challenges in the United States. Other countries experiencing a revolution in information technologies tend to have more uniform and comprehensive legal and regulatory protections in place. Unlike most other industrialized countries, the United States is not pursuing a centralist and coordinated approach to the computerization of health care information.[27] The U.S. information revolution is taking place in a decentralized, fragmented, unregulated environment. Only a few states have adopted laws to protect medical records, and these vary in scope and applicability, sometimes even within the state, depending on the source and type of data. Unlike paper-based records, information in a computerized system will regularly cross state lines, and doing so will be subject to inconsistent legal standards with

---

26. *Ibid.,* 152.

27. Simon Davies, "The Information Revolution in Health Care: New Threats to Privacy," *The International Privacy Bulletin* 2 (January-March 1994): 1.

respect to privacy. Where there are state laws imposing strict privacy and confidentiality standards on data when they cross state lines, for example hospital discharge records, it will be more difficult to ensure their implementation in a computerized environment.

The Office of Technology Assessment evaluates the situation in this country as follows:

> The present system of protection for health care information offers a patchwork of codes; State laws of varying scope; and Federal laws applicable to only limited kinds of information, or information maintained specifically by the Federal Government. The present legal scheme does not provide consistent, comprehensive protection for privacy in health information, whether it exists in a paper or computerized environment.[28]

The Office of Technology Assessment goes on to observe that, as a result of the development of computerized information systems, "the limited protection to privacy of health care information now in place will be further strained. Existing models for data protection, which place responsibility for privacy on individual institutions, will no longer be workable for new systems of computer linkage and exchange of information across high-performance, interactive networks."[29] As noted, the existing legal patchwork does not address many of the significant issues that computerization of medical information pose. The absence of legislation regulating the operation of private sector businesses dealing in computer databases and data exchanges of patient information is particularly problematic because there is no guidance about the responsibilities of secondary users and no recourse for persons who believe they have been wronged by the misuse of data.[30]

Another feature that sets the U.S. apart from most other countries is the amount of personal medical information that is freely available in the private sector for non-health related purposes and the extent to which these data are a valuable commodity. Information brokers gather medical information, process it, and sell the data to insurers, risk assessors, and employers.[31] Some companies obtain information from physicians' computers and

---

28. Office of Technology Assessment, *Protecting Privacy*, 12-13.

29. *Ibid.,* 9-10.

30. *Ibid.,* 15.

31. Davies, "The Information Revolution in Health Care," 13.

pharmacy records, in return for incentives such as low-cost computer hardware and software, and resell the data. Other companies resell information from prescriptions or claims databases. As a sign of things to come, in 1993, Merck & Company purchased Medco Containment Services, a mail-order prescription firm, so as to be able to access its databases to influence physician-prescribing practices.[32] In 1995, Eli Lilly acquired PCS Health Systems so as to be able to access its database of 56 million patients in order to encourage physicians to prescribe Lilly products.[33] It will be very difficult for the directors of future regional health care database organizations to resist reaping economic benefits from allowing access to their data files by third parties.[34]

As noted above, the United States is also the only major industrialized society without a commitment to universal health care or the public underwriting of health care insurance for the entire population. All other major industrialized countries have ratified the *International Covenant on Economic, Social and Cultural Rights,* which recognizes a right to health care.[35] In countries where there is universal access to health care, health information systems tend to cover the entire population. Moreover, universal health insurance reduces incentives to use medical data to lower health insurance risk or for employers to screen prospective and current employees.

Thus the unique situation in this country links realization of the four human rights principles of universality, privacy, nondiscrimination and consent in distinctive ways. While computerized health information systems can potentially provide valuable data for health care reforms designed to achieve greater universality, the development of computerized databases may have the opposite consequence and render access to health care system even more regressive. Given the high cost of health care, private insurers providing traditional, indemnity-based insurance have incentives to lower their risks. Medical insurers will now have new sources of data and ana-

32. Committee on Regional Health Database Networks, *Health Data in the Information Age,* 142.

33. "Eli Lilly Plans to Use PCS Unit's Database to Boost Drug Sales," *The Wall Street Journal,* 11 May 1995 (Dow Jones & Co, Inc. AllNews Plus Database).

34. Committee on Regional Health Database Networks, *Health Data in the Information Age,* 141-42.

35. The 130 state parties that have acceded to the *International Covenant on Economic, Social and Cultural Rights* include Canada, Britain, France, Germany, the Netherlands, Italy, Japan, Russia, and the Scandinavian countries.

lytical tools to assess applicants and reduce risk pools. Unless comprehensive reforms are undertaken to protect privacy, the establishment of a computerized information system may itself deter access to available health services. Finally, the fact that much or all of an individual's most sensitive data may be easily accessed by secondary users may render some patients reluctant to seek care.

In the current political climate the willingness to make a commitment even to the gradual achievement of universality of access to health care appears to be waning and the possibility that data will be used for purposes detrimental to the interests of data subjects is increasing. The passage of Proposition 187 in California, and proposals for imposing significant cutbacks in welfare, Medicaid and Medicare at both the federal and state level point to prospects that, at least in the short term, data from health information systems may be used to limit rather than expand the coverage of the health care system. Currently underserved, excluded, and disadvantaged individuals and groups, responding to a national compassion fatigue bordering on political vindictiveness toward the poor and immigrants, may be reluctant to provide sensitive data about themselves. As middle-class patients become more aware of the potential secondary uses of their health data, they too may be less forthcoming with information that could have an adverse impact on their lives.

Although several studies of privacy issues distinguish between access to data for appropriate statistical research and other questionable uses of data, strengthening the privacy, nondiscrimination, and consent protections governing the health care information system may be a precondition to obtaining accurate and good quality data for any purpose. Protection of the privacy of medical and health records is a prerequisite for trust in the health care delivery system. Testifying to the U.S. Privacy Commission in 1977 on the importance of patients being free of the fear of improper disclosure, the American Medical Association commented that, "Patients would be reluctant to tell their physicians certain types of information, which they need to know in order to render appropriate care, if patients did not feel that such information would remain confidential."[36] The AMA Code of Medical Ethics states that, "The confidentiality of physician-patient communications is desirable to assure free and open disclosure by the patient to the physician of all information needed to establish a proper diagnosis

---

36. Quoted in Office of Technology Assessment, *Protecting Privacy*, 30.

and attain the most desirable clinical outcome possible. Protecting the confidentiality of the personal and medical information in such medical records is also necessary to prevent humiliation, embarrassment, or discomfort of patients."[37]

Moreover, even if more comprehensive legal protections are enacted, legislative reforms by themselves will not assure promotion of human rights standards. Effective implementation of any protections will also require that individuals be informed about the potential for abuses arising from a computerized health information system, their relevant rights and responsibilities, and the means by which they can seek recourse if their rights are abused. Historically, human rights have been claimed from below, not granted from above.

The American Association for the Advancement of Science Project

This overview of the issues that the establishment of health care information systems poses for human rights underscores the need to analyze the problems and develop solutions in a comprehensive human rights framework. There have been several important studies focusing on protecting privacy and confidentiality of computerized medical information, but none of these projects has explored the impact of health information systems in a wider human rights context. *Private Lives and Public Policies*, a 1993 report of the Federal Panel on Confidentiality and Data Access, sought to develop recommendations that could aid federal statistical agencies in their stewardship of data for policy decisions and research. Three areas were of paramount concern to the Panel: protecting the interests of data subjects through procedures that ensure privacy and confidentiality; enhancing public confidence in the integrity of statistical and research data; and facilitating the responsible dissemination of data.[38] The 1993 Office of Technology Assessment report *Protecting Privacy in Computerized Medical Information*, referred to extensively above, examines three topics as well: the nature of the privacy interest in health care information and the

---

37. *Ibid.*

38. Panel on Confidentiality and Data Access, *Private Lives and Public Policies: Confidentiality and Accessibility of Government Statistics* (Washington, D.C.: National Academy Press, 1993).

current state of the law protecting that information; various proposals to computerize health information and the technologies available to both computerize and protect the privacy of information; and models for protection of health care information.[39] *Health Data in the Information Age*, produced by the Institute of Medicine's Committee on Regional Health Data Networks in 1994, examined the potential improvements to the health of individuals and the performance of health care systems offered by existing and emerging health database organizations. In that context, it offered recommendations related to the public disclosure of quality-of-care information and the protection of the confidentiality of personal health information.[40]

As noted earlier, this volume is an outgrowth of a project sponsored by the American Association for the Advancement of Science (AAAS), with the support of the Robert Wood Johnson Foundation, to explore the human rights implications of computerizing health care data and to recommend ways in which it is possible to reconcile the promotion of universality with the protection of privacy, nondiscrimination and consent within the context of health care information systems. The AAAS project builds upon, but also employs a broader human rights frame of reference than, the studies cited above.

A major goal of the project is to identify design criteria and methodologies to enable health care information systems to be consistent with all human rights considerations and resolve the seemingly contradictory requirements of the four human rights principles on which the study focuses. To improve monitoring of access to health care, the project attempts to answer three key questions: what is the minimal amount of information needed to evaluate universality of access, which variables are the most important, and what are the most efficient methodological strategies to attain that goal? Another emphasis is to develop guidelines and mechanisms that provide sufficient data for researchers to monitor health care and study other aspects of the health care system, while adequately protecting the privacy of individuals, preventing the use of individual patient information for discriminatory purposes, and adhering to adequate consent procedures.

The project proceeded under the guidance of an Advisory Committee, whose membership is listed in Appendix 1. At one of its early meetings,

39. See Office of Technology Assessment, *Protecting Privacy.*

40. Committee on Regional Health Data Networks, *Health Data in the Information Age*, 1.

the Advisory Committee decided to commission a series of papers exploring the human rights implication of health information systems. The papers were to address both the problems and opportunities that computerization of health data raises. Members of the Advisory Committee chose the topics for the paper and defined the terms of reference for the authors. Members of the Advisory Committee also wrote several of the papers. This volume is a collection of some of these commissioned papers.

In dealing with issues related to universality, the Advisory Committee concluded that the ability to monitor access to health care requires addressing three sets of problems in relationship to vulnerable and hitherto excluded populations. The first is how to define and enumerate these communities and groups. The second is how to obtain valid information about them. And the third is that successful monitoring requires methodologies to overcome the limitations of current sampling strategies, which often do not provide sufficient sample size to permit estimation of health indicators for some of the groups of interest. The Advisory Committee also recognized that privacy, confidentiality, and consent issues specific to these populations must be given special consideration.

The Advisory Committee also considered the human rights implications of content and confidentiality standards for the health information infrastructure, with the goal of best balancing the availability of data used to monitor access with privacy and security protections. Based on an analysis of current state statutes, legislative models and initiatives, and recommendations of various review panels, the Advisory Committee sought to develop standards which defined the following:

1. The scope of the data to be covered by privacy protections;

2. Limitations on data collection;

3. Violations of health care information privacy related to improper possession, brokering, disclosure or sale of health care information and appropriate sanctions sufficient to deter perpetrators;

4. Requirements for informed consent or notification that protect the security of patient's records but do not unduly impede researchers;

5. An individual's right of access to his/her personal information and procedures to examine, challenge, and correct this information.

As noted, the Advisory Committee also sought to develop guidelines and mechanisms and identify technical measures to reconcile monitoring for the purpose of promoting greater universality with the need to protect privacy and consent and to prevent discrimination. Committee members recognized that doing so is partly a technical issue of making data available for research purposes that are stripped of personal identifiers. It is not always feasible, however, to mask patient identifiers. Moreover, even without personal identifiers, some data are still not protected. Researchers can sometimes identify or trace the individuals behind the records. In addition, for some types of research it may be necessary that researchers have patient identifier information. Therefore human rights concerns require the development of guidelines and mechanisms that will govern access to information by secondary users.

Issues which the Committee sought to address are:

1. How it is possible to protect identified information;

2. What kinds of limitations should be placed on access to use of these data sources by insurers or employers and whether it is feasible to impose such limits;

3. What kinds of mechanisms should be in place to authorize and monitor the use of data;

4. Under what kinds of circumstances the holder of a record should be required to notify the data subject about the records in his or her possession or control and offer the individual an opportunity to deny designated uses; and

5. What types of institutions should be established to oversee the process?

Another topic which the Advisory Committee investigated is linkages made between individuals' records, such as between computerized enrollment and encounter records, for administrative and statistical purposes. Many research studies can be enhanced by linking health care records with records from other systems, such as vital records, social security, taxes, and welfare programs. There may also be reasons to propose linkages between records of providers or insurers. However, linkages pose even greater risks for violations of privacy and the use of data for nonauthorized and potentially discriminatory purposes. Linkages between data that were not originally intended to be collated also raise significant consent issues. The Committee therefore explored the extent to which linkages should be permitted, for what purposes, and under what conditions.

The contributions of, as well as problems associated with new technologies were also explored by the Advisory Committee. Potential technical provisions include encryption techniques to encode data in a way that can be reversed only with the appropriate key, identification techniques to ensure that those accessing a computer or network are authorized to do so, and access control software to maintain records of users' accesses and on-line activities to provide audit trails.[41] The Committee sought to evaluate the feasibility, strengths, weaknesses and costs of various technical measures for purposes of providing greater security for computerized health care data.

Recognizing that the implementation of human rights standards requires knowledge about the rights and the means by which they can be exercised, the Advisory Committee additionally addressed the topics of the level of awareness in the public of the human rights implications of computerized health care information systems and ways to better inform the public about their rights. Existing survey data were used to evaluate the public's knowledge about the scope of current and future health care data collection, the social benefits from research and legitimate use of the data, the difference between research and commercial applications of the data, and potential and actual abuses of privacy and confidentiality of data when health care information systems are created. These data were employed to consider how the public can be better informed about these issues and their relevant rights and responsibilities.

Given the breadth and complexity of the issues it addressed, the Advisory Committee spent much of its time working in two subcommittees. The first focused on monitoring the status of underserved, marginal and disadvantaged communities so as to be able to move toward greater universality. The second dealt with privacy, nondiscrimination and consent within the context of achieving universality. Discussions within the full Advisory Committee on ways to balance and reconcile the competing demands of the four human rights principles reflected many of the differences in priorities of the wider society. Most of the members of the subcommittee on universality emphasized the need to improve data while minimizing the possible risks that these data might entail. The major concern of many of the

---

41. Office of Technology Assessment, *Protecting Privacy*, 89-97.

members of the second subcommittee was to protect privacy, even if this meant blocking or significantly limiting the use of promising methodologies like data linkages. Despite the consensus within the full Advisory Committee that it was theoretically possible to balance and reconcile the demands of the four human rights principles, members often disagreed with one another on particular issues. These tensions are also reflected in the papers which were selected for this volume. Like the two subcommittees, the papers tend to have either a data or privacy emphasis. The major exceptions are the introductory and the final chapters, which were written on behalf of the Advisory Committee. It is hoped that this volume will both illuminate the issues and offer a basis for resolving at least some of these dilemmas.

Editor's Note

As previously explained when the study project that produced this volume began, early in 1994, the possibility of major reforms to the U.S. health care system was still alive. But while the papers included in this volume were being written and reviewed, it became clear that the Clinton Administration's health care reform initiative would not succeed. This drastic change in the policy environment necessitated changes in emphasis in some of the papers, but the fundamental question they address – how to use health care information in ways that are consistent with basic human rights principles – did not go away, and it will continue to be important as further changes occur.

Most of the papers were completed by the end of 1995, and the manuscript was forwarded to the publisher in the Spring of 1996. Later in that year, in August, two major laws with significant implications for access to and use of health care information were enacted. President Clinton signed The Health Insurance Portability and Accountability Act of 1996 (popularly referred to as Kennedy-Kassebaum) on August 21 and on the next day he signed The Personal Responsibility and Work Opportunity Reconciliation Act of 1996 – welfare reform. Some effects of this landmark legislation are just beginning to emerge; it will be many years before a definitive evaluation will be possible.

Organization of the Volume

There are two introductory chapters to the volume. This overview of the issues in developing health care information systems consistent with human rights criteria is followed by a second chapter on the human rights framework. The objective of the latter chapter is to provide a more in-depth exposition of the nature of human rights and the four human rights principles with which the volume is concerned – universality, privacy, nondiscrimination, and consent.

Reflecting the organization of the Advisory Committee, the volume has two major sections. Each of the two sections is preceded by an overview prepared by a member or members of the relevant Advisory Committee subcommittee.

The first of the two major sections of the volume addresses issues related to monitoring access to health care, particularly the status of underserved, vulnerable, and excluded populations. Some chapters focus on specific groups, such as women on welfare and American Indians and Alaskan natives. Others deal with methodological issues and approaches, such as how to collect survey data from hidden, underserved, and vulnerable populations, how to use state-level hospital discharge databases as a source of data to monitor minority and special populations, how to employ information systems to support the delivery of preventive services, and how to design information systems to monitor population access to health care.

The second section of the volume deals with issues related to privacy, nondiscrimination and consent within the wider context of promoting universality in access to health care. Many of the chapters address the development of guidelines and mechanisms consistent with human rights principles for a variety of purposes: designing the health care information infrastructure, regulating access to data by private health insurance providers and by researchers, protecting and promoting privacy, linking health records, and protecting against disclosure and use of genetic data. There is also an examination of the potential contribution of current and future technologies for protecting the privacy and integrity of health care data. The final chapter in this section considers current attitudes among the American public and ways to educate them about rights and responsibilities related to health care information systems.

The final chapter in the volume is a conclusion written by one member of the Advisory Committee on behalf of and with input from the full

Committee. All members of the Advisory Committee contributed their views. Given the differences of perspective in the Advisory Committee that are noted above, however, the particular points made in the conclusion do not necessarily have the support of all members. Nor do all members of the Committee always agree with the manner in which data needs for improved monitoring are reconciled with other human rights protections.

An Epilogue following the concluding chapter provides a brief preliminary discussion of how the 1996 legislation may help or hinder progress toward the establishment of health care information systems that are consistent with the human rights norms of universality, privacy, nondiscrimination and consent. One conclusion is inescapable: the task is just beginning. We believe that the issues identified and the questions posed by the authors of this volume will remain relevant for many years to come.

CHAPTER ONE

The Human Rights Framework

Audrey R. Chapman

The objective of this volume is to identify ways to reconcile the promotion and protection of four human rights principles or norms – universality, privacy, nondiscrimination, and consent – within the development of computerized health care information systems. The first chapter identified three reasons why it is important that health care information systems be consistent with human rights principles. To review them: firstly, human rights express human dignity and worth and, as such, represent the common aspiration and standard of achievement for all peoples and nations in the late 20th century. Secondly, the United States has a rights-based political culture in which rights formulations express the ethical and normative foundations of our society. Thirdly, the United States' government has ratified four international human rights instruments and is, therefore, legally bound to conform to their provisions. This chapter delineates further the human rights framework of the study.

The Nature of Human Rights

Human rights literally are the rights or entitlements that one has as a human being. Rights in moral philosophy and political theory are considered to be high priority claims that a right-holder is justified to make and a duty-bearer obligated to provide. Human rights are a special class of rights, the rights that all persons share by virtue of their common humanity. As various international human rights instruments state, human rights derive from "the inherent dignity of the human person." Human rights define the minimum requirements of a life of human dignity and worth. Conversely, violations of human rights deny the fundamental humanity and worth of victims. Because human rights arise from the inherent dignity of the human person, human rights are held to be universal, to be vested in all persons and applicable in all cultures and nations.

Human rights are considered to be moral norms of the highest priority and status. In designating a human or social attribute as a right, a society underscores that it is regarded as essential to the adequate functioning of the human being within the context of community and accepts responsibility for its promotion and protection.[1] As moral norms, human rights standards provide guidance to behavior, thereby conferring and protecting important freedoms, powers, protections, opportunities and benefits.[2] While human rights are not absolute and without exception, they are sufficiently strong as normative considerations to take precedence over other values and considerations. Like other moral precepts, human rights are considered to exist independently of recognition or legal implementation, at least as standards of argument and criticism.

Human rights are at once an ideal and a guide to realistic practices for implementing this ideal. As an ideal, human rights specify the manner in which human beings should be treated so as to be able to realize their full humanity. For that reason human rights are formulated in absolute and categorical terms, admitting no exceptions. As a guide to implementation, human rights norms provide specific guidelines for action and standards for political systems to achieve.[3] In addition, reporting systems related to international human rights instruments evaluate the performance of countries so as to provide incentives for and advice as to how to conform better to these standards.

A commitment to human rights requires appropriate institutions, laws and social practices to enable a person to realize a life of human dignity. Therefore a right always implies correlative duties, usually by a national government, although it is not always clear in human rights formulations who the duty holder is. Under international law, obligations to implement human rights are primarily assigned to states. States are said to have three types of responsibilities: to respect, protect and fulfill the rights of everyone within their jurisdictions. However, the various human rights instruments

---

1.   Michael Freeden, *Rights* (Minneapolis: University of Minnesota Press, 1991), 7.

2.   James W. Nickel, *Making Sense of Human Rights: Philosophical Reflections on the Universal Declaration of Human Rights* (Berkeley and Los Angeles: University of California Press, 1987), 35.

3.   Jack Donnelly, *Universal Human Rights in Theory and Practice* (Ithaca, New York: Cornell University Press, 1989), 18-19.

frequently do not spell out in detail state parties' obligations relating to the implementation of specific rights. These are only gradually being clarified through the drafting of more specific human rights instruments, the general comments of United Nations human rights monitoring bodies, and court decisions applying international human rights standards. Recently more attention has also been paid to the roles and responsibilities of nonstate actors.

One of the most important functions of human rights standards is to provide protection against "standard threats" to human freedom to dignity. Henry Shue argues that a fundamental purpose of acknowledging basic human rights is to prevent or eliminate, insofar as possible, the degree of vulnerability that leaves people at the mercy of others.[4] According to Shue, by acknowledging basic rights we take the victim's side and the side of potential victims. Historically, the positive content of key security rights, such as the rights not to be subjected to murder, torture, rape and assault, was defined in relationship to relevant "standard threats," in particular the powers of an unlimited or absolute state. In contemporary society, many other institutions and technologies also constitute potential threats, and it is therefore important to provide relevant human rights protections.

Human rights also offer a standard by which to evaluate behavior and an implicit challenge to political systems which fail to protect and promote human rights norms. To make a human rights claim is usually to contend that one is not enjoying the human rights one has. Another way of stating this is to describe rights claims as a form of "last resort," that is, in most circumstances rights are claimed only when the enjoyment of an object, a service or an attribute is threatened or denied.[5] A vision of human rights has time and again rallied and inspired victims to work for a new political order more consistent with respect for human rights principles. Human rights standards also provide a basis for international advocacy efforts on behalf of victims.

Given this framework, a human rights approach entails a special obligation or priority toward the status and rights of the poor, the powerless, and those on the periphery of society. If human rights are conceptualized as instruments to protect and promote human dignity, it follows that their

---

4.   Henry Shue, *Basic Rights: Subsistence, Affluence, and U.S. Foreign Policy* (Princeton, New Jersey: Princeton University Press, 1980), 33.

5.   Donnelly, *Universal Human Rights*, 13-15.

implementation can only be considered effective when those in greatest need of assistance are benefited. The litmus test of whether a specific human right is being implemented is the extent to which the rights of the most vulnerable and disadvantaged individuals and groups are being respected. These groups – the poor, ethnic, racial, religious, and linguistic minorities, immigrants and, in most societies, girl children and women – are most often the victims of human rights abuses and have the most difficulty receiving justice or redress. As a corollary, monitoring and evaluation of human rights need to focus on those whose rights are most likely to be violated rather than the members of society whose rights are more likely to be respected.

The most authoritative document setting forth contemporary understandings of human rights is the *Universal Declaration of Human Rights.* Shortly after the United Nations was founded, its Human Rights Commission drafted an international bill of human rights. This document, the *Universal Declaration of Human Rights,* was unanimously adopted by the General Assembly on December 10, 1948 and proclaimed as "a common standard of achievement for all peoples and all nations." The 27 articles constituting the *Universal Declaration* enumerate both civil and political rights, similar to those found in the Bill of Rights to the U.S. Constitution, and a series of economic, social and cultural rights. Among the civil and political rights listed are rights to freedom from discrimination, life, liberty, the security of the person, freedom of religion, thought, expression, movement, assembly, freedom from torture and cruel punishment, freedom from arbitrary arrest, protection of privacy and a fair trial. Social and economic rights recognized in the *Universal Declaration* include rights to health care, social services, education, housing, marriage and founding a family, freedom from forced marriage, work, equal pay for equal work, and participation in the cultural life of the community. Although declarations and resolutions of the General Assembly are not legally binding, over time the *Universal Declaration* has achieved the status of customary international law.

Human rights norms which have become legal rights in national and international law confer additional protection. Provisions of the *Universal Declaration,* particularly those articles which pertain to civil and political rights, have been codified in the constitutions and laws of many countries, among them the United States. While the *Universal Declaration of Human Rights* does not have formal legal status, a series of international human rights conventions based on the *Universal Declaration* further delineate the content of its constituent rights. When ratifying or acceding to these international human rights instruments, a country becomes a state party and is bound legally to comply with their provisions.[6] As noted in the table below, the United States is currently a state party to four of the seven key international human rights instruments, with a fifth under active consideration.

Table 1. Status of International Human Rights Instruments in the United States		
Instrument	*Scope*	*Status*
Universal Declaration of Human Rights	Enumerates fundamental international human rights, both civil and political, and economic, social and cultural.	U.S. delegates voted in favor in 1948 in U.N. General Assembly. As a General Assembly ruling, it is not legally binding.
International Covenant on Civil and Political Rights	Covers internationally recognized civil and political rights, including privacy and nondiscrimination.	Ratified and, therefore, legally binding.
International Covenant on Economic, Social and Cultural Rights	Covers internationally recognized economic, social, and cultural rights, including rights to health and health care.	Signed, but not ratified.
International Convention on the Elimination of all Forms of Racial Discrimination	Covers both categories of rights – civil and political – and economic, social and cultural, focusing on the elimination of any distinction, exclusion, restriction or preference based on race, color, descent, or national or ethnic origin.	Ratified and therefore legally binding.

Universality

As noted, one of the distinctive features of contemporary conceptions of human rights is that human rights are considered to be vested in all persons on the basis of their common humanity. Twentieth-century human rights documents describe human rights as universal, that is, applicable to every person and all places around the world.[7] Universality, together with non-

---

6.   Nickel, *Making Sense of Human Rights*, 3.

discrimination, equality before the law, and equal protection of the law constitute fundamental core principles undergirding the formulation and realization of human rights. The very title of the *Universal Declaration of Human Rights* attests to the importance of the principle of universality, and the first article declares that "All human beings are born free and equal in dignity and rights." Article 2 recognizes that "Everyone is entitled to all the rights and freedoms set forth in this Declaration,"[8] and the formulation of other articles stresses the universality and inclusivity of their coverage.

Because human rights are grounded in the common humanity of all persons, international human rights standards apply to all cultures and countries. While some Asian and Middle East governments have argued that the norms in the *Universal Declaration* and the major international human rights instruments based on the *Universal Declaration* represent Western rather than universal conceptions, a series of international conferences on human rights have reaffirmed the universality and indivisibility of human rights. Various statements formulated by nongovernmental organizations in the societies claiming exemptions from human rights on cultural grounds also overwhelmingly affirm the universality of human rights standards. For example, the 1993 *Bangkok NGO Declaration on Human Rights,* drafted by some 240 participants from 110 non-governmental organizations concerned with issues of human rights and democratic development from the Asia-Pacific region, stresses that "As human rights are of universal concern and are universal in value, the advocacy of human rights cannot be considered to be an encroachment upon national sovereignty."[9] The *Bangkok NGO Declaration* goes on to state that "those cultural practices which derogate from universally accepted human rights, including women's rights, must not be tolerated."[10] The *Vienna Declaration and Programme of Action,* adopted by the 1993 World Conference on Human Rights, reasserts the full universality of these rights and the applicability of them to all societies and cultures. According to the *Vienna Declaration,* "While the significance of national and regional particularities and various

---

7.   *Ibid.,* 5.

8.   United Nations, *Universal Declaration of Human Rights*, adopted and proclaimed by United Nations General Assembly Resolution 217 A (III) on 10 December 1948.

9.   United Nations, "Bangkok NGO Declaration on Human Rights," 27 March 1993, incorporated within *Adoption of the Report of the Regional Meeting*, World Conference on Human Rights, Regional Meeting for Asia, G.A. Doc. A/CONF.157/ASRM/4, 30 March 1993.

10.   *Ibid.*

historical, cultural and religious backgrounds must be borne in mind, it is the duty of States, regardless of their political, economic and cultural systems, to promote and protect all human rights and fundamental freedoms."[11] The 1993 *Vienna Declaration* also explicitly recognizes women's rights as human rights, thereby compensating for one of the most significant conceptual deficiencies in the understanding of human rights. One expression of the global reach of international human rights is the effort to promote universal ratification of major human rights instruments. None of the seven major international human rights conventions has achieved universal ratification or accession by all 175 United Nations member states, but several have upwards of 75%, including virtually all major nations.

Language in the *International Covenant on Civil and Political Rights,* to which the United States is a state party, reflects the foundational articles of the *Universal Declaration.* The preamble to the *Covenant* grounds human rights in the inherent dignity of the human person and the equal and inalienable rights of all members of the human family. Article 2 mandates each state party to the *Covenant* to respect and ensure to all individuals within its territory and subject to its jurisdiction all enumerated rights, "without distinction of any kind, such as race, colour, sex, language, religion, political or other opinion, national or social origin, property, birth or other status."[12] Article 3 goes on to specify that state parties undertake to ensure the equal right of men and women to all civil and political rights set forth in the *Covenant.*

The principle of universality has both procedural and substantive implications. Procedurally, it requires that each state party ensure or guarantee each human right to all individuals within its territory and subject to its jurisdiction. To do so, it is necessary that a government undertake the necessary steps to frame and give effect to human rights through legislative action and other measures so as to ensure that all individuals are covered and treated equally. In addition, it is important that all individuals should know their rights, and that administrative and judicial authorities should be

---

11. United Nations, *Vienna Declaration and Programme of Action*, World Conference on Human Rights, Vienna, 14-25 June 1993, G.A. Doc. A/CONF.157/23, 12 July 1993, par. 5.

12. United Nations, *International Covenant on Civil and Political Rights*, adopted and opened for signature, ratification and accession by United Nations General Assembly Resolution 2200 A (XXI) on 16 December 1966. Entered into force on 23 March 1976 in accordance with Article 49.

made aware of the obligations that their governments have assumed under the specific human rights instruments that they have ratified or legislated.[13]

A logical corollary of the commitment to universality is the responsibility to identify and rectify failures to achieve full coverage and implementation of human rights. As noted, a human rights approach focuses particularly on the status of the most disadvantaged and marginalized communities – the poor, women and girl children, minorities, the homeless, immigrants, and those with disabilities. Because a human right is by definition a universal entitlement, its implementation is evaluated by the degree to which it benefits those who hitherto have been the most disadvantaged and vulnerable. Evaluation of the extent to which a human right is being implemented requires the careful design of a monitoring strategy that incorporates the most vulnerable groups, that is, those whose rights are the least likely to be respected. In the U.S. context, this means focusing on the 41 million Americans who lack health care insurance and access to health care rather than the members of the population with insurance coverage. This strategy, however, is the converse of current health care information systems that cover those with access to health care, or plans to use computerized information to evaluate the health care being received.

Applied to the health sector, the substantive dimensions of the principle of universality underscore the importance of achieving universal and secure health care access and coverage. Several international human rights instruments recognize an explicit right to health care in the context of a more inclusive right to health. Article 25 of the *Universal Declaration* states that "everyone has a right to a standard of living adequate for the health and well-being of himself and of his family, including food, clothing, housing, and medical care and necessary social services."[14] Article 12 of the *International Covenant on Economic, Social and Cultural Rights,* one of the two international human rights instruments, along with the *International Covenant on Civil and Political Rights,* based on the *Universal Declaration,* "recognizes the right of everyone to the enjoyment of the highest attainable standard of physical and mental health." To that end, it mandates that state

---

13. Fausto Pocar, "The International Covenant on Civil and Political Rights," in *Manual on Human Rights Reporting Under Six Major International Instruments* (Geneva: United Nations Centre for Human Rights and United Nations Institute for Training and Research, 1991), 83-85.

14. United Nations, *Universal Declaration of Human Rights*, Article 25.

parties to the *Covenant* undertake the "creation of conditions which assure to all medical service and medical attention in the event of sickness."[15]

It is difficult to use the formulation of a right to health care as a basis for analysis or monitoring access to health care because the United States, unlike other Western industrialized countries, is not among the 130 countries which have ratified the *International Covenant on Economic, Social and Cultural Rights*. Although initially supportive of the inclusive conception of human rights in the Universal Declaration, various American administrations during the Cold War retreated to a narrower definition of human rights, which focused on civil and political rights. Thus, in the debate on health care in this country, there has been more support for the principle of universality as an ethical obligation or long-term political goal than as a right. One example of this weaker formulation of universality, the *Health Security Act* proposed by the Clinton administration to the 103rd Congress, for example, purported to offer universal coverage but restricted eligibility to citizens, permanent residents, and long-term nonimmigrants (thus excluding some legal and all undocumented aliens). It also envisioned a long time line for achieving the coverage of eligible individuals.[16]

A 1993-94 AAAS project, which explored a right to health care, proposed recognition of a right to a basic and adequate standard of health care consistent with a society's level of resources. The project's two publications, *Exploring a Human Rights Approach to Health Care Reform*[17] and *Health Care Reform: A Human Rights Approach*,[18] elaborate the foundations and implications of this right for health care reform in the United States. Participants in the project concurred that in an advanced industrialized country, like the United States, it is appropriate that all citizens and residents be guaranteed a comprehensive standard of health care. The right to health care was understood as a component of a broader

---

15. United Nations, *International Covenant on Economic, Social and Cultural Rights*, adopted and opened for signature, ratification and accession by United Nations General Assembly Resolution 2200 A (XXI) on 16 December 1966. Entered into force on 3 January 1976 in accordance with Article 27.

16. *Health Security Act*, Bill to 103rd Cong., 1st sess. (Washington, D.C.: U.S. Government Printing Office, 1993), Title I, Subtitle A.

17. See Audrey R. Chapman, *Exploring a Human Rights Approach to Health Care Reform* (Washington, D.C.: AAAS, 1993).

18. See Audrey R. Chapman, ed., *Health Care Reform: A Human Rights Approach* (Washington, D.C.: Georgetown University Press, 1994).

effort to protect and improve the public's health. As defined in the project, a human rights approach acknowledges that all persons, without regard to their purchasing power, social status, or personal merit, are entitled to basic and adequate health care. Participants also agreed that a rights approach confers sensitivity to and places priority on meeting the needs of those groups most disadvantaged by the legacy of unequal access to health care in the United States. Recognition of such a right also underscores the ethical and legal responsibility of society to provide an adequate standard of health care to its members. While participants in the project realized that legal recognition would not automatically guarantee access to health care, the advantage is that it would create an obligation for federal and state governments to establish a broad framework and enact specific policies to promote universal coverage.

One of the objectives of the 1993-94 project was to identify the concrete requirements and implications of affirming a right to a basic and adequate standard of health care. It did so in 10 principles, described as a human rights approach to health care reform. The project's publications elaborate these principles and explore their implications for health care reform:

1. A right to health care mandates that a basic and adequate entitlement be guaranteed to all citizens and residents;

2. Because a human right is a universal entitlement, a rights approach emphasizes the equality of all persons and their inherent right to health care as the framework for health care reform;

3. By employing rights language, the provision of health care is understood as a fundamentally important social good to be treated differently from other goals;

4. A human rights approach focuses particularly on the needs of the most disadvantaged and vulnerable communities;

5. By establishing clear individual entitlements in health care, a rights approach empowers individuals and groups to assert their claims;

6. A meaningful and secure right requires that health care be affordable and publicly financed;

7. A human rights approach underscores the importance of meaningful public participation in setting priorities and shaping health care reform;

8. A rights formulation translates into a series of obligations on the part of the federal and state governments;

9. A rights approach provides a potential recourse for those who experience violations;

10. The rights approach balances individual needs with the common good, thereby making the viability and effectiveness of the health care system a shared concern and responsibility.

As noted, a commitment to universality has many implications, among them a requirement to address barriers to its implementation. This requirement has obvious implications for the design of instruments and methodologies to monitor health care status and coverage, as well as efforts to institute meaningful health care reform. One of the major purposes of this volume is to assess the adequacy of current data for assessing access to health care for vulnerable and disadvantaged groups and to propose alternative methodologies. When the project was initiated, the hope was that the monitoring strategies proposed would facilitate an evaluation of policies intended to expand health care coverage. While a commitment to universal health care in this country now seems more distant, it is no less important to monitor current and future health policies. These data will also enable analysts to track and assess the human rights implications of policies that reduce health care expenditures, eliminate existing entitlements, and/or devolve federal responsibilities to the states. This knowledge may then contribute to the formulation of policies more consistent with human rights standards.

The Right to Privacy

To be consistent with human rights criteria, health care information systems need to have substantial safeguards that protect privacy. The right to protection against arbitrary interference with privacy is enumerated in the *Universal Declaration of Human Rights* and several subsequent international human rights instruments. Article 12 of the *Declaration* states that "No one shall be subjected to arbitrary interference with his privacy, family, home, or correspondence, nor to attacks upon his honour and reputation. Everyone has the right to protection of the law against such interference or attacks."[19] Article 17 of the *International Covenant on Civil and Political Rights* contains essentially the same language as Article 12 of the *Universal Declaration.*

Informational privacy, defined as a state or condition of controlled access to personal information, is a component of the right to privacy. In his book *Privacy and Freedom*, Alan Westin describes informational privacy as "The claim of individuals, groups, or institutions to determine for themselves when, how, and to what extent information about them is communicated to others."[20] According to the federal Panel on Confidentiality and Data Access, "Informational privacy encompasses an individual's freedom from excessive intrusion in the quest for information and an individual's ability to choose the extent and circumstances under which his or her beliefs, behaviors, opinions and attitudes will be shared with or withheld from others."[21]

In 1988, the U.N. Human Rights Committee, the oversight body that monitors the compliance of states parties with the *International Covenant on Civil and Political Rights,* adopted a general comment interpreting the provisions of the right to privacy enumerated in Article 17. According to this general comment, the scope of the right to privacy is comprehensive. It provides protection against all interference and attacks, whether they emanate from state authorities or from natural or legal persons and even guarantees that legally admissible forms of interference be in accordance with the provisions, aims, and objectives of the *Covenant.* Recognizing that protection of privacy is necessarily relative, the Committee opined that competent public authorities should only be able to call for information relating to an individual's private life when the knowledge is essential to the interests of society. The general comment also underscored that "the obligations imposed by this article require the State to adopt legislative and other measures to give effect to the prohibition against such interferences and attacks as well as to the protection of this right."[22]

---

19. See United Nations, *Universal Declaration of Human Rights.*

20. Alan Westin, *Privacy and Freedom* (New York: Atheneum, 1967), 7.

21. Panel on Confidentiality and Data Access, *Private Lives and Public Policies: Confidentiality and Accessibility of Government Statistics* (Washington, D.C.: National Academy Press, 1993), 22.

22. United Nations, Human Rights Committee, "General Comment 16: Article 17 (Thirty-second session, 1988)" in *Compilation of General Comments and General Recommendations Adopted by Human Rights Treaty Bodies,* UN Doc. HRI/GEN 1/Rev.1, 29 July 1994.

The general comment addresses issues related to informational privacy as follows. Firstly, it affirms that provisions of the right to privacy apply fully to the gathering and holding of personal information on computers, data banks and other devices held both by public authorities and private individuals or bodies. According to the general comment, "Effective measures have to be taken by States to ensure that information concerning a person's private life does not reach the hands of persons who are not authorized by law to receive, process and use it, and is never used for purposes incompatible with this Covenant."[23] Secondly, in order for an individual to have effective protection of his/her personal life, the general comment specifies that every individual should have broad rights to ascertain the nature of the personal data that is being stored in computer files, the purposes of these files, and the identity of the public and private authorities which control or may control the files. Thirdly, the general comment accords individuals the right to request correction or elimination of files that contain incorrect personal data or that have been collected or processed contrary to the provision of law.[24]

It is important to note that international human rights instruments enumerate a protection against arbitrary or unlawful interference, not an absolute right to withdrawal, secrecy, or protection. So defined, an invasion of privacy entails an intentional deprivation of the privacy to which one is entitled. Restricted access definitions provide one approach to attempting to delineate a reasonable standard of privacy. Anita Allen, for example, defines personal privacy as "a condition of inaccessibility of the person, his or her mental states, or information about the person to the senses or surveillance devices of others."[25] Restricted access interpretations of privacy generally regard privacy as a matter of degree rather than as an all or nothing concept.[26]

The dilemma, particularly in relationship to health care data, is how to define the boundary or degree of restricted access. For example, what kinds of information is it appropriate to ask individuals to supply in connection with the receipt of health care services and payment for those services?

---

23. *Ibid.,* par. 10.

24. *Ibid.*

25. Anita L. Allen, *Uneasy Access: Privacy for Women in a Free Society* (Totowa, New Jersey: Rowman and Littlefield Publishers, 1987), 15.

26. *Ibid.,* 18.

What uses of this information are appropriate? Who should have access to the information and what kinds of disclosures of these data should be allowed? How much control should individuals be accorded over the uses and disclosures of their information?

The U.S. Constitution does not provide an explicit guarantee of the right to privacy. Nevertheless, the Supreme Court has found a basis for a presumed right to privacy in the First, Third, Fourth, Fifth, and Ninth Amendments to the Constitution.[27] In *Katz v. United States,* the Supreme Court ruled that privacy interests protect an individual against electronic surveillance, but with the following caution:

> . . . the Fourth Amendment cannot be translated into a general constitutional "right to privacy." That Amendment protects individual privacy against certain kinds of governmental intrusion, but its protections go further and often have nothing to do with privacy at all. Other provisions of the constitution protect personal privacy from other forms of governmental invasion.[28]

Overall, constitutional protection for informational privacy is very limited and unlikely to provide an effective line of defense for privacy of health information.[29]

The Privacy Act of 1974 is the most comprehensive federal privacy legislation enacted in the United States. The Privacy Act regulates the collection, maintenance, and disclosure of records about individuals by federal agencies, whether these records are manual or automated. The Act seeks to protect against undue intrusion by requiring an agency, to the greatest extent practicable, to request personal information directly from the data subject (and not a third party) whenever the information may result in adverse determinations about the individual's rights, benefits, and privileges. In making the request, the agency must inform the individual of the legal authority authorizing the request, whether compliance is mandatory or voluntary, the principal purpose for which the information will be used, other routine uses that may be made of it, and the consequences, if any, to the individual for not supplying the information. Under the Act, federal

---

27. Office of Technology Assessment, *Protecting Privacy in Computerized Medical Information* (Washington, D.C.: U.S. Government Printing Office, 1993), 39.

28. *Ibid.*

29. Institute of Medicine, Committee on Regional Health Data Networks, *Health Data in the Information Age: Use, Disclosure, and Privacy*, eds. Molla S. Donaldson and Kathleen N. Lohr (Washington, D.C.: National Academy Press, 1994), 146.

agencies may maintain in their records only such information as is relevant and necessary to their legally defined purposes. The Act provides explicitly for access by the data subject to his/her files. It confers the right for individuals to determine what records pertaining to him/her are collected, maintained, used or disseminated by such agencies. The Act also provides a procedure by which an individual may request the correction or amendment of information pertaining to her/him. With respect to dissemination, personal information may be disclosed within the agency only to those employees who have a need for the records in the performance of their duties. Outside of the agency it may usually be disclosed only through written permission of the data subject. The Act also requires agencies to publish annual notices describing the nature of the personal records they keep and to establish appropriate administrative, technical and physical safeguards.[30]

However, the protections provided by the Privacy Act cover only the health data under the control of federal agencies. As most health data is gathered and maintained by the private sector, it is not subject to the provisions of the Privacy Act.

In 1977, the Privacy Protection Study Commission, established under the Privacy Act, recommended three criteria for effective privacy protection:

1. To create a proper balance between what an individual is expected to divulge to a record-keeping organization and what he seeks in return (to minimize intrusiveness);

2. To open up record-keeping operations in ways that will minimize the extent to which recorded information about an individual is itself a source of unfairness in any decision about him made on the basis of it (to maximize fairness); and

3. To create and define obligations with respect to the uses and disclosures that will be made of recorded information about an individual (to create legitimate, enforceable expectations of confidentiality).[31]

---

30. Jeffrey A. Meldman, "Privacy Expectations in an Information Age," *Computer Security Journal,* Winter 1982, 86-88.

31. Quoted in Sheri Alpert, "Smart Cards, Smarter Policy: Medical Records, Privacy, and Health Care Reform," *Hastings Center Report* 23, no. 14 (November-December 1993), 20.

In an article reviewing medical records and privacy issues in the context of health care reform, Sheri Alpert, a member of the Advisory Committee for this project, proposed 14 principles for federal medical privacy legislation. Some of the provisions Alpert recommends to protect patient privacy effectively are as follows:

1. Clearly define patients' rights with respect to their own medical information (i.e., their rights to gain access to, amend, and correct errors in their records, and have any control over others' access to their records);

2. Define what constitutes legitimate access to personal health/medical information; define the legal and ethical responsibilities of those with legitimate authorization to gain access to that information; and provide training for those persons;

3. Clearly define the types of both allowable and prohibited uses of personal medical information (e.g., in statistical research, for billing and insurance purposes, in employment situations, etc.) and provide an oversight and enforcement mechanism to ensure compliance;

4. Establish civil and criminal penalties for prohibited activities, allowing patients to collect damages;

5. Establish medical record retention schedules for each class of information recipient (i.e., physicians, hospitals, insurers, researchers, auditors, etc.), particularly where patient identifiers are attached to the information;

6. Require notice to patients of health/medical information record use, to include publishing information about the existence of health care data banks, and where and how patients can get access to their medical records;

7. Require extensive audit trails, accessible to patients upon request, to track all disclosures and requests for disclosure of personal medical information (i.e., whose records are released; a copy of the signed patient authorization for such release; names and addresses of the recipients of the records; the reason for the disclosure, such as billing, providing direct medical care, research, etc.);

8. Strictly limit employers' ability to see individual employees' medical/health records and use them to make employment-related decisions;

9. Prohibit the marketing of personal health/medical data;

10. Give patients the prerogative to limit the authorization for the use and disclosure of their medical record information (to include specific references to the records subject to the authorization, the parties allowed access, an expiration date for the authorization, and a right to revoke that authorization).[32]

It should be noted that members of the Advisory Committee do not necessarily subscribe fully to all of the principles cited here. In particular, number 10, to the extent that it could circumscribe legitimate statistical research, would raise problems for some members of the Committee.

Incorporating and implementing safeguards in the complex and fragmented U.S. health care system will be a very difficult undertaking. The second half of this volume will explore options for doing so.

a. Nondiscrimination

The principle of nondiscrimination is also fundamental to human rights. Freedom from discrimination is predicated on the recognition that all members of society have equal moral worth and equal standing. Therefore, it is impermissible to make a distinction in treatment on a basis other than individual merit. Standards of nondiscrimination seek to assure that all persons will be afforded access to rights and freedoms on an equal footing and to provide protection against any person being treated differently solely on the basis of gender, race, ethnicity, social origin, language, or economic standing.

Several articles of the *International Covenant on Civil and Political Rights* obligate each state party to respect and ensure to all persons within its territory the rights recognized within the instrument without distinction of any kind, such as race, color, sex, language, religion, political or other opinion, national or social origin, property, birth or social origin.[33] Article 1 of the *International Convention on the Elimination of All Forms of Racial Discrimination*, to which the United States is also a state party, uses similar

---

32. *Ibid.,* 21.

33. For a discussion on the fundamental importance of the principle of nondiscrimination to the *Covenant,* see United Nations, Human Rights Committee, "General Comment 18 Non-discrimination" (Thirty-seventh session, 1989) in *Compilation of General Comments and General Recommendations Adopted by Human Rights Treaty Bodies.*

language. It provides that the term "racial discrimination" shall mean "any distinction, exclusion, restriction or preference based on race, colour, descent, or national or ethnic origin which has the purpose or effect of nullifying or impairing the recognition, enjoyment or exercise, on an equal footing, of human rights and fundamental freedoms in the political, economic, social, cultural or any other field of public life."[34]

While the *International Covenant on Civil and Political Rights* neither defines the term discrimination nor indicates what constitutes discrimination, a general comment prepared by the Human Rights Committee interprets nondiscrimination under the Covenant as follows:

> The Committee believes that the term "discrimination," as used in the Covenant, should be understood to imply any distinction, exclusion, restriction or preference which is based on any ground such as race, colour, sex, language, religion, political or other opinion, national or social origin, property, birth or other status, and which has the purpose or effect of nullifying or impairing the recognition, enjoyment or exercise by all persons, on equal footing, of all rights and freedoms.[35]

In its general comment on nondiscrimination, the Human Rights Committee emphasizes that the principle of nondiscrimination is consistent with positive measures to guarantee equality of rights. Such steps may take the form of legislative, administrative, or other measures. The Committee also points out that the principle of equality sometimes requires state parties to undertake affirmative action in order to diminish or eliminate conditions which cause or help to perpetuate discrimination, including temporarily granting preferential treatment. According to the Committee, not every differentiation of treatment constitutes discrimination, if the criteria are reasonable and objective and if the aim is to achieve a purpose which is legitimate under the *Covenant*.[36]

Contrary to human rights norms, the United States' health care system institutionalizes two major forms of discrimination. Nondiscrimination

---

34. United Nations, *International Convention on the Elimination of All Forms of Racial Discrimination*, adopted and opened for signature, ratification, and accession by United Nations General Assembly Resolution 2106 A (XX) on 21 December 1965. Entered into force on 4 January 1969 in accordance with Article 19.

35. United Nations, Human Rights Committee, "General Comment 18: Nondiscrimination," par. 7.

36. *Ibid.*, par. 10.

precludes differential treatment on the basis of health status or preexisting medical conditions. However, the absence of a commitment to universal health insurance or coverage provides market incentives to do exactly that. Insurers, both employers and the insurance companies, screen prospective employees and/or claimants so as to identify and refuse coverage to anyone with potentially expensive health claims. Thus the dynamic is the reverse of a human rights approach: relatively healthy individuals are able to gain employment with health insurance benefits and are eligible to purchase individual health insurance policies, while those who potentially have the greatest health care needs are excluded.

The U.S. health care sector also discriminates on the basis of income and operates on the basis of a *de facto* economic apartheid. The structure of the health care system ensures that individuals with a capacity to pay either directly or through their health care insurance are given the most comprehensive and technologically advanced health care anywhere in the world, often with little regard to cost. Those without the means to pay directly or access to the type of employment that offers secure benefits, who are likely to be an increasing proportion of the population, lack secure access to basic health care. Because states determine qualifications for Medicaid, a family income below the poverty line does not assure public assistance. To contain Medicaid costs, states have made eligibility requirements increasingly stringent; as of 1989, 32 states had set the maximum income level for public assistance eligibility at less than 50% of the federal poverty standard.[37] In a period of federal and state cutbacks on social expenditures, the proportion of the population lacking any form of coverage is likely to increase.

A human rights approach also precludes the use of health care information for discriminatory purposes. Again, the present system, by tying health care to employment, encourages employers to use health information in hiring, promotion, and retention of workers. Because of the effect of benefit costs on a company's income, employers who offer health insurance, particularly those who are self-insured, have incentives to obtain very sensitive health information and to use these data for employment-related determinations. Moreover, the increasing availability of health data for a

---

37. The Final Report of the Ad Hoc Committee on Medicaid, "Including the Poor, Health Policy Agenda for the American People," February 1989. Cited in Bioethics Consultation Group, *Health Care Crisis in America Fact Sheet* (Minneapolis, October 1989).

wide range of social applications is likely to result in health status and health-related behavior increasingly becoming a factor in eligibility for other types of insurance, loans and legal decisions.

b. Consent

Because human rights derive from and express the inherent dignity of the human person, autonomy and self-determination are implicit dimensions of human rights norms. Provisions of human rights instruments, like the International Covenant on Civil and Political Rights, seek to eliminate various external constraints on persons, particularly those emanating from the political authorities. The principle of consent is related to and may be derived from these rights.

The principle of autonomy, derived from the Greek *autos* (self) and *nomos* (rule, governance, or law), or self-determination, is fundamental to medical ethics, one aspect of which assures the voluntary consent of human subjects. According to medical ethicists, to respect an autonomous agent is to recognize the right of a person to hold views, make choices, and take actions based on personal values and beliefs. It also involves treating agents so as to allow or enable them to act autonomously.[38] Consent within the medical sphere is equated with autonomous authorization of a medical intervention or involvement in research by individual persons.[39] Informed consent requires the provision of sufficient data to enable an individual to make such a determination. Consistent with the requirements for autonomy, "an informed consent occurs if a patient or subject with substantial understanding and in substantial absence of control by others intentionally authorizes a professional to do something."[40]

Consent measures designed to protect the autonomy of patients and research subjects serve other functions as well. Alexander Capron has identified these as follows:

1. The promotion of individual autonomy;

2. The protection of patients and subjects;

3. The avoidance of fraud and duress;

---

38. Tom L. Beauchamp and James L. Childress, *Principles of Bioethics* (New York: Oxford University Press, 1989), 70-71.

39. *Ibid.,* 76.

40. *Ibid.*

4. The encouragement of self-scrutiny by medical professionals;

5. The promotion of rational decisions;

6. The involvement of the public (in promoting autonomy as a general social value and in controlling biomedical research).[41]

Informed consent is clearly essential for valid experimental research on human subjects. Research protocols require the cooperation of data subjects and data providers. The willingness of people to respond to and provide accurate information depends on relationships of trust. Given the importance that Americans attribute to privacy and confidentiality, compliance with standards of informed consent is a precondition for clinical research.

It is less clear, however, that standards of informed consent developed for clinical research settings are appropriate for statistical research, particularly to data lacking the identification of data subjects. Persons asked to respond to population-based sample surveys are generally given the opportunity to refuse to participate, but are not asked to give explicit written consent for the analysis of data. And participation in at least one survey, the decennial population census, is mandatory.[42]

Standards for informed consent developed for clinical research settings are also difficult to apply to informational rights. Medical and research codes, as well as federal regulations, emphasize two elements as essential for informed consent: the act of consent must be genuinely *voluntary,* and there must be adequate *disclosure* of information. None of the existing medical or legal guidelines, however, specify clear boundaries as to how much information must be disclosed to meet the standard of adequacy. Nor do they define how well the subject must comprehend the situation and options, and whether the absence of impairment can be equated with competence.

Current laws and regulations do not provide adequate or uniform standards of consent or disclosure. The Privacy Act of 1974 sets some minimum requirements for consent, disclosure, and participation rights for record subjects in relationship to the federal statistical system. The Act provides individuals with rights to see, copy, and correct their records, as well as limited control over the collection and disclosure of information.

---

41. Quoted in Beauchamp and Childress, *Principles of Bioethics*, 67.

42. These observations were provided by Tom Jabine, a member of the Advisory Committee.

Although legally the requirements of the Privacy Act apply only to collection of data from individuals, federal statistical agencies have also frequently applied them to data obtained from organizations.[43] Federal regulation for substance abuse programs and nursing facility grants permit individuals access to their health records. State laws regulating patient access to health records are not uniform. Nor do they provide comprehensive coverage. Only 27 states have statutes requiring providers to make records available to patients, most of these under hospital licensing acts.[44]

The American Health Information Management Association (AHIMA) has taken the position that patients should have access to the information contained in their health records so that patients can:

1. Be knowledgeable about the nature of their disease or health status and understand the treatment and prognosis;
2 Be educated about their health status to enable them to participate actively in their treatment process and in wellness programs;
3. Provide a history of their medical care to a new health care provider;
4. Ensure the accuracy of documentation in health records with regard to diagnoses, treatment(s), and their response to treatment(s);
5. Verify that the documentation in the health record supports the provider's bill for services; and
6. Be informed of the nature of the information being released to third parties, such as insurers, when authorizing disclosure of their health information.[45]

As noted in the previous chapter, neither federal nor state laws currently protect data subjects from release of medical data to second and third-party sources. Medical providers typically require patients to sign blanket consent forms that permit the facility to release medical information concerning the patient to broad categories of potential users. Typically, blanket consent forms place no restriction on the amount of information that may be released, the uses to which these parties may put the information, or the length of time for which consent is valid.[46] Even in the absence

43. Panel on Confidentiality and Data Access, *Private Lives and Public Policies*, 64.
44. Office of Technology Assessment, *Protecting Privacy*, 72.
45. Quoted in Office of Technology Assessment, *Protecting Privacy*, 72.
46. *Ibid.*, 73.

of blanket consent provisions, current laws and regulations do not provide protection against the release of information to secondary users.

Given the scope of contemporary medical records, the technical nature of much of the data, and the difficulties for patients and research subjects to comprehend the information, there is considerable debate as to what constitutes valid consent and disclosure procedures with regard to potential uses of medical information. Much of the debate centers on how much information is enough and how it should be conveyed. Some proponents argue against giving persons an extensive information about potential uses of their data, claiming it would be an unwieldy process and result in administrative confusion. Others recommend at a minimum something more than the current situation, where there is little disclosure or restrictions on release of the data. A third position is to set carefully defined boundaries for reasonable use of the data, while requiring informed consent when information would or might be put to other uses.[47] Still other groups argue that all potential data applications should be authorized by the subject. These issues are addressed in many of the chapters of this volume.

Conflicts Among Rights

While human rights are generally described as indivisible, inalienable, and interdependent, the requirements of the fundamental human rights enumerated in the *Universal Declaration* and other human rights instruments are not necessarily consistent. Sometimes, as in the case of the rights considered in this volume, there are evident conflicts among them. In the area of health information, the most obvious is between data requirements for monitoring the achievement of access to basic health services by all persons, without discrimination, and the ability to minimize encroachments on individuals' privacy and maximize their control over uses and disclosure of their own information. Moreover, as noted in the previous chapter, both the need for monitoring and the risks associated with the provision and storage of more comprehensive health data are likely to increase in the near future. A major issue then is how to resolve these conflicts.

Unfortunately, rights theories do not provide a formula or a simple solution to resolve apparent conflicts. Because all human rights are considered to be of equal status and weight, most rights theorists resist either

---

47. *Ibid.*

developing priorities among rights or even dealing with the topic of potential and actual conflicts. A few human rights theorists, Henry Shue for example, have sought to categorize particular rights as basic, fundamental, and therefore of greater importance, but other theorists generally have criticized and resisted efforts to establish a human rights hierarchy. The topic is further complicated by the fact that it is difficult to anticipate potential conflicts among rights. Rights theorists have also argued that a right redefined with sufficient qualifications and exceptions to avoid all possible conflicts would probably be too complex to understand and apply.[48] Formalizing qualifications and exceptions would also risk devaluating the weight and scope of a right.

In the absence of a theoretical solution, it is necessary to develop strategies in concrete situations to reduce conflicts and attempt to reconcile competing rights claims. There are a variety of potential approaches to dealing with the dilemmas which are the subject matter of this volume. Some involve redefining the scope and boundaries of particular rights. Others relate to establishing new legal safeguards, voluntary guidelines, or public policy frameworks to provide additional protection. Another is to rely on technological innovations. The chapters in this volume will explore these alternatives. Each of the chapters makes recommendations based on the views of the author. As might be anticipated, there is a divergence of views as to the feasibility of resolving the apparent conflicts and the most appropriate way to do so. The final chapter in the volume identifies the areas of agreement and disagreement on these issues among members of the Advisory Committee.

---

48. Nickel, *Making Sense of Human Rights*, 49.

Part Two

Moving Toward Universality: Monitoring Underserved and Excluded Populations

CHAPTER TWO

Issues and Methodologies for Monitoring Universality

Douglas A. Samuelson and Floyd J. Fowler, Jr.

If a nation adopts the goal that all of its people should have access to basic medical care, an essential issue is how to evaluate progress in achieving that objective. Even in the absence of an explicit commitment to universal health care, responsible public policy formulation requires an ability to monitor access to health care in order to identify underserved and excluded individuals and communities and to understand the factors shaping the availability of health care. Changes in the health care system, whether through national health care reforms, state level legislation, or private sector initiatives, increase the need for careful monitoring and evaluation. Proposed health care reforms, if enacted, and current market-driven restructuring of the health care system explicitly or implicitly affect some groups within the population more than others. California proposition 187, for example, which would restrict access of undocumented immigrants to public assistance in paying for most health care services, though not yet implemented, has already altered health care utilization, in some cases resulting in severe hardships. Current proposals to move from entitlements to block grants to states is also likely to increase the percentage of the U.S. population lacking secure access to health care services. If this country goes forward into a period of state-level experimentation in providing benefits for and regulating health care, which seems likely at this time, it will be particularly important to have the capacity to collect and analyze the data necessary to assess the strengths and weaknesses of the various approaches.

Nevertheless, there are both difficulties and potential risks involved in development of an information system about the health care people do and do not receive. As the articles in this section of the volume will describe, there are many challenges in designing and implementing an information system that would permit reliable and comprehensive monitoring of the extent to which the nation has achieved universal access to basic medical care. In addition, as more data are collected and stored in computerized databases, it becomes more problematic to protect people from being penalized by the use of their information. These issues are the subject of this section of the book.

We take as a starting point three key areas of interest, as articulated in the Introduction:

- the extent to which access to health care is universal,

- the extent of discrimination in access to health care, and

- the quality and appropriateness of health care people receive.

Each of these three points poses different challenges in the design and implementation of an adequate information system. In addition, there are several fundamental considerations: population coverage, data collection limitations, data quality issues, hard-to-measure topics, and data interpretation problems.

Population Coverage

If one wants to monitor the extent to which health care is universal, the information system must be universal as well. Unfortunately, most information systems that deal with health care and health services are not universal. Moreover, the groups about which one would be most concerned in assessing whether health care is available to all tend to be the ones which are not covered. For example, insurance systems leave out the uninsured, and utilization data, such as hospital discharge records, leave out those who did not receive services. General population surveys, such as the National Health Interview Survey conducted by the U.S. Department of Health and Human Services, do not depend on utilization or insurance coverage for inclusion; but almost all sample surveys utilize housing units for the first stage of sampling. Household-based surveys generally do not provide data about people who are homeless, in institutions, or in transient groups, such as migrant workers.

Data Collection Limitations

Even when data cover the groups of interest, the data often do not enable one to evaluate access to or quality of care for groups of interest. There is inevitably a tradeoff between comprehensiveness of coverage and amount of detail as more detailed information-gathering increases the burden both on the respondents (and data collectors) and on the storage and retrieval capacity of the system. In addition, some types of data are, by their nature, difficult to collect reliably.

In particular, data which could identify at-risk groups tend to be hard to collect. Many characteristics which could put people at risk, such as not speaking English or having low-income or educational attainment, are not available in record-based systems. There are also problems with getting people to provide data that identify them as belonging to a category that puts them at risk with respect to accessing medical care: for example, reporting oneself as an illegal alien or as HIV-positive. Thus even a data collection system specifically designed to identify at-risk groups cannot necessarily do so. Finally, if an information system is based on sampling rather than including all individuals, potentially at-risk groups of interest may be represented by samples that are too small to provide reliable statistics.

Data Quality Issues

Data quality problems are pervasive, especially when one tries to use a database for purposes other than those for which it was designed. Record-based systems intended primarily for billing use tend to have substantial amounts of missing or unreliable data on medical conditions and treatments; data collected for research on a particular condition or treatment tend to be unreliable with regard to other conditions and treatments. In general, data which do not support the primary purpose of the database are much less carefully verified.

In some cases, databases are constructed by matching and linking data sets collected for different purposes, using a variety of populations and selection criteria. Such matching and linkage are usually based on statistical models and checked against known population characteristics, such as racial composition or total expenditure on medical care, to verify the models. These data sets may be much less consistent with other known characteristics which were not considered in the verification process.

Hard-to-Measure Topics

Lack of access to medical care is not easy to measure, even with reliable data. Within limits, use of medical care may be interpreted as an indication of access to care. The converse, however, is not true: those who do not use medical care do not necessarily lack access. Although survey questions have been designed to attempt to identify people for whom medical care is likely to have been beneficial, measuring access to care remains difficult.

Quality of care is even more difficult to measure. Inferring quality of care from quantity of care received or from patient satisfaction cannot be justified. Even outcomes of treatment are not completely informative: patients may recover well from many ailments despite poor care, or die despite good care.

Data Interpretation Problems

In addition to the challenges of having data about the groups of interest in a form that would permit analyzing the results for those groups, there are serious problems in analysis and interpretation. If, for example, analysis of utilization of medical services, broken down by small geographic regions such as census tracts, reveals that certain tracts have little utilization despite population characteristics similar to other tracts with much higher utilization, we can infer that the low-utilization tracts are relatively underserved; but we cannot, without considerable additional information, discern the relative importance of providers' payment policies, availability of transportation, prospective patients' attitudes regarding when to seek care, and other factors in explaining the difference.

Even something as fundamental as the definition of health care can vary in terms of the inclusiveness of its components. To recommend means of monitoring, we would first wish to know exactly what we want to monitor: defining indicators and measures is difficult at best and nonsensical at worst if we start without a clear purpose in mind. What we can do, and attempt here, is to identify some of the ways in which monitoring schemes could be implemented, and to point out some of the policy implications of choices regarding monitoring.

Different Approaches to Monitoring

There are several workable approaches to monitoring access to and quality of health care. They are not necessarily mutually exclusive, but each represents a different view of the overall concept and presents somewhat distinct potential for dispute. The key difference is what one chooses to emphasize as an indicator of adequate health care.

One approach is to examine outcomes of medical treatment. These include mortality, need for additional treatment, and diminished functioning (as, for example, if a patient survives a stroke but is partially paralyzed). Another is to focus on processes: What was done for the patient? What would have been done for the patient elsewhere, or perhaps in the same place if the patient belonged to a different group? Still another is to focus simply on access: Could the patient obtain care when he or she decided it was needed?

These approaches share a common shortcoming: to use them, we focus on persons classified by someone as ill. This means we assume that we agree regarding what medical care is and who needs it, and that we do not consider other factors, outside the medical care system, which also affect health. To overcome these limitations, we can move beyond health *care* and attempt to assess health *status.* Thus we might consider such measures as life expectancy at birth, early childhood mortality, and years of unassisted living.

From the human rights standpoint, however, focusing on health status appears problematic. Does a nation violate its citizens' right to nondiscrimination in health, for example, if its air and water in some regions are badly polluted and its safety record in some industries is particularly poor, but it does offer excellent medical care to all? To what extent should a nation be held accountable for unhealthy habits some groups of its citizens have voluntarily adopted, such as smoking?

We find these complications and the consequent monitoring issues more tangled than we can analyze within the scope of this project. Nevertheless, we consider it important to begin by reminding the reader, and ourselves, that health status, not utilization of health care services, is the ultimate measure of success. Clean air and water, wholesome food, and adequate shelter and clothing are at least as important to health as access to professional services.

We suggest adopting the definition of access as "the timely use of personal health services to achieve the best possible health outcomes."[1]

> This definition forces us to identify those areas of medical care in which services can be shown to influence health status and then to ask whether the relatively poorer outcomes of some population groups can be explained by problems related to access. The definition also emphasizes the need to move beyond standard ap-

---

1. Institute of Medicine, *Access to Health Care in America*, ed. Michael Millman (Washington, D.C.: National Academy Press, 1993), 4.

proaches that rely mainly on enumerating health care providers, the uninsured, or encounters with health care providers to detect health care problems.[2]

With this basis in mind, we now consider what sorts of data are available, and what uses such data can have in the human rights monitoring context.

- Public health agencies at various levels of government collect and utilize data on births, deaths, causes of death, and incidence of diseases (especially those which are infectious and amenable to control by public health measures); these data sets are usually readily available. Comparisons between data sets collected by different agencies, however, can be complicated by differences in reporting practices and standards.

- National compilations of mortality rates, disaggregated to the provider level, such as the one published annually from the early 1980s through 1993 by the U.S. Health Care Finance Administration (HCFA), provide greater standardization and therefore better comparability among small areas. This disaggregation, however, is achieved at the cost of raising serious questions about whether differences in severity of condition at the time of diagnosis have been properly taken into account.

- Data collected in research studies of specific diseases and treatments provide better detail and comparability, but the narrow focus of such studies usually precludes comparisons among regional, ethnic or socioeconomic groups at the national level.

- Billing information tends to be maintained and verified more carefully than data collected for studies and comparisons, but attempts to assess trends or patterns often result in the discovery of numerous missing or invalid diagnostic and treatment codes in the data. Also, billing data sets generally yield little information about poorly served populations.

- Managed care organizations, such as the National Committee for Quality Assurance (in health care), an umbrella organization known as NCQA for short, has identified inconsistent reporting standards as a top-priority problem. In the course of attempting to develop "a

---

2. *Ibid.*

national report card" on health care quality, the NCQA's working groups became increasingly aware of difficulties in comparing diagnostic categories, treatments and outcomes among providers, as the data reporting practices were so different as to require a massive follow-up effort to make comparisons meaningful. NCQA is now updating its standardized Health plan Employer Data and Information Set (HEDIS), including reporting standards for all its members, to facilitate comparisons and trend monitoring in the future. Such data sets offer great promise, but are limited by the differences between subscribers of managed care plans and the population as a whole. In the U.S., where both plans and subscribers have considerable freedom of choice, these differences are highly significant.

• There have been promising efforts to develop key indicators of health status and health care access; these include the Institute of Medicine report, cited earlier, and Thomas B. Jabine's chapter of a book produced by the American Association for the Advancement of Science project on the human rights dimensions of health care reform.[3] Indicators offer the best prospect for meaningful international comparisons, at the cost of focusing on a small subset of all the components of health status.

Summary and Section Overview

Clearly, much additional work will be required to improve data collection and reporting sufficiently to support widely credible monitoring of international human rights to universality and nondiscrimination in health care, no matter how those rights are eventually defined. The chapters in this section are intended to help readers understand the challenges involved in the development of a monitoring system, as well as presenting some ideas for how these challenges might be met.

The initial two chapters in this section of the book deal with issues related to monitoring specific underserved and vulnerable populations. Trude Bennett deals with monitoring welfare and women's health, while Jonathan Sugarman, Martha Holliday, Andrew Roos, and Doni Wilder address improving health data among American Indians and Alaska Na-

---

3. Thomas B. Jabine, "Indicators for Monitoring Access to Basic Health Care as a Human Right," in *Health Care Reform: A Human Rights Approach*, ed. Audrey R. Chapman (Washington, D.C.: Georgetown University Press, 1994).

tives. Given their dependency status, extreme impoverishment, poor health, status, and social stigmatization, women on welfare are a vulnerable group whose plight is likely to increase further if proposals to end welfare as we know it do become enacted. Despite their eligibility for federal assistance, particularly Aid to Families with Dependent Children, Bennett shows that sources of data for monitoring health risks and outcomes among the AFDC population are extremely limited. Lack of interest among researchers and policy makers has stifled initiatives to ensure data quality, achieve adequate sample sizes of recipients, and overcome other methodological barriers; and data will likely become more sparse with budget cuts and the minimized oversight and regulation that are likely to accompany block grants. To attempt to compensate for these deficiencies, the article identifies some existing data that can be utilized for monitoring purposes and the human rights issues related to their use.

The position of American Indians and Alaska Natives is unique in the U.S. health care system. Despite the special obligation of the federal government to provide health services for Indian people, there is a considerable gap between the health status of these groups and that of the general population. Moreover, the presence of over 500 sovereign tribal governments which have entered into agreements with the federal government to operate the health programs in their communities considerably complicates the monitoring of the health status. The chapter by Sugarman et. al. evaluates the inadequacies of current data and describes a demonstration project among Northwest Native Americans to enhance information about Indian health.

The next chapter in this section, written by James Fisher, Jichuan Wang and Joseph Wagner, deals with methodological issues related to "Drawing Samples from Hidden, Underserved and Vulnerable Populations: Methods, Applications, and Ethical Issues." An ability to measure the size and characteristics of persons who are hidden, underserved, and vulnerable with respect to access to health care because of poverty, underemployment, residential instability, undocumented immigrant status, or mental illness, is one prerequisite for successful monitoring. The chapter explores sampling methods which may be useful for state and local governments and service agencies wishing to estimate the size and composition of their target population, as well as the representativeness of their current service population. Considered are trade-offs between the representativeness of probability sampling and the relative feasibility of convenience or non-probability samples.

Next, Barbara Kurtzig discusses some uses of public health data collected and maintained by various states in the U.S. Here there is more detail, but (as she demonstrates) we can also identify more problems with data quality. Even the seemingly simple and widely collected "race/ethnicity" item turns out, upon closer examination, to involve vague definitions, arbitrary coding, and serious potential to mislead analysts who use it for purposes other than those intended by the item's designers. These difficulties complicate monitoring nondiscrimination.

There is some encouragement, however. In the next chapter, Noralou Roos and her coauthors discuss the design of an information system to combine data from various sources in Manitoba, Canada, in mutually compatible and comparable form. They then discuss lessons learned which could be applied to the design of such systems elsewhere. Leslie Roos, David Fedson, Janice Robert, and James Blanchard also present some examples of the analyses which are possible with the Manitoba system, again proceeding to a discussion of lessons learned which have applications elsewhere.

In the final chapter in this section, Douglas A. Samuelson and R. Clifton Bailey review uses and limitations of nationwide outcomes data, as exemplified by public health data, data from large-scale studies, and the mortality data collected and analyzed by the (U. S.) Health Care Financing Administration. Such data provide comparability among regions as well as among providers, but this comparability requires sacrifices of detail and, therefore, of understanding of processes. This chapter also addresses specifically a number of problems of data quality and data interpretation, and ways in which these problems might be handled.

CHAPTER THREE

Monitoring Welfare and Women's Health

Trude Bennett

In the rush to "end welfare as we know it," policymakers have characterized Aid to Families with Dependent Children (AFDC) recipients as an over-protected group in need of incentives, restrictions, or sanctions – not as an underserved population whose health status and access to care require careful monitoring. Yet the disproportionate poverty of women and the attendant threats to their health are well-documented. In the human rights perspective of this volume, vulnerable groups eliciting concern include those discriminated against on the basis of their social position.[1] The dependency status, extreme impoverishment, and social stigmatization of AFDC mothers – as well as the plight of women who will become ineligible as the income support program contracts – warrant renewed attention to the physical and emotional health and well-being of poor women in the U.S.

According to Aday,[2] "The risk [of developing health problems] is ... greater for those with the least social status, social capital, and human capital resources to either prevent or ameliorate the origins and consequences of poor physical, psychological, or social health." In 1994 the average monthly AFDC benefits for a family of three totaled $366; the lowest grant of any state was $120 in Mississippi.[3] Combined income from AFDC benefits and food stamps reached only 62% of the federal poverty level in the average state. Yet AFDC participants have not customarily been iden-tified as a vulnerable group in the health services and health outcomes

---

1. See Audrey R. Chapman, "Introduction: Developing Health Information Systems Consistent with Human Rights Criteria," in this volume.

2. L. A. Aday, "Health Status of Vulnerable Populations," *Annual Review of Public Health* 15 (1994): 506.

3. *Living at the Bottom: An Analysis of 1994 AFDC Benefit Levels* (Washington, D.C.: Center on Social Welfare Policy and Law, 1994).

literature. For example, Aday[4] designates mothers and infants as a high-risk group based on their physical health needs, but does not specify AFDC recipients as high-risk mothers based on their social and economic needs.

Ideological and fiscal interests, not humanitarian concerns, have motivated recent measures to end the AFDC entitlement to subsistence income support for poor mothers. Historically, the AFDC program has penalized single mothers by keeping benefits well below poverty level and attempting to regulate recipients' private lives. The use of AFDC policy to monitor the moral fitness of indigent mothers, deemed the "undeserving poor," has been a consistent theme. Under such conditions, the norms for fundamental human rights (universality, privacy, nondiscrimination, and consent)[5] have not been applied to recipients of AFDC benefits.

The Clintons' and other health reform proposals defeated in 1994 strove for universality of coverage for the sake of equity, as well as for reduction of costs for uncompensated care and preventable illness. Current welfare reform initiatives, in contrast, aim to limit eligibility. The notion of universality in welfare reform resides in the expectation that all heads of households be self-supporting, not in acceptance of a universal right to an adequate standard of living and human dignity. In fact, a majority of single mothers depend on their own earnings rather than public assistance; and many women strive to maintain their families by combining employment with welfare benefits. Single mothers' desire to become self-supporting is often thwarted by lack of education, work experience, child care, transportation, and other resources. Unskilled jobs available to welfare recipients seldom replace Medicaid with private insurance benefits. Thus, the failure of health reform to guarantee universal health coverage compounds the risks associated with new welfare regulations that limit income support.

Privacy of welfare recipients has never been respected or protected; social control functions of welfare run counter to the assurance of privacy rights.[6] Blatant invasions of privacy began under the forerunner of AFDC, the Aid to Dependent Children (ADC) program established as part of the Social Security

---

4. *Ibid.*, 494.

5. See Audrey Chapman, "Introduction: Developing Health Information Systems Consistent with Human Rights Criteria," in this volume.

6. F. F. Piven and R. A. Cloward, *Regulating the Poor: The Functions of Public Welfare* (New York: Random House, 1972). M. Abramovitz, *Regulating the Lives of Women: Social Welfare Policy from Colonial Times to the Present* (Boston: South End Press, 1988).

Act in 1935. The "suitable home" test, which challenged custody rights of many single mothers, was the first in a series of efforts to eliminate the growing number of unmarried and minority women from ADC rolls. Starting in the 1950s, ADC mothers were subjected to increasing scrutiny by states. For example, a man discovered in a recipient's home during a midnight raid could be designated a "substitute father" expected to relieve the state of financial responsibility – regardless of his income, his relationship to the woman and her children, or the woman's wishes. In 1967, welfare rights activists succeeded in eliminating some of the most abusive AFDC regulations, like the "man in the house" rule. However, AFDC benefits continued to imply forfeiture of privacy rights and the right to consent. For example, recent welfare proposals require mothers to identify their children's fathers, even if women believe their safety may be threatened by such identification.

Public assistance programs have traditionally been designed in accord with the "principle of less eligibility," inherited from the British New Poor Law of 1834. Benefits must always be less attractive than the most poorly rewarded employment; in the case of women, welfare is intended to be less desirable than marriage – though factors such as male unemployment and domestic violence complicate the formula. Marriage may fail to provide either economic or social support, but AFDC participation can be perceived as less honorable than even an unhappy or abusive marriage.[7] In recent years, Democrats and Republicans alike have campaigned for an intensification of the stigmatization of "illegitimacy" (and, by association, AFDC status). In this context, the standard of nondiscrimination has little meaning.

In the coming period, poor women on welfare or newly ineligible for assistance should be a key group to monitor for health outcomes and access to health care. Since poverty is widely recognized as an important determinant of morbidity and mortality, one might expect to find a high incidence of health problems among women receiving cash assistance. In September 1995, Senator Edward Kennedy warned: "There is a right way and a wrong way to reform welfare. Punishing children is the wrong way. The Senate is on the brink of committing legislative child abuse."[8] Typical of many advocates for the welfare population, Kennedy spoke exclusively for children without any mention of the abuse of poor women. Women should be the centerpiece of welfare advocacy efforts, both for their own sake and for

---

7. *Ibid.*

8. "Senate OK's Transforming Welfare System," *Raleigh News and Observer*, 20 September 1995, A1, A10.

the sake of their children, since the fate and the health status of women and children are inextricably linked.

Reliable baseline data will be essential for assessing the future impact of welfare reform measures on women and children. However, historical sources of data for monitoring health risks and outcomes among the AFDC population are extremely limited. The emphasis on surveillance of behaviors rather than health indicators of AFDC recipients has influenced the nature of available information. Welfare rolls are carefully maintained for purposes of enumeration, but the collection of information from recipients is usually in a disciplinary context. Validity of self-reported AFDC status in existing health surveys may be threatened by the associated stigma and the fear of losing benefits. Efforts to ensure data quality, achieve adequate sample sizes of recipients, and overcome other methodological barriers will only be undertaken if the influence of welfare policy on health outcomes becomes a topic of greater interest to researchers and policymakers.

Given the prominence of efforts to reduce infant mortality in the U.S., one might expect to find extensive research focused on the health of AFDC recipients as a group of vulnerable mothers. In reality, AFDC mothers have seldom been identified as the focus of public health research on health outcomes and health care utilization trends. A search of MEDLINE, the bibliographic database of the National Library of Medicine, revealed that 1,592 documents made reference to poverty between January 1985 and May 1995. Out of more than 3.7 million articles from over 3,600 journals indexed in this database, only 18 abstracts referred to AFDC. Only three of these abstracts contained references to women and health.

A review of health-related literature in the MEDLINE database found only one study that documented health hazards in the home environments of AFDC recipients; residences of the majority of women and children in a Memphis AFDC sample had neither a functional smoke detector nor tap-water controlled at a safe temperature.[9] Another recent study estimated high rates of alcoholism and drug abuse among a sample of 206 AFDC recipients in Montgomery County, Maryland.[10] The findings of this small study, intended to demonstrate potential barriers to work transitions and

---

9. G. B. Sharp and M. A. Carter, "Prevalence of Smoke Detectors and Safe Tap-Water Temperatures Among Welfare Recipients in Memphis, Tennessee," *Journal of Community Health* 17 (1992): 351-65.

10. C. B. Sisco and C. L. Pearson, "Prevalence of Alcoholism and Drug Abuse Among Female AFDC Recipients," *Health and Social Work* 19 (1994): 75-77.

the unmet need for drug treatment, were reported in the national media and undoubtedly interpreted by many to reflect on recipients' characters rather than their programmatic and health needs.

Not surprisingly, outbreaks of vaccine-preventable diseases followed declines in childhood immunization in the 1980s. According to a study by Teitelbaum and Franklin,[11] "This decline coincided with vaccine price increases, an increase in the percentage of children in poverty and a decline in the rate of poor children receiving Aid to Families with Dependent Children (AFDC) and Medicaid." They attributed 100,000 cases of disease to the drop in immunizations; 55,000 cases, 11,000 hospitalizations, and 130 deaths occurred in the measles epidemic from 1989-91. One can imagine, but not easily measure, the effects on these children's mothers in terms of caretaking, anxiety, time lost from work or other responsibilities, and grief.

A study of childhood mortality (ages 1-18) in North Carolina used AFDC eligibility as a surrogate measure for poverty.[12] Because the author was interested in income status and not program participation, he grouped AFDC participants together with children ascertained to be AFDC-eligible from Medicaid records, and discovered that the mortality risk of this combined group was almost three times as great as the risk for non-eligible (i.e., higher income) children. Relative risks were higher for deaths in certain age groups for particular causes; for example, deaths from perinatal conditions (during the period surrounding childbirth) were 5.4 times more likely among AFDC-eligible children, and deaths from fire were 9 times as likely to occur to AFDC-eligible children, ages 1-4, compared with their more affluent counterparts.

This analysis provided powerful evidence of the relationship between poverty and childhood mortality, but missed an opportunity to explore differences among poor children based on their AFDC status. If children at similar income levels were more likely to suffer early deaths when they were not enrolled in AFDC, it is possible that AFDC benefits may have played a protective role in the family environment. If the mortality rates were higher or similar for AFDC children, the detailed information on ages

11. M. A. Teitelbaum and P. C. Franklin, "Vaccine-Preventable Illness in U.S. Children: 1980-1992," *Statistical Bulletin of the Metropolitan Insurance Company* 75 (1994): 2-9.

12. M. D. Nelson, "Socioeconomic Status and Childhood Mortality in North Carolina," *American Journal of Public Health* 82 (1992): 1131-33.

and causes of death could be used to define interventions that could be targeted to recipient families. For example, more rigorous inspection of subsidized housing could be mandated in order to reduce fire hazards, and landlords receiving subsidies for eligible tenants could be penalized for not providing and maintaining smoke detectors.

If the intent of welfare programs were truly to provide a public safety net and enhance self-sufficiency, participation could be used as an opportunity for health promotion and disease prevention. Such an orientation towards welfare would require not only a major shift in social values, but a reorientation towards the collection and utilization of data related to welfare recipients. In the rest of this chapter, I will review the availability of data for monitoring health status and health care access of AFDC recipients, identify potential women's health problems associated with welfare reform measures, and suggest changes necessary to improve existing databases or develop new information sources on health indicators for participants in AFDC and future income support programs.

Beyond administrative counts, sociodemographic descriptors, and accounting of costs, current sources of information for key issues are limited. AFDC participation has not always been included as a variable in national health surveys, though notable exceptions exist. The National Medical Expenditure Survey (NMES), which dates from 1987, asks about AFDC participation and includes numerous questions regarding health status, access, usage, and expenditures. Each year since 1990, the National Health Interview Survey (NHIS) has gathered information about AFDC as a source of household income, along with extensive data about health and medical care. The National Survey of Family Growth (NSFG), which is predominantly a fertility survey, has an AFDC question but fairly limited health information. The National Health and Nutrition Examination Survey (NHANES) asks respondents how much of their income, if any, comes from "welfare and other forms of public assistance," but does not ask explicitly about AFDC. The 1988 National Maternal and Infant Health Survey (NMIHS) asked women about AFDC status, but gathered limited diagnostic and service utilization data due to low provider response rates.

National sample surveys that focus on AFDC and other government program participation patterns tend not to question respondents in depth about their health, and certainly are not designed to detect program effects on health. Program evaluation research often measures "high-risk" characteristics of women, such as poverty and unmarried motherhood, which may overlap with but are not equivalent to AFDC status. Without specific data on AFDC enrollment, it is not possible to distinguish between AFDC-eligible women who receive other benefits (e.g., Special Supplemental Food Program for Women, Infants, and Children, or WIC) and those who do not, or between participants in other programs such as WIC who are AFDC recipients and those who are not.

The failure to identify AFDC participation has been especially problematic in evaluations of the Medicaid program for coverage of prenatal care and delivery costs. Though averted at least temporarily, the proposed conversion of the federal-state Medicaid program into state block grants heightens the importance of assessing the strengths and weaknesses of Medicaid maternity coverage. A major reform strategy since the late 80s has been the extension of Medicaid maternity benefits to pregnant women of low and moderate income who lack private insurance coverage but do not qualify for AFDC. Prior to these expansions, the vast majority of Medicaid-eligible pregnant women were on AFDC, and Medicaid coverage was a reasonably good proxy for AFDC status for purposes of monitoring and evaluation. In recent years, however, pregnant women and new mothers with Medicaid coverage have become a much more diverse group. In spite of their lack of private insurance, women who are newly included in Medicaid might be expected to have fewer health risks, better resources for obtaining care, and more favorable outcomes than AFDC mothers.

Initial evaluations showed that although rapid state implementation of the expansions extended coverage to many previously uninsured women, entry into prenatal care was still markedly delayed for Medicaid patients. Further evaluations confirmed the persistence of poor access to care for women with Medicaid coverage. Research has failed to demonstrate any improvements in birth outcomes for the Medicaid population relative to women with private insurance coverage in this recent period.[13]

---

13. B. Schwethelm, L. H. Margolis, C. Miller, and S. Smith, "Risk Status and Pregnancy Outcome Among Medicaid Recipients," *American Journal of Preventive Medicine* 5 (1989): 157-63. C. N. Oberg, B. Lia-Hoagberg, E. Hodkinson, C. Skovholt, and R. Vanman, "Prenatal Care Comparisons Among Privately Insured, Uninsured, and Medicaid-Enrolled Women," *Public Health Reports* 105 (1990): 533-35. J. M. Piper, W. A. Ray, and M. R. Griffin, "Effects of Medicaid Eligibility Expansion of Prenatal Care and Pregnancy Outcome in Tennessee," *JAMA* 264 (1990): 2219-64. *Prenatal Care: Early Successes in Enrolling Women Made Eligible by Medicaid Expansions* (Washington, D.C.: U.S. General Accounting Office, 1991). P. Braveman, T. Bennett, C. Lewis, S. Egerter, and J. Showstack, "Access to Prenatal Care Following Major Medicaid Eligibility Expansions," *JAMA* 269 (1993): 1285-89.

Lack of improvement for the Medicaid population as a whole could reflect declining trends for women on AFDC, who might be crowded out of the limited Medicaid provider pool. The stalling of progress might alternatively (or additionally) indicate a system so overloaded and dysfunctional that it engenders rather than reduces risks for the near-poor. To get a clear view of the situation, it would seem essential to analyze separately the trends in prenatal care and birth outcomes for the AFDC population and the newly-eligible women at higher income levels. Yet none of the published evaluation studies attempts this type of comparative analysis by focusing separately on women who qualify for Medicaid based on AFDC enrollment.

What explains the lack of focused attention in medical and public health research on the health status and health service utilization of women on AFDC who are living in severe poverty? A number of factors undoubtedly influence both the capacity and the motivation of researchers in the public health community. A major limitation is the lack of appropriate data, a deficit which mirrors more fundamental ideological and policy realities. Population-based maternal and child health studies frequently rely on vital statistics records, specifically birth certificates, which are now linked for all states with infant death records. Despite significant weaknesses, reporting in birth and death certificates is deemed acceptably complete and accurate for monitoring of vital events and trends in relation to sociodemographic characteristics. Insurance coverage, however, is noted on birth certificates in only 12 Registration Areas – 11 states and New York City. Insurance status is a key element in hospital discharge records because of their accounting function; with considerable effort, hospital discharge data can be linked to birth certificates. However, AFDC status is not recorded in either vital statistics or hospital records, for obvious and significant reasons of confidentiality.

Other technical problems interfere with the best intentions to monitor the health of AFDC participants. The recipient population is ever-changing, with people cycling on and off, and many other influences on their health continually change as well. Longitudinal studies would be needed to assess effects of program participation. Government-funded longitudinal surveys exist for other purposes. The Survey of Income and Program Participation (SIPP), conducted by the U.S. Bureau of the Census, and the Panel Study of Income Dynamics (PSID), contracted by the National Science Foundation to the Survey Research Institute at the University of Michigan, are rich sources of information about AFDC recipients' circumstances over time;

but they do not include detailed queries about women's general and reproductive health.

Without more extensive longitudinal data, we cannot establish the causal direction between poor health and welfare status. We do not know the extent to which medical problems precipitate or prolong AFDC participation, or whether any aspects of AFDC status increase the likelihood of physical or mental disability. Even without better longitudinal studies, more adequate cross-sectional information about the health of the AFDC population would be very useful to assess women's problems and needs and to design appropriate preventive health programs.

The apparent disregard for information about AFDC recipients' health status cannot be attributed wholly to technical difficulties. Since the hope is that women's welfare status will be transitory, accompanying risks may not be seen as enduring, even though poor health is a major barrier to self-sufficiency and departure from the welfare program. More importantly, welfare status is increasingly considered blameworthy. If women are blamed for the conditions that cause their entry into income support programs, they will also be held accountable for problems that ensue from their impoverishment and discriminatory treatment as recipients. Since data collection, monitoring, and evaluation of program effects are motivated by accountability, it is not surprising that an abdication of public responsibility would correspond to a lack of information.

In the moralistic view, welfare mothers are seen as irresponsible not only towards their children but also towards society because of their reproductive decisions. Harsh disincentives to childbearing among teenagers, single women, and poor women are prominent among welfare reform measures currently being implemented at the federal and state levels. Proposals have been widely disseminated to enforce economic penalties against single mothers and even establish government-run orphanages for the placement of their children. If prevention of additional pregnancies among women in the income support program is a major policy objective, monitoring indicators of reproductive health for recipients is not likely to be a high priority.

Numerous researchers, most notably under the sponsorship of the Kids Count Project of the Annie E. Casey Foundation, have developed and disseminated social indicators of children's health and well-being that should be useful for monitoring. Less attention has been focused on indicators of women's well-being, although many welfare reform proposals are

designed to influence women's incentives, behaviors, and social and economic status. The direct consequences of such policies on women's health
cannot be detected solely through their effects on children.

The Personal Responsibility and Work Opportunity Reconciliation Act
of 1996 (PL 104-193) eliminates AFDC as an entitlement, leaving significant discretion to states in administering Temporary Assistance for Needy
Families (TANF) as a block grant program. Among the federal mandates
to be implemented by July 1, 1997 is a cumulative time limit of five years
for cash assistance. Work requirements take effect after two years of
benefits; after two months of program participation, non-working adults
must perform community service.

Teen parents are not eligible for TANF benefits unless they are living
with their parents or in an "approved, adult-supervised setting," and states
are not required to assist unmarried teen parents or their children. States
are allowed, but not required, to deny additional benefits to women who
become pregnant while on public assistance (i.e., child exclusion of the
"family cap"). Legal immigrants become eligible for cash assistance, nonemergency Medicaid, and other federal means-tested benefits only after
five years of residence; undocumented immigrants cannot qualify for any
benefits.

In an attempt to meet its objectives of reducing out-of-wedlock childbearing and promoting two-parent families, PL 104-193 establishes an
"illegitimacy bonus" to states that decrease out-of-wedlock births without
increasing the number of abortions. However, states are no longer required
to provide family planning services to welfare recipients. Instead, abstinence education programs are mandated to teach students that "sexual
activity outside of the context of marriage is likely to have harmful psychological and physical effects." Women's eligibility for TANF is contingent on establishment of paternity, and child support enforcement is
strengthened.

Many elements of the1996 federal welfare reform legislation have
already been implemented by states. According to *The New York Times*,[14]
"The Administration has generally denied waivers only when it consideres
changes unconstitutional." Nineteen states have already obtained waivers

---

14. "Tighter Welfare in Massachusetts," *New York Times*, 4 February 1995, A1, A6.

for child exclusion.[15] At least dozen states now have two-year limits on AFDC benefits. North Carolina's "Work First" welfare reform package requires the first wave of recipients (a third of the state's total) to start working at a paid or unpaid job within 12 weeks of enrollment. AFDC applicants must sign personal responsibility contracts, and any violation of the contract (e.g., failure to get children immunized, children's absence from school) will result in penalties – including revocation of Medicaid benefits for nonpregnant women.[16] Under the provisions of the Personal Responsibility and Work Opportunity Reconciliation Act for continuing waiver programs, it seems likely that states will continue to receive encouragement for such experiments.

In the current "reform" environment, attempts are being made to leverage changes in health care utilization by applying sanctions through state welfare programs. Several states have already received federally approved waivers to limit welfare benefits based on numerous criteria, including compliance with recommended schedules of prenatal care, immunizations, and other preventive health services. Concerns have been raised about inequities among states or coercive practices resulting from such policies, as well as the potential loss of welfare benefits by families that cannot meet these utilization criteria because of their limited access to health care. If states provide information about the number of persons losing eligibility for specific reasons, these data could be examined in conjunction with statistics about availability of the targeted services.

It will be essential to monitor trends in addition to those for the intended outcomes, especially in relation to women's health. For example, the loss of AFDC eligibility for unmarried teen mothers is intended to reduce out-of-wedlock childbearing, a trend which can be assessed easily (if not totally accurately) from birth certificate data. However, the overall policy impact cannot be understood without examining birth outcomes. Currently, the mortality rate for infants of married teen mothers under 18 is slightly higher than the rate for infants of young unmarried teens.[17] It is possible

15. "The New Welfare Reform Law: Provisions Affecting Reproductive Health," The Alan Guttmacher Institute (New York and Washington, D.C., September 1996).

16. "Gov. Hunt Launches 'Work First' Welfare Reform," State of North Carolina, Governor's Press Office (Raleigh, North Carolina, 14 September 1995).

17. T. Bennett and Division of Analysis, National Center for Health Statistics, Centers for Disease Control, "Infant Mortality by Marital Status of Mother – United States, 1983," *Morbidity and Mortality Weekly Report* 39 (1990): 521-23.

that teen birth rates could decline or more pregnant teens might marry subsequent to the change in welfare policy; in either case, the stated objective would be achieved. However, it is also possible that the infant mortality rate might rise for single teen mothers losing income supports, or for teens bearing children in the often precarious circumstances of teen marriage. Though infant mortality data specific to AFDC recipients are generally not available, gains or losses resulting from welfare reform might be reflected in indicators for the general population and especially for low-income and vulnerable groups.

The rest of this discussion will speculate about insults to women's health and well-being that may result from the different areas of welfare reform being enacted, and will suggest some information sources and techniques for monitoring women's health to marshall the evidence. Critics have expressed concerns that current welfare experiments may threaten reproductive autonomy for poor women and enhance risks to women's health through increasing the likelihood of homelessness, inadequate nutrition, domestic violence, and exposure to physical and psychological hazards of workplaces associated with low-wage employment. It is critically important for public health and welfare rights advocates, supported by feminist allies and other human rights activists, to monitor these and other areas of potential harm.

Such efforts will suffer from the lack of past data collection and analysis, and also from the likelihood that data will become more sparse with budget cuts and the minimized oversight and regulation that are likely to accompany block grants. Official data efforts will concentrate on the explicit policy goals. Other social perspectives – feminist, humanistic, and non-punitive – should be brought to bear on future surveillance. Indicators of health and well-being in an era of radical government restructuring must be designed to capture fully the complementary needs of women, children, and families.

In the sections below I indicate some existing data that can be utilized for monitoring purposes. These are actually "wish lists" in which I have tried to imagine the optimal range of information. In some areas I am unaware of available information, but I am sure that a collaborative effort of researchers and advocates could uncover valuable sources. In other cases, the collective undertaking would have to be the actual collection of primary data through various means or the organization of campaigns to demand improved data collection by government agencies. Surveys, focus groups, ethnographic studies, and other qualitative research methods will need to be employed to supplement analysis of routine vital statistics and program administrative data, such as hospital discharge data, Medicaid claims files, and WIC records. However, it will be important to seek possible interrelationships between health and welfare policy in routine analyses of those existing data sources and to develop new strategies for analysis and reporting of policy-relevant data.

Since it is difficult to find information about the actual health status of AFDC recipients, it will be important to assess characteristics of the changing welfare population that indicate the presence of reproductive and other health risks. Data prior to welfare reform should be obtained whenever available, but regular monitoring should be implemented as quickly as possible, regardless of earlier gaps. Information on aggregate changes in the age, parity, and racial/ethnic composition of the welfare population, as well as average length of time receiving benefits, should be available through program records. Levels of funding and the number of eligible applicants turned away should be tracked, in addition to the level of participation in TANF, WIC, and other programs. Decreases in the number of participants should not be assumed to be signs of success, but should be considered in conjunction with city- or neighborhood-level census data reflecting community need, such as poverty, unemployment, and literacy rates.

As eligibility restrictions and work requirements are implemented, it will be important to monitor the health status of the TANF population and also the larger population of Medicaid-eligible and other low-income women who previously might have qualified for AFDC benefits. Overall population trends should be evaluated, whether or not AFDC or TANF participants can be identified and analyzed separately. Relevant trends would include the incidence of low birthweight, maternal and infant mortality, premature death of women from various causes, and cases of HIV and other infectious diseases reported for women. The effects of welfare policy changes could be severe enough to have an overall impact on population rates, though their importance should not be discounted if this is not the case.

A study by the Southern Institute on Children and Families[18] confirmed that potential loss of Medicaid coverage is an important disincentive in

---

18. S. C. Shuptrine, V. C. Grant and G. G. McKenzie, *A Study of the Relationship of Health Coverage to Welfare Dependency* (Columbia, South Carolina: Southern Institute on Children and Families, March 1994).

AFDC recipients' decision to seek employment. To be meaningful in terms of providing security, work requirements must be premised on continuation of Medicaid coverage if work-related insurance is not provided. Under the federal-state Medicaid system, non-AFDC applicants often face extended delays in certification for coverage, especially if they are not pregnant. Medicaid coverage in the transition from welfare to work may be administered differently by various states. Rosenbaum and Darnell have noted that "Unless individuals losing their welfare have an alternative eligibility pathway under federal law, they may lose their Medicaid eligibility once their eligibility for welfare ends."[19] For these reasons, it will be critical to keep track of the number of uninsured women ages 15-44 (as well as the entire uninsured population) through monitoring of hospital discharge records, national surveys, and other available sources. It may also become necessary to track the Medicaid eligibility status of TANF recipients in states with varying regulations.

One promising source of data is Medicaid claims files. Like hospital discharge records, they are primarily compiled for billing rather than research purposes; but they may identify different eligibility categories, including welfare status. The author is currently involved in a Cooperative Agreement[20] with the Centers for Disease Control and Prevention, the University of North Carolina at Chapel Hill, the North Carolina State Center for Health Statistics, and the North Carolina Division of Medical Assistance to accomplish a linkage between birth certificates and Medicaid claims files for services provided to new mothers during a two-year period surrounding the deliveries of their newborns. This project requires resources and interagency cooperation that are not easily attainable; the resulting database will allow comparative analyses of multiple health and health services issues for AFDC recipients and other low- and moderate-income women eligible for Medicaid financing of maternity care. Such efforts could contribute to the establishment of baseline indicators to assess the impact of future changes in AFDC and Medicaid.

---

19. S. Rosenbaum and J. Darnell, "An Analysis of the Medicaid and Health-Related Provisions of the Personal Responsibility and Work Opportunity Reconciliation Act of 1996," *Health Policy and Child Health* 3 (Summer 1996): 1-8.

20. Cooperative Agreement U48-CCU409660-04 between Centers for Disease Control and Prevention, Health Promotion Disease Prevention Research Center, Reproductive Health Division; and University of North Carolina at Chapel Hill, Center for Health Promotion and Disease Prevention and Department of Maternal and Child Health (FY 1996-97).

We hope to repeat this data linkage in the future for the purpose of comparing cross-sectional profiles of low-income women over time. Longitudinal analyses of health and welfare issues for poor women are complicated by continuous changes in individual women's program participation and needs, as well as administrative changes in welfare programs. Sequential analyses of large-scale databases, however, may suggest ecologic influences on the health of poor women. If welfare reform succeeds in promoting economic independence among low-income women in a health-enhancing manner, one would expect to see favorable trends – especially among the Medicaid-eligible women who are not TANF recipients. On the other hand, if welfare cuts and restrictions are injurious, the harmful effects may be discernible in these data among both the TANF and the broader Medicaid populations. Even though the technical tasks involved in such a data linkage require research facilities beyond the capacity of most advocacy groups, similar projects, where feasible, should be useful for the work of advocates, community organizers, and health planners.

It is not possible to make precise predictions about the effects of new state Medicaid options in terms of data availability, access to services, or health outcomes. Whether or not consistent data and reporting requirements prevail at the national level, it will be extremely important to document the effects of each state's particular strategies. In 1982, an 18% reduction of Medicaid funding in California resulted in closures of emergency rooms and trauma centers. Preventable morbidity and mortality attributed to lack of access to services incurred before an influx of federal Medicaid dollars rescued California from this severe crisis. Congressional proposals that were defeated in 1996 would have reduced the average state's Medicaid budget by 30%, with no possibility of a federal bailout.[21] States will surely be searching for any means of controlling Medicaid costs; North Carolina's plan to penalize noncompliant welfare recipients by withdrawal of Medicaid coverage may gain broader appeal as a cost-saving measure. The documentation of Medicaid cuts and their consequences may be left to patients and their advocates as systems and agency personnel rapidly "downsize" and change.

The Department of Health and Human Services currently mandates external research evaluations, including impact analysis of state waiver

---

21. J. Finberg and S. Dorn, *Unraveling the Mystery of Medicaid Block Grants* (San Francisco and Washington, D.C.: Consumers Union, Inc. and National Health Law Program, July 1995).

programs, as well as quarterly reporting on program implementation. The methodological difficulties of evaluations are compounded as waivers become more complex.[22] One can only speculate about the reporting and evaluation requirements for TANF block grants, and the likelihood of isolating separate program effects is low. The first imperative is to register the number of women in each state who lose eligibility or benefits for any reason. Myriad other measures may be culled from various sources to document possible effects of welfare restrictions: changes in the number of homeless women (with and without children), increases in foster care placements, arrests of women for petty economic crimes, rising numbers of women's psychiatric hospitalizations in public hospitals. With the possible exception of psychiatric hospitalization, many of these are not typically considered health indicators. However, the stresses associated with abandonment, loss, and coercion present drastic risks to mental health. Severe health consequences are well-documented for homelessness, as well as for the continuum of deprivation leading to a homeless state.

The objective of reducing out-of-wedlock fertility is the basis of broad political consensus. The claim at the crux of the welfare debate that AFDC provides incentives to out-of-wedlock childbearing and marital dissolution has spawned voluminous research. A critical review of the literature shows the findings to be inconsistent and largely inconclusive; overall, no effect has been demonstrated for the impact of AFDC on out-of-wedlock fertility. Perhaps more importantly, large increases in nonwhite poverty have been shown to result from termination of benefits.[23]

Frequent claims are made that out-of-wedlock childbearing is a primary cause of infant mortality. In fact, research indicates that single mothers are at high risk due to related causes, such as poverty and inadequate prenatal care.[24] Unmarried motherhood has been associated with infant mortality in numerous studies, but the effect of marital status on birth outcomes has been shown to differ by mothers' age and race/ethnicity. Research has generally failed to show a disadvantage for unmarried adolescent mothers

22. M. C. Laracy, "If It Seems Too Good To Be True, It Probably Is," The Annie E. Casey Foundation, 21 June 1995.

23. S. Danziger, R. Haveman, and R. Plotnick, *Antipoverty Policy: Effects on the Poor and the Nonpoor* (Williamsburg, Virginia: Institute for Research on Poverty and U.S. DHHS, 1984).

24. T. Bennett, "Marital Status and Infant Health Outcomes," *Social Science and Medicine* 35 (1992): 1179-87.

vis-à-vis their married counterparts, and the heightened risk of unmarried women appears to be greater for whites than for blacks.[25] These findings confirm that risks associated with out-of-wedlock births are neither uniform nor inevitable. Unmarried status *per se* may not be a good predictor of health risk among women who are disadvantaged by low socioeconomic status and discriminatory treatment.

Nonmarital births are often presumed to be unintended or unwanted. Such a general assumption is unwarranted; though marital status is associated with pregnancy intentions, a substantial proportion of out-of-wedlock births are reported by women as wanted.[26] Completed fertility, however, is lower for single mothers than for married women. In the AFDC recipient population, the average family size including parents and children dropped from 4.0 in 1969 to 2.9 in 1992. Over the same time period, the proportion of AFDC families with only one or two children increased from 49.6% to 72.7%.[27]

The 1967 Social Security amendments directly challenged the right to choose unmarried motherhood by approving the use of funding for birth control "for the purpose of preventing and reducing out-of-wedlock births." Now states will be offered financial incentives for lowering their "illegitimacy ratio," as long as abortions do not increase. In other words, sanctions will be imposed at the state level against single motherhood and against abortion for all women, not just for welfare recipients. The inclusion of abortion in this formula reveals the underlying agenda attacking reproductive rights. If the policy objective is a reduction in out-of-wedlock childbearing, but abortion is not considered an acceptable option, then the assumption is that abstinence must prevail unless effective contraceptive is widely utilized.

In the absence of adequate family planning and medical services, disincentives for childbearing among welfare recipients might exert coercive pressure towards utilization of Norplant or other long-acting contraceptives or irreversible sterilization. Though these are popular methods

25. *Ibid.*

26. S. R. DePersio, W. Chen, D. Blose, R. Lorenz, W. Thomas, and P. N. Zenker, "Unintended Childbearing: Pregnancy Risk Assessment Monitoring System – Oklahoma, 1988-1991," *Morbidity and Mortality Weekly Report* 41 (1992): 933-36.

27. United States Department of Health and Human Services, Administration for Children and Families, Office of Family Assistance, *FY 1992 Aid to Families with Dependent Children.* (Washington, D.C.: U.S. DHHS, 1994).

chosen voluntarily by many women, the availability of such reproductive technologies raises many ethical questions. Awareness of the potential for coercion has triggered intensive monitoring efforts of state legislation, litigation, and the availability and promotion of long-acting hormonal contraceptives with publicly-funded patients.[28] Funding for this purpose from the Kaiser Family Foundation to the Alan Guttmacher Institute has now expired, which may herald the end of coordinated national monitoring. Continued vigilance is especially important since there seems to be a shift in patient demand from Norplant to Depo-Provera, an injectable contraceptive that may receive less public scrutiny than Norplant because it does not require surgical insertion or removal.

Vital statistics data on teen pregnancy and out-of-wedlock births are routinely collected and reported by the states and the National Center for Health Statistics. Most states also report the number of induced abortions. The Alan Guttmacher Institute monitors levels of abortion funding, availability of abortion providers, proxy measures of unintended pregnancy, and unmet needs for family planning. Whether or not welfare recipients can be distinguished, family planning data from clinics and health departments should be reviewed for trends in the number of patients and visits, and the contraceptive methods chosen by different subgroups of women (e.g., teens). Focus groups with family planning clinic nurses and with TANF and other clients about method selection and utilization would be helpful to detect pressures on providers and patients. In addition, the relative risk of single compared with married mothers for outcomes such as low birthweight and infant mortality should also be noted as welfare reform progresses. The existing disadvantages of single mothers may be exacerbated by the public campaign against out-of-wedlock childbearing.

Finally, the Medicaid waivers to extend the postpartum eligibility period for family planning services (so far approved in Maryland, Rhode Island, and South Carolina) should be evaluated in relation to patient satisfaction, inter-birth intervals, and other fertility trends. Evaluations should also address the question of whether isolated eligibility for family planning enhances general health status and utilization of other primary health care services. If other states receive approval for waivers to extend

---

28. S. E. Samuels and M. D. Smith, eds., *Dimensions of New Contraceptives: Norplant and Poor Women* (Menlo Park, California: Henry J. Kaiser Family Foundation, 1992).

postpartum eligibility for a broader range of services, comparative evaluations may be possible.

Most welfare reform proposals require hospitals to establish paternity and create various mechanisms for tracking fathers and collecting child support. While making fathers accountable for their parental responsibility, such measures threaten other consequences for women. In the past, AFDC benefits have provided an escape hatch for women fleeing abuse. Both the House and Senate welfare reform bills propose the creation of national data banks using Social Security numbers for surveillance purposes. While the stated intent is to track down "deadbeat dads," the rest of us would also be traced every time we changed jobs or obtained a driver's or occupational license. Garfinkel[29] points out that among the other people who might be located against their wishes are victims of domestic violence who have fled from their attackers. The risk of domestic violence could also increase as a result of pressures for teen mothers to stay in their parental homes. Changes in reported incidents of domestic abuse and requests for services at battered women's shelters could provide data to verify these fears.

The more restrictive the new welfare laws become, the greater the potential for electronic surveillance. If lifetime limits of five years or less on TANF are to be enforced, sophisticated national data systems will have to be developed. It doesn't take a great deal of imagination or paranoia to spell scenarios of risk to individual civil liberties. For example, the release of a woman's medical records to a potential employer might reveal previous welfare status. Ironically, a history of public assistance could undercut a woman's efforts towards employment and economic independence.

Given the current U.S. economy, the emphasis on employment to replace income subsidies is destined to concentrate many former recipients in low-wage, low-status jobs; to displace other women who have managed to avoid welfare by working at such jobs; and to weaken unionization and other worker organizing efforts. The fear of losing a job without any other safety net will deter attempts to improve working conditions, including health and safety provisions. Little is known about the health risks that may be introduced by workfare programs because there have been few occupational health studies of low-wage service workers in the U.S.[30] Among the

---

29. S. Garfinkel, *San Jose Mercury News*, 17 July 1995, 1F.

30. A. Dula, S. Kurtz, and M. L. Samper, "Occupational and Environmental Reproductive Hazards: Education and Resources for Communities of Color,"

potential sources of work-related stress that could be detrimental to women, in addition to toxic exposures and physical hazards, are rigid work schedules, necessity of working at more than one job, isolation, fatigue, multiple role strain, and disrespectful treatment. Both health and welfare policy should be based on a comprehensive understanding of the effects of service sector employment on women's health and well-being, since this is likely to be the nature of mandatory private or public sector jobs for welfare recipients.

Workfare program administrative data should indicate the levels of employment attained. Additional efforts might track the patterns in women's employment-related insurance coverage, unemployment rates for women once they enter the workforce, rates of injuries, and workers' compensation and work-related disability claims filed by women workers. Newly attained employment status must be assessed to determine if it enhances women's health or if there may be detrimental effects of the types of employment required and the stresses of combining low-wage work with family responsibilities.

The Food Research and Action Group (FRAC) and other nutrition and hunger advocacy groups, as well as the American Public Health Association (APHA), mobilized successfully in 1996 to prevent the dismantling of the WIC, Food Stamp, and other nutrition programs essential for maternal and family health. The proposal to fold these programs into a nutrition block grant would have eliminated not only program dollars, but also uniform requirements for high-quality nutritional content, broad eligibility, and monitoring for quality assurance. However, the new welfare law did reduce the Food Stamp budget by $27.7 billion over six years by cutting eligibility to legal immigrants and adjusting other eligibility and benefit rules. President Clinton's attempt to reverse some of these cuts after his re-election was met by resistance in Congress from both Republicans and Democrats who had committed themselves to the compromise.[31]

In addition to the concrete areas mentioned in this discussion, the potential for loss of human rights and civil liberties looms large in the campaign to end "welfare as we know it." Consider the quality of life for a teen mother in Delaware, a state which has received approval for a waiver

---

Environmental Health Perspectives 101, Suppl. 2 (1993): 181-89.

31. "Clinton Considers Move to Soften Cuts in Welfare," *New York Times,* 27 November 1996, A1.

that will "require teen parents to live in an adult-supervised setting, attend school, immunize their children and take part in parenting and family planning education." Delaware teens are required to sign a "contract of mutual responsibility" to receive benefits for a maximum of two years, which are contingent on participation in job training. Massachusetts legislation requires that teens desiring benefits must finish school and live either at home, in a group home, or in an alternative state-approved setting.

In 1994, Clinton overrode the California legislature to allow Los Angeles welfare officials to fingerprint AFDC applicants.[32] New York City is currently taking fingerprints of persons receiving Home Relief (General Assistance) and plans to start fingerprinting AFDC recipients. City officials interpret the extremely low rate of duplicate fingerprints as a sign that screening is an effective deterrent to fraud; to welfare rights advocates, this is a sign that accusations of fraud are grossly exaggerated.[33]

In the face of this kind of social disciplining of poor women, the public health and feminist communities cannot afford to ask whether monitoring of health effects will make a difference. The question must be how to make the information matter – to policymakers, to the public, and to the health professionals who serve the communities being targeted. A group of prominent feminist scholars and activists formed the Committee of One Hundred to proclaim solidarity with poor women, stating that "We think that it is urgent that women speak out *as women* against punitive welfare legislation. . . . This legislation will primarily wreak its havoc on poor women and their children. . . . But the provisions concerning reproductive and familial choices for those needing welfare suggest a broader effort to pressure all women into a repressive sexuality, limited reproductive choices, and conventional family arrangements."[34]

These are public health issues, and the task for concerned women and others within public health is to join the two areas of health and welfare policy. Multisectoral cooperation will be required at the state and local levels to monitor health-related data in many areas. The challenge is to devise strategies that will document the health-related needs of TANF recipients and other poor women while protecting their rights to privacy,

32. "Welfare Program Requiring Parents to Be Fingerprinted," *New York Times*, 31 March 1994, A13.
33. "Welfare Fingerprinting Finds Most People Are Telling Truth," *New York Times*, 29 September 1995, B1, B4.
34. Statement in a flyer published by Committee of One Hundred (May 1995).

consent, and nondiscrimination. We can perform a service to welfare rights advocacy groups by providing evidence of the health consequences of so-called welfare reform. Presentation of the same data to health care providers can heighten their sense of social responsibility and the need to advocate for their patients, with a focus on women in their own right as well as in their role as mothers.

CHAPTER FOUR

Improving Health Data Among American Indians and Alaska Natives: An Approach from the Pacific Northwest[1]

Jonathan R. Sugarman,
Martha Holliday, Andrew Ross, and Doni Wilder

While generally unrecognized amid the conventional wisdom that there was little progress in the arena of government-sponsored health reform in the early 1990s, the health care system for American Indians and Alaska Natives (AI/AN) is in the process of tumultuous and exciting change. Although hardly the fodder for front page national news reports or radio talk shows, the process of change within the Indian health system reflects in microcosm the national mood for increased local control, reducing the federal bureaucracy, and moving resources to the service delivery level. These changes are likely to impact the collection and reporting of Indian health data on a national level.

In considering the health status of vulnerable and excluded populations, the situation of AI/ANs deserves particular attention because of the unique position of Native Americans[2] in the U.S. health system. At least three characteristics result in this unique position. The first is the special obliga-

1. This work was supported in part through a cooperative agreement (U83/CCU008678-01) from the National Center for Health Statistics of the Centers for Disease Control and Prevention.

2. In this paper, we use the terms American Indian and Alaska Native (AI/AN), Native American, and Indian interchangeably. While there are varying opinions regarding the appropriateness of these labels, many consider AI/AN to be the preferred terminology, because it is less ambiguous than "Native American," which is often understood to include Native Hawaiians and American Samoans, or misunderstood to refer to persons born in the United States.

tion of the federal government to provide health services for Indian people. The second is that, despite this federal obligation, there remains a considerable gap between the health status of AI/ANs and that of the general population. This gap clearly highlights the vulnerability of AI/AN populations and suggests the existence of persistent inequities in appropriate access to timely and appropriate health care. The third feature is the presence of over 500 sovereign tribal governments, whose ability to exercise tribal self-determination by entering into agreements with the federal government to operate the health programs in their communities has recently been enhanced through legislative changes. In this paper, we will briefly review several special challenges in monitoring the health of AI/ANs, and describe the application of an analytical strategy which can be used to address these challenges for a broad range of health status indicators.

American Indian and Alaska Native communities have a political relationship with the U.S. federal government which differs from that shared by other Americans in a number of respects. The differences follow from the special status of Indian tribes as sovereign nations with intrinsic rights to self-governance, and a government-to-government relationship with the U.S. An important aspect of this relationship is the obligation of the U.S. to assure the availability of health services to American Indians and Alaska Natives, an obligation that is not due to other Americans. Specific statutory authority for Congress to appropriate funds for health services to Indian tribes was authorized by the Snyder Act (25 U.S.C. 13) in 1921 and was reaffirmed and significantly enhanced in 1976 with the passage of P.L. 94-437, The Indian Health Care Improvement Act. Although there are disagreements between tribes and the federal government regarding the extent to which the federal trust responsibility for Indian tribes extends to health services, courts have generally accepted the premise that the trust responsibility extends to the arena of health services. Some have described the trust responsibility as the nation's first comprehensive pre-paid health policy, the premium for which was the (often forced) transfer of aboriginal Indian lands to the U.S. In order to gauge the needs of AI/AN people and to assess the success of interventions, comprehensive and accurate data regarding their health status are necessary. Readers interested in a more complete discussion of the Federal-Tribal relationship with regard to health through the 1980s are referred to a 1986 report prepared by the Office of Technology Assessment.[3]

The Indian Health Service (IHS), an agency of the Public Health Service, has been the lead federal agency charged with addressing the health needs of AI/AN. Since the establishment of the IHS in 1954, the health status of AI/AN has improved considerably. For instance, between 1973 and 1990, IHS reported a 54% decrease in infant mortality, an 81% decrease in mortality from gastrointestinal diseases (primarily infectious diarrhea), a 74% decrease in tuberculosis mortality, and a 36% decrease in mortality from alcoholism.[4] Despite these improvements, however, the health status of AI/AN lags far behind that of the general population. IHS reported that the alcoholism mortality rate among AI/AN in 1990 was 5.3 times that for the all-races population, the tuberculosis rate 5.4 times greater, and deaths rates from injuries were 2.6 times those for the all-races population. IHS reported that infant mortality rates in 1990 were only slightly higher than those for all races (10.2 compared to 9.2 deaths per 1,000 live births), although data from other sources[5] suggest that the discrepancy is far greater.

The adverse health status among AI/ANs is closely associated with socioeconomic deprivation.[6] According to the 1990 Census, nearly one third of the 1.9 million persons who identified themselves as AI/AN lived in poverty, compared to 13% for the nation as a whole. The median family income for AI/AN was $21,750, compared with $35,225 for the total population. AI/ANs were half as likely as other Americans to have a bachelor's degree or higher. In addition, the AI/AN population is young: 39% are less than 20 years of age, compared with 29% of the all-races population.

In the late 1960s and 1970s, Indian tribes began to reassert their right to control their own affairs and to end the paternalistic domination by the federal government who administered programs in Indian communities. While much of the dissatisfaction was directed towards the Bureau of Indian Affairs, tribes were also frustrated by the perceived unwillingness

3. See Office of Technology Assessment, *Indian Health Care,* OTA-H-290 (Washington, D.C.: U.S. Government Printing Office, April 1986).

4. See Indian Health Service, *Trends in Indian Health 1994,* (Rockville, MD: U.S. Department of Health and Human Services, 1994).

5. R. A. Hahn, J. Mulinare, and S. M. Teutsch, "Inconsistencies in Coding of Race and Ethnicity Between Birth and Death in U.S. Infants: A New Look at Infant Mortality, 1983-1985," *JAMA* 267 (1992): 259-63.

6. E. L. Paisano, *We the First Americans*, U.S. Department of Commerce, Bureau of the Census (Washington, D.C.: U.S. Government Printing Office, 1993), 350-631.

and opposition of the IHS to allowing tribal governments to exercise sufficient control over health care programs operating in tribal communities. Consequently, in 1975 Congress passed P.L. 93-638, the Indian Self-Determination and Education Assistance Act. This Act enabled tribes to enter into contracts with the federal government to operate for themselves programs provided for their benefit by the federal government. By 1990, approximately 50% of IHS programs were operated by tribes or tribal organizations.

The passage of P.L. 93-638 did not end the frustration of tribes. Extensive federal regulations and policies continued to allow for federal oversight of tribal-operated health programs. Excessive reporting, purchasing, and contracting regulations, which tribes believed restricted rather than enhanced health care delivery, created frustration. However, most troublesome to tribes was the perception that increased resources provided to the IHS by Congress in the late 1980s and early 1990s were disproportionately directed to headquarters-level administrative operations rather than directly to local communities.

In 1988 Congress passed a comprehensive amendment to P.L. 93-638. These amendments attempted to eliminate many regulatory and contract restrictions previously associated with tribal contracting of health programs. However, these amendments did not address the concern of tribes that much of the resources appropriated by Congress for the benefit of the Indian people were consumed by administrative layers above the tribal community. Consequently, in the late 1980s tribes initiated a dialogue with Congress to work toward the transfer of federal resources used for Indian programs to the direct control of the tribes themselves. This process came to be known as "self-governance."

Among the goals of self-governance are to recognize the right of sovereign tribes to determine internal priorities, to redesign and create new tribal programs, and to reallocate financial resources in a manner which the tribes felt would be more effective and efficient in meeting local needs.[7] Tribes reasoned that elimination of government personnel, procurement, and reporting regulations would free up resources for direct services to Indian people.

---

7. Lummi Nation Self-Governance Communication and Education Project. *Self-Governance: A New Partnership*, (Bellingham, Washington: Lummi Nation, 1995), 7.

The Tribal Self-Governance Demonstration Project was established in the Indian Self-Determination Act Amendments of 1988, with legislation focusing on the Bureau of Indian Affairs (BIA) in the Department of Interior. The demonstration project permitted the negotiation of compacts which transferred to tribes the responsibility to administer and manage services and functions previously managed by the BIA. In 1991, the Tribal Self-Governance Demonstration Project Act (P.L. 102-184) extended the authority to negotiate contracts between the federal government and tribes to the IHS, and 17 tribes began the self-governance negotiations with IHS. In 1994, Congress authorized up to 30 new tribes per year to enter into IHS compacts for the succeeding 10 years of the Demonstration Project. Each increase in the number of beneficiaries served under self-governance compacts results in a corresponding decrease in the number of beneficiaries to whom IHS provides service directly or through tribal contracts, along with a decrease in personnel and resources managed or overseen by IHS.

How might self-governance affect efforts to monitor the health of Indian people? One of the reasons tribes sought legislation was relief from cumbersome federal reporting requirements, which in the view of many tribal leaders did not return useful information to the local level. Tribes participating in the Self-Governance Demonstration Project have not been required to report patient care data (such as diagnosis-specific ambulatory care or inpatient hospitalization information) to existing IHS data systems. These systems, however, have been the main source of patient care data for Indian people across the nation for the past several decades. Most data regarding health care utilization of AI/AN are derived from the inpatient and ambulatory care data sets, which describe visits to hospitals and ambulatory care facilities operated directly by IHS or for visits paid for by the IHS Contract Health Services program. Data from the national surveys currently used to monitor ambulatory and inpatient care are not useful sources of data regarding Indian health for several reasons. First, federal facilities (including IHS and many tribally-operated hospitals) have not been included in the sampling frame of such surveys as the National Hospital Discharge Surveys and the National Hospital Ambulatory Medical Care Survey.[8] Likewise, the National Ambulatory Medical Care Surveys

---

8. E. J. Graves, "National Hospital Discharge Survey: Annual summary, 1992," National Center for Health Statistics, *Vital and Health Statistics,* Series 13, no. 119 (Washington, D.C.: U.S. Government Printing Office, 1994), 1-63. L. F. McCaig and T. McLemore, "Plan and Operation of the National Hospital Ambulatory Medical

have excluded from the sampling frame physicians in federal service and hospital-based physicians, who provide the majority of care in the Indian health system.[9] Even if the sampling frames for these surveys did include IHS and tribal facilities and physicians, the sampling strategies currently used would be unlikely to provide useful national data for AI/AN. At best, only a few Indian health facilities would be included, unless significant oversampling occurred, and data from a small number of Indian health facilities would not be generalizable to the nation as a whole. Even crude regional estimates for AI/AN would not be possible for the same reasons. Few state hospital discharge systems report data separately for AI/AN, so state-specific Indian hospitalization data are not uniformly available.

Although IHS databases describing medical care utilization have limitations with regard to their completeness and representativeness, they remain the most complete data sets available describing health care utilization among AI/AN. In addition to providing national data, reports are available which present information separately for large geographic areas of Indian country. While the extent of the eventual participation of Indian tribes in a central Indian health reporting system is difficult to predict, it is likely that any such system will be less inclusive and representative of the overall AI/AN population than is the current IHS system.

Along with the transfer of resources and responsibility afforded by self-governance, tribes have inherited the need for accurate population-based data about their constituencies in order to best plan and implement health programs. Thus, even as the IHS infrastructure previously associated with the collection and analysis of health data is being diminished, many tribes have recognized the critical importance of developing and maintaining health data systems designed to describe the health status of small populations.

Two technical issues, although not unique to Indian health data, have a disproportionately unfavorable impact on the validity and utility of available information regarding the health status of AI/AN. The first issue is that persons who consider themselves to be American Indian are often

Survey, Series 1: Programs and Collection Procedures," *Vital and Health Statistics,* Series 1, no. 34 (Washington, D.C.: U.S. Government Printing Office, 1994), 1-78.

9. E. Bryant, I. Shimizu, "Sample Design, Sampling Variance, and Estimation Procedure for the National Ambulatory Medical Care Survey," *Vital and Health Statistics,* Series 2, no. 108, DHHS Pub. No. (PHS) 88-1382 (Washington, D.C.: U.S. Government Printing Office, 1988).

recorded as non-Indian in health data sets, including morbidity registries and vital records. When present, this type of racial misclassification almost always results in underestimation of morbidity and mortality rates among Native Americans. The second issue is that even health data systems which attempt to separately identify AI/AN rarely attempt to assess tribal affiliation. Thus, tribal-specific health data, in which many tribes are extremely interested, are seldom available. (The homologous issue for other ethnic minorities is that reporting systems often fail to allow for sufficiently fine division of large groups, so diverse groups such as Hmong, Laotians, Samoans, Chinese, and Koreans are included under the rubric of "Asian and Pacific Islanders.") As we will describe, these technical issues can effectively exclude Indian populations in some parts of the U.S. from accurate monitoring of health data.

Racial and Tribal Classification of American Indians in Vital Records and Morbidity Registries

In recent years, increasing attention has been directed to the scientific and logical inadequacies of the concepts of race and ethnicity with respect to health statistics and public health surveillance.[10] Stroup and Hahn have argued that the system of classification used in most U.S. demographic and health statistics fails to meet a number of basic standards (such as validity, exclusivity and exhaustiveness, meaningfulness to respondents, measurability, consistency, and reliability) which should be applied to such systems.[11] Interested readers are referred to the above-referenced works for more thorough presentations of these issues. In the present context, however, two aspects of the issue of "racial classification" of AI/AN deserve further exploration. The first is that, regardless of how accurately (validly) a racial descriptor provides information about the genetic or cultural characteristics of an individual, any description of disease or death rates must assign an individual to the same category in both the numerator and the denominator in order for the rate to be meaningful. The second aspect

---

10. Centers for Disease Control and Prevention, "Use of Race and Ethnicity in Public Health Surveillance: Summary of the CDC/ATSDR Workshop," *Morbidity and Mortality Weekly Reports* 42, No. RR-10 (1993): 1-17. R. A. Hahn, "The State of Federal Health Statistics on Racial and Ethnic Groups," *JAMA* 267 (1992): 268-71. N. G. Osborn and M. D. Feit, "The Use of Race in Medical Research," *JAMA* 267 (1992): 275-79.
11. Centers for Disease Control and Prevention, "Use of Race and Ethnicity," 5-6.

pertinent to definitions of race and ethnicity among AI/AN is that, in addition to the racial (biological) and ethnic (cultural) dimensions which are usually discussed, there is an important political dimension to the identification of AI/AN.

a. Inconsistent Classification Between Numerator and Denominator Data Sets

Among persons who self-identify as AI/AN, it is frequently the case that race is designated differently for the same individual in numerators and denominators of health data sets. We use the term "racial misclassification" to refer to situations in which persons recorded as AI/AN in a reference data set (such as IHS records or tribal enrollment registries) are recorded as a race other than AI/AN in vital records or disease registries. Although the term "inconsistent racial classification" may be argued to be more accurate because of the lack of a valid and reproducible criterion standard for Indian race, others may consider that such terminology obscures the political dimension of AI/AN identification. In addition, because federal and tribal systems exist that are specifically designed for the purpose of delivering health care to AI/AN, and because persons defined by these systems to be AI/AN are the populations among whom health status should be measured, the word "misclassification" can be appropriately applied when inconsistencies result in inappropriately low estimates of morbidity and mortality.

The classification of American Indian race on birth and death certificates has recently been the object of critical examination. Although racial identification for the Census is based on self-report, race on death certificates is recorded by an observer, often a funeral director or a coroner. Several studies have suggested that a significant percentage of persons who are considered to be Indian during life are coded as non-Indian on death certificates. In a linkage of 12 Current Population Surveys from the Bureau of Census with the National Death Index for the years 1979-1985, race identified during life was compared to race on death certificates.[12] Among decedents identified in the National Death Index who were recorded as AI in the Current Population Surveys, only 73.6% were recorded as AI on the death certificate. (About 90% of persons listed as American Indian on death certificates were listed as Indian on the Current Population Surveys.) After

---

12. P. D. Sorlie, E. Rogot, and N. J. Johnson, "Validity of Demographic Characteristics on the Death Certificate," *Epidemiology* 3 (1992): 181-84.

applying the appropriate weighting, the authors concluded that AI mortality rates based on death certificates may be underestimated by as much as 22-30%. Among clients of an urban Indian health clinic in Seattle from 1973-1988, nearly one-third of deceased persons who had identified themselves to clinic staff as American Indians were listed as non-Indian on death certificates.[13]

In several studies, computerized patient registration files from the IHS have been linked with other data systems to assess potential misclassification of race in surveillance systems. For instance, in the Pacific Northwest, the patient registration file for Washington, Oregon, and Idaho was linked with a database of persons receiving kidney dialysis maintained by the Northwest Renal Network. End-stage renal disease rates among IHS-registered Indians were underestimated by over 20% when racial classification as recorded in the database was used.[14] In a similar study of a Surveillance, Epidemiology, and End Results cancer registry, including 13 counties in western Washington state, approximately 40% of IHS-registered American Indians included in the tumor registry were coded to a race other than AI/AN.[15] In a statewide injury surveillance system in Oregon, 35% of persons in the registry who were American Indian, according to IHS records, were listed as white.[16] A recent study linking IHS patient registration data to Washington state death records, in which 12.8% of IHS-registered AI/AN were listed as other races on death certificates, found that IHS enrollees with cancer were less likely to be classified as AI/AN than those with alcohol-related deaths.[17]

---

13. J. R. Sugarman, G. Hill, R. Forquera, and J. Frost, "Coding of Race on Death Certificates of Patients of an Urban Indian Health Clinic, Washington, 1973-1988," *IHS Provider* 17 (1992): 113-15.

14. J. R. Sugarman and L. Lawson, "The Effect of Racial Misclassification on Estimates of End-stage Renal Disease among American Indians and Alaska Natives in the Pacific Northwest, 1988 Through 1990," *American Journal of Kidney Diseases* 21 (1993): 383-86.

15. F. Frost, V. Taylor, and E. Fries, "Racial Misclassification of Native Americans in a Surveillance, Epidemiology, and End Results Cancer Registry," *JNCI* 84 (1992): 957-62.

16. J. R. Sugarman, R. Soderberg, J. E. Gordon, and F. P. Rivara, "Effects of Racial Misclassification of American Indians on Injury Rates in Oregon, 1989-1990," *American Journal of Public Health* 83 (1993): 681-84.

17. F. Frost, K. Tollestrup, A. Ross, E. Sabotta, and E. Kimball, "Correctness of Racial Coding of American Indians and Alaska Natives on the Washington State Death Certificate," *American Journal of Preventive Medicine* 10 (1994): 290-94.

Other evidence for possible misclassification of race on death certificates has been obtained in studies using linked infant birth and death certificates. Infant race is currently assigned by NCHS on the basis of maternal race listed on the birth certificate, although until 1989 race was assigned using an algorithm, which included both maternal and paternal race. Among infants classified on birth certificates as AI/AN born in the U.S. from 1983-1985, almost 40% of infants who died within the first year of life were classified as another race on the death certificate. Using a consistent definition of infant race at birth and death resulted in an infant mortality rate for American Indians which was 46.9% higher than that calculated using the race of the infant as listed on the death certificate.[18]

IHS continues to report infant mortality rates in its annual statistical publications, using unlinked birth and death certificates, although it has conducted an analysis using linked data sets which, while printed as an in-house (although publicly available) statistical report has not been widely distributed.[19] If one accepts the unlinked data, Indian infant mortality rates compare favorably with those for the entire nation. However, appropriately analyzed data suggest a persistent and disturbing gap in Indian infant mortality rates. This discrepancy is perhaps the most powerful example of the implications of inconsistencies in racial classification on different data sets with respect to our ability to monitor the health of a vulnerable population of AI/AN.

In its annual statistical reports, IHS excludes data for the Portland area (which includes Washington, Oregon, and Idaho), from California, and from Oklahoma in presenting national mortality data for American Indians because of a presumption that rates of racial misclassification on death certificates in these states are high. To the extent that resources for health services are at least partially allocated on the basis of mortality data, racial misclassification presents a dilemma for policy makers in appropriately directing these resources.

---

18. R. A. Hahn, J. Mulinare, and S. M. Teutsch, "Inconsistencies in Coding of Race and Ethnicity Between Birth and Death in U.S. Infants: a New Look at Infant Mortality, 1983-1985," *JAMA* 267 (1992): 259-63.

19. Indian Health Service, *Trends in Indian Health 1994*, (Rockville, Maryland: U.S. Department of Health and Human Services, 1994). Indian Health Service, *Indian Babies Who Die: A Comparison with Those Who Survive the First Year of Life*, data from the linked birth/infant death data sets 1983-1986 (Rockville, Maryland: U.S. Department of Health and Human Services, October 1992).

b. The Political Dimension to American Indian Designation

The political dimension follows from the sovereignty of tribal governments. A basic right of all governments is to establish membership criteria for its citizenry. For instance, individual tribes can (and do) determine the proportion of Indian heritage (blood quantum) which is necessary for tribal membership, and can define how Indian heritage is assessed. Many tribes, for instance, require as much as 1/2 tribal blood quantum for membership, whereas others grant membership to persons with far lower blood quantum. As discussed above, significant entitlements (for instance, to health services) can be attached to those aspects of "Indianness" which accrue from tribal membership.

As increasing attention is directed toward the role of socioeconomic status rather than race and ethnicity *per se* as factors associated with the adverse health status of minority populations, future public health surveillance activities may deemphasize attention to race. However, even if AI/AN were not socioeconomically disadvantaged, it would still be important to maintain health information systems designed to elucidate the health status of AI/AN in order to insure that the federal obligation to enhance the health of Indian populations has been met.

Lack of Tribal-Specific Data

A second major issue of concern related to monitoring the health of vulnerable and underserved AI/AN populations is the relative inability to derive tribal specific data from most data sets. National data describing Indian health obscure some extremely important intertribal variations. For instance, mortality from lung cancer among American Indians in the United States is, in aggregate, similar to that among the general population. However, mortality rates from lung cancer among American Indian women vary greatly among geographic regions served by the IHS. In some areas, such as Alaska and the Northern Plains, the lung cancer mortality rate is more than double that for the U.S.[20] In parts of the Southwest, lung cancer mortality rates among Indian women are less than one-sixth those for the U.S.

---

20. Indian Health Service, *Cancer Mortality among Native Americans in the United States: Regional Differences in Indian Health, 1984-1988 and Trends Over Time, 1968-1987*, ed. S. Valway (Rockville, Maryland: U.S. Department of Health and Human Services, 1991).

Even within regions, there is substantial variability of disease prevalence for some conditions. Diabetes is more common among American Indians than among the general population. Although the prevalence of non-insulin-dependent diabetes mellitus among American Indians in Washington, Oregon, and Idaho is three times greater than that for the all-races U.S. population, there are significant differences within and among cultural groups consisting of related tribes.[21] (Although no classification system is ideal, anthropologists have described cultural groups as groupings of tribes or bands that shared significant traditional, religious, and language traits prior to European contact. In the Northwest, there are three distinct cultural groups: Coastal, Great Basin, and Plateau.) In a study of diagnosed diabetes, which included 10 reservations in the Northwest, the prevalence of diabetes on tribal reservations from the Great Basin cultural group was 3.6 times that for the U.S. Among the nearby Northwest Coast reservations, diabetes prevalence was only 1.9 times that for the U.S. Within the Plateau cultural group, the prevalence of diabetes among the Nez Perce Tribe was twice that among the Colville Tribe. Therefore, diabetes prevalence data aggregated by state or region in the Pacific Northwest would fail to illuminate important differences among tribes in the region. With the notable exception of New Mexico, state vital records systems rarely include tribal identifiers.[22]

"Improving Health Data Among Northwest Native Americans:" A Demonstration Project to Enhance Information about Indian Health

Efforts by Indian tribes in the Pacific Northwest to improve health data regarding AI/AN in the region were summarized in a 1988 document, published by the Northwest Portland Area Indian Health Board (NPAIHB).[23] The NPAIHB is a nonprofit tribal advisory board representing 38 of the 40 federally recognized Indian tribes in Washington, Oregon and

---

21. W. L. Freeman, G. M. Hosey, P. Diehr, and D. Gohdes, "Diabetes in American Indians of Washington, Oregon, and Idaho," *Diabetes Care* 12 (1989): 282-88.

22. C. Halasan, P. Totkamachi, L. Towles, A. Mueller, and T. Ortiz, *1990-1991 New Mexico Tribe Specific Vital Statistics* (Sante Fe, New Mexico: New Mexico Department of Health, Public Health Division, Bureau of Vital Records and Health Statistics, November 1992).

23. *Information to Improve Health Care for Indian People* (Portland, Oregon: Northwest Portland Area Indian Health Board, September 1988).

Idaho. Its purpose is to promote improved health care for Indian people served by the Portland area IHS. The document, entitled "Information to Improve Health Care for Indian People," called for steps to enhance IHS data systems and to improve tribal-specific health data. Tribal leaders were particularly concerned that IHS did not publish tribal-specific health data using tribal affiliation recorded in its data systems. However, the accuracy of tribal enrollment data in the IHS data system in the Northwest had not been validated, so the validity of tribal-specific data from existing data systems could not be assured.

In 1992, the NPAIHB and the IHS entered into a collaborative agreement with the National Center for Health Statistics, Centers for Disease Control and Prevention, under a Minority Health Statistics Grants Program entitled "Advance the Understanding of Racial and Ethnic Populations." The project, "Improving Health Data for Northwest American Indians," was funded for a three-year period, ending in September of 1995.

The specific aims of the project were:

1. To determine the feasibility of compiling a comprehensive registry of enrolled members of the 40 federally recognized tribes in Washington, Oregon, and Idaho, using enrollment records maintained by the tribes;

2. To prepare a comprehensive computerized data base of members of the 40 tribes in order to serve as a well-defined denominator to use in conducting studies of health status, using existing data sets;

3. To link the computerized data base of tribal members with existing data sets, such as vital records and disease registries in Washington, Oregon, and Idaho in order to obtain estimates of tribal-specific rates describing morbidity and mortality among AI; and

4. To link the tribal enrollment database with a separate database of AI enrolled with the IHS, in order to obtain improved regional estimates describing morbidity and mortality among AI from linkage studies with vital records and disease registries.

In the following sections, we will describe the methods used to achieve these aims and present the results of tribal recruitment activities, linkage of tribal rolls with IHS systems, and will present some findings regarding the extent of misclassification of race on vital records in Washington, Oregon and Idaho. Finally, we will present data which provide insight into the value of an approach which uses linkage studies with tribal rolls to obtain tribal-specific data.

The first step in conducting linkages using tribal rolls was to obtain permission to conduct the project from each tribal council (the tribe's governing body). The complexity and effort required to complete this process varied widely among tribes, as some tribal councils granted permission to conduct the study on written request, while others required several visits by study personnel to present the proposal to various council committees and sessions. In some cases, competing priorities in tribal business (because of issues such as economic development and natural resource management) resulted in long delays in scheduling presentations. In other cases, council members were concerned about confidentiality of tribal rolls and possible adverse consequences which might be associated with publication of tribal-specific health data. Concerns about data ownership were also frequently expressed, as some council members believed that previous anthropological and medical research projects among Indian communities have often been used to the detriment of tribes, or simply was of no benefit to tribes. The study protocol (which was approved by the appropriate IHS and state Institutional Review Boards) stipulated that no identified tribal-specific data would be disseminated without explicit tribal approval, and rigorous standards to protect the confidentiality of tribal rolls were adopted. These standards required that the research team maintain physical and electronic control of tribal rolls. In response to tribal concerns, analyses were conducted by the study team rather than by agencies who maintained the health data sets to which tribal rolls were linked. The names of tribes participating in the study were not released by the study team without tribal permission. Representatives from tribes were frequently apprised of the status of the study, and data were released to Indian groups before they were released (even in aggregate form) to general audiences.

The IHS maintains a computerized data file, including names and other identifying data for all persons who have registered to receive services from the Agency. Registration requires proof of tribal membership or descent from a member of a federally-recognized tribe. Persons register in order to receive a broad range of services, such as primary medical care, dental care, engineering services related to water supplies and waste disposal, and social and behavioral health services.

The Portland Area IHS (which includes the states of Washington, Oregon and Idaho) began to maintain a centralized computer registration file in 1984, although data from prior years were used to establish the registry. Records of deceased patients or persons who have not used health services for some time are not deleted from the file. The Patient Registration File includes information on tribal affiliation and Indian blood quantum, in addition to a variety of demographic and personal identifiers.

The IHS Patient Registration File is not population-based, as it requires that individuals actively enroll for services, rather than being automatically registered by virtue of tribal membership or descendancy. While the population of persons registered with IHS has relevance in terms of the delivery of health services, the number of American Indians registered with IHS is only about half the number of persons who identified themselves to be American Indian in the 1990 Census. Many of these self-identified persons may not register for IHS because they live in areas (including many urban centers) which are not near IHS facilities, or because they prefer to use other sources of care. Others may be ineligible because they are affiliated with tribes not recognized by the federal government. Although previous linkage studies have utilized the IHS file to conduct record linkages, the extent to which data from IHS registrants can be generalized to all AI/AN has rarely been evaluated. For instance, the proportion of tribal members who are enrolled with IHS has not been systematically evaluated in the Pacific Northwest, and previous studies have not examined the accuracy of tribal affiliation as recorded in IHS records compared to tribal rolls. On the other hand, tribal enrollment registries define populations which are not based on registration for health services. Although most tribes require application for membership and approval of applications by the tribal council, health status or the need for health services is not considered in membership decisions. In the Pacific Northwest, many AI/AN are members of tribes indigenous to areas outside Washington, Oregon or Idaho, and are not included in tribal rolls of local tribes, despite permanent residence in Indian communities. Thus, linkage studies using a combination of tribal rolls and IHS records is likely to include a more comprehensive perspective on Indian health in the region than either data system alone.

Tribal rolls were converted from a variety of manual, desktop computer, and mainframe computer systems to a single ASCII file format suitable for use on desktop computers. Data linkage was conducted using the AutoMatch computer system (MatchWare Technologies Inc., Silver Spring, MD). AutoMatch uses probabilistic matching algorithms to link data sets, and permits the user to overcome analytic challenges, such as digit transpositions in birth dates or numerical person identifiers or slight spelling differences in names.[24] Matches were called if Social Security number, date of birth, surname, and given name were identical across the data sets. When all of these data items were not present in both data sets, or if values were slightly different, a hierarchy was developed using the weighting capacity of AutoMatch, and possible matches were reviewed manually to make conservative estimates of true matches. The clerical review process, although by its nature somewhat subjective, yielded similar results when matching was done independently by two investigators. (The subjectivity arises in part from the fact that persons with slightly different identifying data who have unusual names were more likely to be considered matches than persons who had more common names. That is, if the date of birth differed by 2 digits for records with the name Littlefeather Chases-buffalo [a fictitious example], one would be more likely to call a match than in a similar situation in which the name was John Smith.)

Of the 40 federally-recognized tribes in Washington, Oregon and Idaho, 22 tribal councils passed resolutions agreeing to participate in the project. However, rolls could not be obtained from three tribes, so linkage studies were conducted using 19 tribal rolls.

There was wide variability in the data items provided by the tribes to the NPAIHB. Some tribes provided databases with a broad range of variables and personal identifiers (including Social Security numbers), and had historical records of deceased members, which included dates of death. Others provided only minimal data which could be used for record linkage (given name, surname, and date of birth), and did not include separate designation from deceased members. Thus, the *a priori* likelihood of successful data linkages with vital records and disease registries differed substantially among tribes.

The 19 sets of tribal rolls included 32,205 records. Of these, 4215 (12%) were listed by the tribes as deceased. Tribal rolls varied in size from 166 (126 not listed as deceased) to 9,122 (7,935 not listed as deceased). The mean number of members per tribe was 1,853 (SD = 4996); the mean number not listed as deceased was 1,631 (SD = 4,557).

---

24. M. A. Jaro, "Advances in Record-Linkage Methodology as Applied to Matching the 1985 Census of Tampa, Florida," *Journal of the American Statistical Association* 84 (1989): Issue #406, 414-20.

The Portland Area IHS Patient Registration file contained 122,768 records as of August, 1994. Approximately 6.5% of the IHS records were duplicate entries for the same individual. Of the 35,205 enrolled tribal members, 23,116 (65.7%) were linked to the IHS Patient Registration file. When restricted to persons not listed as deceased on the tribal rolls, 22,249 (71.8%) of tribal records were linked. However, the proportion of tribal members linked to the IHS files varied substantially among tribes. (Range 52.9%-85.2%, mean = 70.6%) (Table 1). (In order to maintain tribal confidentiality, but to preserve an understanding of the variability across tribes, tribal data in the table are aggregated into three groups according to number of persons listed on tribal enrollment databases submitted for the project.)

The IHS file contains an entry for tribal affiliation. However, because descent from a member of a federally-recognized tribe confers eligibility for IHS services, proof of tribal enrollment is not required in order for a registrant's claim of tribal affiliation to be recorded on IHS records. Of the 23,116 tribal members linked to IHS records, only 15,300 (66.2%) were listed on IHS records as affiliated with the tribe in which they were actually enrolled. This proportion varied among tribes from 20.9% to 90.4% (Table 1). However, review of the IHS tribal codes suggested that there were systematic discrepancies in coding for 11 of the 19 tribes. That is, for these tribes, substantial proportions of tribal members were coded by IHS to another tribe (usually in another part of the U.S.) with no logical cultural or geographic association, suggesting that persons were truly associated with the other tribe (for instance, because of differing maternal and paternal tribal membership).

On further investigation, we learned that the IHS coding scheme for tribal affiliation changed in the mid-1980s, but that the computer files were not systematically updated to reflect the changes (personal communication, Steven Kauffman, August 23, 1995). Thus, the same tribal code may refer to two completely unrelated tribes in the IHS Patient Registration file, and the correct tribe can only be ascertained through inferences based on residence or linkage studies, such as the one under discussion. However, careful review of the coding suggested that most of the inconsistencies were due to systematic entry of entirely incorrect tribal codes, rather than ambiguous codes which could refer to more than one tribe.

The number of persons coded to each participating tribe in the IHS file exceeded the number of records matched using the computer linkage, and for several tribes exceeded the total number of living and deceased members. Again, there was variability among tribes with less than 25% to more than 95% overlap between IHS-designated tribal affiliation and documented tribal membership (Table 1).

Death certificates were obtained from the states of Washington, Oregon and Idaho for the years 1984-1992 (although the 1992 data for Washington were incomplete). Additionally, we linked 1993 death records for Idaho, 1980-1983 records for Washington, and 1983 records for Oregon. The combined IHS and tribal roll file was linked individually to death records from each state.

Annual mortality rates (both cause-specific and all-cause) are reported for the U.S., and frequently for states. However, few (if any) of the participating tribes had enough deaths to permit annual assessment of mortality rates for the purpose of year by year comparison (Table 2). Even when tribes were grouped together by size, the number of annual deaths for most years was too sparse for calculation of mortality rates, except for the larger tribes. Only 5 of 19 tribes had more than 100 death certificates identified during the years in which death certificates were linked.

Among tribes with 20 or more deaths, the proportion of tribal members recorded as American Indian on death certificates ranged from 55% to 95% (Table 2). Using the entire combined file of IHS enrollees and tribal members, 85.6% linked decedents were listed on the death certificate as Native American (Table 2). The proportion of IHS enrollees or tribal members coded as Native American differed by state, from a low of 80.1% in Oregon to a high of 91.3% in Idaho. These proportions were maintained when the analysis was restricted to the years 1984-1991, for which complete death files were used for all three states (data not shown).

Although a full discussion of differences in mortality rates and patterns among the various populations studied is beyond the scope of this chapter, selected data on the proportions of deaths due to selected causes by various subpopulations studied are shown in Table 3. Regardless of which population of American Indians is considered, patterns of mortality were strikingly similar. For instance, the proportion of deaths from heart disease among the groups included in the table ranged from 20.5% to 25.7%, with the exception of the statewide data for Oregon, where 30.3% of deaths were from heart disease. A lower proportion of deaths among American Indians was attributable to malignant neoplasms than was the case for other races in the states studied. Conversely, higher proportions of deaths among the

Table 1
Linkage of 19 tribal rolls to IHS Patient Registration file by vital status and tribal affiliation

Population	Number on tribal rolls (living and deceased)	Number listed as living [N, (%)]	Total linked to IHS (living and deceased) [N, (%)]	Living linked to IHS [N, (%)]	Number and percent of tribal members listed on IHS files as members of same tribe.	Number and percent of people listed as affiliated with a specific tribe on IHS files who were linked to that tribe's rolls
Large Tribes[i] (N=5)						
Total	22286	19349 (86.8%)	14252 (64%)	13666 (70.6%)	10075 (70.7%)	14563 (69.1%)
Range	2670-9122	2266-7935 (79.6-98.5%)	1750-6360 (48.4-69.7%)	1515-6034 (60.6-76%)	1023-4807 (56.6-81.4%)	1723-5903 (56.6-81.4%)
Medium Tribes[ii] (N=3)						
Total	6926	6197 (89.5%)	4874 (70.4%)	4713 (76.1%)	2855 (58.6%)	4337 (65.8%)
Range	2057-2461	1490-2461 (72.4-100%)	1160-2021 (56.4-70.3%)	1077-2021 (71.9-82.0%)	807-1025 (50.7-69.6%)	1305-1733 (54.6-78.5%)
Small Tribes[iii] (N=11)						
Total	5993	5444 (90.8%)	3990 (66.6%)	3870 (71.1%)	2370 (59.4%)	3794 (62.5%)
Range	166-977	126-901 (64.0-100%)	148-574 (42.9-83.7%)	88-634 (52.9-85.2%)	78-476 (20.9-90.4%)	145-811 (18.5-95.4%)
ALL TRIBES (N=19)	35205	30990 (88.0%)	23116 (65.7%)	22249 (71.8%)	15300 (66.2%)	22694 (67.4%)

[i] 2,500-10,000 listed on tribal rolls / [ii] 1,000-2,499 listed on tribal rolls / [iii] <1,000 listed on tribal rolls

Table 2
Number of deaths by population and year, and proportion of deaths in population coded as AI/AN on death certificate

Population	N	1980	1981	1982	1983	1984	1985	1986	1987	1988	1989	1990	1991	1992	1993	% Coded AI/AN
Large Tribes[iv] (N=5)	956	60	53	74	65	87	74	73	77	90	98	84	84	28	9	86.9
Medium Tribes[v] (N=3)	231	3	1	4	19	27	19	24	15	27	26	29	18	19	0	78.8
Small Tribes[vi] (N=11)	157	6	12	6	13	12	14	16	14	10	25	15	11	2	1	80.3
ALL TRIBES (N=19)	1344	69	66	84	87	126	107	113	106	127	149	128	113	49	10	84.7
Persons included on tribal rolls but not linked to IHS records	553	50	49	67	79	88	51	43	30	28	26	23	15	4	0	77.6
Combined IHS patient registration & tribal rolls	3660	109	102	133	140	220	277	327	354	424	446	451	440	184	53	85.6
Persons listed on IHS file	3107	59	53	66	61	132	226	284	324	396	420	428	425	180	53	87.1
Washington death certificates-[vii]	2462	109	102	133	114	162	184	214	236	287	285	295	286	55	—	86.1
Oregon death certificates	704	—	—	—	26	34	50	59	67	82	101	107	92	86	—	80.1
Idaho death certificates	494	—	—	—	—	24	43	54	51	55	60	49	62	43	53	91.3

[iv]2,500-10,000 listed on tribal rolls / [v]1,000-2,499 listed on tribal rolls / [vi]<1,000 listed on tribal rolls / [vii]State death certificates restricted to those linked to IHS patient registration file, tribal rolls, or both.

Indian populations were attributable to cirrhosis and motor vehicle accidents. As expected, most of the variance among populations for proportionate mortality occurred among small tribes with few deaths. Although future analyses will focus on mortality rates (rather than proportions), it is clear from the analyses to date that the leading causes of death among Northwest tribes do not differ markedly across tribes, and that specific causes of death are consistently more prominent among Indian communities.

The linkage studies summarized above have yielded important insights into methodological and substantive issues regarding the monitoring of health status among American Indians in the Pacific Northwest. These insights are most striking with regard to the utility and feasibility of consolidation of tribal rolls for data linkage, the variability in the accuracy of tribal affiliation as listed in IHS records, the variable results across tribes in success of data linkage with death certificates, and the variability of racial classification on death certificates by tribe and among states.

The first aim of the NPAIHB health statistics project was to determine the feasibility of preparing a consolidated database of tribal enrollment registries in the Pacific Northwest for the purpose of improving health data. The environment and resources available for the project were extremely favorable: the project was conducted by an organization consisting of tribal representatives, eligible tribes had long recognized the importance of tribal-specific data and were motivated to seek solutions to the problem of inadequate data, many of the study personnel were Native American, and adequate financial, logistical, and technical resources were available for the project. Despite these nearly ideal circumstances, fewer than half of the eligible tribes ultimately participated in the project. The project has demonstrated the technical feasibility of preparing a consolidated data set, including data from many tribes, and shown that record linkage is quite feasible. However, the generalizability of the aggregate tribal data cannot be determined with respect to all members of tribes indigenous to the region because of the high proportion of non-participating tribes. In order for the approach to have validity with regard to population-based surveillance over the long term, vigorous efforts to seek the participation of the remaining tribes would be required. The single database afforded by the IHS file yielded data comparable to that for tribal enrollees and, based on results from the participating tribes, probably includes over two-thirds of members enrolled in the Northwest tribes. Unfortunately, the completeness of the

Table 3
Distribution of leading causes of death (percent) by selected populations

Cause of death	19 participating tribes, all states (N=1,342)	Members of 19 tribes who were linked to IHS patient registry (N=1,090)	Idaho tribal deaths (N=79)	Oregon tribal deaths (N=963)	Washington tribal deaths (N=963)	Tribe A (Large tribe)	Deaths to AI/AN[x] in counties near Tribe A	Tribe B (Small tribe)	Deaths to AI/AN[x] in counties near Tribe B	Deaths coded as AI/AN on Washington death certificates, 1989-1991 (N=1,314)	Deaths coded as other races on Washington death certificates, 1989-1991 (N=112,185)
Heart disease	24.2	24.4	21.5	30.3	22.5	20.5	25.7	25.0	22.6	22.9	30.5
Malignant neoplasms	13.7	13.0	12.7	16.7	12.9	13.1	12.2	8.9	14.7	13.1	24.5
Motor vehicle accidents	11.3	10.6	15.2	7.7	12.0	10.6	8.6	10.7	9.5	7.5	2.3
Other accidents	5.9	6.4	3.8	6.0	6.0	5.4	4.7	8.9	5.7	5.0	2.4
Cirrhosis	5.7	6.7	3.8	7.0	5.5	5.8	6.8	1.8	7.2	6.1	1.1
Cerebrovascular disease	4.9	5.1	6.3	4.3	5.0	5.2	6.8	14.3	4.4	5.2	7.4

[x]Persons coded as AI/AN on state death certificates residing in counties included in the same IHS Service Unit, including the selected tribe.

IHS data set is likely to diminish in succeeding years, so it does not represent a long-term solution to the problem.

Tribes want tribal-specific data. In this respect, the approach described above has yielded favorable results. The study has shown that tribal affiliation, as recorded on the Portland Area IHS patient registration file, has only a moderately high concordance with that shown on the tribal rolls. While the concordance was very high for some tribes, it was unacceptably low for others. This situation results in part from the distinction between tribal enrollment and tribal affiliation. Many persons who are descended from tribal members and who live in and are identified with tribal communities may not meet blood quantum requirements for enrollment. In addition, some persons who do meet tribal enrollment criteria may have chosen not to enroll, especially in tribes where enrollment is not perceived to confer any specific benefits. Some of the variance between IHS and tribal records may be due to dispersion of potential members off of reservations, and consequent geographic barriers to enrollment. Some may be due to the effect of termination of federal recognition of tribes, and failure of persons to enroll after subsequent reinstatement of recognition. In any case, the tribal rolls are data sets to use for obtaining *tribal-specific* data in preference to IHS records. If tribes wish to continue participating in the IHS data system and to seek tribal-specific information from that system, considerable effort will be needed to define and assure accuracy of tribal affiliations included in the IHS data system.

There was considerable variability across tribes in the number of members linked to death certificates. Some of the variability was clearly related to population size. However, potential elements for data linkage differed among tribes, and may have accounted for some of the difference. For instance, linkage was facilitated by the availability of Social Security numbers, which were not included in all tribal data sets. This problem was partially compensated for by linkage of tribal rolls with the IHS data system, which included Social Security numbers for most registrants.

Previous studies by specific tribes have demonstrated the utility of linking tribal rolls to vital records. For instance, the Seneca Nation of Indians in New York has linked tribal records to New York death certificates in order to derive tribal-specific mortality rates,[25] and the Warm

25. M. C. Mahoney et al., "Mortality in a Northeastern Native American Cohort, 1955-1989," *American Journal of Epidemiology* 129 (1989): 818-26. A. M. Michalek, M. C. Mahoney, G. Buck, and R. Snyder, "Mortality Patterns among the Youth of a

Springs Confederated Tribes of Oregon have analyzed infant mortality patterns using tribal records maintained over four decades.[26] The present study complements previous work by demonstrating that, even in relatively small areas, linkage of tribal rolls with other data sets may meet with different levels of success.

The study was not designed to assess reasons for differential rates of racial misclassification among participating states. However, rates of inconsistent classification between state death certificates and IHS or tribal enrollees ranged from 8.7 -19.9%. The reasons for these differences are not clear. States in which there are a higher proportion of AI/AN who live in urban areas or off reservations may be less likely to classify tribal members appropriately on death certificates. For instance, many Indians in western Oregon live in or near metropolitan areas, may seek care in non-IHS or non-tribal facilities, and therefore may not be recognized as Indian by funeral directors or others filling out death certificates. Another possible explanation is that differences in Indian blood quantum across states, or differences in blood quantum requirements for tribal membership, may account for systematic differences across states.

Recommendations

Linking tribal enrollment registries with health data sets is a promising strategy to enhance health data regarding AI/AN. While the results described in this paper focus on linkages with death certificates, studies are currently underway using state databases, including reportable communicable diseases and other morbidity registries, such as a state-wide cancer registry. Future efforts in this arena deserve attention in the following areas.

First, studies similar to those described here should be conducted in other regions of the country where the problems of racial misclassification and lack of tribal-specific data are believed to exist. There is likely to be considerable variation in the extent of misclassification across regions. For instance, in California and Oklahoma, states with large but diverse Indian

Northeastern American Indian Cohort," *Public Health Reports* 108 (May-June 1993): 403-407.

26. R. Nakamura, R. King, E. Kimball, R. Oye, and S. Helgerson, (1991) "Excess Infant Mortality in an American Indian Population 1940 to 1990," *JAMA* 266 (1991): 2244-48.

populations, misclassification is likely to be an important problem.[27] In parts of the Southwest, such as the large Navajo Nation, these challenges may be less acute because of the existence of large geographic areas inhabited primarily by members of a single tribe. Also, because many AI/AN live in urban areas rather than on reservations or tribal lands, and many urban Indians are not registered with the IHS, linkages with tribal rolls should be explored as a method of improving health data regarding urban Indians.

Second, individual tribes should be encouraged to work directly with state authorities to conduct record linkage studies intended to better characterize health patterns of tribal members. Although the financial costs of the technical steps needed to conduct linkage studies need not be great, issues of data access, confidentiality, and dissemination are likely to require the establishment of collegial relationships between tribes and states. For the most part, it would be appropriate for interested tribes to initiate contacts with the states, as the experience from the project described above suggests that many tribes are cautious about participating in projects which require access to tribal rolls. In order for the linkage studies to be successful, however, tribes should be encouraged to maintain their enrollment files in electronic formats that are easily transported to standard computer formats (such as ASCII files), and should include data items (such as birth and married surnames for women, and Social Security numbers) which can facilitate data linkages.

Finally, the small population sizes of most tribes have important implications for monitoring the health of AI/AN populations in general. Unless Indian health statistics continue to be aggregated in order to highlight gaps between the health status of AI/AN and the general population, it is possible the continuation of a past record of effective use of data for advocacy purposes may be hampered. That is, IHS patient care and other data have been successfully used to focus attention and resources on specific health problems (such as diabetes and unintentional injuries) which disproportionately affect AI/AN across the nation. Tribes should give consideration to continuing to report data to some aggregate Indian health data system

---

27. R. E. Deapen and R. D. Kennedy, "Differences Between Oklahoma Indian Infant Mortality and Other Races," *Public Health Reports* 106 (1991): 97-99. D. O. Farley, T. Richards, and R. M. Bell, "Effects of Reporting Methods on Infant Mortality Rate Estimates for Racial and Ethnic Subgroups," *Journal of Health Care for the Poor and Underserved* 6 (1995): 60-75.

maintained by a national Indian organization, if not by the IHS. Thus, sovereign tribes which have entered into self-governance compacts will need to be vigilant to ensure that the advantages of improved local control over health resources and the elimination of burdensome administrative regulations do not result in a diminished capacity to monitor the health status of potentially vulnerable AI/AN populations throughout the U.S.

CHAPTER FIVE

Drawing Samples from Hidden, Underserved and Vulnerable Populations: Methods, Applications and Ethical Issues

James Fisher, Jichuan Wang, Joseph Wagner

I. Introduction

Recent legislative debates over health care reform in America highlight the trade-offs between a human rights goal of guaranteeing universal coverage and fiscal conservatism that seeks to reduce the size of government and the impact of unfunded mandates on the private sector. Health care reform will probably be a process consisting of many public and private decisions, rather than a single, well-defined package. The 1990s have seen dramatic growth in information systems which are increasing the potential for monitoring much of the nation's health. The decennial census, more frequent sample surveys, insurance and service provider records all contribute to our understanding of potential and actual demands placed on health care providers. These systems are evolving very rapidly. The integration of health information with geographic coding has fueled an explosion of research on the spatial patterns of health. Management and geographic information systems have been particularly effective in the study of families with stable residence, telephones, regular doctors and health insurance.

Unfortunately, these same systems are poorly designed for enumerating and understanding the health needs of persons in hidden, underserved and vulnerable populations. The term hidden refers to persons who often missed when a census or survey is conducted using standard procedures. Hidden populations include, among others, persons who are homeless, transient, undocumented foreigners, and evading law enforcement. Underserved refers to persons who are not receiving adequate health care, such as basic immunizations, preventative care and treatment for illness or injury. Vulnerability refers to a lack of access to resources, which puts people at heightened risk of harm to health and well-being.[1] In some respects the movement to integrate information systems may distract analysts from the task of monitoring health and use of health services by persons who are not readily located on a map, have no formal ties to the information system and often don't want to be counted.

Uncertainties over the size and characteristics of hidden, underserved and vulnerable populations have particular significance for local governments. The rise of underemployment and homelessness challenges local governments and social service agencies to meet rising demands, often without adequate financial backing. From the perspective of local governments, knowing how many people live in a particular place is instrumental to the day-to-day effort of providing services, such as education and health, and ameliorating negative consequences of activities, such as waste removal and crime. Local governments are trapped between mandates from higher-level governments to provide adequate services, demands from constituents to freeze or reduce taxes, and the demands of their service agencies for resources to assist vulnerable populations. Given this demanding climate, local governments and service providers are not always disposed to seek out and advocate for the needs of vulnerable populations. A recent manifestation of voter anger at providing subsidized services emerged in California's Proposition 187, restricting access of undocumented immigrants to health, education and welfare services.

The goal of this article is to describe sampling methods which can provide baseline and subsequent measures of health care demands and service utilization, and thus improve our understanding of the impacts of the reform process, particularly on hidden, underserved and vulnerable populations. A research plan for measuring the impacts of health care reform should identify:

1. A target population, that is the population of interest;

2. A sampling frame, or a list of the persons from whom a sample may be drawn to represent the target population;

---

1.   A thorough discussion of these terms can be found in Audrey R. Chapman, ed., *Health Care Reform: A Human Rights Approach* (Washington, D.C.: Georgetown University Press, 1994).

3. A sample which is drawn from the sampling frame; and

4. The instrumentation which will guide the questions to be answered.

Our goal in this article is to augment the second and third steps in order to obtain data on populations who are frequently missed using standard data collections systems. This process is particularly challenging for hidden, underserved and vulnerable populations, as will be indicated. Without a sound methodology for policy evaluation, uncertainty as to whether reform moves us closer to meeting human rights objectives in health care will remain.

II. Collecting Data on Hidden, Underserved and Vulnerable Populations

Our discussion of three broad methods for gathering data begins with the census, which attempts to survey everyone in the target population, roughly equating the target population, the sampling frame and the sample. This is followed by probability-based sampling, which seeks respondents that are believed to be representative of the target population, based on knowledge of the likelihood of their selection within the sampling frame and knowledge of the representativeness of the sampling frame itself to the target population. The third method, non-probability or convenience sampling, surveys respondents without specific knowledge of the likelihood of individuals being selected, and often without a sampling frame. The choices of how to develop a sampling frame and then how to select respondents from within that frame are handled simultaneously.

a. Census

A census is an enumeration of the entire population which is presumed to include the target population. In the case of the U.S. Census of Population, a sampling frame is currently established through detailed maps of all residential locations for the entire country, contained in the Topographically Integrated Geographic Encoding and Referencing (TIGER) System. The census has numerous appealing qualities. In principal, few statistical assumptions about representativeness are required, and the results are easily interpreted. Problems with conducting a census include the extraordinary financial and logistical requirements for the data collection effort, the limited scope of questions that can be included in the instrument, and the earlier-mentioned difficulties of successfully interviewing hidden populations.

The U.S Census of Population has a long history. The decennial census is the benchmark upon which most sample surveys are compared. Unfortunately, the short form census does not request health information, and the long form sample has little bearing on matters of health service utilization. In fact, recent indications are that the 2000 Census will contain fewer, not more, questions. However, many significant administrative and fiscal decisions, including apportionment of some federal grants in aid, hinge on population estimates from the census. Of particular interest are counts of persons who fall within our research target population. Knowledge of the number of homeless, undocumented immigrants, substance abusers, and so on would provide a basis for establishing sample quotas for health surveys.

In the late 20th century, traditional criticism of the census has given way to more extreme forms of condemnation. Choldin provides a thorough and illuminating discussion of the 1990 census process, illustrating many factors which affected decisions of how to enumerate homeless persons and whether to adjust census counts in final tabulations.[2] Among the most publicized controversies in the 1990 census were related to the undercount of hidden populations, such as undocumented immigrants and homeless. Census enumerators, engaging in one-night sweeps through inner city neighborhoods attempted to gather at least skeletal information from homeless persons. Some homeless shelters were hostile to census takers, arguing that undercounts were inevitable and that the enumeration process itself was at fault. Far more homeless persons were simply missed as they slept, hidden from view. Following release of census findings, many large and medium-sized cities protested loudly that census enumerators missed large numbers of residents.

Complete enumeration of hidden, underserved and vulnerable populations, like the homeless, for the study of health care reform would be very expensive, if not impossible, and is an unlikely prospect in the future. The census is costly, infrequent and subject to the capability of enumerators to locate and successfully interview respondents from the hidden categories in a relatively brief period of time. An additional concern is the unstable, and often cyclical nature of homelessness can lead to radically high or low

---

2. Harvey M. Choldin, *Looking for the Last Percent: The Controversy Over Census Undercounts*, (New Brunswick: Rutgers University Press, 1994).

sub-population estimates, depending on the season, regional economic conditions and even the weather conditions on the enumeration day. The census strategy is thus an unlikely choice for monitoring health care reform.

b. Probability Sampling

Probability sampling purports to select individuals, households or other sampling units with a known probability or likelihood of being chosen. Complex sampling designs may employ information on probability of being selected to balance or weight responses. Detailed discussions of probability sampling are provided in numerous texts.[3] Kish has developed rolling sampling methods which can spread resource costs more efficiently than large, simultaneous enumerations.[4] While Kish's methods show promise, they lie beyond the scope of this study.

Simple random sampling attempts to select persons from a sampling frame, such as a list of names or address, with equal probability. A common strategy is to number all of the names in the list sequentially, and then use a table of random numbers to select who will be included in the survey. Simple random sampling is far less costly than conducting a complete enumeration, permits the use of more detailed instruments, and maintains ready interpretability of findings.

Several enhancements to simple random sampling further reduce costs, while maintaining representativeness of the target population. Systematic sampling is often employed in household surveys and is characterized by beginning with a randomly selected household, and then contacting every n[th] household along that street. The same strategy can be employed in sampling service utilization, where every third or every fourth customer is interviewed. Caution should be exercised that the interval of selection does not bias results. A sample taken of every fourth household on a street might result in taking only households located on corner lots, or samples taken every third hour might exclude certain patterns of activity.

---

3.   A brief introduction to sampling is presented in Jichuan Wang and James H. Fisher, "Sampling," in *Magill's Survey of Social Science: Sociology*, (Pasadena, Texas: Salem Press, 1994). Harold A. Kahn and Christopher T. Sempos, *Statistical Methods in Epidemiology* (New York: Oxford University Press, 1989) presents a good overview of sampling issues as well statistical methods for assessing risk.

4.   Leslie Kish, "Rolling Samples and Censuses," *Survey Methodologies* 16, no. 1 (June 1990): 63-79.

In stratified sampling, a population can be separated based on some characteristic(s) of interest, such as age or race. Separate samples, optionally using different sampling probabilities, can then be drawn from each strata. For instance, oversampling, or intentionally selecting a higher percentage of a relatively rare population, such as persons of particular economic, religious or ethnic groups, can assure that a sufficient sample size is achieved for that group. If African Americans are relatively rare in a target area, sampling 1% of European Americans might be combined with a 50% sample of African Americans. Subsequent statistical adjustments can then be used to appropriately analyze oversampled groups with the rest of the population.

Cluster sampling refers to prior selection of subpopulations from which to select individuals. For example, health care utilization data might be collected from patients from a subset of the hospitals located in the survey area, rather than attempting to gather data in all hospitals. Census blocks might be selected from which respondents would be surveyed. In order to maintain representativeness of clusters, attention must be paid to selecting many clusters using random processes, or employing judgement in selecting clusters which are believed to represent the target population. Clustering significantly reduces travel time and field costs for enumerators. However, poorly selected clusters, such as locations with large institutions or homogeneous economic classes, can lead to distorted results.

Multistage sampling generally employs some combination of stratification, clustering and random sampling. An example of two-stage sampling, for instance, is randomly selecting census blocks (clustering), and then randomly selecting respondents from within the selected blocks. The extent to which data are considered representative depends on how well we can estimate the probability of individuals or households being in the sample.

A basic criticism of probability-based sampling, when applied to hidden, underserved and vulnerable populations, is the lack of information needed to establish a sampling frame. There are no lists of potential respondents nor maps showing their locations. The lack of a bench mark, such as would be provided by a successful census, increases uncertainty over the representativeness of samples. In the absence of a well-defined sampling frame, probability sampling places heavy reliance on enumerators to locate, identify and recruit respondents from these populations. When significant numbers of respondents cannot be located, identified or recruited, the representativeness of findings is further compromised.

To overcome these problems, researchers suggest that a sampling frame can be generated through large-scale screening. After the sampling frame is established, probability samples can be drawn with relative ease. Kalton presents a useful overview of more complex sample designs for rare and stigmatized populations.[5] Methods discussed in Kalton's article, specifically disproportionate stratification, multistage sampling, multiple frames, multiplicity sampling, and two-phase screening, are designed to generate probability samples. Each technique requires some preliminary population data, usually derived from screening, to identify members of the rare or stigmatized populations in sampling areas or at least the estimated distribution of persons in each sampling area, in order to create the sampling frame.

Kalton also describes time/space location sampling, which can be employed without preliminary population estimates, but requires sampling to occur in specific locations and times, such as soup kitchens or gay bars, where the rare population is most likely to be found. Time/space location sampling is analogous to measuring the flow of people through a location, rather than a crosssectional snapshot of persons of a specific group at a specific time, irrespective of location. This latter technique is an important method for measuring utilization rates of health services and the composition of the service-using population, but yields no information on persons who do not use the service.

Unfortunately, these sampling methods may not work with many non-institutionalized, vulnerable populations. With rare populations, representing less than 1% of a population, screeners might have to contact 10,000 households to identify 100 members of the category. Large-scale screening is also unlikely to be effective for persons associated with illegal and stigmatized activities. An overall refusal rate of only 5% during screening or actual enumeration may mask much higher refusal rates for persons in the stigmatized populations. Would-be respondents from the target population are often more likely to refuse participation or deny being in a

---

5. Graham Kalton, "Sampling Considerations in Research on HIV Risk and Illness," in *Methodological Issues in AIDS Research,* eds. David G. Ostrow and Ronald C. Kessler, (New York: Plenum Press, 1993). See also Seymour Sudman and Graham Kalton, "New Developments in Sampling Special Populations," *Annual Review of Sociology* 12 (1986): 401-29.

particular classification, such as criminally involved, HIV-positive or undocumented immigrants, wishing to be left alone or seen as being part of the mainstream. If screening fails to attain reasonable coverage of the target population, probability samples based on a partial-coverage frame constructed from the screening are apt to be biased.

Some hidden, underserved and vulnerable populations, such as the homeless, are not spread evenly within the general population, but are concentrated within specific locations. In these cases, spatially targeted or clustered sampling methods may reduce screening costs. The savings in data collection costs must be balanced with the loss of useful information on more dispersed members of the target population. Rural homelessness, for example, has received minimal attention.

Nonspatial characteristics of subpopulations, such as having a mental illness, are known to correlate with being hidden. Sampling in mental health and law enforcement programs can increase our understanding of the relationship between mental illness and being hidden, but even among these subpopulations there are large numbers who do not seek or receive institutional assistance, such as persons with symptoms of paranoia. Further, an arrest or admission to treatment can occur far from the residential location of the respondent, enhancing the perception of spatial concentration of hidden populations.

c. *Nonprobability Sampling*

Kalton divides nonprobability sampling methods into those based on convenience, judgement and quotas.[6] Convenience sampling can be considered the non-probability extreme, where data are collected which may not represent any particular population. Judgement and quotas are strategies to improve the representativeness of data without incurring all of the costs associated with probability sampling. In practice these methods may be combined, and all three strategies are relevant to hidden, underserved and vulnerable populations. Convenience methods for this population can include data collected where services are delivered, such as health clinics and homeless shelters, street corner studies, using posters to recruit study volunteers, and snowball, or chain-referral sampling.

---

6.   Graham Kalton, *Introduction To Survey Sampling*, (Thousand Oaks, California: Sage Publications, 1983).

Judgement inevitably plays a role in conducting probability and non-probability surveys. It refers to the decision on the part of some authority to select locations or respondents rather than allow such selection to occur based purely on probability. Judgement may be employed to select spatial clusters, which will then be randomly sampled in proportion to subpopulation size, in which case the data may still have strong probabilistic properties. On the other hand, when judgement leads to the selection of individuals as representative of class of people, the sample clearly falls into the nonprobability group. Service provider studies are often hampered when clinical judgement overrides research criteria, very often in the name of client well-being. A study of homeless shelter populations is affected by admission criteria which exclude people who are visibly intoxicated, arrive late or have broken shelter rules in the past. Random assignment of participants to medical treatment may be overridden by clinical judgement that a particular client would really benefit by getting a particular treatment strategy.

Quotas are also a part of many sampling strategies. They refer to prior establishment of target sample size, often stratified across categories of the population. A study of persons using health care services might target five white-male, five black-male, five white-female, five-black female clients each day rather than simply selecting a random sample of users. Quotas are very useful in establishing group samples that are of sufficient size to permit statistical analysis, and the use of quotas will not necessarily make a sample nonprobabilistic. For instance, stratified sampling will often require oversampling of a particular group of people in order to insure sufficient size. The sample can then be weighted in order to be representative of the population. However, when quotas are employed in nonprobabilistic samples, they may mitigate but not eliminate concerns about sample representativeness. Within each of the sample groups, the persons selected may be the most accessible or most willing to participate, and therefore not representative of their group.

One of the clearest examples of existing convenience data used to measure the impacts of health care reform is data collected by service providers tracking total numbers of patients by their method of payment, admission status (emergency v. nonemergency), client socioeconomic information, out-of-pocket charges to clients and payment default rates. Data are designed to meet the administrative and clinical needs of the agency, but also may meet existing reporting requirements on specific infectious diseases or criminal activities such as child abuse. The sheer volume of information can be staggering, particularly in large hospitals and social service agencies, and the data are often formatted to facilitate transactions, such as seeking payment of bills, as opposed to a research or evaluation-oriented format. As such, this information would be only partially suited to the task of monitoring impacts of health care reform. Critical variables describing the patients and their health status may be missing or recorded in narrative patient charts. Clinical and administrative data may be fragmented across several unconnected departments or organizations. Historical data may be lost, with new information overwriting old information rather than being appended.

Persons who are older, less healthy, less criminally involved and less anxious about being contacted are likely to be overrepresented in health service populations. Weights can be applied to nonprobability data to mitigate sample bias in some instances. For instance, the frequency with which an individual uses a service affects the probability that (s)he will be interviewed. A weight, such as an inverse function of this frequency, can be used to reduce their representation in the sample.[7] There are no procedures for weighting to compensate for the large number of people who never use a service, though it is hypothetically possible to pool data from a variety of health service providers, public and private, to develop broader representation. In practice this is extremely difficult at any but the most aggregate level. Still missing are persons who use no health services or have no continuity of care, and therefore no continuity of data. Thus, three principle criticisms of service provider data are that they only capture an in-treatment population, that clinical consideration may interfere with research objectives and that providers may have a strategic interest in inflating service demand estimates.

Snowball or chain-referral sampling can be a particularly useful non-probability technique for screening or sampling noninstitutionalized populations. Typically, respondents in a survey are asked to identify other members of the target population and/or encourage members to participate. Participation may be encouraged through financial or in-kind compensation for time required to complete the survey instruments.[8] In cases where the

7.   Marjorie J. Robertson, Alex Westerfelt, and Irving Piliavin, "Research Note: The Impact of Sampling Strategy on Estimated Prevalence of Major Mental Disorders Among Homeless Adults in Alameda County, California," (paper presented at the annual meeting of the American Public Health Association, Atlanta, November 1991).

target population is composed of socially cohesive groups or the target population is especially motivated by financial compensation, snowball samples can grow very quickly. The process can be very efficient, with the number of persons who are screened and found not to be eligible typically very low when compared with probability sampling techniques. Snowball sampling can provide added insight into informal networks within the target population, as well as insight into epidemiological patterns with respect to infectious diseases. These strategies are often employed in contact tracing, such as sexual and/or needle-sharing partners, to name a few.

The probabilities that individuals in the target population will be included in a snowball sample are not equal, but rather a function of connectedness to others in the population. The use of partner identification and notification in tracing sexually transmitted diseases produces a snowball of persons who may have been exposed. The final composition of this snowball is likely to depend on the first few persons enumerated and subsequent patterns of sexual contact. As such, the process of selective identification and volunteering for participation can produce biased, unrepresentative findings. Kalton suggests that the snowball strategy is more acceptable when employed to build a sampling frame. In some populations it may be possible to snowball a virtually exhaustive list of all persons in the target population. A random sample drawn from that list would probably be considered representative, though concerns about changes that occur in a population during the snowballing process and potential contamination of the data resulting from the snowballing process or financial compensation remain. Some connections are themselves illegal or stigmatized and can be difficult, if not dangerous, to pursue. The outreach process in sensitive areas, such as substance abuse or use of illegal abortion services, has to be respectful of the privacy of respondents, a matter which will receive greater attention later in this chapter.

---

8.   Sherry Deren et al., provide an interesting account of the impacts of monetary and nonmonetary incentives for recruiting and maintaining study participation. The authors conclude that monetary incentives were more effective in soliciting participation from two drug-using samples. The ethical implications of providing money to drug users are explored. See Sherry Deren et al., "The Impact of Providing Incentives for Attendance at AIDS Prevention Sessions," *Public Health Reports* 109, no. 4 (July-August 1994).

d. Capture-Recapture Strategies for Estimating Population Size

If the primary objective of research is estimating the size of hidden populations, rather than their characteristics or behaviors, then capture-recapture techniques used in nonsedentary populations are potentially less costly. These methods are characterized by taking two or more successive samples from the same population and attaining the percentage of individuals that appear in both samples. The amount of overlap can be used to estimate the prevalence of particular subpopulations within the target population. The technique can provide only limited additional information about the population of interest, depending on the level of detail collected in each of the samples.[9]

Capture-recapture methods in social studies have been challenged as inaccurate and nonrepresentative.[10] Two underlying requirements are of paramount importance. First, these methods assume that each of the samples is collected in probabilistic sweeps through the entire population. As discussed earlier, in the absence of a sampling frame, probability-based samples are difficult to collect. If any of the samples is convenience-based or nonrepresentative, then the resulting estimates of population are likely to be inaccurate. The use of service programs, such as methadone clinics and jails, as places of enumeration provides some information, but not the prevalence of the target population. The requirement of multiple samples can present additional problems in interpreting findings, particularly if there are significant events, such as seasonal, macroeconomic or political changes occurring between the samples which differentially affect migration in or out of the sampling area.

The second requirement is that individuals enumerated in one sample can be identified again in subsequent samples. In animal populations this is accomplished through tagging or banding. In human populations, use of

---

9. Mastro et al., provide an application of capture-recapture to estimate the size of the opiate-using population in Bangkok, Thailand. They collected two samples, one from a methadone treatment program and another from urine tests run at the time of arrest by Thai police. The two samples totalled 4064 (s_1) and 1540 (s_2), with 171 (m_{12}) persons identified as being in both samples. The formula (s_1s_2) / m_{12} provides an estimate of total opium- using population in Bangkok. In this case (4064*1540)/171 = 36,600 is the estimate of total opiate users in Bangkok. See Timothy Mastro et al., "Estimating the Number of HIV-Injection Drug Users in Bangkok: A Capture-Recapture Method," *American Journal of Public Health* 84, no. 7 (July 1994).

10. Richard Neugebauer and Janet Wittes, "Annotation: Voluntary and Involuntary Capture-Recapture Samples-Problems in the Estimation of Hidden and Elusive Populations," *American Journal of Public Health* 84, no. 7 (July, 1994).

social security numbers or some other reliable identifier is required. Persons in hidden, underserved and vulnerable populations may lack reliable forms of identification. Matching names is difficult, though not impossible, if names of individuals and their family members are accurately recorded. The impact of missing actual matches between the two samples is to increase the estimate of the target population size. Thus, while capture-recapture techniques can be an efficient means for estimating the size of specific populations, they generally will not produce sufficient information on the population to measure impacts of health care reform.

III. Application of Service-Based and Targeted Sampling

The challenge for studying hidden, underserved and vulnerable populations is to develop a strategy that can provide better representation than non-probability sampling and a more feasible strategy for data collection than probability sampling. Two strategies, clinic-based sampling and targeted sampling implemented for substance abusers, will now be compared.

a. Service Provider Sampling: Enhanced Treatment Project (ETP)

A five-year study, funded by the National Institute on Drug Abuse (NIDA Grant Number DA06944), has been investigating enhanced treatment for persons entering drug addiction treatment at the Department of Veteran Affairs Medical Center in Dayton, Ohio (DVAMC). Funding and the interinstitutional arrangements for the project restricted participation to drug-abusing veterans seeking treatment in one particular program. New participants were admitted to the study over a three-year period.

The sampling procedure was typical of a service provider study. The research team attempted to include all persons who were admitted to treatment and who had a recent history of drug use, but were not recently attending other drug treatment programs. Clients who agreed to enter the study were interviewed at intake, then 6, 12 and 18 months following admission. During the course of the 90+ minute interviews, data about drug use, family and residential history, criminal activities, health and employment were recorded. Respondents were compensated financially for participating in each of the four interviews. The refusal rate for participation remained low for persons clinically assigned to inpatient drug treatment. Persons who were clinically assigned to outpatient treatment were less likely to follow through on treatment or participation in the study. Among persons missing from this sample are persons referred to other treatment programs, nonveterans, out-of-treatment drug abusers, persons selecting private care, persons in long-term incarceration. This sample represents a narrow, though important segment of the drug-using populations in this metropolitan area.

The resulting 566 clients in this study were nearly all male (99%), primarily African American (73%), or white (26%), with an average age of 37 years. The DVAMC program did not dispense methadone, and thus was not a major treatment center for opiate addiction. Most clients reported either crack-cocaine as their drug of choice (65%) or used crack in combination with other drugs and alcohol. Injection drug use in this sample was relatively low, with fewer than 15% injecting in the year prior to entering treatment. Many respondents were residentially unstable, but generally able to stay off the street and out of homeless shelters. Many went from one home to another, some nights with their mothers, some nights with a girlfriend, some nights in a crack-house. During the period immediately preceding admission to drug treatment, many of the clients were burning all of their bridges, stealing in order to buy drugs and behaving erratically. This would have been a difficult group to enumerate in household surveys.

Though 88% of respondents had graduated from high school or passed GED examinations, and many held full-time jobs in the year preceding entry into treatment (61%), most were unemployed at the time of entry (79%). Their work histories included considerable amounts of informal and under-the-table work, as well as illegal activities for income. As such, there appears to be little promise in picking up this population in work-place enumeration either. Some clients were not "bottoming out" as such, but were experiencing intense problems in more specific life domains.[15] Some were in trouble with the law and were compelled by probation officers to enter treatment, while others were destitute and homeless after a sustained period of unemployment, and primarily needed a place to live. Many of the clients, the older ones in particular, were experiencing a variety of chronic physical and mental health problems. For many clients, the combination of deteriorating social, occupational and health status all contributed to their decision to enter treatment. These clients, who by their own admission had

---

15. Harvey A. Siegal et al., "Presenting Problems of Substance Abusers: Implications for Service Delivery and Attrition," *The American Journal of Drug and Alcohol Abuse*, Vol. 21, no. 1 (winter 1995), pp. 17-26.

bottomed out, are likely to be overrepresented in a clinic-based sample. Many, by their own admission, came out of hiding in order to deal with their multiple problems.

b. Stratified Targeted Sampling: AIDS Prevention Program (AIDS)

The AIDS Prevention Program, funded under the National Institute of Drug Abuse (Research Grant 1U01DA07305-01), studied alternative means of providing AIDS prevention education to high-risk drug users. Field workers in the Columbus, Ohio and Dayton, Ohio metropolitan areas targeted persons actively injecting drugs or smoking crack-cocaine. During the period from 1992 through 1993, 920 drug users who were not in drug treatment for the past 30 days were recruited for the study.

A modified version of Watters' and Biernacki's targeted sampling was designed and employed.[16] The essence of this approach was to use information on observable area characteristics and secondary data as markers of the prevalence of the target population in the target subareas. Sampling quotas were then established for target subareas, based on the estimated relative prevalence of the target population and needed total sample size for the program.

1. Subareas (zip codes) within the primary target area (county) were chosen for organizing sampling quotas. Alternative subareas might have been census tracks or blocks. In this case the availability of existing marker variables based on zip code made this a better choice.

2. In this step a series of risk indicators were gathered to measure potential drug-related activities in a subarea, and a risk index was estimated from the risk indicators to estimate the potential density of drug users. An ethnographer worked with local field workers to estimate the number of crack-houses, crack-copping areas, shooting galleries, etc., in each zip code. Secondary data on other drug-related activities were gathered from drug treatment programs, County Departments of Health, and security systems. Simple combinations of

---

16. The basic targeted sampling strategy is laid out in John K. Watters and Patrick Biernacki, "Targeted Sampling: Options for the Study of Hidden Populations," *Social Problems* 36, no. 4 (October 1989). A variation of this strategy is applied to noninstitutionalized drug users in Detroit in Mildred S. Braunstein, "Sampling a Hidden Population: Noninstitutionalized Drug Users," *AIDS Education and Prevention* 5, no. 2 (1993): 131-39.

the risk indicators or factor scores estimated from the risk indicators were used to create the risk index.

3. The zip code areas were then stratified into three risk density zones, or sampling zones based on the risk index. In this case high, medium and low-risk zones were established. The summation of the rescaled risk index was then used as the sampling weight for each zone.

4. Target groups, such as injection drug users and crack users, were identified, and sampling quotas for each target group in each sampling zone were developed on the basis of the sampling weight.

5. An outreach process was employed to collect the quota of interviews from each sampling zone. The outreach process combined use of local informants, networking and snowballing to recruit participants.

The stratified targeted sampling strategy attempted to make the sample more representative of the target drug population, when compared with Watters' and Biernacki's targeted sampling. Most importantly, this approach encourages data collection in even low-risk or low-prevalence zones. This targeted approach would appear to be more representative than service provider sampling, such as the Enhanced Treatment Project. This aided the collection of more representative data on a noninstitutionalized drug-using population, one of the most hidden and difficult to enumerate populations in America. A more complete description of this process is presented by Carlson, et al., and Wang, et al.[13]

Most respondents in this sample were male (72%), African American (77%), with an average age of 38. Fifty-four percent graduated from high school, and 18% were employed at the time of the interview. Heroin and crack-cocaine were used in the past month by 60% and 72%, respectively. Injection drug use was considerably higher for this group, as it was a targeted behavior for inclusion in the study.

---

13. Robert G. Carlson, Jichuan Wang, Harvey A. Siegal, Russel S. Falck, and Jie Guo, "An Ethnographic Approach to Targeted Sampling: Problems and Solutions in AIDS Prevention Research among Injection Drug and Crack-Cocaine Users," *Human Organization* 53, no. 3 (fall 1994). See also Jichuan Wang, Robert Carlson, Harvey Siegal, Russel Falke, and Jie Guo, "Sampling 'Hidden' Populations: A Stratified Targeted Sampling Strategy," (paper presented at the Annual Meeting of the Population Association of America, Cincinnati, April 1993).

c. Comparing Results

Table I compares clients from the samples across several basic social and demographic indicators. The data indicate that while the samples were taken very differently, there is evidence of overlap. Notably, the ETP sample is limited by eligibility for DVAMC services, which accounts for the paucity of female patients and the higher percentage of high school graduates. The AIDS program targeted not-in-treatment injection drug and crack-cocaine users, while the ETP clients were in a drug-free treatment program, typically less popular among heroin addicts. Thus it is not surprising to note the much higher prevalence of heroin users in the AIDS sample. Similarities also exist between the two samples. Racial composition of the samples is very similar. Mean age in the two samples suggests that both procedures identified a population of older, confirmed drug users. Marital status appears similar, though somewhat different categories were employed. Despite differences in levels of high school completion, the samples have very similar reported levels of employment. Except for heroin use, other drug use patterns between the two samples are very similar. A majority of the participants in both programs reported recent use of alcohol and crack-cocaine.

The spatial distributions for best available address of the clients is similar for both samples. Addresses, elicited from clients who had any address at all, were compiled, and zip code information mapped for the Dayton-Springfield Metropolitan Area. Figures I and II are dot density maps of Montgomery County zip code areas. Each dot represents one client in the study. As can be seen, the density patterns are quite similar, with participants most concentrated in Dayton's west side and a secondary area east of the center.

Estimates of the relative costs of these two strategies are difficult to generalize. The service provider sample was initially a matter of having an interviewer in position when clients arrived for services. The stratified-targeted sampling strategy required additional research to develop target quotas for sampling areas and staff time for recruiting clients into the study. However, the recruitment process worked well, and the pace of interviewing was brisk when compared to the slower pace of admissions to the DVAMC treatment program. Follow-up interview procedures were essentially the same for both projects, with staff time divided between locating clients and reinterviewing them. In both projects, the cost in time and effort of locating clients for follow-up interviews increased dramatically for a

	Table 1	
	Comparison of Two Samples	
Recruitment Method	ETP DVAMC Patients	AIDS Outreach Recruitment
Number analyzed	570	920
% White	26%	23%
% Black	73%	77%
% Male	99%	72%
Mean Age	37	39
Single	26%	34%
Married	18%	20%
Living with partner	—	9%
Divorced/Separated/Widowed	56%	37%
High School Graduates	88%	54%
% Currently Employed	21%	18%
% Who Used Drug in Past Month		
Alcohol	86%	86%
Marijuana	49%	55%
Crack-Cocaine	75%	72%
Heroin-Opiates	10%	60%

percentage of highly mobile clients. Persons who were homeless at intake were among the most difficult to find for reinterviewing.

IV. Issues for Combining Results and Inferring Results to Larger Populations

While the service based sampling and stratified, targeted sampling appear to have produced similar demographic compositions, the stratified-targeted procedure delivers a broader cross section of the population of interest. Most importantly, the service-based sample is determined by basic service eligibility criteria which have little to do with being hidden, underserved or vulnerable. However, there may be merit in combining results of several such methodologies, particularly when this reduces the cost of producing a sufficiently large sample. In this case, combining findings for an in-treatment sample with an out-of-treatment sample may be desirable. The same may be true for comparing persons eligible for subsidized medical services with those not eligible for subsidized services. Changes in the composition

Figure 1
Distribution of ETP Respondents

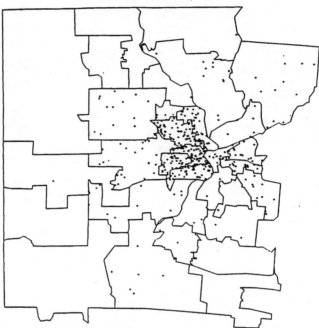

Figure 2
Distribution of AIDS Respondents

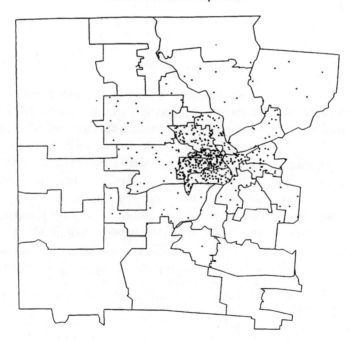

of these two populations will be very important in assessing the impact of health care reform.

Data can be combined at several levels. Often the most basic level, that of literally concatenating raw, microdata among sites, is impossible due to insufficient comparability of variables, time scales and sampling methods. A level up from this is merging tabulated data. This approach, as evidenced in Table I, permits comparisons across studies, but limits more advanced, inferential tests. Research conclusions may also be compared without any specific reference to data. Megastudies often operate at this level. Van Meter discusses more rigorous methods for comparative, cross-classification analysis of nonprobability, or in his terms, "ascending" data.[14]

Selectivity of the samples turns out to be one of the crucial impediments to combining data, tabular analyses or research conclusions. In these studies clients have opt-out provisions, with potentially biasing effects. Additionally, administrative eligibility criteria for a service, and thus enumeration, may not be relevant to the sampling scheme and often differ across sites. Finally, there are historical factors which influence patterns of service enrollment. For instance, lack of funds may result in long waiting lists or required copayments.

V. Ethical Issues in Sampling Hidden, Underserved and Vulnerable Populations

There are at least two levels on which ethics should be considered in sampling. At a macrolevel, demographers, epidemiologists and others in the research community are professionally obligated to produce scientifically representative, unbiased samples. Failure to adequately represent significant portions of a population discredits the process and the people who designed it. Two factors interfere with gathering good sampling. As Choldin reflected,

> The undercount is not a feature of the census; it is a feature of our society. Changing the census has not eliminated our undercount. In order to eliminate the undercount, we would have to change the

---

14. Karl M. van Meter, "Sampling and Cross-Classification Analysis in International Social Research," in *Comparative Methodology: Theory and Practice in International Research*, ed. Else Øyen (Thousand Oaks, California: Sage Studies in International Sociology 40, 1990).

society. Our society abides by great material inequality. Despite the nation's wealth, every city has destitute homeless people. Furthermore, freedom and inequality conspire to create disorder. Poverty and disorder are great obstacles to census-taking.[15]

The inherency of the problem of undercounts is such that the debate moves from how to fix the census process for data collection to how to weight the results to compensate for errors. The second factor interfering with the 1990 census was political interference in the decision of whether to weight results to compensate for undercounts. Like clinical interference in conducting research with service providers, political decisions on whether to employ weights affect outcomes of research in ways that can reduce the validity of the results. The impact of health care reform on universality of coverage must be evaluated with respect to meeting the needs of the entire population. Identification of winners and losers in the reform process depends on an enumeration process which can compensate for societal and political processes which interfere with data collection and analysis.

A second, microlevel ethical concern is the protection of privacy of respondents. In the course of conducting normal population sampling, a process of random selection and masking of identifying information can insure the privacy of respondents. Alternative processes, such as using service provider data, targeted sampling and capture/recapture all require more careful identification of respondents to eliminate redundancy and estimate coverage. These processes, particularly when applied to persons who may be engaging in illegal activities, can trigger the interest of immigration and law enforcement authorities. The frustration of law enforcing agencies in identifying persons who are law-breakers is understandable, yet efforts to conscript research organizations and force them to turn over information can undermine the credibility of both organizations. The line separating research from intervention is often difficult to define, yet must be maintained if research is to succeed. When an enumeration process fails to protect respondent privacy, not only is the potential for abuse increased, but respondent willingness to cooperate is threatened.

15. Choldin, *Looking for the Last Percent*, 230.

VI. Conclusion

Recent trends in health care reform are not further integrating service provision, but rather appear to be market-driven, minor adjustments designed to correct specific consumer and provider concerns. Many changes do not appear to favor hidden, underserved and vulnerable populations. While any loss of health care for these populations is lamentable, the process of monitoring these impacts is even more important. These populations, like the current process of health care reform, are highly segmented. They include persons who are homeless, impoverished, undocumented, criminally involved, informally employed or housed. Members of these subpopulations have particular lifestyles, preferences and behaviors.

The differentiation of providers and consumers will continue to challenge monitoring efforts, often requiring multiple and complex strategies for data collection and analysis. Strategies for surveying the growing population of undocumented persons in the United States, for instance, are unlikely to work for urban homeless populations, or drug users, or any of a multitude of other difficult to reach subpopulations. While specifying strategies to particular subpopulations may increase program effectiveness, the monitoring function becomes far more complex. Aggregating information across fragmented data collection efforts is often precluded by inconsistent data structures and sampling procedures.

Measuring the impacts of health care reform involves identifying a target population, developing a sampling frame and collecting data on a wide spectrum of health-related information from a representative sample. The techniques discussed in this study are generally well-suited to working with specific, hard-to-reach subpopulations within a locally controlled, dynamic, market-driven health care system. These small, targeted studies can play an important role in informing local policy and incremental reform. Highly integrated, national reform of the health care system would benefit from better integration of data collection and dissemination on the populations discussed in this study. Methods for encouraging integration range from financial support for simultaneous, regional monitoring of health care utilization, using uniform research protocol, to less costly strategies for the design and dissemination sampling methodologies and research instrumentation which are adaptable to monitoring specific target populations by local health providers.

This chapter presents a brief introduction, the merits and limitations of census, probability and nonprobability sampling methods for hidden, underserved and vulnerable populations, and compares convenience with stratified-targeted sampling. The objective of stratified-targeted sampling is to address concerns with traditional sampling procedures. Neither study was designed to draw a sample from the full spectrum of drug abusers, while each samples from a segment of that larger population. The differences in clinical demands of each study, one to monitor treatment enhancements with an initially in-treatment population and the other to monitor the reduction in HIV risk behavior in an out-of-treatment population, need not be sacrificed in promoting the use of coordinated sampling strategies and data instrumentation. With better planning and coordination of research protocol, the potential for combining results from the samples would be facilitated. While the examples in this chapter are limited to the study of substance abuse intervention, the processes are not.

CHAPTER SIX

Using State-Level Hospital Discharge Data Bases: A Source of Race/Ethnicity Data to Monitor Minority and Special Populations

Barbara S. Kurtzig

Overview

The challenges for monitoring the access, appropriateness and efficacy, quality, and value of health care for minority and special populations at the state level are significant. State agencies that collect information on vulnerable populations confront issues such as defining minorities, standardizing the definitions, standardizing coding practices, and determining an effective paradigm for collecting the information.

One way several states currently attempt to capture information on minority populations is on their state-level hospital discharge data bases. At this time there are 38 states with mandates to collect, analyze, and disseminate hospital discharge data. These hospital discharge data sets are mandated by the states, and they are not part of federal information reporting requirements. As of 1991, 15 state agencies with state-mandated responsibility for collecting hospital discharge data reported they collect a race/ethnicity data element.[1] These states are: California, Connecticut, Delaware, Georgia, Maine, Maryland, Massachusetts, New Hampshire, New Jersey, New York, Rhode Island, South Carolina, Utah, Vermont, and Wisconsin. While a state may indicate that race/ethnicity information is

---

1. National Association of Health Data Organizations, *State Health Data Resources Manual: Hospital Discharge Data System* (Falls Church, Virginia: NAHDO, May 1993).

collected, the state may not (or may not have the authority to) enforce the collection of the information.

States use the race/ethnicity data they collect to monitor minority health issues, such as percentage of low-birthweight infants, length of hospital stay, age distribution of mothers, expected source(s) of prenatal care pay-ment, injury morbidity and mortality, and communicable diseases (includ-ing sexually transmitted diseases, HIV, AIDS, tuberculosis, etc.). This information helps state legislators, researchers, governors' offices and public health officials design policy, make clinical and demographic deter-minations, and monitor the success (or determine the failure) of a health program or procedure.

Some states use their hospital discharge data sets in combination with other data sets to help determine the need for primary care practitioners in a particular area, to better distribute available resources where they are most needed, and to better define, understand, and address high-crime-area issues.

State Data Organizations

The term "state data organization" (SDO) is used here to define that [public] organization mandated by the state to collect, analyze and disseminate hospital discharge data. Some state data organizations also are responsible for maintaining hospital financial data, nursing home discharge-level data, nursing home financial data, and outpatient surgery data from either hos-pitals, free-standing surgery centers, or both. Other state-level data sets may include data from physicians' offices, public health data, vital and health statistics, birth and death records, and maternal and child health data sets.

Historically, states created these data organizations for several reasons: to regulate health care costs, to support competition, to ensure the provision of pertinent information to policy-makers, to understand and improve the quality of patient care and provider practice patterns, to monitor health status of the population, and to promote effective decision-making[2]. The development of these organizations reflects the trend in the health care system to shift from regulation to competition as a way to control health care costs. Regardless of the reasons these agencies were created, often

---

2. *Ibid.*

SDOs are the only source of comparative information on all patients discharged from nonfederal, acute care hospitals in a state.

Annual operating budgets for these agencies range from approximately $0.5 million to more than $2.5 million; total staff size ranges from one to more than 21. Generally, SDOs are funded from the state's general fund or from provider (hospital) assessments. Some supplement their budgets with revenue from data sales.[3] SDOs are designed as free-standing organizations, or agencies within state departments of health, or agencies within the office of insurance commissioners. Some states, like Virginia, created public/private not-for-profit agencies to collect, analyze, and disseminate hospital discharge data. Many SDOs use commercial vendors to process their data.

Statewide Hospital Discharge Data Bases

Hospital discharge data bases are the most common type of data bases maintained by state data organizations. As of today, there are 40 states with mandates to collect hospital discharge data, that is, information on an individual's experience in a (nonfederal) hospital. Attachment A is a list of these states. Of these, approximately 22 have been collecting data long enough to have viable data sets. The other 18 have mandates, but little or no funding; or the collection effort is in its infancy.

A hospital discharge data set includes demographic data (age, gender, residence by zip code, and in some cases, race/ethnicity); clinical data (diagnoses and procedures); identifier data, which includes hospital, physician, and patient identifiers; and billing and payer data (expected source of payment, total charges billed to the payer, and length of stay). These data sets are encounter-level, that is, they contain information on all patients discharged from a hospital in a state, regardless of payer.

A hospital discharge data set *does not* contain cost information; that is, the actual cost to the hospital for treating an individual. The data set also does not contain information on an individual's contacts with public health agencies and providers outside the hospital setting (e.g., clinic visits,

---

3. National Association of Health Data Organizations, *State Health Data: A Tool for Health Reform and Consumer Information* (report researched and compiled for the Public Policy Institute of the American Association of Retired Persons, Washington, D.C., In draft).

physician office visits, etc.); and usually does not contain information collected from speciality hospitals, such as psychiatric or childrens' speciality hospitals. However, these data bases are a source of state-wide comparative information on hospital charges (prices) and use.

While most of these state organizations use standardized forms to collect the information, the Uniform Bill (UB) or the Uniform Hospital Discharge Data Set (UHDDS), there are significant variations among the data collected. The variations across states are a result of inconsistencies and idiosyncrasies in classification codes, coding methods, or data element definitions. The UB and the UHDDS forms are hospital billing forms, and are the instruments hospitals use for reimbursement purposes and have limited clinical value. And, in some states, such as California, Oregon and New York, a state-specific collection form is used instead of the UB or UHDDS form. These dissimilarities make interstate comparisons difficult.

Data Acquisition

Every state will protect the confidentiality and privacy of individuals. Each SDO has policies and procedures for the release of data which ensure confidentiality and privacy. These policies guide what data elements may be released to whom, under what conditions, and for what purpose. Some states require the data purchaser to appear before an institutional review board (IRB) or data committee to explain the reasons for which the data are requested and how the data are to be used and protected. Each state may have a different set of confidential or patient-identifiable data elements which may not be released. For example, states may not release patient date of birth, the date a procedure was performed, date of admission, extended zip code, or race/ethnicity element(s) because a combination of these elements could identify a patient. Most states have policies on how and if their data may be re-released.

Data are acquired from SDOs through a state-specific application process; and data are usually available in several formats. Some states have a "public use" data base, i.e., a data base that contains no individual identifiers, or elements which, in combination, could identify an individual or an institution. The "public use" data can be purchased directly from the state agency in tape form, cassette, and in some cases on CD Rom. Some states will perform special computer runs for a data purchaser. The special runs will, to the best of the agency's ability, meet the specific needs of the purchaser. States that do not have a "public use" data base may make aggregate data tapes available or publish reports using the data collected. Several SDOs make a confidential hospital discharge data set available to bona fide researchers. The researcher's application for these data is subjected to rigorous reviews by the state, and he or she must abide by all state confidentiality and privacy rules and regulations. States levy stiff penalties for any breech of confidentiality or privacy.

The cost of acquiring data from a state varies across states and depends on, among other things, the number of discharges or records. The price for a year of data ranges from approximately $300 to $18,000 among the states. The state agency will provide the data purchaser with data documentation which includes the agency data layout format and data definitions. However, for staff to better assist users of hospital discharge data sets, they will need to know the following:

- Type and year(s) of data requested;

- Type of research to be performed, along with protocols;

- Data elements required for research and rationale (especially if deniable or confidential data elements are requested).

The state data organization may require that a copy of the final or published research performed using their data be filed in their office and that the appropriate data source citations be included in the published research.

There are several private, for-profit organizations that purchase data from state agencies. These organizations usually enhance the data, adding value, and then sell information developed from using the data, or resell the data obtained from states that will permit resale.

Confidentiality and Privacy

To track an individual's health care across settings and time, a data base must have a mechanism for linking or following an individual through the health care system. The most efficient way to track this information is by using a unique patient identifier number (UPIN). Several issues related to UPINs and confidentiality, privacy, and data security must be given special attention when health care issues for special populations and minorities are being addressed.

California uses an encrypted Social Security number as a base to develop a record linkage number on all hospital inpatients to allow for tracking of readmissions. The state, using its discharge data sets, is beginning to track hospital use and charges by vulnerable populations. For example, the state is beginning to determine the birth rate (and rate of uncompensated care) of undocumented workers. However, many of these studies are preliminary because the state suspects heavy use of fictitious or duplicate Social Security numbers. California and other border states recognize their health systems provide care to a large undocumented, often non-English-speaking population, and they are trying to better understand how to (and if they should) accommodate these populations.

The economic concern of swelling Medicaid roles and uncompensated care in California led to Proposition 187 (1994). After an emotional and divisive debate, the proposition which, in effect, denied health care in California to undocumented workers and residents without proof of U.S. citizenship, was passed. However, the constitutionality of the proposition has yet to be tested in the courts. A major concern of those opposing Proposition 187 is that using the race/ethnicity identifier on a medical record will open the gates for rampant discrimination in the provision of health care to those who need it the most. It follows that migrant and undocumented workers, as well as the homeless, runaways, and HIV-positive populations, etc., may feel compelled to use false Social Security numbers, names, and addresses, and other means of identification, in order to obtain care.

Data Collection Considerations (Race/Ethnicity Codes)

A major problem with race/ethnicity data is how this information on the patient is reported to the hospital. In many states, the race and ethnicity of the patient is self-reported. That is, the patient is asked to identify his or her race and ethnicity. Some patients misrepresent this information because they are afraid they will not give the "right" answer to obtain care. Some misunderstand questions of race and ethnicity, confusing citizenship with ethnic background, or reporting religion as race or ethnic background (e.g., Muslim, Irish Catholic, Russian Orthodox). This may be especially true of non-English speaking patients. However, the Office of Management and Budget (OMB) contends that self-identification by the applicant is the preferred method of obtaining characteristic data. An alternative method is to collect the data by observation.

In some states, the race/ethnicity information is reported by the intake clerk upon observation. Often undertrained in these issues, a clerk may indicate race or ethnicity by observing skin color, surname, or language spoken. Many states allow each hospital to determine how the information will be collected.

Another barrier to collecting valid information concerns those patients of mixed race or mixed ancestry. While most intake forms have a category labeled "other," this category has the potential of being the largest and least useful of all. Unfortunately, any one or all of these practices and problems can be found in the same hospital system or even in the same hospital. While there have been no scientific studies on these issues, many SDOs suspect that vulnerable populations, however defined, are those populations who find questions of race and ethnicity threatening. They are the least-equipped to understand the health care system – and, it is suspected, receive less preventative care and come to a hospital sicker and require a larger number of health care services than those not defined as "vulnerable." This adds to the health care financial morass.

Because reimbursement is not an issue with the race/ethnicity code (that is, hospitals do not get reimbursed for collecting this information), hospitals have no reason to pursue race/ethnicity accuracy. Many SDOs, therefore, check only for completeness (has the element been reported) rather than for accuracy. This is especially true in states where the reporting of this element is mandatory rather than voluntary. These issues and the others mentioned pose a threat to the validity and reliability of reported race/ethnicity data. Whether the reporting of race/ethnicity data is a mandated or a voluntary effort, the validity and accuracy of the information is suspect.

A state agency collects hospital discharge data on a regular basis from hospitals within 6 months to 1 year after the close of a calendar or (state) fiscal period (year or quarter). The SDO edits, processes and analyzes the data. The agency then returns the data to the hospital for confirmation or correction before the data are released to the public or aggregated for use in public reports. Each state sets a required level of accuracy, and hospitals that have submitted erroneous data must resubmit the corrected data to the agency within a specific time period. The time between the initial collection of the data from the provider and the release of the data may take as long as 18 months.

Race/Ethnicity Validity Considerations

There are a few ways to verify race/ethnicity, and none is accurate. One way would be a check on race-specific or ethnic-specific diagnoses. For example, it was once thought that only the black American population suffered from sickle cell anemia, an inherited form of anemia which causes crystallization of the blood cells, resulting in blocked blood vessels. Recently, however, there have been cases of sickle cell anemia documented in the white population. Carriers of Tay-Sachs disease, which is an inherited disease that destroys the nervous system, is usually associated with the Eastern European Jewish population. However, the disease is being found in the Western European and North African populations (Jewish and non-Jewish), probably as a result of interreligious and crosscultural marriages. These examples show how clinical studies of certain diseases could be compromised if race/ethnicity only is used as a nonvariable indicator.

Another way to check the accuracy of race/ethnicity data is to track readmissions for consistency. Some states have performed reabstraction studies, where medical records are manually cross-checked with a previously collected data set. Reabstraction studies require a UPIN; however, even if a UPIN is available, it is an expensive and labor-intensive process.

Another issue to consider is that in some states, race and ethnicity are entered on the data base as two separate codes; in others, race/ethnicity is a single code. This compromises the usefulness of both race and ethnicity information. Table 1 is a comparison of race/ethnicity categories and codes among three states, Massachusetts, New Jersey and New York.

Defining race(s) also varies from state to state. For example some states define "ethnicity" as either Hispanic, non-Hispanic, or other. California is one of the few states that defines "white" as "A person having origins in or who identifies with any of the original Caucasian peoples of Europe, North Africa, or the Middle East." Some states do not define race, but list choices instead, e.g., American Indian or Alaskan Native, Asian or Pacific Islander, Black, White, Other, Unknown. In New Mexico, the term "American Indian" or "Native American" may be broken down even further to be tribe-specific or to describe the location of a tribe. Attachment B is a compilation of all the race categories from all the states that collect this element on their hospital discharge data bases.

Other Issues Related to Race/Ethnicity Codes

The Office of Management and Budget's (OMB) Statistical Policy Directive 15[4], "Race and Ethnic Standards for Federal Statistics and Adminis-

Table 1 Data Element Comparison Table: Race/Ethnicity Categories and Codes					
Massachusetts		New Jersey[1]		New York[2]	
Category	Code	Category	Code	Category	Code
White	1	White (non-Hispanic)	1	White	1
Black	2	Black (non-Hispanic)	2	African American (Black)	2
Other	3	Other	7	Other Race	88
Unknown	4	Unknown	6	Unknown	99
American Indian	5	American Indian/ Alaskan Native	4	Native American (American Indian, Eskimo/Aleut)	3
Asian	6	Asian/Pacific Islander	5		4
Hispanic	9	Hispanic	3		
Missing	Blank				

[1]New Jersey: Hispanic is coded as race; however, other Hispanic ethnicities are codes as separate ethnic elements: 0=not Hispanic, 1=Mexican, 2=Puerto Rican, 3=Cuban, 4=Central or South American, 5=Other Hispanic, 6=Unknown.
[2]New York: Ethnicity is coded as a separate element: 1=Spanish/Hispanic Origin; 2=Not of Spanish/Hispanic Origin; 3=Unknown

From information gathered for the Healthcare Cost and Utilization Project, 1989-1994 (HCUP-3). May, 1995. Agency for Health Care Policy and Research, U.S. Department of Health and Human Services, Public Health Services, Rockville, Maryland.

4.   U.S. Department of Commerce, Office of Federal Statistical Policy and Standards, "Directive No. 15: Race and Ethnic Standards for Federal Statistics and Administrative Reporting," *Statistical Policy Handbook* (Washington, D.C.: Department of Commerce, 1978).

trative Reporting," is responsible for categorizing race and ethnicity for federal statistics. Directive 15 is designed, not as a scientific document, but rather as a way to standardize data collection and publication among federal agencies, with hopes that the states will adopt the same standards.

Currently, OMB is grappling with whether to add multiracial and multiethnic categories to the directive and to redefine some current classifications. An example is a suggestion to change "Black" to "African American."[5] This change may lead to some interesting data collection options. For example, if the color of a patient's skin is not white, if he or she is not a U.S. citizen, or if they are a citizen but were not born in the United States, they are not Native American, Hispanic, etc., how will they respond to the question? The same holds true of an individual born of parents of two different "minorities." As the complexion of the U.S. population changes, the race/ethnicity identification and coding issues become even more complicated. In addition, definitions may change over time, making longitudinal studies using race as an indicator more fragile. The result may be that the cost of collecting and verifying this element (for federal or state data bases) may exceed its usefulness. The OMB debate is ongoing.

Examples of Uses of Hospital Data by States to Address Health Issues of Vulnerable Populations

While state agencies understand the limitations of race/ethnicity data collected on a hospital discharge data base, they use the information as a starting point to help them understand issues of access to care by vulnerable populations. Most of these agencies do not have the resources to collect data that further identifies vulnerable populations on their state-level data bases. Analyses of health care needs could be further enhanced with the application of geo-coding (pinpointed geographic areas of need using zip codes or extended zip codes), linking other state-level or federal data bases which are used to identify areas of need, or having cooperative data agreements with the criminal justice system to help provide appropriate outreach and care in high-crime areas. However, these enhancements are costly and often prohibited by federal or state laws. For example, many federally-funded programs prohibit a state agency sharing data collected

---

5.   Suzann Evinger, "How Shall We Measure Our Nation's Diversity?" *Chance* 8, no. 1 (1995).

for that program, citing the federal Privacy Act of 1974, which prohibits identifying individuals and requires that the data be used only for the reason they are collected.

Several state laws mirror the federal Privacy Act of 1974. By not sharing information, data collection has become fragmented, duplicative and costly.

State agencies use published reports as the most common format to disseminate information collected and analyzed on state-level data. Examples of reports on minorities and special populations by state agencies follow:

1. The California Office of Statewide Health Planning and Development's (OSHPD) mission is to plan for and support the development of a health care system which meets the needs of California citizens. The agency produces annual reports on hospital use by minorities.[6] The state's hospitals are required to identify the race/ethnicity of each patient discharged. Discharges have clinical coding identifying principal and secondary diagnoses and procedures, and tables are produced displaying information by race/ethnicity on the most frequently occurring diagnoses, patient disposition (routine, transferred to acute hospital unit, transferred to long-term, death, etc.), and percent of newborns with low birth weight by county, among others. The reports are an example of how the state uses its hospital discharge system to support their efforts to monitor and assess health issues of relevance to minorities in California.

   California also has a method for linking vital statistics data with hospital discharge data to better understand the incidences of low birth-weight babies. The state is using, among other variables, the data element for the neonate's race and ethnicity from the vital statistics data set; and the patient's race/ethnicity element from the hospital discharge data set. Concentrating on this element, the state found that the race/ethnicity coding on the hospital discharge data file and the vital statistics linked birth/death file is not coherent[7], making this element a "weak" link and of marginal value.

---

6. California Office of Statewide Health Planning and Development, *Hospital Utilization Summaries: California Hospital Discharge Data for Minorities* (Sacramento, California, March 1994).

7. Beate Herrchen, Jeffrey B. Gould, and Thomas S. Nesbitt, "A Probabilistic Method for Linking Vital Statistics Linked Birth/Death and Hospital Discharge File with Results

2. South Carolina's *Healthy Start Management Information System* provides an integrated, retrospective view of utilization, infant mortality, and risk factors across medical, social, and psychosocial services. An objective of the program is to provide comparative analysis for physicians, case managers, and hospitals for treatment protocols. Data from several state agencies contribute to the information system. These agencies include Medicaid; the South Carolina Health Department, which contributes Vital Records, Women, Infants and Children programs and Immunization, Case Management, and Family Planning; South Carolina Department of Mental Health; the South Carolina Department of Social Services, which contributes Aid to Families and Dependent Children, and Food Stamps; Community Health Centers; and the South Carolina Department of Alcohol and Other Drug Abuse Services. Linking this information with census data and applying an address match program (geo-coding), the state can identify geographic areas (to the block-level) of need. For example, the state can now determine whether a low birth-weight baby was born in a high-crime, low-income neighborhood. The mother's prenatal care (if any) can be tracked, along with hospital use, including emergency room. The need for and placement of outreach programs can be determined and implemented.[8]

3. The Wisconsin Center for Health Statistics produces, among other publications, information about racial and ethnic minorities in the state, and reports on the basic health issues and concerns of vulnerable populations.[9] Recognizing that the minority population in Wisconsin is growing, the state looked at several issues to address the needs of a diverse population. This publication concentrates on the developmental stages of life and is divided by health concerns by age cohorts. Findings for each racial/ethnic population are compared to findings for the Wisconsin population as a whole. Each section

for the 1990 California Birth Cohort," (working paper presented at the Annual Meeting of the Information for State Health Policy Program, Robert Wood Johnson Foundation, Chicago, May 1995).

8. Beth Corley and Walter P. Bailey, "Examples of Integration of Health and Human Services Data Bases," (paper presented at the Annual Meeting of the Information for State Health Policy Program, Robert Wood Johnson Foundation, Chicago, May 1995).

9. Wisconsin Department of Health and Social Services, Center for Health Statistics, Division of Health, *Minority Health in Wisconsin: Toward a Health Diversity* (Madison, Wisconsin, 1993).

contains information not only on health care access problems, but also on the prevention and health promotion efforts underway in the state. Among the data bases used to compile the information in the report, the state uses birth certificates, U.S. Census information for Wisconsin, death certificates, state surveys on prenatal care and family health, the Wisconsin Behavioral Risk Factor Survey, the Wisconsin Cancer Reporting System, and reportable disease programs in the Bureau of Public Health.

4. North Carolina health officials undertook an analysis of the health of minorities in the state, and discovered a disproportionate illness and death rate among this population. To better disseminate information on their findings and plans to improve the health and health care of minorities, the state produced a series of reports to help affect health policy decisions.[10]

5. Massachusetts released a report containing information on Chinese and Southeast Asian infant and maternal health in the commonwealth. Using data from the U.S. Census Bureau, the state Registry of Vital Records, and hospital data, the report details incidences of low birth-weight, jaundice, and whether prenatal care was received from private physicians, HMOs, community health centers, or not at all.[11]

Massachusetts also produced a report on preventable hospitalizations (PH) in the commonwealth. A major role of the Massachusetts Office of Health and Human Services, Division of Healthcare Finance and Policy (formerly the Massachusetts Rate Setting Commission), the SDO for the commonwealth, is to enhance the performance of the competitive marketplace in Massachusetts, and to improve health policy development and assessment. Analyses of the rates of preventable hospitalizations or ambulatory care sensitive conditions can warn of potential problems in the primary care delivery system and can provide information for creating and targeting strategic interventions to reduce PH rates and measure the success or failure of the

---

10. For further information on CHES Studies, contact the North Carolina State Center for Health and Environmental Statistics, P.O. Box 29538, Raleigh, NC 27626-0538.

11. Massachusetts Department of Public Health, *Chinese & Southeast Asian Births in Massachusetts* (Boston, Massachusetts, June 1993).

interventions. Massachusetts identified the following factors that may be causing PH:

- Inability to obtain services because of transportation and child care difficulties, as well as restricted office hours;

- Underinsurance or no insurance;

- Cultural and linguistic barriers;

- Fear or distrust of medical community;

- Lack of patient follow-up, inadequate equipment, etc.;

- Inappropriate diagnoses.

Among the data sources used to develop the report, Massachusetts used data from their hospital discharge data set, data from the U.S. Census Bureau, and the Medicaid Management Information System. In addition, the commonwealth employed geo-coding, using the Massachusetts zip codes.[12]

Examples of Uses of Hospital Data by Nonstate Agencies to Address Health Issues of Vulnerable Populations

Federal agencies and other national organizations often use state hospital discharge data to study health issues of concern to vulnerable populations. The Agency for Health Care Policy and Research, U.S. Department of Health and Human Services, Public Health Service (AHCPR) is using hospital discharge data sets to examine trends in hospital procedures performed on black and white patients.[13] This report compares rates of all diagnostic and therapeutic procedures received by black and white patients discharged from a national sample of U.S. hospitals.

AHCPR is also in the process of building a multistate hospital discharge data base for researchers [14] as part of their Healthcare Cost and Utilization

---

12. Massachusetts Rate Setting Commission, *Preventable Hospitalization in Massachusetts*, (Boston, Massachusetts, January 1994).

13. U.S. Department of Health and Human Services, Public Health Service, Agency for Health Care Policy and Research (AHCPR), *Trends in Hospital Procedures Performed on Black Patients and White Patients: 1980-1987*, Provider Studies Research Note 20, AHCPR Publication Number 94-0003. (Rockville, Maryland: DHHS, April 1994).

14. For more information, contact the Division of Provider Studies, Center for

Project, 1988-1994 (HCUP-3). The data base is designed to be a 20% sample of U.S. hospitals, and contains records for all stays in the sample hospitals. The initial data base was released in June 1995 and contains a sample of hospitals from 11 states; the data base will be updated annually, depending on the resources available to AHCPR for the project. Among the data elements contained on the data base is race/ethnicity. AHCPR developed algorithms which allow them to code consistently race and ethnicity, as well as other hospital discharge data elements, across the states participating in the project. For the first time, hospital discharge data sets can be compared among states.

Among other agencies and organizations using state-level information to study health care for vulnerable populations are the National Academy for State Health Policy, the Association of State and Territorial Health Officials, the Robert Wood Johnson Foundation, and the Milbank Memorial Fund.

Conclusions

State data organizations are anxious for their data to be used. However, state agency staff understand what the data can and cannot do. State-level data sets generally are patient-level, and because health and health care is local, there are regional differences in definitions, coding practices, uses, and requirements for collecting and releasing health data within states as well as across states. Collecting information as close to the source of care is critical to help ensure accuracy; however, this practice leads to disparate data sets with limited comparability. National data standards for uniformity in collecting, coding, defining and ensuring accuracy of patient-level data would not only allow for comparability across states, but also allow the research community and policy-makers a more accurate information base from which to work. AHCPR's HCUP-3 Project is a step toward standardizing hospital discharge data sets, but federal guidelines are needed to ensure uniformity among the states.

Race and ethnicity data present problems that go beyond the technical considerations of standardized coding and definitions. The emotional and psychological issues of identification cannot be forced into matrices or

Intramural Research, AHCPR at 301-594-1410 or the National Association of Health Data Organizations (NAHDO) 254-B North Washington Street, Falls Church, Virginia, 20046. Telephone 703-532-3282.

tables. Nor can the intangible concerns of the undocumented worker, the illegal resident, the homeless, and those with "socially unacceptable" conditions, such as AIDS. Fear and mistrust must not be underrated. As states try and better understand the health care needs of their residents, they must first reach out to the communities in the states, as well as to federal agencies for guidance and support. Community health centers must convey the needs of their populations to state-level agencies. Federal agencies setting guidelines on race/ethnicity data should do so in partnership with state and local agencies, and recognize that SDOs are state-funded agencies with restricted resources and often limited by their mandates. Federal and state agencies must also consider whether race/ethnicity data with their inherent limitations are the best means by which to study the health care issues of minority and special populations.

Attachment A
States With Legislative Mandates To Gather Hospital-level Data

Arkansas
Douglas R. Murray
Director
Arkansas Center for Health Statistics
Group
4815 West Markham Street, Slot 19
Little Rock, AR 72205-3867
501-661-2633
FAX: 501-661-2464

Arizona
Joseph Brennan
Economist, Cost Reporting and Review
Offc. of Pub. Hlth., Eval. & Stats.
Arizona Department of Health Services
1651 East Morton, Suite 110
Phoenix, AZ 85020
602-255-1140
FAX: 602-255-1135FAX: 203-566-5663

California
Homero Lomas
Manager
Data Users Support Group
California Office of Statewide Health
Planning and Development
818 K Street, Room 500
Sacramento, CA 95814
916-322-2814

Connecticut
Michael Hofmann
Senior Research Analyst
Connecticut Office of Health Care Access
1049 Asylum Avenue
Hartford, CT 06105-2431
203-566-7793
FAX: 203-566-5663

Delaware
Donald Berry
Manager
Division of Management Services
Bureau of Health Planning
P.O. Box 637
Dover, DE 19903
302-739-4776
FAX: 302-739-3008
Internet: dberry@dhss.state.de.us

Florida
Debra Gressel
Administrator for Research and Analysis
Florida Agency for Health Care Administration
State Ctr. for Health Statistics
325 John Knox Road
Suite 301, The Atrium
Tallahasee, FL 32303
904-922-5572
FAX: 904-921-0973

Georgia
Hope Woodward
Research Unit Supervisor
Georgia Dept. of Human Resources
655 Willeo Rd.
Roswell, GA 30075
770-993-0345

Illinois
Joseph Bonefeste
Executive Director
Illinois Health Care Cost
Containment Council
4500 South Sixth Street Road
Suite 215
Springfield, IL 62703-5118
217-786-7001
FAX: 217-785-8461

Indiana
Tom Reed
Director, Health Planning Division
Indiana State Board of Health
1330 West Michigan St., P.O. Box 1964
Indianapolis, IN 46206-1964
317-633-8541
FAX: 317-633-0776

Iowa
Jeff Petrie
Vice President
Health Management Information Center
601 Locust, Suite 330
Des Moines, IA 50310
515-244-1211
FAX: 515-288-9143

Kansas
Elizabeth Saadi
Director
Office of Health Care Information
Kansas Department of Health and Envi-
ronment
109 SW 9th Street
Mills Building, Suite 400A
Topeka, KS 66612-2219
913-296-5639
FAX: 913-296-7025
Internet: USKANJDV@IBMMAIL.COM

Kentucky
Michael J. Hammons
Member
Kentucky Health Policy Board
909 Leawood Drive
Frankfort, KY 40601
502-564-4040
FAX: 502-564-5931

Bob Van Hook
Executive Director
Kentucky Health Policy Board
909 Leawood Drive
Frankfort, KY 40601
502-564-4040
FAX: 502-564-5922

Maine
Marianne Ringel
Director, Division of Research & Data
Management
Maine Health Care Finance Commission
State House Station #102
Augusta, ME 04333
207-287-3006

Maryland
Theressa Lee
Administrator
Maryland Health Services
Cost Review Council
4201 Patterson Avenue, 2nd Floor
Baltimore, MD 21215
410-764-2577
FAX: 410-764-5987

Massachusetts
Jean Delahanty
Data Analyst, Hospital Bureau
Massachusetts Rate Setting Commission
2 Boylston Street
Boston, MA 02116
617-451-5330
FAX: 617-451-1878

Minnesota
Jim Golden
Manager, Data Analysis Program
Health Care Delivery Policy Division
Minnesota Department of Health
121 East 7th Place, Suite 400
P.O. Box 64975
St. Paul, MN 55164-0975
612-282-5640
FAX: 612-282-5628
Internet: jim.golden@health.state.mn.us

Walter Suarez
Director of Operations
Minnesota Health Data Institute
910 Piper Jaffray Tower
444 Cedar Street
St. Paul, MN 55101
612-228-4372
FAX: 612-222-4209

Missouri
Barbara Hoskins
Chief
Bureau of Health Statistics
Missouri Department of Health
P.O. Box 570
Jefferson City, MO 65102
314-751-6279
FAX: 314-526-4102

Nevada
Chris Thompson
Chief
Health Care Financial Analysis Unit
Nevada Department of Human Re-
sources
505 East King Street, Room 604
Carson City, NV 89710
702-687-4176
FAX: 702-687-4733

New Hampshire
Kenneth Roos
Supervisor, Health Services Unit
New Hampshire Division of
Public Health Services
6 Hazen Drive
Concord, NH 03301
603-271-4617
FAX: 603-271-3745

New Jersey
Anne Davis
Policy Analyst
Office of Health Policy & Research
New Jersey State Department of Health
CN 360, John Fitch Plaza #800
Trenton, NJ 08625-0360
609-292-7837
FAX: 609-292-0085

New Mexico
Ron Dirks
Systems Analyst Manager
New Mexico Health Planning Commission
435 St. Michael's Drive, Suite A-202
Santa Fe, NM 87501
505-827-4488
FAX: 505-827-4481

New York
Gene Therriault
Director, Bureau of Biometrics
New York State Department of Health
Empire State Plaza, Concourse Room C-
144
Albany, NY 12237-0044
518-474-2377
FAX: 518-486-1630

Michael Zdeb
Research Scientist
New York State Department of Health
Empire State Tower, Room 890
Albany, NY 12237-0657
518-474-2079
FAX: 518-473-2015

North Carolina*
Jim Hazelrigs
Director
North Carolina Medical Database Commission
112 Cox Avenue, 2nd Floor
Suite 208
Raleigh, NC 27605
919-733-7141
FAX: 919-733-3682
Internet: MEDJAH@mail.doi.state.nc.us

North Dakota
Gary Garland
Health Planning Administrator
North Dakota State Health Department
State Capitol, Judicial Wing, 2nd Floor
Bismarck, ND 58505
701-328-2894
FAX: 701-328-4727

Ohio
Lorin Ranbom
Chief of Health Services Research
Bureau of Medicaid Policy
Ohio Department of Human Services
30 East Broad Street
Columbus, OH 43266-0423
614-466-6420
FAX: 614-266-2908
Internet: Lorin_Ranbom@health.ohio. gov

Oklahoma
Matthew K. Lucas
Director
Division of Health Care Information
Oklahoma Health Care Authority
4545 North Lincoln Boulevard,
Suite 124
Oklahoma City, OK 73105
405-530-3439
FAX: 405-528-2786

Oregon
Ala Mofidi
Oregon Health Plan Administrators
Office
255 Capitol St., NE
Salem, OR 97310
503-378-2422
503-378-5511

Pennsylvania
Ernie Sessa
Director
Pennsylvania Health Care Cost
Containment Council
225 Market Street, Suite 400
Harrisburg, PA 17101
717-232-6787
FAX: 717-232-3821

Rhode Island
Jay Buechner
Chief, Office of Health Statistics
Rhode Island Department of Health
3 Capitol Hill
Providence, RI 02908
401-277-2550
FAX: 401-277-6548

South Carolina
Walter P. Bailey
Chief, Health and Demographic
Statistics Sections
South Carolina Budget & Control Board
1000 Assembly Street
Suite 425, Rembert C. Dennis Building
Columbia, SC 29201-3117
803-734-4022
FAX: 803-734-3619

South Dakota
Sally Van Den Berg
Manager, Research & Statistics
South Dakota Department of Health
445 East Capitol Street
Pierre, SD 57501-3185
605-773-3361
FAX: 605-773-5683

Tennessee
George Wade
Health Statistics and Information
Section
Tennessee Dept. of Health
Cordell Hull Bldg.
426 Fifth Ave., N. 4th Fl.
Nashville, TN 37247-5261
615-741-1954
FAX: 615-532-7904

Texas
Ann Henry
Director, Data Management
Texas Department of Health
1100 West 49th Street, M660
Austin, TX 78756-7261
512-458-7261
FAX: 512-458-7344

Utah
Denise Love
Director
Office of Health Data Analysis
Utah Department of Health
288 North 1460 West
PO Box 16700
Salt Lake City, UT 84116-0700
801-538-6689
FAX: 801-538-7053
Internet: hlhsi.dlove@email.state.ut.us

Vermont
Michael Davis
Health Planner II
Vermont Health Care Authority
89 Main Street, Drawer 20
Montpelier, VT 05620
802-828-2900
FAX: 802-828-2949

Virginia
Michael Lundberg
Executive Director
Virginia Health Information
The Plantation House
1108 East Main Street, Suite 1201
Richmond, VA 23219
804-643-5573
FAX: 804-643-5375
Internet: vhi@freenet.vcu.edu

Ann McGee
Director
Virginia Health Services
Cost Review Council
805 East Broad Street, 6th Floor
Richmond, VA 23219
804-786-6371
FAX: 804-371-0284

Washington
Vicki Hohner
Data Products Manager
Washington Department of Health
P.O. Box 47811
Olympia, WA 98504-7811
360-705-6027
FAX: 360-705-6020
Internet:
VKH0303@HUB.DOH.WA.GOV

West Virginia
David Forinash
Executive Director
West Virginia Health Care
Cost Review Authority
100 Dee Drive, Suite 201
Charleston, WV 25311
304-558-7000
FAX: 304-558-7001

Wisconsin
Bernie Tennis
Research Analyst
Office of Health Care Information
Office of the Commissioner of
Insurance
121 East Wilson Street
P.O. Box 7984
Madison, WI 53707-7984
608-266-7568
FAX: 608-264-9881

*The North Carolina Medical Database
Commission is de-authorized as of
October 1, 1995.
For further information, contact:
National Association of Health Data
Organizations (NAHDO)
254-B North Washington Street
Falls Church, Virginia 22046-3593
703-532-3282
FAX: 703-532-3593

Attachment B
Compilation of Race Categories Used by States that Collect Race on Their Discharge Data Sets

White*
Black*
Native American, Alaskan Native*
Asian, Pacific Islander*
Chinese
Japanese
Hawaiian
Filipino
Other Asian, Pacific Islander
Hispanic
White Hispanic
Black Hispanic
Other/Unknown
Other
Unknown

* = These categories replicate the OMB Directive 15 categories.

CHAPTER SEVEN

Designing an Information System to Monitor Population Access to Care, Health and Health Care Use[1]

Noralou P. Roos, Charlyn Black*, Norm Frohlich**,
Carolyn DeCoster, Marsha Cohen***, Doug Tataryn*,
Cameron A. Mustard*, Leslie L. Roos*, Fred Toll, K.C.
Carriere*[†], Charles Burchill, Leonard MacWilliam,
Bogdan Bogdanovic, Kathleen Decker*

Introduction

The opening of new hospitals in Canada and elsewhere has historically been made in response to population growth, increases in volume of use, technological imperatives, and political pressure. The numbers and specialties of physicians and their practice locations have seldom been linked to health needs of populations.

Critical assessments of care typically focus on the clinical outcomes of individual treatments and quality of care delivered by institutions, not on the health of populations. In the United States (U.S.), despite some interesting applications by public health epidemiologists,[2] health services' re-

1.   This work was supported by the Health Services Development Fund, via a contract establishing the Manitoba Centre for Health Policy and Evaluation, and by a grant from the National Health Research and Development Program (6607-1579-57P). All authors are part of the Centre's Population Health Information Systems Group.
   *Members of the Department of Community Health Sciences, Faculty of Medicine, University of Manitoba.
   **Member of the Faculty of Management, University of Manitoba.
***Member of the Sunnybrook Health Science Centre.
   [†]Member of the Department of Mathematical Sciences, Faculty of Science, University of Alberta
The authors would like to thank Amy Zierler for her editorial help with this manuscript.

search funding has been heavily directed to micromanaging health care delivery.[3] Micromanaging may have a role in improving system efficiency, but this approach is unduly costly. For example, the Hartford Foundation is supporting a multimillion dollar effort across several states to develop a Community Health Management Information System (CHMIS). The primary focus of this effort is not on population use, risk characteristics, and health status, but on making claims processing more efficient.

Policy makers now, however, need tools to assess and communicate to the public answers to such questions as:

1. What are the levels of health in different regions?

2. What is the level of investment per capita in acute care for different areas?

3. Are high-risk populations poorly served or do they have poor health outcomes despite being well-served?

4. Does high utilization represent overuse or utilization related to high need?

5. Does high need respond positively to added health care resources?

6. Where might financial cuts be made without jeopardizing "at risk" populations?

7. What is the appropriate level of various kinds of health care resources in a given region?

We have developed a population health information system[4] to help the public understand that more health care is not necessarily better, and to help planners identify the levers for combining the concerns of population health with those of cost-containment. The Population Health Information System (POPULIS) facilitates comparing the health characteristics of defined populations with the use of the health care system. Researchers and

---

2. G. Dever, *Epidemiology in Health Services Management* (Rockville, Maryland: Royal Tunbridge Wells, 1984). R. Williams, G. Cunningham, F. Norris, and M. Tashiro, "Monitoring Perinatal Mortality Rates: California 1970-1978," *American Journal of Obstetrics and Gynecology* 136 (1980): 559-68.

3. D. M. Steinwachs, A. W. Wu, and E. A. Skinner, "How Will Outcomes Management Work?" *Health Affairs* 153 (1994): 153-62.

4. This paper represents further development of a paper originally prepared for the Honda Foundation, Discoveries Symposium, October 1993. An earlier version was published in the *Milbank Quarterly,* 74 (1996): 3-31.

policy-makers can simultaneously relate characteristics which affect a population's need for health care to that population's use of health care, to that area's supply of health care resources, and finally, to the health status of the population.

This information system builds on administrative data generated while paying hospitals, nursing homes, and physicians. Three types of information are essential to refocus policy on the determinants of health: health status, socioeconomic status, and health care use. These elements must be available and arranged to permit the integration and comparison of meaningful groups. We have used geographically defined groups, but this is not always necessary. The principles underlying the system are applicable to nongeographically defined populations such as Medicare, Medicaid, and health maintenance organization patients in the U.S. Indeed, the need for this type of information has become especially acute as the U.S. seeks to address its health care issues, particulary for underserved and disadvantaged populations.

This article describes our approach, its use in one health care jurisdiction – the province of Manitoba, Canada – and its application to other jurisdictions in the United States. The quality and the utility of the Manitoba data for addressing important questions in health services research have been discussed at length elsewhere.[5]

Key Concepts

Our conceptual model (Figure 1) represents an expansion of that proposed by Evans and Stoddart.[6] The model combines a range of background factors which, influenced by individual responses, leads to initial health status and well-being. Health status, again mediated by individual responses, affects demand for health care services, with utilization co-determined by supply and practice pattern factors. The individual response to care leads to a new outcome: a subsequent health status and level of well-being which feeds back into the model iteratively.

5. N. P. Roos, "Predicting Hospital Utilization by the Elderly: The Importance of Patient, Physician, and Hospital Characteristics," *Medical Care* 27 (1989): 905-919. L. L. Roos, N. P. Roos, S. M. Cageorge, and J. P. Nicol, "How Are the Data: Reliability of One Health Care Data Bank," *Medical Care* 20 (1982): 266-76.

6. R. G. Evans and G. L. Stoddart, "Producing Health, Consuming Health Care," *Social Science and Medicine* 31 (1990): 1347-63.

Figure 1
The Conceptual Model Underlying the Population Health Information System

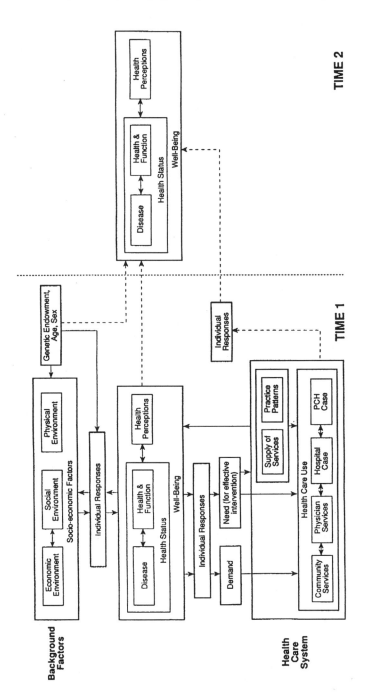

Not long ago we assumed that use of the health care system was almost completely determined by ill health, and that such utilization was effective in reducing ill health. The importance of the supply of physicians and hospital beds and of practice variations has since been recognized: physicians of the same specialty practice medicine in markedly different ways. The role of patient demand – independent of physician supply and practice style – is less well understood. Furthermore, ill health is not a random event. Biological factors (including genetic predispositions to develop specific diseases), environmental factors (such as pollution), and individual socioeconomic characteristics (poverty, lack of education, unemployment) have a strong negative impact on the health of the population. Our initial focus has been on the socioeconomic determinants of health and their relationship to utilization, supply, and health status indicators. Social determinants are thought to have substantially greater impact than do environmental pollutants;[7] the evidence for the role of social determinants is stronger than that for genetic impacts.[8] Baird has argued that the gene pool must be distributed similarly across social classes, but that individuals in the lower socioeconomic groups likely experience more stressors, such as poor diet or lack of self-esteem, which will in turn trigger more disease in these groups.[9]

The population-based POPULIS system is designed to track the health status and health care use of populations (regardless of where such usage takes place) (Figure 2). Standardizing the age and sex characteristics of a population across geographic areas adjusts for two of the important determinants of health and use of the health care system. Data on the usual supply parameters of health planning (hospital beds, nursing home beds, and physicians) are presented, but our system also directly measures access, or the proportion of individual residents in a given area who use a service (i.e., contact a physician), regardless of where the service is obtained.

The system is organized around issues relevant for policy-makers. For example, questions concerning intensity of use can easily be answered: How much do residents of regions vary in their use of high-tech teaching

---

7. G. Rose, *The Strategy of Preventive Medicine* (London: Oxford University Press, 1992).

8. J. Horgan, "Trends in Behavioral Genetics: Eugenics Revisited," *Scientific American* 268 (June 1993): 123-31.

9. P. Baird, "The Role of Genetics in Population Health," in *Why Are Some People Healthy and Others Are Not? The Determinants of Health of Populations*, eds. R. G. Evans, M. L. Barer, and T. R. Marmor (New York: Aldine de Gruyter Press, 1994).

Figure 2
The Manitoba Population Health Information System

Organizing Principles

- Population-based

- Describe:
  - supply
  - access to care
  - intensity of use
  - differential use across areas

- Juxtapose indicators of:
  - socioeconomic risk
  - use
  - health

- Assess contributions to costs per capita of:
  - differential access
  - $ per service (visit, day of care)
  - services per user

- Relevant to managers of system

- Sum use across sectors

- Create regional profiles

hospitals versus their use of small rural hospitals for their acute care? What is the relative use across regions of resource-intensive procedures (i.e., hysterectomy versus less intensive procedures, such as hysteroscopy)? We also compare usage patterns across regions whose residents have similar levels of good health, allowing policy-makers to approach the question of "which rate is right?" in terms of "what is the least costly rate associated with good health?"

This system also facilitates comparing discretionary use of services across geographic areas. We have calculated expected length of stay of nursing home patients based on the age, sex, and level of care at entry to a nursing home.[10] The degree to which one region admits younger, healthier individuals with a much longer expected length of stay to nursing homes suggests more discretionary use of resources, as does the extent to which hospitals admit patients for diagnoses whose admission patterns vary markedly across areas.[11] Similarly, physician visits can be separated into conditions classified as "posing a serious threat to health" versus those classified as "less serious."

Costs incurred by a region's residents will be affected by how often residents access a type of care (are admitted to hospital or contact a physician at least once during the year), the average cost of the service incurred (whether the physician was a specialist or whether the hospital day was spent in a teaching hospital or a small rural institution) and the number of services per user. How each of these factors interact in determining cost per resident is assessed.

Indicators have been selected because of their potential value for health care system management. The hospital indicators distinguish between medical, surgical, pediatric, psychiatric, and obstetrical admissions, while use which takes place in the region of residence can be compared with that occurring out-of-region. The physician supply indicators distinguish between the physicians available to area residents because they live in the area, and the physicians effectively available to area residents because patients travel (as do physicians sometimes).

This information system permits adding usage across sectors, using a dollar figure where possible and, in the case of nursing home and hospital use, summing total days of chronic institutional care. Finally, regional profiles showing how each region's health, socioeconomic risk, and use characteristics differ from the provincial norm can be readily created.

a. Developing the Population Health Information System

The steps for developing a population-based system to compare health status, various key risk indicators, and hospital use are straightforward:

1. Create meaningful geographic areas using postal code identifiers, which can be linked to public use census tapes. "Meaningful" will

---

10. E. Shapiro and R. Tate, "Survival Patterns of Nursing Home Admissions and Their Policy Implications," *Canadian Journal of Public Health* 79 (1988): 268-74.

11. J. E. Wennberg, K. McPherson, and P. Caper, "Will Payment Based on Diagnosis-Related Groups Control Hospital Costs?" *New England Journal of Medicine* 311 (1984): 295-300.

vary depending on the purpose for which the analyses will be made. To date we have developed areas based on regions (presented here), physician service areas, procedure-specific hospital service areas (tonsillectomy), and socioeconomic-based neighborhoods for the city of Winnipeg.

2. For each geographic area, obtain data for the denominator – the number of area residents, as well as their age and sex characteristics (from the most up-to-date census information or from provincial population registries, as available).

3. For each geographic area, obtain indicators of socioeconomic risk (as a first step, use census data to develop indicators such as household income, unemployment, education and cultural diversity).

4. For each geographic area, develop indicators of health status for area residents from various sources, including all cause, cause-specific and premature mortality rates from Vital Statistics files.

5. For each area, describe the utilization of health care by area residents, including hospital use, nursing home use, and use of physician services.

Health United States provides population-based data by state on health status measures, health care use, and socioeconomic status, but the data are presented independently, with no attempt to identify relationships across the elements.[12] However, many states have hospital, nursing home, and other discharge data-based programs which include the key variable, place of residence by zip code, making it possible to build a population-based system.[13] Population-based data bases can also build on information currently available to answer similar questions about specific populations within the U.S. Data routinely created as part of the government-funded Medicare and Medicaid programs and information from health maintenance organizations can be used. Siu et al. have advocated a population-based approach to comparing quality of care provided by health plans.[14] The

12. National Centre for Health Statistics, *Health United States 1992* and *Healthy People 2000 Review* (Hyattsville, Maryland: Public Health Service, 1993).

13. M. H. Epstein, "Guest Alliances: Uses of State-Level Hospital Discharge Databases," *Journal of AHIMA* 63 (1992): 32-35.

14. A. L. Siu, E. A. McGlynn, H. Morgenstern, and R. H. Brook, "A Fair Approach to Comparing Quality of Care," *Health Affairs* 10, no. 1 (spring 1991): 62-75.

challenge in the U.S. will be compiling information across health care sectors because of the fragmented health insurance system.

Putting the System Together

Figure 2 outlines the system. The major parts of the system are described, and results from the first set of annual reports on care across the regions of Manitoba (Figure 3) are presented.[15] It is important to remember that these concepts and analyses can be applied to examine health care use and health status in other populations. We then illustrate how the population-based approach has been used for needs-based planning for physicians in the province.

a. Socioeconomic Risk

Systematic relationships between socioeconomic characteristics and health status have been observed for roughly 100 years in England and France;[16] they are currently being rediscovered in North America.[17] Figure 4 shows Thompson residents to be at highest risk for poor socioeconomic status, followed by Norman and Parklands residents (the socioeconomic risk index is described in an attachment following this chapter). It was created from several indicators describing characteristics of neighborhood residents, such as unemployment, educational level, dwelling values, etc. Residents of the five remaining regions score similarly and are at low risk for poor socioeconomic status. If a region has a more vulnerable population, we expect health to be poorer and the need for health care use rates to be higher (just as if one region had more elderly residents).

b. Indicators of Health Status

Available instruments to measure health status can be classified into those focusing on individual health and those emphasizing the health of popula-

---

15. The original reports can be obtained by contacting the MCHPE. An abridged version of the reports with editorial comments about what we learned has been published *Medical Care* 33 (1995).

16. P. Liberatos, B. G. Link, and J. L. Kelsey, "The Measurement of Social Class in Epidemiology," *Epidemiology Review* 10 (1988): 87-121.

17. G. Pappas, S. Queen, W. Hadden, and G. Fisher, "The Increasing Disparity in Mortality Between Socioeconomic Groups in the United States, 1960 and 1986," *New England Journal of Medicine* 329 (1993): 103-109.

Figure 3
Regions of Manitoba

tions or communities. The Population Health Information System draws heavily on indicators developed to measure the health of populations (U.S. Health 2000, Statistics Canada Health Indicators Working Group and so forth). Using administrative data to assess health status has the major advantage over surveys in that the entire population's health status can be

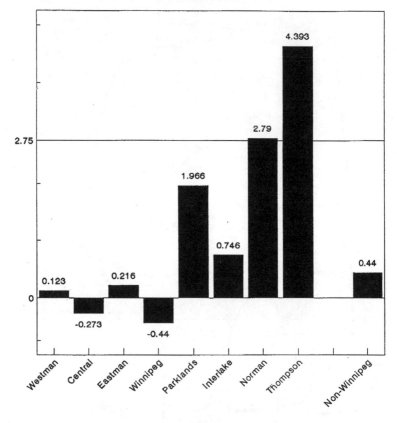

Figure 4
Regional Scores on the Socio-Economic Index*

Standard Deviations from Provincial Mean

*A high score on the index means poor socio-economic status (SES) relative to the province. Regions with scores of 2.75 or greater have significantly poorer SES than that of Province alpha = .05

assessed repeatedly over time. This proved critical for the physician re-source project described below, since some of the areas in northern Mani-toba consist of widely dispersed communities of 1000-2500 individuals. Collecting interview-based health status data across the 54 physician serv-ice areas would have required a large investment of time and money; the committee responsible for identifying areas of physician undersupply and oversupply required a plan to be in place within a six-month time frame.

We have developed multiple indicators of health status from adminis-trative data, using vital statistics mortality data, hospital discharge diagnoses, and the single diagnosis submitted on claims for physician visits.[18] These indicators include various aspects of community health, such as mortality from cancer, injuries, and chronic diseases. The incidence of births under 2500 grams was also available from administrative data sources. In addition, we focus on the prevalence of medical conditions (such as hypertension) and musculoskeletal conditions (such as rheumatoid arthritis) associated with poor functional status and poor self-perceived health.[19] Another set of indicators relates to treatments, hospitalizations, and deaths which should be avoidable, given timely and appropriate medical intervention or public health action.[20]

The standardized mortality ratio (SMR) based on deaths occurring among individuals aged 0-64 has been suggested as the best single indicator of health status capturing the need for health care (Figure 5).[21] The SMR for those 0-64 has been used for allocating health care funds across different parts of Scotland. Norman and Thompson regions show SMRs which are both above the provincial average and much higher than for the rest of Manitoba (Figure 5). Across the various indicators, the two northern regions (Norman and Thompson) generally show very poor health status, while residents of five of the southern regions enjoy quite good health status. Comparing regional scores on health status with regional scores on the Socio-Economic Risk Index (SERI, Figure 4) results in identical rankings. In fact, 87% of the variation in health status (measured by the standardized mortality rate for those aged 0-64) is explained by differences in the socioeconomic risk index. This relationship was observed both at the

---

18. For a complete listing, see M. M. Cohen and L. MacWilliam, *Population Health: Health Status Indicators,* vol. 1, *Key Findings,* (Winnipeg: Manitoba Centre for Health Policy and Evaluation, 1994).

19. G. C. Pope, "Medical Conditions, Health Status, and Health Services Utilization," *Health Services Research* 22 (1988): 857-77.

20. J. R. H. Charlton, R. M. Hartley, R. Silver, and W. W. Holland, "Geographical Variation in Mortality from Conditions Amenable to Medical Intervention in England and Wales," *Lancet* 26 (March 1983): 691-96. J. S. Weissman, C. Gatsonis, and A. M. Epstein, "Rates of Avoidable Hospitalization by Insurance Status in Massachusetts and Maryland," *Journal of the American Medical Association* 268 (1992): 2388-94.

21. V. Carstairs and R. Morris, *Deprivation and Health in Scotland,* (Aberdeen, Scotland: Aberdeen University Press, 1991). J. Eyles, S. Birch, J. Chambers, J. Hurley, and B. Hutchinson, "A Needs-Based Methodology for Allocating Health Care Resources in Ontario, Canada: Development and an Application," *Social Science and Medicine* 33 (1993): 489-500.

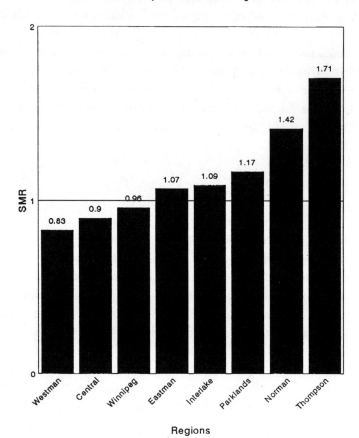

Figure 5
Standardized Mortality Ratio for Reasons Aged 0-64 Years

regional level and across the 54 smaller physician service areas, (although less variation is explained for the latter area).

Survey data from the Manitoba Heart Health Survey (1992) have provided general confirmation of the conclusions on health status drawn from mortality data. The two northern regions are characterized by relatively high proportions of smokers, diabetics, and people who are obese.[22]

---

22. D. E. Gelsky, T. K. Young, and S. M. MacDonald, "Screening with Total Cholesterol: Determining Sensitivity and Specificity of the National Cholesterol Education Program's Guidelines from a Population's Survey," *Journal of Clinical* Epidemiology 47 (1994): 547-53.

c. Use of Hospitals

Using the POPULIS system, the rate of hospitalization for individuals during a given year can be distinguished from the number of hospital separations per 1000 residents, the latter being approximately 44% higher (Table I). Because patients are sometimes transferred from small rural hospitals to larger centres, episodes of hospital care (hospital-to-hospital transfers being counted as one episode) are also calculated. In rural Manitoba (the non-Winnipeg regions), patients are admitted to hospital at much higher rates, and rural residents spend more days in hospital per year than do Winnipeg residents (743 days per 1000 Winnipeg residents to 1532 days per 1000 Thompson residents). Although residents of the two Northern regions had the highest level of socioeconomic risk and the poorest health status, they are clearly not without access to medical care, spending more days in hospital than residents of any other region. Hospital use across the Southern regions of the province also deserves comment; although residents of the five Southern regions of the province demonstrated similar health and socioeconomic status, Winnipeg residents spend substantially fewer days in hospital per capita than do residents of the rural regions.

The hospital use module permits replicating Table I for the following subanalyses:

- where individual was hospitalized (in-region/out-of-region, Winnipeg/out-of-region, other);
- type of hospital to which admitted (teaching, community, etc.);
- service to which admitted (surgical, obstetrical, etc.);
- resource intensity of care received (using DRG weights);
- complexity of case (whether individual had major comorbidities or not);[23]
- discretionary nature of admission (high variation conditions).[24]

---

23. M. E. Charlson, P. Pompei, K. L. Ales, and C. R. McKenzie, "A New Method of Classifying Prognostic Comorbidity in Longitudinal Studies: Development and Validation," *Journal of Chronic Diseases* 40 (1987): 373-83. P. S. Romano, L. L. Roos, and J. G. Jollis, "Adapting a Clinical Comorbidity Index for Use with ICD-9-CM Administrative Data: Differing Perspectives," *Journal of Clinical Epidemiology* 46 (1993): 1075-79.

24. J.E. Wennberg, K. McPherson and P. Caper, "Will Payment Based on Diagnosis-related Groups Control Hospital Costs?," *New England Journal of Medicine* 311 (1984): 295-300.

Table 1 – Regional Use of Hospital Resources[1]:
Use of Short Stay[2] Inpatient Care 1991/92

	Central	Eastman	Interlake	Norman	Parkland	Thompson	Westman	Winnipeg	Non-Winnipeg Comparison	Manitoba
Number of residents	94,484	85,180	71,939	24,952	46,056	45,019	117,724	655,055	485,351	1,140,406
Active treatment beds per 1000 population located in region.	4.3	2.4	2.8	7.7	6.8	4.8	6.4	4.9	4.7	4.8
Number of persons hospitalized per 1000 population.	101	98	99	142	123	159	106	75	110	90
Number of episodes of hospital care per 1000 population.[3]	140	139	139	210	184	231	149	99	157	124
Number of hospital separations per 1000 population.	149	148	148	224	195	263	160	101	168	130
Average length of stay per hospital separation.	6.3	6.1	6.4	5.4	6.3	4.4	6.6	7.3	6.1	6.6
Number of days of hospital care per 1000 population.	920	946	938	1351	1108	1532	985	743	1018	861

[1] All rates (except for average length of stay per hospital separation and bed ratios) are age- and sex-adjusted to the Manitoba population using an indirect method of standardization.
[2] Stays of 1-59 days are defined as short stays.
[3] An episode of hospital care is defined as a continuous period of hospital care which may involve one or more transfers between facilities.

d. Nursing Home Care

Table II presents an overview of Manitoba nursing home use, concentrating on the 85% of nursing home admittees who are 75 years of age and older. Since new nursing home beds are opened according to a planning ratio based on 90 beds per 1000 population, aged 70 years or more, existing inequities are historical. Norman has a high per capita rate of nursing home use. Thompson's apparently low per capita rate is misleading since the availability of a federally funded home (outside the provincial data system) brings the area rate up to the provincial average. These two "outlier" regions with very small elderly populations aside, the availability of nursing home beds per 1000 population varies only moderately across regions. These supply differences lead to Westman's elderly residents spending approximately 27% more days in nursing homes than Parklands' residents; statistical tests confirm much greater variation in hospital use across regions than in use of nursing homes.

Manitoba's centralized assessment procedures to control nursing home placement also minimize the amount of discretionary use; regions vary relatively little in expected length of stay (as defined above), regardless of the type of home examined (secular/non, proprietary/non). The estimated cost per day of nursing home care differs only slightly (Table II), from $75.06 in Westman to $79.01 for Winnipeg. Variation in costs per day of nursing home care is largely influenced by the proportion of residents at each care level. The information system permits replicating Table II for all ages and age-specific groups, level of care to which patient is admitted, and type of home.

e. Use of Physician Services

Figure 6 illustrates supply of, access to, and use of physician services across the province. We have included all physician visits except those to hospitalized patients: physician office visits, ambulatory clinic care occurring in hospitals, emergency room visits, physician visits to a patient's home or to nursing home residents, and all consultations which occur in any of these settings. Although physician availability ranges from 14.6 physicians per 10,000 population in Winnipeg to 5 physicians in Eastman, access to physicians is remarkably uniform across regions; almost 80% of the residents in every region contact a physician at least once over the course of the year. Thompson, the region with the lowest proportion of the population in contact with a physician (77.7%) receives 50% of its primary care from nurses at nursing stations in remote areas. These contacts (and costs) are not reflected in our data. The physician contact rate ranged from a low of

Table 2 – Utilization of Personal Care Home Resources, 1991/92: Age 75+

	Central	Eastman	Interlake	Norman	Parkland	Thompson	Westman	Winnipeg	Non-Winnipeg Comparison	Manitoba
Population (Age 75+)	6,223	3,826	4,038	811	4,108	497	9,761	36,488	29,264	65,752
PCH beds per 1000 population	121	118	125	160	122	52	144	128	130	128
Residents of PCH per 1000 population (number)	130.6 (834)	136.2 (489)	137.3 (526)	161.3 (115)	120.0 (496)	87.2 (38)	142.0 (1,471)	130.8 (4,747)	134.8 (3,969)	132.6 (8,716)
Admissions to PCH per 1000 population (number)	28.8 (183)	24.4 (90)	31.8 (123)	26.6 (20)	32.2 (134)	19.3 (9)	27.1 (277)	27.1 (277)	28.3 (836)	27.7 (1,819)
Days of PCH care per resident of region	37.9	39.6	39.0	48.8	33.0	23.3	41.9	41.9	39.0	38.6
Estimated costs of PCH care per resident of region ($).	2,903	3,081	3,060	3,762	2,495	1,766	3,144	3,144	2,977	3,000
Estimated costs per PCH day ($)	77	78	78	77	76	76	75	75	76	78

[1] Rates are age- and sex-adjusted to the Manitoba population using an indirect method of standardization. All are based solely on the population aged 75 years and older.
[2] Excludes one federally funded nursing home.

4.1 visits per Central region resident to a high of 5.3 per Winnipeg resident (data not presented). This was a relatively small (30%) difference given the large (290%) variation in physician supply. However, 41% more per capita was spent on physician contacts for Winnipeggers in 1991/92 than for Central residents ($123 per resident vs. $87 per resident); both visits per user and cost per visit (more Winnipeg care is delivered by specialists) are higher in Winnipeg. The three biggest contributors to Winnipeg's high expenditure patterns were visits to psychiatrists, pediatricians, and internists; over a third of the additional expenditures related to psychiatric contact alone.[25]

Types of Analysis

a. Demographic Patterns

The population registry permits tracking movement to and from regions of the province by such key characteristics as age and socio-economic risk status. Although population growth, particularly increases in the numbers of the very young or very old, might be used for planning health services, Carstairs has argued that change in the number of individuals in a population at high socio-economic risk is at least as important in estimating health care needs.[26] Well-off elderly will have fewer health care needs than those who are at risk. The system describes demographic changes across geographic areas (migration, births and deaths) according to the age of individuals and the socioeconomic characteristics of the neighbourhood from which residents leave/arrive.

b. Use Across Sectors

Focusing on the number of days which the elderly population of a region spends in a nursing home or in a nonacute hospitals permits examining the degree to which the two services substitute for one another across regions. Unexpectedly, areas (Westman and Norman) whose residents are among the highest users of hospital beds for nonacute stays (stays of 60 days or longer) also tend to be high users of nursing home resources (Figure 7).

---

25. These figures are based on those practitioners receiving payments of $40,000 per year or more and exclude radiologists, pathologists and anesthesiologists, most of whom practice in Winnipeg but do not deliver ambulatory care.

26. V. Carstairs and R. Morris, *Deprivation and Health in Scotland*, (Aberdeen, Scotland: Aberdeen University Press, 1991):691-96.

Figure 6
Physician Use Across Regions
Physician Supply
(Physicians/10,000 Population)

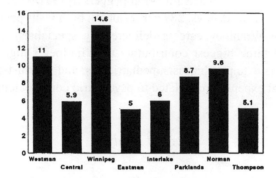

Access to Physicians
(% with Visit)

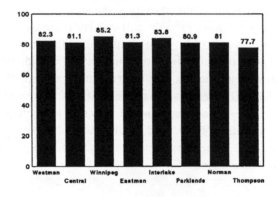

Expenditures on Physicians
($ per capita)

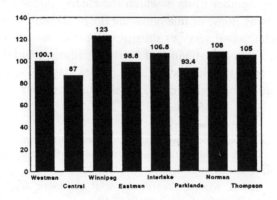

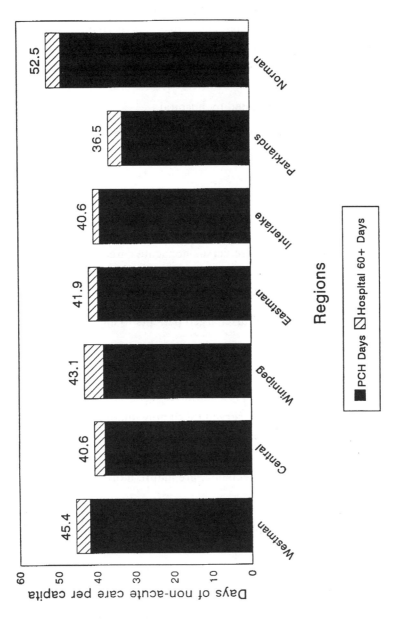

Figure 7
Use of Nursing Homes and Hospitals
(60 + Day Stays*) (Age 75+)

*Excluding Day 1 to Day 59, Due to the small number of elderly (497) and missing data, Thompson is excluded from analyses.

c. Using Existing Indicators to Assess Hospital Performance

Ministries of Health have a special interest in assessing hospital performance. Rural hospitals are a good place to start, since indicators for such
hospitals are not generally contaminated by the referral of patients from
outside their catchment areas. Thus, two sets of indicators of hospital
performance have been or are being developed.

The first set, based on cases treated by a given hospital, includes such
measures of hospital function as:

- number of people treated by hospital,

- neediness of population treated (based on percent age of cases from
  high socioeconomic risk postal codes),

- case intensity,

- cost efficiency for average case treated,

- discharge efficiency (length of stay),

- proportion of acute care versus nonacute care (many acute hospitals
  have long-stay wards),

- outpatient/inpatient surgery ratios,

- readmission rates (of discharged patients to any other hospital), and

- occupancy rates.

A second set of measures facilitates assessing hospital performance in
relation to the population served and includes:

- size of the population served (assigning small geographic units to a
  hospital service area based on a plurality rule of which hospital is
  used most frequently by area residents),

- health status (life expectancy, premature mortality),

- socioeconomic risk characteristics of the population,

- the percentage of physician visits which result in hospitalization
  (adjusted in various ways), and

- the percentage of low-severity patients who are hospitalized (adjusted in various ways)

Rural hospitals can be expected to differ on these dimensions. Two
hospitals might appear to operate equally efficiently but serve populations

of very different health status. Hospitals serving populations with the same needs might operate at quite different levels of efficiency. At a time when major changes are occurring across Canada, the Ministry of Health has recognized the utility of such descriptive data on hospitals.

d. *Longitudinal Research*

Tracking indicators over time permits monitoring the direction in which the health care system is moving, changes in the intensity with which care is delivered, and changes in health status over time. We recently analyzed four years of data on acute hospital use to assess whether the closure of 16% of the beds at the Winnipeg teaching hospitals adversely affected access to hospital services, the quality of care delivered, or the health of the population. We reported that the system adapted very well; we found no decrease in patients treated (due largely to an expansion of outpatient surgical facilities), no increase in adverse events due to too-early discharge or system cutbacks (as judged by mortality rates, readmission rates, emergency room contacts, and physician office visits within 30 days of discharge). Finally, we observed no adverse impact on the health of the population, even after separate analyses focusing on high-risk groups, including the poor and the very elderly.[27]

e. *Vulnerable Populations*

The Manitoba data base will also be used to monitor the health care use and health status of specific disadvantaged populations, such as natives. This is possible because treaty status aboriginals have a special status and a federal entitlement permitting identification by code on the population registry. For this group, analyses can proceed at the individual level. Other at-risk groups (for example, areas with a high proportion of recent immigrants from countries where there is a high prevalence of tuberculosis) can be identified using census data, or by using income quintiles for neighbourhoods in urban areas.

With population-based data, individuals who are not using the system can also be identified. By examining the rate of individuals not contacting a physician according to the risk characteristics of the community, esti-

---

27. N. P. Roos and E. Shapiro, "Using the Information System to Assess Change: The Impact of Downsizing the Acute Sector," in "Assessing the Relationship Between Health Care and Health: Experience with a Population Based Health Information System," *Medical Care,* 33 (12; suppl.) DS109-DS126 (1995).

mates can be made as to whether low contact rates represent good health or poor access. We have already used the information system to assess the adequacy of prenatal care across groups of differing socio-economic status[28] and for assessing immunization rates.

The system is also useful for assessing who delivers care to the high-risk populations. While general practitioners at walk-in clinics are thought to be symptomatic of the oversupply of physicians in Winnipeg, our analyses suggest that high-risk populations are much more likely to receive care from general practitioners than from specialists (as are the elderly). Such data have led to a rethinking of which physician groups should be targeted as contributing to the Winnipeg physician surplus: pediatricians, general internists and psychiatrists, those specialties who underdeliver care to the most vulnerable groups and overdeliver to the more affluent groups have become the focus of the physician-surplus discussion.

f. Using Population-Based Data for Policy Development

The insights from these analyses should be useful not only to administrators in other single-payer systems but also to managers of health maintenance organizations responsible for the delivery of care to "populations" and to those concerned about access to health care and the health status of excluded and vulnerable populations. Our most recent use of the POPULIS system has been for physician resource planning.

In January 1994, the Manitoba government and the Manitoba Medical Association (the group which bargains on behalf of physicians with the province over the setting of fee-for-service payment schedules) agreed on capping the total amount of money to be paid to fee-for-service physicians and restricting the number of billing numbers to be made available to physicians wanting to practice in the province. Without a billing number a physician has no access to the fee-for-service payment pool, and effectively cannot practice. A Physician Resource Committee was established to develop a comprehensive plan for how many physicians, of what type, are needed where in Manitoba. For the first year, until this plan was in place, new physicians, primarily new medical school graduates, were issued provisional billing numbers with no guarantee of conversion to regular billing numbers.

---

28. C. A. Mustard and N. P. Roos, "The Utilization of Prenatal Care and Relationship to Birthweight Outcome," *American Journal of Public Health* 84 (1994): 1450-57.

The Manitoba Centre was asked to be a member organization on the Resource Committee (along with representatives from the medical association, Manitoba Health, the College of Physicians and Surgeons, the Faculty of Medicine, medical student and intern and resident associations, and several public representatives). The Centre was also asked to provide analytic support to the Committee.

Using the POPULIS system, we proceeded to divide the province into 54 physician service delivery areas. We identified which area's residents were in the poorest health and best health, using the premature mortality and low birthweight indicators, and noting those areas in the highest and lowest quintiles on the measures. The Committee viewed socioeconomic risk scores as particularly important, not only in identifying communities at high-risk of poor health, but in specifying communities likely to have problems attracting and keeping physicians because of a lack of amenities.

Using the POPULIS, we noted areas well-supplied and poorly-supplied with physicians. We worked with three measures of physician supply:

1) the relative supply of physicians (full-time equivalent per 1000 residents) in the area;

2) the relative supply effectively available to area residents (since patients travel, if area A residents used 20% of Area B physicians, area A was attributed .2 of a FTE physician and area B .8); and

3) area residents' contact rate with physicians (visits per resident), regardless of where the contact took place.

A series of map transparencies highlighted the high-need areas (i.e., those in poor health and at high socioeconomic risk) and low-need areas, and the high-supply/low-supply areas. These analyses enabled the Committee to identify what they began to refer to as "hot spots," those few areas of the province with low supply and high needs.

They also confirmed the high physician supply in Winnipeg. Our earlier analyses (such as those in Figure 4 and 5) had been criticised for treating Winnipeg as one region, masking the relatively large and very poor core area of the city. We divided Winnipeg into 9 areas for physician resource planning, designed around the differing socieconomic neighborhoods. This approach identified Winnipeg's inner core as not only the poorest health area of the province, but also as an area whose residents had the highest rate of physician contact, averaging over 6 visits per resident per year. This provided further confirmation of Winnipeg's ample supply, if not oversupply of physicians.

These analyses helped the Deputy Minister deal with negative publicity surrounding a supposed exodus of physicians from some rural communities. The population-based data showed that one of the communities from which loud complaints were coming was both one of the healthiest communities in the province and well-served by physicians.

Because the Committee had not finalized its plan by the end of the year, there was strong pressure to grandfather in all physicians given provisional billing numbers. Instead, the Committee used the population-based data to argue that only if physicians practised for at least a four-month period in the north or for a somewhat longer period in the south outside Winnipeg would they receive a regular billing number. Physicians remaining in Winnipeg would remain on provisional numbers until the final plan was formulated. Despite frequent press stories about the exodus of physicians from the north and rural areas caused by the new process' uncertainty, comparing six-month periods before and after the plan showed a desirable increase in physicians in the north and rural south and a decrease in the Winnipeg physician supply.

Discussion

This information system has evolved through close interaction of Centre staff with government managers and policy-makers. Developing data for use by policy-makers requires great attention to detail: stakeholders will challenge aspects which do not support preconceptions. The tendency to produce volumes of indicators and cross tabulations must be balanced by the commitment to produce timely information. More detailed analyses do have a clientele. Manitoba Health's Capital Planning group and Centre investigators have conducted population-based analyses for 10 rural hospital service areas interested in "repatriating" care currently delivered in urban centres to rural hospitals. Manitoba Health can request these analyses on a one-off basis or develop their own internal capabilities for implementing the analytic programs after design of the basic system. Over time, analyses are being used to assess the impact of major health reform initiatives; a separate module focusing on use of mental health services across the province has been developed.

What conclusions can be drawn to date? First of all, the Canadian system, which provides first-dollar coverage of health use for hospitals, nursing homes, home care and physician services, appears to be partially need-driven and to work reasonably equitably in Manitoba. The two regions whose residents have the highest levels of hospital use (the northern, geographically isolated Thompson and Norman regions) are also those whose residents have the poorest health and the highest scores on the socio-economic risk index.

Thompson residents are hospitalized frequently, despite having only an average availability of hospital beds in the region and the most limited supply of physicians. However, fully 30% of Thompson residents' hospitalizations occur in other regions; such hospitalizations would not seem to be supply-driven. On the other hand, while much of the high use may be related to need, Norman has both more hospital beds per capita than any other region and a rich supply of physicians (9.6 physicians per 10,000 population versus 6.9 in rural Manitoba more generally). Future analyses will try to separate the proportion of use which appears need-driven from that associated with supply and/or practice patterns.

The health of the population should be the cornerstone for challenging and improving health care. While measuring health status may be imperfect, the indicators we used clearly picked up marked health differences across Manitoba's regions. Large, consistent differences across a wide variety of measures document the poor health status among Thompson and Norman residents. The strong, statistically significant differences in mortality rates across Manitoba regions can be compared with the failure of many popular and expensive medical therapies to show a positive impact on reducing all-cause mortality. Cholesterol lowering, screening for prostate cancer, and breast screening mammography have not been shown to reduce overall mortality in a population.[29] (There appear to be no data to

29. J. E. Russouw, B. Lewis, and B.M. Rifkind, "The Value of Lowering Cholesterol after Myocardial Infarction," *New England Journal of Medicine* 323 (1990): 1112-19. I. Holme, "An Analysis of Randomized Trials Evaluating the Effect of Cholesterol Reduction on Total Mortality and Coronary Heart Disease Incidence," *Circulation* 82 (1990): 1916-24.

M.D. Krahn, J.E. Maloney, M.H. Eckman, J. Trachtenberg, S.G. Pauker, and A.S. Detsky, "Screening for Prostate Cancer: A Decision Analytic View," *Journal of the American Medical Association* 272 (1994): 773-80.

J. G. Schmidt, "The Epidemiology of Mass Breast Cancer Screening – A Plea for a Valid Measure of Benefit," *Journal of Clinical Epidemiology* 323 (1990): 215-25.

date demonstrating an impact of breast screening mammography on overall mortality. Thus screened women "saved" from dying of breast cancer seem to die just as early as unscreened women – but of another cause.) Future analyses will systematically attempt to estimate the strength of the relationships among risk factors, health status, supply and practice patterns outlined in Figure 1.

Clearly the health care system is supposed to care for those who are ill, and Manitoba provides a remarkably high level of care for residents of disadvantaged regions. However, given the strong relationship between socioeconomic risk factors and health status and usage, what is the most effective way to ensure access to health? High use of the health care system does not guarantee health. Ongoing longitudinal analyses will help sort out the extent to which high health care expenditures over time are associated with improving population health. However, current expenditure patterns both pose the danger of driving out the ability to fund other programs and appear unlikely to resolve the underlying problems creating poor health. While the health problems of Norman and Thompson residents should not be ignored, our analyses raise fundamental questions about the role of the health care system in improving the health of the population.

In both the United States and Canada, much effort has been expended on fine-tuning the existing system by developing practice guidelines to help physicians use more effective treatments and by focusing enormous attention on hospital-based quality of care. Arguably there is a need for monitoring quality of care in the United States. Grisso et al. found that elderly inner city blacks receive little if any rehabilitative and follow-up care for hip fractures, resulting in poor recovery, continued pain, and disability 5-10 months after their fall.[30] Nevertheless, focusing so much attention on quality of care diverts us from asking the more important question: How much contribution does this very expensive care make to the health of the population?

The Physician Payment Review Commission articulated a national data strategy which is not population-based and which ignores the key data elements necessary to refocus health policy on the determinants of health: health status, socioeconomic status and health care use.[31] Instead, the

---

30. J. A. Grisso et al., "The Impact of Falls in an Inner City Elderly African American Population," *Journal of American Geriatric Society* 40 (1992): 673-78.

31. Physician Payment Review Commission, *Annual Report to Congress* (1994).

Commission details the principal requirements for a national data strategy for health system reform as:

1) monitoring utilization and costs,

2) monitoring quality of care,

3) establishing accountability for quality and access,

4) supporting outcomes research, and

5) profiling and measuring risk.

Such a national data strategy neither leads towards a focus on the health of populations nor facilitates considering the link between use, expenditures and health. The flagship publication of the National Center for Health Statistics, *Health United States in 1993,* provided population-based data by state on health status measures, health care use, and socioeconomic status (at least to the extent that race serves as a proxy), but the data were presented independently, with no attempt to identify relationships across these elements.

Population-based analyses are not new to the United States; Wennberg's small area analysis, demonstrating marked differences in treatment patterns across neighbouring communities, led directly to the focus on outcomes assessment and the Patient Outcomes Research Teams (PORTs).[32] While the original design of this effort included a strong population focus, administrative data effective at the population level have been found wanting for capturing subtle clinical differences. Research capable of addressing population health issues appears to have been de-emphasized.

The strengths of population-based information become much more obvious in a single-payer system. To the extent that health maintenance organizations and the Veterans Administration serve populations and act as single payers, they should also benefit from this approach. In targeting and monitoring expenditure/use patterns, health status and socioeconomic risk are key.

---

32. J. E. Wennberg, "Outcomes Research, Cost Containment, and the Fear of Health Rationing," *New England Journal of Medicine* 323 (1990): 1202-04. J. E. Wennberg and A. Gittelsohn, "Small Area Variations in Health Care Delivery," *Science* 182 (1973): 1102-09. J. E. Wennberg and A. Gittelsohn, "Variations in Medical Care among Small Areas," *Scientific American* 246 (1982): 120-34.

The role of the health care system as a determinant of health seems overemphasized. To improve the health of the population, resources must be reallocated from health care to activities which more directly prevent illness. But where to direct these funds? Into social policy to improve standards of living (sewage treatment and better housing on native reserves is a long-unanswered call)? Into education – particularly early childhood education – in an attempt to raise more effective adults? Into private sector efforts to create meaningful jobs so that families can become more functionally viable? Now is clearly time for more fundamental and applied research on the determinants of health from a broad social policy perspective. Needed funds can come at least partially from basic biomedical research, historically much better-funded than work directed towards the social determinants of health.

The type of analyses presented here can be of considerable use to policy-makers. Our research, and work on population health generally, seems to have encouraged some new thinking in Manitoba. Funds from the Manitoba Health budget have been used to support interdepartmental planning among the Ministries of Health, Education, Justice, and Family Services (which provides welfare) for an initiative on single mothers. This followed a Centre study suggesting that socioeconomic differences in birth weight are primarily attributable to factors other than use of early prenatal medical care.[33] A broadened information system will permit monitoring the health outcomes of this initiative.

Finally, this approach offers policy-makers and the public the ability to separate issues of health from other factors. By directly measuring socioeconomic risk status and demonstrating its strong link to population health, an independent set of social levers outside the health care system is identified. Unfortunately, the growing literature suggestive of what these policy initiatives might be is not mainstream to health services research. Grantham-McGregor et al. compare nutritional supplementation, psychosocial stimulation and mental development of stunted children.[34] The World Bank suggests investing in maternal education as a means of improving children's health.[35] The Perry Preschool Study demonstrated that inner-city

---

33. Mustard and Roos, "The Utilization of Prenatal Care and Relationship to Birthweight Outcome," *American Journal of Public Health* 84 (1994):1450-57.

34. S. M. Grantham-McGregor, C. A. Powell, and S. P. Walker, "Nutritional Supplementation, Psychosocial Stimulation, and Mental Development of Stunted Children: The Jamaican Study," *Lancet* 338 (1991): 1-5.

children, randomly assigned to a "preschool" group, received major long-term benefits relative to their contemporaries not receiving the "treatment."[36] Nineteen years later, group had higher rates of school graduation, higher rates of college attendance, fewer arrests, fewer teenage pregnancies, higher rates of employment and a lower reliance on welfare. While health measures per se were unavailable for the two groups, the strong association between socioeconomic status and health strongly suggests the health benefits of such a program.

Such initiatives and an appropriate information base are important for breaking the cycle of the "medicalization of social ills."[37] Deteriorating social conditions in both the United States and Canada call for systems which highlight the health impacts and health care costs of an increasingly two-tiered society. Whole cohorts of clinicians and health services researchers have come to believe that outcomes research, guidelines, and quality of care are what really matters. A change of paradigm threatens many entrenched interests but suggests a path towards both improved health and a better society. Look at the data!

Attachment

Using census data gathered and published by Statistics Canada, we obtained a variety of measures of socioeconomic status for residents in each of the eight regions. A set of five poor health and usage indicators deemed to be particularly sensitive to differences in socioeconomic status were used to construct a test index against which to measure the explanatory power of candidate socioeconomic indicators. The socioeconomic measures most highly associated with our poor health status index were: the percentage of the population between the ages of 25 and 34 having graduated high school, the percentage of the labour force between the ages of 15 and 24 unemployed, as well as the percentage between ages 45 and 54 who were unemployed, the percentage of single-parent, female-headed households, the percentage of females participating in the labour force, and the average

35. World Bank, *World Development Report: Investing in Health* (New York: Oxford University Press, 1993).

36. D. P. Weikart, "Early Childhood Education and Primary Prevention," *Prevention in Human Services* 6 (1989): 285-94.

37. J. C. Hurowitz, "Toward a Social Policy for Health," *New England Journal of Medicine* 329 (1993): 130-33.

dwelling value. The indicators used in the test health status index included admission rate to hospitals of females for injuries, admission to hospitals of males for injuries, admission to hospitals of children age 0-4 for respiratory infections, admission to hospitals of persons greater than age 65 years for respiratory infection, and fertility rates. Removing fertility from the test index, in response to observations that it was not a measure of "poor health," led to similar results. The indicators were weighted on the basis of the strength of their association with the health status index.

CHAPTER EIGHT

Supporting the Delivery of Preventive Services Through Information Systems: A Manitoba Example[1]

Leslie L. Roos, David S. Fedson, Janice D. Roberts, and James F. Blanchard

Introduction

The use of computers and administrative databases to support health care administration and personal health services has grown markedly, but computers' potential for improving public health services has not been realized. Thacker and Stroup (1994)[2] have outlined future directions for public health information systems in the United States. In Canada, recent tightening of health care budgets provides an incentive to improve the management of preventive programs.[3]

1.   This work was supported by a National Health Research and Development Program Career Scientist Award (to L. Roos), by the Manitoba Centre for Health Policy and Evaluation, by the Canadian Institute for Advanced Research, by HEALNet (Health Evidence Application and Linkage Network – A Network of Centres of Excellence program) and by the St. Boniface General Hospital Research Centre. The authors gratefully acknowledge the assistance of Manitoba Health, Winnipeg, Manitoba, Canada. The results and conclusions are those of the authors, and no official endorsement by Manitoba Health is intended or should be inferred. Some of this chapter has appeared in Healthcare Management Forum.
2.   Stephen B. Thacker and Donna F. Stroup, "Future Directions for Comprehensive Public Health Surveillance and Health Information Systems in the United States," *American Journal of Epidemiology* 140 (1994): 383-97.
3.   Robert Steinbrook and Bernard Lo, "The Oregon Medicaid Demonstration Project – Will it Provide Adequate Medical Care?" *New England Journal of Medicine* 326 (1992): 340-44. Morris L. Barer and Robert G. Evans, "Interpreting Canada: Models,

This paper reviews the information systems and administrative data for health care in the Canadian province of Manitoba, emphasizing how they could be used to better manage the delivery of preventive services to the entire population. Since 1988, Manitoba has used these data to support a program of childhood immunizations. Information systems to support the delivery of two other relatively cost-effective preventive services, influenza immunization of the elderly and cervical cancer screening, have not yet been developed.[4] Comparatively little attention has been paid to reaching the people most in need of such services. As new strategies for prevention are implemented, Manitoba data can give a picture of the situation "before" the inauguration of these efforts, provide the information base for helping to deliver these services, and aid in evaluating the impact of these strategies.

Public Health Information Systems

a. Multiple Needs

A public health information system should be able to address multiple needs for management, surveillance, and evaluation. Three Canadian provinces (Manitoba, Saskatchewan, and British Columbia) have developed population registries and health care databases comparable to those in such European countries as Denmark, Iceland, and Sweden. As these administrative databases expand their coverage and content, they should be increasingly able to serve as health information utilities, providing multipurpose data for health services research, epidemiology, and public health.

In Manitoba, registries and utilization databases needed to integrate several traditionally separate areas of health and health care already exist. These components include:

Mind-Sets, and Myths," *Health Affairs* 11 (spring 1992): 44-61. Louise B. Russell, "Some of the Tough Decisions Required by a National Health Plan," *Science* 246 (1989): 892-96. C. David Naylor, "A Different View of Queues in Ontario," *Health Affairs* 10 (fall 1991): 110-28. Robert J. Blendon and Jennifer N. Edwards, "Caring for the Uninsured: Choices for Reform," *Journal of the American Medical Association* 265 (1991): 2563-67.

4. Tammy O. Tengs et al., "Five-Hundred Life-Saving Interventions and Their Cost-Effectiveness," *Risk Analysis* 15 (1995): 369-90. Louise B. Russell, *Educated Guesses: Making Policy About Medical Screening Tests* (Los Angeles: University of California Press, 1994).

- A population registry which incorporates necessary information on birth, death, mobility within the province, and in- and out-migration. This registry accurately defines the health insurance status for each resident for each day from 1970 to 1994. It has been set up to facilitate translating between each individual's (scrambled) personal health identification number (PHIN) and the same individual's other identifiers (family identification number, date of birth, gender, and initials). Because the PHIN has been used only since 1984, while family identification number changes with age and family status, building such a universal translation capability has been a major project. This work was done by a university-based research group (the Manitoba Centre for Health Policy and Evaluation) in association with Manitoba Health.

- Timely information bearing on each substantive public health problem. Specifically, a record of each event (such as an immunization or a test), characteristics of the event, and each individual's relevant identifiers are present. Of interest are laboratory files (to provide information on tests performed and results), communicable disease registries, physician claims for reimbursement (to indicate diagnoses and tests performed), hospital discharge abstracts, and vital statistics (death and cause of death).

- Organization of the data so as to minimize bias. In immunization studies, for example, immunization and hospitalization events are examined simultaneously, even though they were ascertained independently. This eliminates an important source of bias which may inadvertently create or overestimate associations between vaccine use and adverse events.[5]

- Software to link across data files. If the same personal identifier (e.g., PHIN in Manitoba) is used in two or more files, linking data files is quite easy. However, software to help translate between two or more systems with different personal identifiers has proven essential.[6]

---

5.   Paul E. M. Fine and Robert T. Chen, "Confounding in Studies of Adverse Reactions to Vaccines," *American Journal of Epidemiology* 136 (1992): 121-35.

6.   Leslie L. Roos et al., "Record Linkage: An Overview," in *Medical Effectiveness Research Data Methods*, eds. H. A. Schwartz and M. L. Grady (Rockville, MD: U.S. Department of Health and Human Services, 1992), 119-29. André Wajda, *LinkPro User's Manual, Version 1* (Winnipeg, MB: InfoSoft Inc, 1992).

- Software to select appropriate control groups for retrospective cohort and case control studies of efficacy and clinical effectiveness. Such programs aid in matching of controls to cases based on such variables as age, gender, and place of residence. Flexible criteria (such as date of birth, plus or minus one year) are included in the software.

b. *Software for Data Analysis*

Government, community, and university researchers need user-friendly programs to flexibly calculate population-based rates of disease, health care utilization, and mortality. Manitoba researchers have produced software with a graphical interface to generate crude and adjusted rates across any file having substantive information and patient residence codes. Researchers can choose from a menu or develop their own options. The geographic areas to be compared can be easily changed for the study of different problems, while a variety of graphics and statistics can be chosen within the program. Individual patient identifiers are not necessary, but they can be used if available.[7]

Because health care utilization data are characterized by multiple records per person, researchers need flexible methods to summarize information on preventive health interventions, such as immunizations and Papanicolaou tests. One software module developed in Manitoba tracks individual records to search for user-defined conditions, rearranging such data into one record per individual.[8] Another module produces individual histories from files with multiple records per person, counting the number of specified events and summarizing variables across the events. Such software has been developed using a fourth-generation language (SAS was the choice for the software used by the Manitoba Centre for Health Policy and Evaluation) and structured to be as general as possible. This has simplified training and maintenance, allowing the same programs to be used by managers, professionals, and scientists across the fields of public health, epidemiology, health services research and clinical investigation.

7.   Charlyn Black, Charles A. Burchill, and Leslie L. Roos, "The Population Health Information System: Data Analysis and Software," *Medical Care* 33, Suppl. (1995): DS127-DS131.

8.   Leslie L. Roos et al., "Software for Health Analysts: A Modular Approach," *Journal of Medical Systems* 11 (1987): 445-64.

Childhood Immunizations

Although a number of studies have emphasized that childhood immunizations are actually cost-saving,[9] such analyses have not dealt with designing
systems that can be used to ensure that a high percentage of children are
immunized, to support appropriate surveillance for adverse effects, and to
assess the clinical effectiveness of vaccination.

In Canada, a recent review has noted the need to understand successful
provincial immunization programs.[10] Computerization has been recommended for all such programs, but thus far has been implemented only in
Manitoba, New Brunswick, and (partially) Ontario. The availability of
computerized data would greatly facilitate the interprovincial comparisons

	Infancy Schedule Recorded as Complete by First Birthday, % (No.)			
	Winnipeg			
	Outside Winnipeg	Inner City	Suburbs	Total
Non-Indian				
Continuous enrollment from birth to at least the first birthday	90.3 (6,120)	87.3 (3,273)	93.6 (5,460)	90.8 (14,853)
Interrupted enrollment in the first year of life*	42.3 (442)	33.5 (340)	43.8 (377)	40.0 (1,159)
Indian				
Continuous enrollment from birth to at least the first birthday†	38.6 (1,519)	65.2 (368)	62.9 (70)	44.5 (1,957)
Interrupted enrollment in the first year of life*†	12.8 (47)	30.0 (30)	50.0 (2)	20.3 (79)

Table 1
1989 Birth Cohort: Proportion with Immunization Schedule Complete by Indian Status, by Enrollment Status and by Place of Residence

*Recorded rates underestimate actual immunization rates because of migration.
†Recorded rates underestimate actual immunization rates because the Federal Health department did not fully participate in the Manitoba Immunization Monitoring System.
Reprinted from J.D. Roberts et al., "Monitoring Childhood Immunizations: A Canadian Approach," *American Journal of Public Health* 84 (1994): 1666-68, with the kind permission of the American Public Health Association, 1015 15th St. NW, Washington D.C. 20005.

9.   Tengs et al., "Five-Hundred Life-Saving Interventions," 369-390.

10.   Theresa W. Gyorkos et al., "Practice Survey of Immunization in Canada," *Canadian Journal of Public Health* 85, Suppl. (1994): S31-S36.

suggested by Gyorkos et al. (1994).[11] Issues involving migration and aboriginal populations, with their effects on both numerators and denominators in rate calculations, can most efficiently be addressed by such data.[12] By comparisontion data are collected by survey,[13] the estimated immunization rates are almost certainly too high.

a. Manitoba Immunization Monitoring System

In Manitoba, a population-based registry and monitoring system help manage provincial programs for vaccine purchase and immunization by tracking the delivery of each dose of each vaccine. In 1989, at least 85% of the children resident in Manitoba during their first year of life received a full set of childhood immunizations (three diphtheria-tetanus-pertussis (DTP) and two oral polio immunizations) (Table 1). There is some under-reporting of immunization of treaty-status Indians by federal public health nurses and more general difficulty in ascertaining the immunization histories of children migrating into Manitoba.[14] Among non-Indians born in 1989 and continuously enrolled in Manitoba during their first year of life, 90.8% completed the full set of recommended immunizations by their first birthday. The value of the Manitoba Immunization Monitoring System (MIMS) could be further improved by an effective computer interface between the federally-funded services provided to treaty-status Indians and the provincially-funded childhood immunization program.

   The Manitoba Immunization Monitoring System combines data produced by physicians for billing purposes with data entered by public health nurses into terminals located at public health offices. New information is generated each time a child is immunized, allowing tracking of each dose of vaccine delivered in childhood. Immunization status is monitored by comparing, in the month of the first, second, fifth, and sixth birthdays, the system record and the recommended schedule. Missing immunization produce a letter to the family (fifth birthday) or to the last provider (other birthdays), requesting completion. The direct effectiveness of the system can be estimated only after the first birthday, when "reminders" begin. A direct examination of monitoring efficacy found it to increase coverage

---

11. Ibid.

12. Janice D. Roberts et al., "Monitoring Childhood Immunizations: A Canadian Approach," *American Journal of Public Health* 84 (1994): 1666-68.

13. Roberts et al., "Monitoring Childhood Immunizations," 1666-68.

14. Gyorkos et al., "Practice Survey of Immunization in Canada," 531-36.

among one- and two-year olds by approximately 6%, from 92% to 98%,[15] a cost-effective increase in terms of disease prevention.

Because the Manitoba Immunization Monitoring System has a number of capabilities not available elsewhere, it is difficult to judge its total benefits in increasing immunization rates in the province. Like other computerized immunization systems, MIMS can measure the cumulative percentage of immunizations completed by certain ages in specified birth cohorts and calculate percentages of children who are up-to-date for their recommended immunizations. In addition, the Manitoba system allows a closer look at the data; for example, the percentage of children receiving all scheduled immunizations within 30 days of the recommended age can be calculated to determine the proportion who are age-appropriately immunized. Finally, MIMS can define population subgroups by demographic characteristics and calculate immunization rates by indicators of known influence on uptake (urban/rural residence, native/non-native status, etc.).[16] Jurisdictions outside Manitoba typically lack the ability to measure immunization rates among migrants or certain minority groups.[17]

The cost of MIMS is less than $2.00 per child (aged six and under) annually. These costs include those associated with separately capturing immunizations by public health nurses, combining these data with immunization data obtained from physician payment claims, merging new information with that previously recorded, maintaining the resulting file in a form which permits public health nurses to review the immunization status of individual children, and sending out reminders. When the costs of running the Manitoba system are allocated across the various functions performed, the incremental improvement in immunization rates resulting from the system appear to be cost-saving in directly preventing illness.[18]

---

15. Ibid.

16. Ibid.

17. Norman T. Begg, O. N. Gill and Joanne M. White, "COVER (Cover of Vaccination Evaluated Rapidly): Description of the England and Wales Scheme," *Public Health* 103 (1989): 81-89. Hans P. Verbrugge, "The National Immunization Program of the Netherlands," *Pediatrics* 86, Suppl. (1990): 1060-63. Elizabeth R. Zell et al., "Low Vaccination Levels of US Preschool and School-Age Children: Retrospective Assessments of Vaccination Coverage, 1991-1992," *Journal of the American Medical Association* 271 (1994): 833-39.

18. Janice D. Roberts, "The Manitoba Immunization Monitoring System (MIMS): Cost Effectiveness," (Department of Community Health Sciences, University of Manitoba, 1992).

Table 2
Designated Diagnostic Codes Showing Statistically Significant Increases Among Hospitalization Following DTP/DT Immunization in the First Year of Life; Children Born in 1987, 1988 and 1989

Designated Code	Number of Codes		P Value	Time Interval (Days) Following Immunization
	Before Immunization	After Immunization		
047.9 Unspecified viral meningitis	7	3	.6446	28
320.0 Hemophilus meningitis	2	4	.7540	28
345.6 Infantile spasms	0	5	.0125	28
780.3 Non-epileptic convulsions	1	11	.0019*	7
780.6 Pyrexia of unknown origin	0	7	.0040*	2
999.5 Other serum reaction	0	4	.0228	28
999.9 Complication of medical care	0	6	.0071*	2

Designated codes appearing 4 or more times in the appropriate time period (before and after all DTP immunizations) were chosen for statistical analysis. The P-value was ascertained using McNemar's chi-square test.

*Significant at .05 level using Bonferroni correction (critical value of .05/7 = .0071)

Reprinted from: J.D. Roberts, et al., "Surveillance of Vaccine-Related Adverse Events in the First Year of Life: A Manitoba Cohort Study," *Journal of Clinical Epidemiology* (1996): 51-58, with the kind permission from Elsevier Science Ltd, The Boulevard, Langford Lane, Kidlington OX5 1GB, UK.

Moreover, the system may help providers (particularly public health nurses) concentrate on other important health-related activities.

b. Surveillance of Vaccine-Associated Adverse Events

Adverse events following vaccination have been the subject of much concern and controversy. Their apparent temporal association with routine childhood immunizations, particularly pertussis (given as diphtheria-tetanus-pertussis [DTP]) and oral polio vaccination, has been extensively reviewed.[19] Hodder and Mortimer (1992)[20] have stated that "one of the most perplexing and difficult problems in epidemiology, one that has required and received maximum attention during the past 10 or 15 years, is whether pertussis vaccine is sometimes responsible for major neurologic disasters and, in rare cases, death."

Previous work using MIMS has defined subgroups of the 1987, 1988, and 1989 birth cohorts in the first year of life. Immunization data on the non-Indian children were linked with hospital and mortality files to determine population-based incidence rates of adverse events temporally related to vaccination and to assess the nature of the association between routine immunization with DTP and oral polio vaccines and hospitalization. Rates of adverse events were compared before and after immunization. Such comparisons are appropriate only when nonimmunized individuals in the population are few.[21] The Manitoba data do not suffer from problems associated with other studies' incomplete coverage; coverage levels for the province were high and adverse events were not concentrated among children with less than the full series of immunizations.[22]

Analysis of the relationships between vaccine exposure and serious adverse events showed no increase in overall hospitalization rates following DTP/poliomyelitis vaccine use. However, DTP immunization was associated with hospitalization with fever and non-epileptic convulsions within two and seven days, respectively, of immunization. Hospitalization for the "complication of medical care" ICD-9-CM code also showed a

---

19. James D. Cherry et al., "Report of the Task Force on Pertussis and Pertussis Immunization, 1988," *Pediatrics* 81, Suppl. (1988): 938-84. Christopher P. Howson and Harvey V. Fineberg, "Adverse Events Following Pertussis and Rubella Vaccines: Summary of a Report of the Institute of Medicine," *Journal of the American Medical Association* 267 (1992): 392-96. Paul V. Varughese et al., "Eradication of Indigenous Poliomyelitis in Canada: Impact of Immunization Strategies," *Canadian Journal of Public Health* 80 (1989): 363-68. Benjamin M. Nkowane et al., "Vaccine-Associated Paralytic Poliomyelitis: United States: 1973 through 1984," *Journal of the American Medical Association* 257 (1987): 1335-40. Roland W. Sutter, I. M. Onorato, and Peter A. Patriarca, "Current Poliomyelitis Immunization Policy in the United States," *Pediatric Annals* 19 (1990): 702-706.

20. S.L. Hodder and E. A. Mortimer, "Epidemiology of Pertussis and Reactions to Pertussis Vaccine," *Epidemiologic Reviews* 14 (1992): 243-67.

21. Fine and Chen, "Confounding in Studies of Adverse Reactions to Vaccines," 121-35.

22. Janice D. Roberts et al., "Surveillance of Vaccine-Related Adverse Events in the First Year of Life: A Manitoba Cohort Study," *Journal of Clinical Epidemiology* (1996): 51-58.

statistically significant increase following vaccination. Although the relative odds of being hospitalized in the periods before and after immunization closely approximated the relative risks, the magnitudes of risk could not be stated with assurance because the numbers of events were few and corresponding confidence intervals were very wide.

To assemble cohorts of greater size, we plan to merge relevant data from the 1990-1994 Manitoba birth cohorts with those from the 1987-1989 birth cohorts. The eight years of information will be used to more accurately determine population-based rates for vaccine-associated adverse events leading to hospitalization and to better assess the temporal association between DTP immunization and hospitalization, with fever, non-epileptic convulsions, and complications of medical care. Several additional diagnoses (such as those noted in Table 2) will be investigated, although certain rare diagnoses, such as encephalopathy, will remain difficult to study. Finally, the possibilities of analyzing ambulatory visits in the same way that hospitalizations have been studied will be explored.

How do the results from surveillance based on administrative data compare with those produced using other methodologies? In an earlier chart review, a passive approach (where the physician records on the hospital chart a possible immunization-related adverse event following DTP vaccine) noted only 13 such instances, compared with 48 such events found from linked administrative data on hospitalizations within the same cohort.[23] The administrative data seem highly sensitive, since diagnostic codes in the administrative record were accurately reflected in the clinical information recorded on the hospital chart. The physician's recognition of a possible relationship with immunization was what was missing.

In summary, sound, workable, and relatively inexpensive strategies for actively monitoring vaccine delivery and evaluating vaccine safety can be developed using administrative data. These data lend themselves to the continual interaction between surveillance and research. The ongoing accumulation of such information promises studies powerful enough to yield accurate baseline incidence rates and detailed assessments of temporal relationships between putative adverse events and vaccine use.

---

23. Ibid.

c. The Clinical Effectiveness of Childhood Vaccination

The efficacy of a particular vaccine is usually assessed prior to licensing. Once it becomes widely used, ongoing assessment of efficacy and effectiveness is uncommon. However, recent outbreaks of vaccine-preventable diseases, such as measles and pertussis ("whooping cough"), have occurred in well-immunized populations in Canada and the United States.[24] During such outbreaks, rapid epidemiologic assessment of vaccine efficacy could be helpful to indicate strategies for action. For example, if overall vaccine effectiveness is shown to be unexpectedly low, then questions regarding vaccine transport and storage might be raised. Additionally, if the vaccine proves to be ineffective, strategies which emphasize accelerated vaccine delivery may be misdirected.

In 1994 Manitoba experienced a substantial outbreak of pertussis, with the number of reported cases exceeding that reported in any year since 1970. We have proposed using administrative data to evaluate this outbreak, selecting cases of disease based on several criteria. The gold standard would be cases identified by means of culture of *B. pertussis* (almost 400 cases in 1994). As long as the total number of cultures done remains constant, pertussis identification through positive cultures ensures that observed increases are not due to wider surveillance.[25] A second list of pertussis cases could be identified from the records of the Manitoba Health Communicable Disease Surveillance System (600 cases were recorded in the first nine months of 1994). This system accepts as a case of pertussis any illness as defined by:

1) a positive culture for *B. pertussis*,

2) an antibody detection by direct fluorescence,

3) a serological test of antibodies, or

4) a clinical case definition (an unexplained cough lasting more than two weeks).

Cases with an ICD-9-CM diagnosis of pertussis or whooping cough on either a physician claim or (infrequently) a hospital abstract would

---

24. Celia D. Christie et al., "The 1993 Epidemic of Pertussis in Cincinnati: Resurgence of Disease in a Highly Immunized Population of Children," *New England Journal of Medicine* 331 (1994): 16-21.

25. Noel W. Preston, "Pertussis Vaccination: Neither Panic nor Complacency," *Lancet* 344 (1994): 491-92.

202 \ *Moving Toward Universality*

constitute a third list. Eight hundred and eight such individuals were identified by these administrative data in 1993, and considerably greater numbers are expected for 1994. The Manitoba population registry can be used to select control subjects for each list of cases, and can accurately assess loss to follow-up and mortality information on all subjects.[26] Case-control studies can then be undertaken to see the extent to which judgements as to immunization efficacy vary with the criteria used to select cases.

Supporting the Delivery of Other Preventive Services

Opportunities exist to extend the approach of the Manitoba Immunization Monitoring System to other programs for primary and secondary disease prevention.[27] Both influenza immunizations for the elderly and cervical cancer screening involve efforts at targeting certain patient groups and focusing reminders on particular individuals and their physicians. As emphasized in a recent review, preventive activities such as these are usually more effective with selective use.[28]

a. Influenza Immunization for the Elderly

Although analyses of existing administrative data can avoid the expense of setting up a registry, achieving a high level of influenza vaccination by introducing a reminder system (targeted towards the elderly and other high-risk groups) may be more difficult than ensuring an appropriate level of childhood immunization. The time pressures are severe, since the "vaccination season" is limited to the three months before the influenza season. Physician payment claims would have to be processed unusually quickly in order to generate similar reminders for those not immunized in the current season. By contrast, American health maintenance organizations with high levels of automation might be able to enter vaccination information into a database shortly after the event. Reminders might be sent to elders and high-risk individuals at the beginning of the influenza vaccination season; those who were not vaccinated the previous year might receive several reminders. Alternatively, since some provincial information sys-

26. Leslie L. Roos et al., "Registries and Administrative Data: Organization and Accuracy," *Medical Care* 31 (1993): 201-12.

27. Tengs et al., "Five-Hundred Life-Saving Interventions," 369-90.

28. Kristin Leutwyler, "The Price of Prevention," *Scientific American* 272 (1995): 124-29.

tems permit linking doctors with specific patients to determine the primary care-givers, physicians who tend not to give influenza vaccine could be identified and urged to do so by an appropriate organization (e.g., the provincial College of Physicians and Surgeons). Data based on physician claims would probably need to be supplemented by information from other sources. For example, previous work to assess whether appreciable numbers of patients received influenza vaccine in the hospital setting involved checking with hospital pharmacies. The number of inpatient immunizations was small; many hospital immunizations of the elderly were done by fee-for-service doctors in outpatient clinics and were consequently recorded in the claims database. If in-hospital immunization increased markedly, obtaining information on immunizations for the elderly performed outside of the fee-for-service system would be important and would require special arrangements, perhaps data entry similar to that done in Manitoba for childhood immunizations.

Currently, considerable variation both in rates of influenza vaccination and in hospitalization for influenza-associated respiratory conditions exists across 58 Manitoba physician-service areas (Figure 1). As is the case with childhood immunizations, the lower recorded rates of vaccinations tend to occur in areas with relatively high Indian populations. In many of these areas, a large proportion of health care services are delivered through nursing stations. Some influenza immunizations might be carried out without physician billing, but health care providers familiar with the situation think the numbers are small. Analyses separating native and non-native populations could reduce uncertainty about immunization in the non-native population, while highlighting the difficulties in making inferences about native immunization rates. Because rates for hospitalization for influenza-associated respiratory conditions are high in some of these areas, Figure 1 suggests the need for attention to both immunization and validation of the data regarding this important preventive measure.

The cost-effectiveness of an information system directed towards reminders and monitoring would primarily depend upon its ability to lower the hospitalization and mortality associated with influenza. Increasing Manitoba immunization rates would appear to have considerable potential to do so.[29] The cost-effectiveness of such a system would also partially

---

29. David S. Fedson et al., "Disparity Between Influenza Vaccination Rates and Risks of Influenza-Associated Hospital Discharge and Death in Manitoba in 1982-1983," *Annals of Internal Medicine* 116 (1992): 550-55. David S. Fedson et al., "Clinical Effectiveness of Influenza Vaccination in Manitoba in 1982-1983 and 1985-1986," *Journal of the American Medical Association* 270 (1993): 1956-61.

Figure 1
Estimated Manitoba Rates of Influenza Vaccination and Hospitalization for Influenza – Associated
Respiratory Conditions [1993-1994, Ages 65 and older]

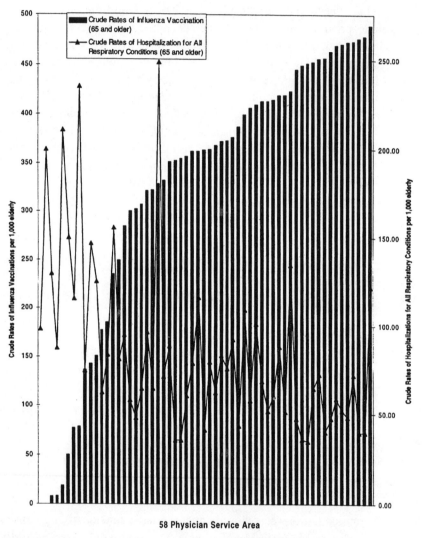

Respiratory conditions were defined as Pneumonia and Influenza; 1CD9-CM codes 480-487.
*Manitoba Influenza Vaccination rate was 410.75 per 1,000 (ages 65 and over)
†Manitoba hospitalization rate for Influenza-Associated Respiratory Conditions was 23.64 per 1,000 (ages 65 and over)

depend upon its usefulness in reducing the costs of distributing provincially-funded vaccine and in monitoring the effectiveness of influenza
vaccination. In addition, if pneumococcal vaccine were to be distributed
provincially (as argued by Fedson [1995]),[30] an information system to
facilitate both influenza and pneumococcal immunization might be well-
justified by splitting costs between the two programs.

b. Screening for Cervical Cancer

The cost-effectiveness of Papanicolaou testing for cervical cancer screening varies markedly with the testing schedule and the risk status of the
patient.[31] Improving the effectiveness of screening efforts by concentrating
resources on certain individuals is particularly important for cervical cancer. For example, screening all elderly women every three years seems quite
cost-effective (perhaps U.S. $1,500 to $4,000 per life-year gained). Screening previously unscreened elderly women may be cost-saving; i.e., early
identification of cervical cancer might lower treatment costs more than the
expense of screening.[32] However, increasing the frequency of screening can
be a very expensive way to extend lives. Compared with screening every
three years, screening every year might cost from roughly $100,000 per
life-year gained among elderly women to more than $1 million per life-year
gained for younger women.[33]

Cohen et al. (1992)[34] have applied criteria from the Canadian Task
Force report on cervical cancer screening in their assessment of screening
in Manitoba. Using four years of population-based data for women aged 25
to 64 years, only 56% were judged to have been tested appropriately
(approximately once every three years). Both over-testing (15%) and under-testing (29%) were found. Individual physician testing practices also

---

30. David S. Fedson, "Influenza and Pneumococcal Vaccination in Canada and the
United States, 1980-1993: What Can the Two Countries Learn From Each Other?"
Clinical Infectious Diseases 20 (1995): 1371-76.

31. Charlotte J. Muller et al., *Costs and Effectiveness of Cervical Cancer Screening in
Elderly Women* (Washington, D.C.: Government Printing Office, 1990). Marianne C.
Fahs et al., "Cost Effectiveness of Cervical Cancer Screening for the Elderly," *Annals
of Internal Medicine* 117 (1992): 520-27.

32. Fahs et al., "Cost Effectiveness of Cervical Cancer Screening for the Elderly,"
520-27.

33. Louise B. Russell, "The Role of Prevention in Health Reform," *New England
Journal of Medicine* 329 (1993): 352-54. Russell, *Educated Guesses.*

34. Marsha M. Cohen et al., "Assessing Physician's Compliance with Guidelines for
Papanicolaou Testing," *Medical Care* 30 (1992): 514-28.

varied considerably, with some physicians usually over-testing and others markedly under-testing. As Russell (1994)[35] has emphasizelth from screening the roughly one-quarter of all women who are under-tested are much greater than the gains possible from more frequent screening of the remaining 75%.

Geographic differences in rates of Papanicolaou testing among Manitoba women 18 to 69 years in age are shown in Figure 2. By looking at any entry for an individual – either a physician bill or a laboratory bill – an effort is made to capture all women screened for cervical cancer. The lower rates of recorded testing have again been observed in areas with native populations, where nursing stations deliver much of the care. Because the Health Sciences Centre in Winnipeg performs laboratory work for Manitoba as a whole, we are currently trying to determine how much Papanicolaou testing, particularly of natives, might escape the billing system. Preliminary analyses of claims data suggest that almost all patients are picked up through physician billing, with laboratory records noting relatively few cases not previously identified. Sensitivity testing – eliminating native women from consideration in both numerator and denominator of rate calculations – made little difference in the overall results, but some of the small area rankings did change.

Outside Canada, successful screening programs for cervical cancer are being conducted in Finland and the United Kingdom.[36] British Columbia Task Force Report on Cervical Cancer Cytology Registry, with follow-up of patients having appreciable cellular abnormalities; each patient's physician is notified if smears have not been received by the cytology service within two years of the last negative smear. Over the last 30 years large reductions in morbidity (78%) and mortality (72%) from invasive carcinoma of the cervix have been attributed to this follow-up program.[37]

With rates of invasive cervical cancer in British Columbia approximately one-half those in Alberta and Manitoba, the British Columbia

35. Russell, *Educated Guesses.*

36. Matti Hakama and Kirsti Louhivuori, "A Screening Programme for Cervical Cancer that Worked," *Cancer Surveys* 7 (1988): 403-16. A. J. Robertson et al., "Evaluation of a Call Programme for Cervical Cytology Screening in Women Aged 50-60," *British Medical Journal* 299 (1989): 163-66.

37. George H. Anderson et al., "Organization and Results of the Cervical Cytology Screening Programme in British Columbia, 1955-85," *British Medical Journal* 296 (1988): 975-78. George H. Anderson, "The British Columbia Experience," *Chronic Diseases in Canada* 13, Suppl. (1992): S5.

Figure 2
Estimated Rates of Papanicolaou Testing

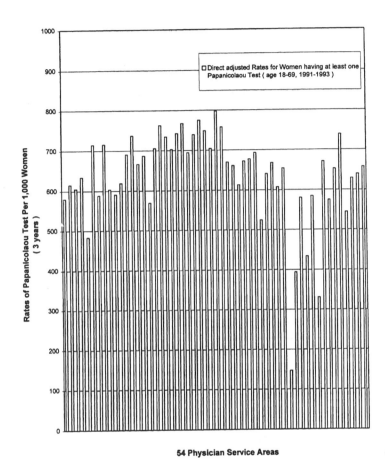

54 Physician Service Areas

*Manitoba Papanicolaou Test mean value is 704.97 per 1,000 women (age 18-69, having at least one test in three years).

example suggests possibilities for other provinces. The number of laboratories handling Papanicolaou smears and capabilities for linking test histories with cervical cancer cases vary markedly across Canadian provinces.[38] Given different provincial strategies to reduce cervical cancer, experimentation across these sites could improve learning. Several lines of research have suggested the importance of efforts to improve Papanicolaou test sampling and reading.[39] On the other hatem in Manitoba need not require additional changes in the organization of testing; a case-control study has shown Papanicolaou testing to be effective, even with decentralized testing and no provincial cytology registry.[40] The operation of the information system, the degree of centralized testing, the extent and effectiveness of quality control efforts, and whether or not a cytology registry is incorporated into the program are all relevant for each insurance plan.

Operational questions are important. To avoid sending reminder notices to women who have recently left or arrived in the province, accessing the Manitoba population registry is desirable. Given Manitoba's recording of Papanicolaou smears on physician payment claims, running an information system and generating reminders for cervical cancer testing could cost less than operating the Manitoba Immunization Monitoring System (approximately $150,000 Canadian annually). Adding information on test results and contacting women with abnormal smears would increase both costs and benefits. Sensitivities connected with informing women of their test results might be alleviated if the organization with a legal mandate for cancer care, the Manitoba Cancer Treatment and Research Foundation, ran the program. As Miller (1995)[41] has noted, although Canada is slowly moving towards a more organized approach to cervical cancer screening, a long distance remains to be travelled.

---

38. Health and Welfare Canada, "Proceedings of the Second National Workshop on Cervical Cancer Screening, Edmonton, Alberta, November 24-25, 1992," *Chronic Diseases in Canada* 13, Suppl. (1992): S1-S41.

39. Michael T. Fahey, Les Irwig and Petra Macaskill, "Meta-Analysis of Pap Test Accuracy," *American Journal of Epidemiology* 141 (1995): 680-89. Russell, *Educated Guesses.*

40. Marsha M. Cohen, "Using Administrative Data for Case-Control Studies: The Case of the Papanicolaou Smear," *Annals of Epidemiology* 3 (1993): 93-98.

41. Anthony B. Miller, "Failures of Cervical Cancer Screening," *American Journal of Public Health* 85 (1995): 761-62.

Discussion

a. Managing an Information System for Preventive Services

The coverage, content and quality of available information resources will greatly affect their helpfulness in managing public health services. A single-payer health insurance system minimizes problems of coverage and content; such systems have the ability to compel providers to submit information in a standardized fashion. As more provinces build population registries and organize their health care databases for multiple purposes, both government professionals and researchers need to develop expertise in using these resources. The benefits to health which can result from a well-designed information system must be made readily apparent to assure adequate support for development and management. Such a system must be successfully marketed to provincial health authorities to improve both population health and the cost-effectiveness of Canadian health care.

Creative strategies for using information to manage both health care services and health maintenance programs need to be identified. Compatibility of computer languages, data representation, and hardware should be discussed from the beginning. Organizational factors will also be important. Because hospital delivery of preventive services may be noted on independent databases or not recorded at all, attention must be paid to incorporating such information into provincial systems. In many instances, improving the federal-provincial interface will be critical for recording data for the Canadian aboriginal population. Often university-government relationships must operate smoothly to facilitate sharing of data, software, and personnel.

Integrating individual patient reminders with a public health information system raises several technical issues. For example, given the current reliance of the Manitoba Information Monitoring System on a mainframe computer, planning for its eventual replacement should be coordinated with the development of improved information systems to support new preventive services. In the meantime, record-linkage software that helps determine whether the same individual exists in two or more databases will have to be used for management and research purposes.[42]

Considering the potential benefits of targeting and the small costs of transferring software, appropriate health information systems can effi-

---

42. Roos et al., "Record Linkage: An Overview," 119-29.

ciently support new methods of delivering preventive and screening services. Building on and working with existing administrative data is usually easier than developing entirely new systems. Most current systems can already be used to study geographic variations among various preventive and screening programs; such information may highlight where improvements in delivery are particularly needed. Administrative data with unique identifiers can document health outcomes associated with receiving or not receiving these services.

b. Future Possibilities

Timeliness is a continuing issue for users of information systems and administrative data. There are inevitable delays from the time when events occur to the time when data documenting these events become available. Further delays occur from the time when data are ready for use to when reminders could be sent out. In Manitoba, the Centre for Health Policy and Evaluation has arranged with Manitoba Health to receive data at either six-month or twelve-month intervals (depending on the file). Where appropriate, the Centre could also update the population registry and utilization files on a high priority basis for relevant users.

Although the utility of administrative databases has been demonstrated for evaluating the clinical effectiveness of influenza vaccination,[43] stronger research designs are possible. One approach would be to introduce several competing vaccines (e.g., acellular pertussis vaccines) in a controlled fashion so that clinical effectiveness and adverse events could be monitored prospectively. This potential application could be very important because it is unlikely that randomized controlled trials directly comparing different vaccine preparations will ever be undertaken.[44] Identifying adverse events for existing and new vaccines can be accomplished more efficiently using administrative data. Setting up an "early warning" system based on analyses of hospitalization and immunization data that would be updated monthly is feasible and would be relatively inexpensive. As a supplement to WHO and national activities, a population-based administrative database such as Manitoba's could assess both the effectiveness of each vaccine and adverse events following immunization on a timely basis.

43. Fedson et al., "Clinical Effectiveness of Influenza Vaccination," 1956-61.

44. Wayne A. Ray and Marie R. Griffin, "Letter: Re: Confounding in Studies of Adverse Reactions to Vaccines," *American Journal of Epidemiology* 139 (1994): 229. Fine and Chen, "Confounding in Studies of Adverse Reactions to Vaccines," 121-35.

The cost-effectiveness of targeting individuals at high-risk of specific diseases is a matter of considerable debate.[45] The case for targeting women who have not had regular Papanicolaou testing has been made earlier. The information system and database can also be used to evaluate different approaches to sending reminders to patients who need testing. Although several randomized controlled trials of reminder systems have been carried out, none has been undertaken for an entire population.[46] Screening programs for cervical cancer for women in the 18 to 69 years' age group are recommended in Canada;[47] there is great potential for experimentation on how much should be invested in which type of reminders for Papanicolaou testing. Should they be single or multiple? Should they be sent to the patient, to the last physician seen, or to a health care unit, such as a nursing station in a remote area? Within an overall experimental framework, researchers can stratify the design according to area, a woman's age, and her prior screening history.

New knowledge of human genetics has expanded the possibilities for developing programs for genetic screening and counselling for several diseases. For example, by linking the Manitoba population registry with data from the Cancer Foundation, children of parents diagnosed with different types of cancer within the last 24 years could be identified; depending on the risk associated with being a first-degree relative, they could be targeted for various screening or counselling programs. Not only specific cancers but other conditions, such as early-onset heart disease, might be selected for attention.[48] The benefits of this strategy would depend on the relative risk borne by such individuals, as well as the efficacy and effectiveness of screening and treatment. The costs of contacting the children of Manitobans with these conditions would be low, given the investments already made in the population registry and in computer software.

45. Geoffrey Rose, *The Strategy of Preventive Medicine.* (London: Oxford University Press, 1992).

46. Steven M. Orenstein et al., "Computer-Generated Physician and Patient Reminders. Tools to Improve Population Adherence to Selected Preventive Services," *Journal of Family Practice* 32 (1991): 82-90.

47. Anthony B. Miller et al., "Report of a National Workshop on Screening for Cancer of the Cervix," *Canadian Medical Association Journal* 145, Suppl. (1991): 1301-25.

48. Arno G. Motulsky, "Nutrition and Genetic Susceptibility to Common Diseases," *American Journal of Clinical Nutrition* 55, Suppl. (1992): 1244S-45S.

c. Variations in Program Delivery

Considerable variation in the organization, effectiveness, and equity of programs for preventive health care is to be expected. Research into avoidable illness may provide clues as to which preventive services can be cost-effectively expanded and where major health improvements could be produced. Within the United States, variations across states in delivering childhood immunizations suggest great opportunities for learning.[49] The "natural experiments" in health care financing and delivery currently underway in developed countries would inform such work, aiding in the cross-national assessment of health care technologies.[50]

Canada's preventive programs reflect several different influences. Greater acceptance by the public of government responsibility for planning health care services probably underlies Canada's success with childhood immunizations.[51] Although the Canadian provinces manage childhood immunizations in a variety of ways, they all rely on public health nurses to supplement immunizations given by physicians under fee-for-service arrangements. At the same time, despite major differences in both the mix of physician specialties and access to medical care, Canada and the United States show similar rates for preventive services delivered through standard fee-for-service mechanisms (as is done with influenza vaccination of the elderly and Papanicolaou testing).[52] On the other hand, Canadian physicians and provincial funders have been less convinced of the importance of pneumonococcal immunization of the elderly; Canadian rates are well below those in the United States.[53]

---

49. Gary L. Freed, W. Clayton Bordley and Gordon H. DeFriese, "Childhood Immunization Programs: An Analysis of Policy Issues," *Milbank Quarterly* 71 (1993): 65-96. Marilyn Moon and John Holahan, "Can States Take the Lead in Health Care Reform?" *Journal of the American Medical Association* 268 (1992): 1588-94. Jonathan A. Showstack et al., "Health of the Public: The Academic Response," *Journal of the American Medical Association* 267 (1992): 2497-02.

50. Morris L. Barer, W. Pete Welch and Laurie Antioch, "Canadian/U.S. Health Care: Reflections on the HIAA's Analysis," *Health Affairs* 10 (fall 1991): 229-39. George J. Schieber, Jean-Pierre Poullier and Leslie M. Greenwald, "Health Care Systems in Twenty-four Countries," *Health Affairs* 10 (fall 1991): 22-38. Michael F. Drummond et al., "Issues in the Cross-National Assessment of Health Technology," *International Journal of Technology Assessment in Health Care* 8 (1992): 671-82.

51. See Institute of Medicine, *The Future of Public Health* (Washington, D.C.: National Academy Press, 1988).

52. Fedson, "Influenza and Pneumococcal Vaccination," 1371-76. Cohen et al., "Assessing Physician's Compliance with Guidelines for Papanicolaou Testing," 514-28.

In the last several years, all Canadian provinces have restrained their health care budgets and encouraged moving care to noninstitutional, community-based settings.[54] The extent to which the traditional orientation toward treatment will change toward an increased emphasis on cost-effective disease prevention is as yet unclear. In Canada, the nonimmunized and unscreened have a high probability of visiting a physician for other reasons and many opportunities for delivering preventive services are missed.[55] However, the Canadian provinces, increasingly blessed with good administrative data, are only beginning to try to profit from each other's experiences and to develop systems to better manage preventive services.

d. Implications for the United States

In Manitoba, an information system combines childhood immunizations provided by fee-for-service physicians with those done by public health nurses. Although the single-payer system clearly facilitates this, coherent systems designed for monitoring all influenza immunizations and Papanicolaou tests are not in place in Manitoba. Not only do our three examples highlight difficulties in monitoring preventive services for Indians, but having multiple providers (both public and private) makes it difficult and time-consuming to generate information relevant for the entire population. Once again, organizational cooperation will be key to developing better systems.

Both problems of getting better information and those of developing reminder systems are germane for the United States. In most American settings, data from a large number of insurers and providers would have to be integrated. Although competitive pressures make such cooperation problematic, some sharing of information and efforts at integration have begun.[56]

---

53. Fedson, "Influenza and Pneumococcal Vaccination," 1371-76.

54. Manitoba Health, *Quality Health for Manitobans – The Action Plan: A Strategy to Assure the Future of Manitoba's Health Services System* (1992). Raisa B. Deber, John E. F. Hastings and Gail G. Thompson, "Health Care in Canada: Current Trends and Issues," *Journal of Public Health Policy* 12 (1991): 72-82.

55. Jana M. Mossey and Leslie L. Roos, "Using Insurance Claims to Measure Health Status: The Illness Scale," *Journal of Chronic Diseases* 40, Suppl. (1987): 41S-50S. Roberts et al., "Monitoring Childhood Immunizations," 1666-68. Fedson et al., "Disparity," 550-55.

56. Edward L. Baker et al., "Health Reform and the Health of the Public: Forging Community Health Partnerships," *Journal of the American Medical Association* 272

In the United States, coverage issues will be critical for tracking and notification systems; setting up local registries will be more expensive in the United States than in Manitoba.[57] Deciding on relevant identifiers will be difficult, since many children will not have Social Security numbers. Enrolling and tracking eligible individuals has proven to be a major problem in the American Medicaid program.[58] States with more advanced insurance systems (such as Hawaii and Minnesota) are at an advantage since most of their populations are already enrolled.[59] Without unique personal identifiers, building nationwide databases for children's immunizations would be very difficult in both the United States and Canada.

The possibilities for developing reminder systems to deliver preventive services would seem greatest in health maintenance organizations (HMOs), where information on enrolled individuals can be readily organized and updated. Agreement on the kinds of information collected and the format for recording this information can also facilitate the evaluation of delivering preventive services to this section of the population. For persons not enrolled in HMOs, data available from private (Blue Cross/Blue Shield) and public insurers (Medicare and Medicaid) can provide a resource for evaluating service delivery, but reminder systems may be difficult to implement in such situations.

Getting estimates for the uninsured population poses very different problems. Before a child enters the school system, contact with public or private health care providers is likely to be erratic. Although attention to reducing missed opportunities for immunization may help improve immunization levels, the data gathering and management challenges are formidable. The effectiveness of recent efforts towards better delivery of immunizations has been called into question because of just these issues.[60]

(1994): 1276-82. Freed, Bordley and DeFriese, "Childhood Immunization Programs," 65-96.

57. W. Wayt Gibbs, "Preventing the Preventable," *Scientific American* 266 (1993): 135. Cohen, "Using Administrative Data for Case-Control Studies," 93-98.

58. Roselie A. Bright, Jerry Avorn and Daniel E. Everitt, "Medicaid Data as a Resource for Epidemiologic Studies: Strengths and Limitations," *Journal of Clinical Epidemiology* 42 (1989): 937-45.

59. Roos et al., "Registries and Administrative Data," 201-12.

60. J. Michael McGinnis and Phillip R. Lee. 1995. "Healthy People 2000 at Mid Decade," *Journal of the American Medical Association* 273: (1995) 1123-29. Philip K. Russell, "Heading Off a Crisis in Vaccine Development," *Issues in Science and Technology* 9 (1995): 26-32. "Clinton Two Strikes Down," *Nature* 375 (1995): 707-08.

Ideally, population-based data will facilitate experimentation with different ways of delivering and evaluating preventive health care. If the cost-effectiveness information underlying the preventive services discussed here is reasonable, improved health with little extra cost is attainable. Although the possibilities for improving population health may be even greater in the United States than in Canada, established practice patterns have influential advocates in both countries. Regardless of the setting, better allocation of resources takes political will if substantial sections of the population are to achieve their full health potential.[61] However, without use of the new information systems, services will continue to be delivered inefficiently. Organizational change will be necessary for both better preventive services and better measurement of such care for vulnerable populations.

---

61. Margaret Whitehead and Göran Dahlgren, "What Can be Done About Inequalities in Health?" *Lancet* 338 (1991): 1059-63.

CHAPTER NINE

Issues Regarding Appropriate Uses of Outcomes Data in Monitoring Universality and Nondiscrimination in Access to Health Care

Douglas A. Samuelson and R. Clifton Bailey[1]

Introduction

To monitor universality and nondiscrimination in access to health care, some measures or indicators will have to be accepted as representing the overall situation. These measures can be based on the *structure* of health care delivery systems, the *processes* by which care is provided within these structures, and the *outcomes* of treatment. Of these, outcomes are generally the least culturally dependent and the easiest to quantify. Therefore it is important to consider ways in which outcomes data can be used in monitoring, taking into account both the potential and the difficulties of quantifying this complex subject.

Any meaningful monitoring of universality and nondiscrimination in health care must incorporate a comprehensive understanding of which health care activities and resources actually benefit patients. There is no benefit in mandating universal and nondiscriminatory access to useless or even harmful care. Even when certain health care activities are clearly beneficial, but minimally so and extremely expensive, we may choose to

---

1. The opinions expressed in this paper are those of the authors and do not necessarily reflect the views of the Health Care Finance Administration or of any other agency of the United States Government.

avoid improving access to those activities if doing so would preclude broadening other, more cost-effective care.

Structure and process measures alone, therefore, offer little hope of providing a defensible basis for monitoring access to or quality of care. As studies of quality improvement and practice guidelines have shown, experts often disagree about how to treat ailments. One recent comprehensive review concluded that 80 to 90% of common medical practices for a broad selection of conditions had no published basis in the scientific literature:[2] experience and conventional wisdom prevail. This review also found that what was thought to be a well-defined process could be implemented in many different ways, producing varying results. In this case, only careful analysis of unexpected variation in outcomes brought the process variations to light.

There may be several competing views of "best" process, even within a single hospital; disparities are additionally magnified when we attempt assessments among many providers and patient population groups. Comparisons among population groups must, therefore, include various uses of outcomes data. Especially when we want comparisons among different cultures, with different concepts of what constitutes health care, examining the health status which follows health care (or lack of it) is critical to understanding what health care is needed.

Outcomes data, therefore, will be essential for comparisons among countries. Such data will also be essential for comparisons within a country, among racial, ethnic and income groups, among beneficiaries of different payment sources, among groups exposed to different levels of environmental hazards, and among recipients of different authorized plans of care for given ailments. In addition, outcomes data greatly facilitate evaluating the effectiveness and cost-effectiveness of alternative treatments, improving the quality of care, and identifying emerging problem areas. In the U.S., health promotion goals have been stated and monitored primarily in terms of outcomes measures.[3]

Unfortunately, outcomes data do not necessarily make such comparisons easy and clear. Problems with data collection and verification, ques-

2.   Brent C. James, "Implementing Practice Guidelines through Clinical Quality Improvement," *Frontiers of Health Services Management* 10, no. 1 (fall 1993): 20.

3.   Donald L. Patrick and Pennifer Erickson, *Health Status and Health Policy: Quality of Life in Health Care Evaluation and Resource Allocation* (New York: Oxford University Press, 1993), 292-312.

tions about definitions (of conditions, severity, treatments and outcomes), unobserved factors which turn out to be important, and random variation all make analysis and interpretation difficult. While we will illustrate these problems with U. S. data, the same difficulties can be expected worldwide – and all the more so in international comparisons.

Outcomes data also make possible a number of abuses. They could be used by insurers and employers to discriminate in access to health care services, in employment, and in other areas. They could also be misused in ways which would diminish choice of treatments and, consequently, quality of care. Overly broad restrictions on use and dissemination, on the other hand, could diminish the benefits obtainable from outcomes data. Choosing the best policy requires a detailed understanding of the uses of outcomes data.

Some Sources of Outcomes Data in the U.S.

Measures of outcomes of medical treatment include mortality, need for additional treatment, and diminished functioning (as, for example, if a patient survives hip replacement surgery but can no longer walk). There are various sources of outcomes data. In the United States, which does not have a single-payer system and does have much clinical and public health research, these sources are especially numerous and varied. They include:

- vital statistics (data on births, deaths, causes of death, and incidence of diseases, especially those which are infectious and amenable to control by public health measures) collected by public health agencies at various levels of government;

- life expectancy tables used in insurance underwriting, and the outcomes statistics on which these tables are based;[4]

- national compilations of mortality rates, disaggregated to the provider level, such as the one published annually from the early 1980s through 1993 by the U. S. Health Care Finance Administration (HCFA);

---

4. See, for example, R. D. C. Brackenridge, *Medical Selection of Life Risks* (New York: The Nature Press, 1985).

- similar collections of data at the state and local government level, including compilations of vital statistics and registries of causes of death;

- data collected in research studies of specific diseases and treatments (double-blind clinical trials are respected most by U. S. physicians), and in longitudinal analyses, such as the well-known Framingham, Massachusetts study of heart disease;[5]

- results of intensive medical reviews of effects of different treatments of a specific condition, such as the Patient Outcomes Research Teams' (PORT) studies, sponsored by the Agency for Health Care Policy and Research (AHCPR);[6] and

- billing information from individual providers, and collections of such information by provider networks, payment sources and managed care organizations.

The diversity of sources leads to problems in consistency and comparability. Even the definition of "outcome" varies, as some data sets use only mortality, while others include one or more degrees of diminished functioning. Coding for diagnosis and treatments is still more disparate, not only among data sets but often within them. Nevertheless, the increasing availability and quality of outcomes data have made possible better analysis of treatments' effectiveness.

a. *Some Uses of Outcomes Data in the U. S*

There is a long history of collection and use of outcomes data. One of Florence Nightingale's contributions to medicine was her insistence on careful recording of deaths and outcomes of hospitalizations. The collection and analysis of vital statistics, beginning in England in the early 19th century, became ". . . the foundation upon which rests the modern, humani-

---

5.   Ralph B. d'Agostino and William B. Kannel, "Epidemiological Background and Design: The Framingham Study," *Proceedings of the American Statistical Association, Sesquicentennial Invited Paper Sessions*, 1989. Thomas R. Dawber, *The Framingham Study: The Epidemiology of Atherosclerotic Disease,* (Cambridge: Harvard University Press, 1980). Thomas R. Dawber, William B. Kannel, and L. Lyell, "An Approach to Longitudinal Studies in a Community: The Framingham Study," *Annals of the New York Academy of Sciences* 107 (1963): 539-56.

6.   See, for example, Marilyn J. Field and Kathleen N. Lohr, eds., *Clinical Practice Guidelines: Directions for a New Program* (Washington, D.C.: National Academy Press, 1990), 7. See also Agency for Health Care Policy and Research, *Report to Congress: Progress of Research on Outcomes of Health Care Services and Procedures,* AHCPR Publication No. 91-0004 (Washington, D.C., May 1991).

tarian, scientific movement for the development and application of the laws of public health and sanitation" and hence for "the protection of people against a thousand insidious sources of infection."[7] Physicians, especially surgeons, have centered their reviews of quality of care on outcomes, dating back at least to the pioneering work of Codman[8] early in this century. More recently, medical science has increasingly focused on clinical trials to determine which treatments work. These studies require clear, operationally defined end points (outcomes), as well as experimental designs including randomization, balance and blinding, case control and other strategies whose common feature is the attempt to clarify what could have caused the observed variation in outcomes.

Another long-standing use of outcomes data is the life expectancy tables used to set premiums for health and life insurance.[9] These compilations include statistical estimates, based on incidence and mortality statistics, of the differences in life expectancy attributable to ethnic group membership, occupation and various medical conditions. While these data give little insight into treatment processes, they are at least a good first indicator of whether certain groups appear to be at increased risk.

Donabedian, in the culmination of nearly 30 years of work which was instrumental in the current outcomes assessment movement, analyzed a number of process and outcomes studies, which resulted in significant improvements in care in a number of provider organizations, mostly hospitals.[10] This "annotated chartbook," as he called it, is perhaps the best example available of how to use outcomes and process data to assess the quality of health care. In summing up, he concluded that process and outcomes measures should be regarded as complementary rather than competing approaches: "It is enough to say that process and outcome are members of a symmetrical pair; that neither is inherently more valid than the other, since validity resides in the bond that ties them; that the choice

---

7.   S. N. D. North, "Seventy-Five Years of Progress in Statistics: The Outlook for the Future," *The History of Statistics: Their Development and Progress*, ed. John Koren (New York: Macmillan, for the American Statistical Association, 1918), 30-31.

8.   See, for example, Avedis Donabedian, *The Criteria and Standards of Quality* (Ann Arbor, MI: Health Administration Press, 1982), 21, citing Ernest A. Codman, *A Study in Hospital Efficiency* (Boston: Thomas Todd Co., Printers, circa 1916).

9.   See, for example, Brackenridge, *Medical Selection of Life Risks*, op. cit.

10. Avedis Donabedian, *The Methods and Findings of Quality Assessment and Monitoring: An Illustrated Analysis* (Ann Arbor, MI: Health Administration Press, 1985).

of one in preference to the other is mainly based on practical considerations, such as the availability, costliness, accuracy and timeliness of information; and that where possible there is safety and persuasiveness in obtaining information about both."[11]

In the early 1980s, HCFA began publishing mortality statistics, by diagnostic group, for all hospitals which participate in the Medicare program. Adjustments were made for various risk factors, based on the administrative data at HCFA. These adjustments included demographics of age and sex (not race), medical condition based on the ICD-9 code for the reason for admission, comorbidities as defined by collections of secondary diagnoses, and health history as indicated by prior admissions with a discharge within the prior six months. As the modeling evolved, it included more refinement of the reason for admission for any ICD-9 code that had occurred more than 300 times per year. The source and type of admission were also included in the models; but they were subject to considerable problems, as they were not considered part of the payment checking process and were, therefore, not edited by HCFA on submission. Hence local variation in the attention paid to these codes undermined the very valuable information about whether the admission was via emergency department, physician referral, or other sources.

HCFA's efforts gave rise in turn to several methods of adjusting for difference in severity of the patients' condition upon admission to the hospital. Taking these differences into account, there are, in turn, a number of ways to interpret the data to gain insight into differences in providers' performance and changing patterns of mortality. Fleming et al. reviewed some of these methods, using the 1992 release of 1990 mortality statistics.[12]

Fleming et al. went on to evaluate, as a case study, the performance of one outlier hospital in terms of predicted and observed mortality rates and mortality model determinants. Proportionately more patients treated in the study hospital were women and had cerebrovascular degeneration or chronic renal disease; fewer patients had cardiovascular disease. Substantially more patients from this hospital were transfers from a skilled nursing facility. Fewer patients were admitted through the emergency department.

11. *Ibid.,* 452.

12. Steven T. Fleming, Lanis L. Hicks, and R. Clifton Bailey, "Interpreting the Health Care Financing Administration's Mortality Statistics," *Medical Care* 33, no. 2 (February 1995): 186-201.

Although patients tended to be more seriously ill overall, compared with other hospitals in the country, observed mortality rates were still higher than predicted. Possible explanations Fleming et. al. found for the discrepancy were coding inconsistencies, inability to control adequately for the severity of illness of transfers from skilled nursing facilities, or quality of care problems.

The analysis of changing patterns of mortality can be expanded and extended to provide useful guidance regarding the spread and severity of ailments, not necessarily limited to well-known infectious diseases. For instance, Krakauer and Bailey[13] applied epidemiologic methods to HCFA data to analyze patterns and quality of care offered to Medicare beneficiaries.

Combining mortality statistics with other variables provides additional information. For example, the observation of some clinical variables during hospitalization leads to better explanation and prediction of outcome.[14] In addition, rather than considering simply the occurrence of an event (such as death, recover function, onset of complication, etc.) within a certain time interval, we can also consider the time until the event occurs. If the full-time course is measured, then outcomes that look good in the short term may look bad in the long term, and vice versa. Introduction of time course enables the analyst to separate the long and short-term effects, as was demonstrated in the HCFA mortality model.[15]

Outcomes analysis can also be extended and expanded to yield better understanding of the effects of different treatments for specific ailments,[16] and of patterns of incidence.[17] In the same way as the latter study's

---

13. Henry Krakauer and R. C. Bailey, "Epidemiologic Oversight of the Medical Care Provided to Medicare Beneficiaries," *Statistics in Medicine* 10, no. 4 (April 1991): 521-40.

14. D. W. Smith, M. Pine, R. C. Bailey, B. Jones, A. Brewster, and H. Krakauer, "Using Clinical Variables to Estimate the Risk of Patient Mortality," comment in *Medical Care* 31, no. 5 (May, 1993): 469-70.

15. Henry Krakauer, R. C. Bailey, K. J. Skellan, J. D. Stewart, A. J. Hartz, E. M. Kuhn, and A. A. Rimm, "Evaluation of the HCFA Model for the Analysis of Mortality Following Hospitalization," *Health Services Research* 27, no. 3 (August 1992): 317-35.

16. For example, Henry Krakauer, E. K. Spees, W. K. Vaughn, J. S. Grauman, J. P. Summe, and R. C. Bailey, "Assessment of Prognostic Factors and Projection of Outcomes in Renal Transplantation," *Transplantation* 36, no. 4 (October 1983): 372-78.

17. For example, Eleanor R. Cross and R. C. Bailey, "Prediction of Areas Endemic for Schistosomiasis Through Use of Discriminant Analysis of Environmental Data," *Military Medicine* 149, no. 1 (January 1984): 28-30.

consideration of different incidence in different geographic areas, we can also analyze rates of incidence in different populations, provided each patient's population membership is accurately coded in the data set.

Especially for ailments which are not usually fatal, outcomes analysis can improve understanding not only of treatments' effectiveness, but also of underlying clinical science.[18] Professional associations' efforts to develop treatment guidelines have generated both improved data and analytical innovations, as well as the intended recommendations for improved treatment.[19] The health care profession in general has come to view outcomes analysis as an essential component of assessing quality of care.[20]

There have been promising efforts to develop key indicators of health status and health care access. These include the Institute of Medicine report, cited earlier, and a chapter in an American Association for the Advancement of Science study on a human rights approach to health care reform.[21] Indicators offer the best prospect for meaningful international comparisons, at the cost of focusing on a small subset of all the components of health status.

Another such effort, somewhat broader in scope of data but narrower in the population covered, is the "national report card" on health care quality being developed by the National Committee for Quality Assurance (in health care), known as NCQA. NCQA is an independent, nonprofit Washington, D.C.-based organization which assesses the quality of managed care plans. A partnership among purchasers, consumers and health plans, it includes approximately 550 managed care organizations as members; it exists to provide industry-wide services and analyses which are

---

18. Joyce C. West and Deborah Zarin, "Practice-Relevant Research Findings: APA's Psychiatric Research Network," *Behavioral Healthcare Tomorrow*, May-June 1995, 38-39.

19. American Academy of Orthopaedic Surgeons, Committee on Outcome Studies, "Fundamentals of Outcome Research," (Rosemont, IL: American Academy of Orthopaedic Surgeons, 1994). L. E. Kazis, "Health Outcomes Assessments in Medicine: History, Applications, and New Directions," *Advances in Internal Medicine* 36, (1991): 109-30.

20. Joint Commission on Accreditation of Healthcare Organizations, "A Guide to Establishing Programs for Assessing Outcomes in Clinical Settings," (Chicago, IL: Joint Commission on Accreditation of Healthcare Organizations, 1994).

21. Thomas B. Jabine, "Indicators for Monitoring Access to Basic Health Care as a Human Right," *Health Care Reform: A Human Rights Approach*, ed. Audrey R. Chapman (Washington, D.C.: Georgetown University Press, 1994).

beyond the scope of individual managed care providers. NCQA is now updating its standardized Healthplan Employer Data and Information Set (HEDIS), including reporting standards for all its members, to facilitate comparisons and trend monitoring in the future. The member health plans use these data in their efforts to select more cost-effective forms of care.[22]

When we have data on patterns of care, however, we can also infer patterns of noncare, if patients' origins are accurately identified. For example, area-wide data on utilization of common types of care, if it includes accurate origin data, can be compared with overall population densities and locations to identify apparently underrepresented locales. Census data on these areas support inferences about the nature of the subpopulations which thus appear to be underserved. One study utilizing this approach, which was based primarily on providers' billing records rather than the kinds of outcomes data sources we have considered here, ultimately foundered on the poor quality of diagnosis and treatment coding in these records.[23] Nevertheless, the analytical approach is promising, if applied to better data.

So we see that outcomes data can be useful in monitoring rights to universality and nondiscrimination in health care. These uses, however, are subject to a number of data quality problems and analytical difficulties, to which we now turn our attention.

Quality and Limitations of Some Outcomes Data

The HCFA Standard Analytic File covers inpatient and outpatient Medicare claims, and the HCFA MedPar file includes skilled nursing home claims, as well as additional hospital inpatient claims. These data sets include patient demographics, diagnoses, procedures, and dates of services; MedPar also includes tests and length of stay. The data are based on bill transactions and are fairly complete for the Medicare population. There is one exception: the managed care portion of the Medicare population has been funded through various special demonstration projects and – more recently – most often via risk contracts. The consequence of this form of

22. Margaret E. O'Kane (President, NCQA), panelist comments in "Managed Care Incentives and the Market for Better Data and Information," National Committee on Vital and Health Statistics 45th Anniversary Symposium, Washington, D.C., July 1995.

23. Joy Clay, D. A. Heckert, W. C. Schmidt, D. A. Samuelson, P. M. Ward, and S. D. Skinner, "Policy Issues in Indigent Health Care: A Case Study" (paper presented at Southeast Conference on Public Administration [SECOPA] conference, October 1992).

funding is that the billing transactions are no longer available for this growing sector of the Medicare population. The files maintained by HCFA are linked to the administrative data at the Social Security Administration. The need to terminate payments to beneficiaries upon death provides a strong incentive to capture date of death or at least to know the month in which death occurs; consequently, the mortality outcome is very reliable. This is in contrast to most state and provider data sources, where very little effort is made to capture dates of death outside of the institution or the state.

Billing data provides fairly comprehensive information on the coded principal diagnosis or reason for hospital admission for acute care. There is also information on secondary diagnoses. The files use identifiers, so multiple events comprising both inpatient (Part A) and outpatient (Part B) are known. By linking records, a prior history can be constructed and summarized, including additional important information, such as risk adjustment factors. Also, outcomes such as time to readmission or other events can be created from the linked records. Since the population is well-known, population estimates can be used for monitoring. This is a consequence of the fact that there is an enrolled population and specific information, such as address, sex, race and scope of enrollment (Part A, or part B, and plan number for risk Health Maintenance Organizations.)

HCFA's enrollment data base includes a "race" variable, obtained from Social Security enrollment. It is usually either self-reported or reported by the enrolling official. This variable is of uneven quality; it depends on subjective judgment and on the cultural environment at the time and place of enrollment. The Medicare Current Beneficiary survey contains more information on race and ethnicity, but only for a sample of Medicare beneficiaries. This sample also has income information for the beneficiary. It differs from many other sources of income data (surveys) in that the questions are about the income of the beneficiary and spouse, not total household income; this complicates comparisons with other income data.

These data can be linked to other government data on income and ethnicity using Social Security number and other identifiers. It is technically feasible to link Internal Revenue Service (IRS) income data to Medicare data and to link to occupational data from Social Security. In practice, this has not generally been done, and the source agencies have resisted such linkages as a matter of policy. One reason is that Medicare data is freely available because of research provisions in the enabling legislation, so linking would involve significant risk of disclosure of individuals' income and occupation. Also, since these linkages have not been done and analyzed, experience with other linkages indicates that probably some unforeseen technical problems would come to light once a linkage was attempted.

Identifying race or ethnicity is very difficult because it is critically dependent on how the question is posed and how the possible answers are defined. The person's own racial self-identification may change with circumstances or over time; it may differ from other persons' perception; and both may differ from a "true" identification based on genetic analysis. In recent years, registration of births has switched from race of father to race of mother. There has also been a large increase in multiracial, multicultural births, which present serious problems in operational definitions, as the variable in its usual form forces the choice of one major racial or ethnic group: black Hispanics, for example, are shown as either black or Hispanic, but not both.

Income is also complex, as many sources of financial support (such as alimony, welfare, and some business and investment income) may not be considered income for tax purposes. Generally the data about ethnicity is not reliable, and the links to income are not made as a matter of policy. These problems are present in state and local data, as well.

The Veterans Administration (VA), in contrast to HCFA, also has good data on medical treatments and conditions, but does not have an enrolled population. The population seeks care on an as-needed basis. In addition, some veterans are covered by private health plans and prefer to seek treatment outside the VA system. Hence any population estimates from these data sets are difficult.

The lack of population data greatly complicates monitoring universality and nondiscrimination in access. If the population is fully accounted for, then health status and outcomes for the entire population have value as evidence of whether some large subpopulations are underserved, even if individual records do not include race and income data. If one wishes to focus on specific subpopulations defined by race, gender, religious belief, ethnic group, or occupation, then the file would ideally be linked or linkable to these classification variables at the individual level; however, even linkages at the group level (for example, 15% of this regional group is known to be black) permit some inferences. These inferences can be made more precisely and reliably when population proportions on all variables of interest are known.

State data sources are more inclusive, especially for the under-65 poor, since the Medicaid program (assistance for poor people in paying for health care) is administered by the states. The Medicaid data, assembled nationally, include patient demographics, diagnoses, tests, procedures, and dates of service. Various states have nursing home data as well, including the same data elements, plus measures of functional status and detailed measures of selected conditions. These data sets, however, do not track migration among states and may, therefore, miss deaths or other key events; this creates considerable difficulty with continuity for monitoring purposes. In addition, eligibility for Medicaid can change from month to month, so key events for monitoring are easily missed. Linkages to national data sets which include income and occupation data would be harder, since the best national-level identifier, the Social Security number, is more likely to be absent or miscoded in data sets collected by institutions which do not have to have a correct Social Security number to get paid.

Individual providers usually don't have a defined population. Hence population estimates are impossible. Furthermore, outcomes data are limited to short-term outcomes, since follow-up is generally difficult, expensive and incomplete. Managed care providers do have defined populations, but transitions among providers in and out of the managed care system may be frequent. In all these cases, both race/ethnicity and income data are usually not available, either directly or by linkage to other data sets.

Medicare allows monthly transitions among providers. If there are frequent transitions, then the summary of these frequencies may be an important indicator to monitor. Other outcome measures will be compromised by the transitions.

Systems for monitoring must factor in the bias inherent in the system. Some systems will be selective against the unhealthy or unfit. This is true of employer-sponsored plans, since there is a selection factor for being employed. Systems for the subsets of the population are biased in many unknown ways. Consequently, monitoring based on information from such systems may be informative regarding the status within the system, but not informative regarding the access to health care across systems. Since the U.S. has a heterogeneous population, health care system and data systems, monitoring of the right to health care across all age groups and populations within the U.S. is limited to our common systems of vital health statistics. Even these systems contain considerable state-to-state variation, such as the differing requirements in who specifies cause of death.

A recent report prepared for the Agency for Health Care Policy and Research (AHCPR) summarized efforts to compare these and a number of

228 \ *Moving Toward Universality*

other data sources for quality monitoring. The other data sources included the National Hospital Discharge Survey, which has broad population coverage and provides certain medical information in a readily comparable form, but omits much of the patient demographics; the Kaiser Center Research Database, which provides unusually good outpatient information, but only for a not-necessarily-representative subset of the population; and a few large health plans' claims-based files, which to some extent duplicate and to some extent supplement the public-source data, again for a subset of the population. However, as the authors pointed out, although these data bases have been used for performance measurement, "Many measures cannot be used with these databases because the needed data are unavailable in the form required by the measure." They go on to state that increasing use of the data for performance measurement will no doubt lead to improvements in the data bases, which will make performance measures easier to construct and use.[24] We can make a similar prediction of what would happen if these data sets were used for monitoring of universality and nondiscrimination in access to health care; but the same reasoning also implies that these data sets are unlikely to be of much help in their present form, since they were never designed to answer the questions in which we are interested.

Even with a national health care system, some of these difficulties remain. In Canada, for example, data on health services are generally fairly extensive within a province, but the funding system is such that information does not freely pass from province to province. This complicates monitoring statistics. The British health care system seems to lack a central file of health data that can be used. This also seems to be true of Sweden. The race/ethnicity and income/occupation variables have the same definitional problems and the same difficulties with linkage to other data sets that we noted earlier in our discussion of HCFA data.

More global monitoring is achieved from sample surveys; these surveys can also include race/ethnicity and income/occupation questions, at the risk of reducing respondents' cooperation and veracity. However, monitoring from surveys tends to be short on solid outcome measures. Sample surveys generally cannot provide the detailed regional level summaries, such as

---

24. Center for Health Policy Studies, "Understanding and Choosing Clinical Performance Measures for Quality Improvement: Development of a Typology" (report prepared for the Agency for Health Care Policy Research, U.S. Department of Health and Human Services, 31 January 1995, pp. 6-5 and 6-6).

state-by-state or institution-specific summaries. Nevertheless, sampling may be the only effective way to prime the process for the formation of national monitoring systems.

Analytical Considerations and Limitations

The variety of sources of outcomes data in the U. S. provides opportunities for cross-checking somewhat independent data sources, but it also hinders combining data for more global analysis. Comparisons between data sets collected by different agencies are complicated by differences in reporting practices and standards. As we noted earlier, even the definitions of outcome may be inconsistent, and coding of diagnoses and treatments is much more inconsistent.

There are also trade-offs between breadth of coverage and depth of detail. Studies of individual diseases tend to include especially accurate data on the variables of interest, but the narrow focus of such studies usually precludes comparisons among regional, ethnic or socioeconomic groups at the national level. Similarly, studies which utilize additional clinical variables are likely to include them for only a fraction of the population of interest. If this fraction is chosen by a suitable sampling scheme, we can make inferences about the other members of the population; but neglect in the sampling design can make such inferences meaningless. At the very least, we would want to have good data on "matching variables," such as membership in subpopulation of interest, for all members of the population to be able to determine whether the sampled members were atypical in some significant way. Unfortunately for our purposes, such "matching variables" data are unlikely to be included in many research-oriented studies.

When available, "matching variables" present other difficulties. Racial, ethnic and income data are sensitive and subject to various interpretations. Cultural and language differences complicate definition of health indicators, pain, degree of disability, and many other factors one might wish to consider in risk adjustment, assessment of vulnerability, and matching.

Also, when one attempts to analyze data in a way or for a purpose not contemplated when the data were collected, problems often appear. A common example is the unpleasant discoveries analysts often encounter when trying to use medical information from billing records. For instance, the study of patient origins and facilities utilization in Shelby County,

Tennessee, cited earlier,[25] found that many providers simply did not have accurate diagnosis data for most of the patients whose pay sources did not insist on such data and review it. Data which are not used soon after collection usually are not verified; data which are not verified are usually unreliable. The Shelby County study also noted considerable difficulty in tracking patients through the multiple-provider system, since patients did not have unique identifiers. This problem was especially acute for children from low-income households, as these patients were less likely to have Social Security numbers, stable addresses, or even consistent surnames.

Even for data sets based on health plan membership, for which patient identification and data verification are not as troublesome, diversity of reporting standards among providers can cause considerable difficulty. NCQA, in its effort to combine and compare data from its member organizations, identified inconsistent reporting standards as a top-priority problem. The NCQA's working groups became increasingly aware of difficulties in comparing diagnostic categories, treatments and outcomes among providers, as the data reporting practices were so different as to require massive follow-up effort to make comparisons meaningful.[26]

The success of NCQA's efforts would not produce a panacea either. The utility of such restricted data sets for overall monitoring is limited because of the differences between subscribers of managed care plans and the population as a whole. In the U.S., where both plans and subscribers have considerable freedom of choice, these differences are highly significant.

Even if data inconsistencies and limitations could be resolved, there remain serious definitional issues. For some ailments, especially those which are rarely fatal, quality of life after treatment is what is important. It is possible for the health care system to produce an unacceptable result, even if each provider does a good job: one well-known example (hypothetical, but consistent with real experience) is that of a preventable death from cancer because a radiology report got lost.[27] This is, of course, precisely why tracking processes alone, without considering outcomes, is insufficient; but it also indicates the complexity of assessing just what health care

---

25. See Clay et al., "Policy Issues in Indigent Health Care."

26. Randall K. Spoeri, "NCQA, HEDIS 2.0, and the Report Card Project: A Partnership for Quality Improvement in Managed Care" (presented at the Annual Meeting of the American Statistical Association, 1995).

27. Donald M. Berwick, A. Blanton Godfrey, and Jane Roessner, *Curing Health Care* (San Francisco: Jossey-Bass, 1990), Chapter 1.

processes and activities contribute to outcomes. Both process-based and outcomes-based monitoring are additionally complicated by time lags: although we know immediately what treatment processes were used (this is one of the attractions of process-based monitoring), the full effects of processes – combined, inevitably, with other factors we may not have measured – usually will not be known until some time afterward.

Furthermore, monitoring a right to access to health care will be confounded with environmental and occupational policy. Our engineering systems (civil and sanitation engineering, for example) provide infrastructure for drinking water and sanitation that improve health in many aspects; but if improperly maintained, they can go astray, in which case these very systems can jeopardize the health of many. Occupational exposures to harmful agents and community exposure can have important effects, from improved dental health via sodium fluoride in the water systems to harmful effects of lead in water pipes and of asbestos dust in the workplace. Since health outcome measures are inherently confounded by these environmental and occupational factors, even a comprehensive, complete system of statistics on health care would leave many open questions about the true fairness and universality of the country's overall approach to its citizens' health. Resolving these questions will require the improvement of data on environmental and occupational factors.

These difficulties are magnified several-fold when we try to use indicators to compare among regions or cultures. Consider, for example, an isolated rural area populated by two different splinter religious groups. Suppose that all health care is provided by faith healers, who are mostly ineffective but widely available. While this area's overall health status would be poor, it would have commendable universality and nondiscrimination in its provision of health care: everybody gets pretty much the same services.

Now suppose that the county health department opens a clinic in the area, but most people in the area would need cars to get there; and suppose that one group's leader permits the use of motorized vehicles, while the other group's leader forbids them. Now many members of the first group would generally utilize health care services which remained unused by members of the other group. Presumably our monitoring group would consider these services desirable (with or without asking the people in the area!), so the county would now be found to have a serious violation of both universality and nondiscrimination. If we considered only process measures based in the clinic, such as a cross-tabulation by group of the people who get treated there, a naive monitoring organization might recommend that the county improve its human rights performance by closing the clinic.

Note, however, that adding outcomes measures adds some information but does not completely clarify the situation. Outcomes measures would show that the more mobile group had longer life expectancies and reduced mortality and morbidity from certain diseases. Only by combining these outcomes measures with information about the difference in treatment can we really understand what caused the difference. In this case, the best policy would be to add one or more other clinics, or to buy some cars and make house calls, extending the benefits to more members of the immobile group – assuming that they want the services. (Such a policy might be limited by other factors, of course, such as lack of resources. Neither our measures nor the processes and resources they measure will ever be perfect.)

This example illustrates both the difficulty and the necessity of using outcomes measures as part of monitoring. Outcomes measures alone cannot tell us why disparities exist; without outcomes measures, we can notice disparities in processes, and perhaps relate these disparities to group membership, but find ourselves unable to determine which process provides better health care.

While the benefit of the new service was assumed to be significant and obvious in this example, it is not at all obvious in other cases; and in many real-life situations, the difference would be confounded with other factors, such as differences in environmental conditions, occupational hazards, eating habits, and so on. In such cases, only noticing a significant difference in outcomes between populations would have directed our attention to the difference in processes.

For clinical studies of diseases, medical outcomes are meant to be well-defined and unambiguous measures, or events that can be used to evaluate a clinical intervention. Death within a specified time interval is a widely recognized and generally available measure; but this may not always be well-defined for chronic diseases and some medical procedures. If one focuses on whether or not a patient died within a preselected time, there may be a temptation to prolong life, perhaps at considerable cost in suffering, to make the numbers look good. Using a more complete measure, such as time from treatment to death, is more informative and less likely to result in a "gamed" or distorted result.

We must recognize, therefore, that outcomes analysis takes place in the context of understanding how health care processes and providers affect people; it does not and cannot replace such understanding. Statistical indicators defined or interpreted without understanding of the goals and processes of measurement can easily mislead, and they can easily be used to mislead.

A closely related concern is expressed in the old industrial engineering maxim, "What gets measured gets done." Activities which are important but difficult to measure may be slighted in a system overly focused on a limited set of indicators. Similarly, measurements which affect payment are more likely to be done well and quickly than those which do not: for example, effective treatments based on diet or lifestyle may take far longer than new medications to be medically evaluated, simply because the financial incentives to evaluate medications are so much greater. (Of course, another reason is that studies of medications are easier to control.)

Even when both the outcomes measures and the processes are clearly defined, we must still consider the scope of effect we can reasonably expect health care to have. In a highly developed country with generally good health care, deaths preventable by direct medical intervention constitute a rather small minority – perhaps 10% in the U.S. – of all deaths.[28] Should a region with higher death rates from, for example, cardiovascular disease be considered to violate its citizens' human rights because they have chosen less healthy diets and lifestyles than citizens of other regions? If not, then our measures must reflect only those deaths which are clearly related to universality and nondiscrimination in access to and quality of care.

It is critical, therefore, that any measures we use be based on a well-defined theory of the processes and outcomes being assessed, so that there is a clear context or basis for comparison. Dimensions of measurement must be driven by the theory, not just a selection of the visible numbers that are most available (and consequently most subject to tampering, or most responsive to tampering with the processes, to the detriment of both the information system and the patients.)

The measures must also have a theoretical context that includes understanding of variation. How much variation is associated with the measurement technique? How much variation is associated with the process or

---

28. J. Michael McGinniss, and W. Foege, "Actual Causes of Death in the United States," *Journal of the American Medical Association*, 10 November 1993, 1207-12.

intervention? Is the change following the intervention much bigger than we could have expected by chance just from the random variations in the measure? Without such an understanding, we cannot use the outcomes as an indicator of current status or as a guide to future improvements.

Potential Harm

While outcomes data clearly provide many benefits, widespread use of outcomes data has the potential to be harmful in a number of ways. Inappropriate disclosure of raw data, without adjustment for such factors as severity of condition upon first examination, can lead to poor choices of treatments, thereby harming both patients and providers. In a setting in which patients or payers pay close attention to summary indices of treatment effectiveness, such disclosures could also induce some patients to switch from better to poorer providers, again harming patients, providers and payers. These were among the considerations which led HCFA to abandon publication of its annual outcomes report, cited earlier – although there is ample room for disagreement as to whether simply abandoning the report, and many of the associated data quality efforts, was the correct response.

If society becomes more attuned to outcomes-based effectiveness indices, laws could be enacted requiring disclosure of more raw information. Such legislation, however, could have a negative effect: the potential for compulsory disclosure of data intended for in-house quality reviews, and the potential for legal actions using such data, could cause providers to refuse to collect such data at all, thereby severely hampering quality improvement. Again patients, providers and payers would all be harmed.

An even more serious possibility, from the public policy standpoint, is the potential outcomes data could have to enable third-party payers to restrict access by some patients to some providers, or even to some types of care, for financial rather than medical reasons. In turn, providers might systematically distort their reports of outcomes and related data to protect their patients' financial interests – and their own. There is some evidence that such misreporting does occur now, in the U.S., for mental ailments.[29]

---

29. Kathryn Rost, G. R. Smith, D. B. Matthews, and E. Guise, "The Deliberate Misdiagnosis of Major Depression by Primary Care Providers," *Archives of Family Medicine* 3 (1994): 333-337. Carla D. Willams, and K. Rost, "The Deliberate Misdiagnosis of Major Depression in Primary Care," *Proceedings of the 25th Public*

Obviously any difficulties one encounters in intergroup comparisons are magnified when the scope of analysis is expanded to include many countries and cultures. The very definition of "health care" varies among cultures, as do a number of lifestyle factors (such as diet, exercise patterns, acceptance or avoidance of accident risks) which affect life expectancy but do not fall within most definitions of health care. Hence international comparisons, not adjusted for differences in other factors which affect health, could be extremely misleading.

Broad restrictions on collection, use and dissemination of outcomes data pose other problems. Policy analyses using outcomes data generally fall outside the usual definitions of "medical research," and may consequently run afoul of broadly drafted rules intended to protect privacy. Strict restriction of dissemination and use of such data, on the other hand, could preclude innovative epidemiological and public health analyses which would improve many people's health. For example, according to at least one authoritative source, the spread of AIDS via homosexual activity within the U.S. was aggravated by public officials' reluctance to discuss high-risk sexual practices openly and candidly, and by gay men's resistance to public health advisories.[30] If, in addition, the diagnosis itself had been suppressed, in many cases to protect the patients' privacy regarding sexual preference, tracking the disease's spread and identifying its means of transmission would also have taken much longer, increasing its eventual toll even more.

This example illustrates the difficulty of finding the socially optimal balance between collecting and analyzing data to improve public health and protecting against harmful use and disclosure. Overprotection of privacy and individual choice makes identification of disease agents and vectors of spread take longer, resulting in a bigger and worse epidemic. Underprotection, in addition to violating individual rights directly, undermines quality of data and credibility of results and recommendations. Either way, both public health and individual rights suffer.

Health Conference on Records and Statistics (Washington, D.C.: U.S. Department of Health and Human Services, Centers for Disease Control, 1995), 60-62.

30. Randy Shilts, *And the Band Played On* (St. Martin's Press, 1987; revised edition: Penguin Books, 1988, especially 276-77 of the Penguin version).

Systems Considerations

In addition to the problems of defining measurements, maintaining and improving data quality, and performing meaningful and effective analysis, we need to pay attention to some issues regarding the health information system. In the increasingly specialized environment typical of most developed countries' health care, diagnoses and treatments which used to be performed by one person (usually a physician) may now be divided among several persons with a variety of backgrounds. The growing incidence of complex disorders, which require more collaboration to diagnose and treat, and the movement toward managed care approaches further accelerate this trend.

This means that the completeness and accuracy of the patient's medical record, and of its counterpart in large-scale surveys and similar data bases, will assume much greater importance: in a large and growing number of instances, the record will be the only information shared by all persons who have a role in diagnosis and treatment. These records in larger-scale data sets provide the basis for studies of incidence and spread of disease, effectiveness and cost-effectiveness of treatments, and inter-group differences in treatments and outcomes. Therefore, increased efforts to ensure the accuracy and completeness of medical records will be critical to both cost containment and quality improvement – and, of course, to monitoring as well.

Note that the monitoring thus affected is not limited to human rights. Care managers, payment sources, and medical professionals have exactly the same concerns: which treatments are effective for given ailments? Which are more cost-effective than others? What are the trends and patterns in disease and care which will affect the health care system in the future? Who is covered, and who is excluded? Are some providers doing a better job than others? Do some groups have much better access to the better providers? Thus, for example, the authors of "managed competition" recently concluded, "Attempts at federal health care reform last year showed that the health system data available were neither timely nor accurate." They went on to advocate a federal role in improving and standardizing the national health information system as an essential step toward quality improvement and cost containment in health care.[31]

---

31. Paul Ellwood and Alain C. Enthoven, "'Responsible Choices': The Jackson Hole Group Plan for Health Reform," *Health Affairs* 15, no. 2 (summer 1995) 24-39.

As we have seen, however, some policies and practices create incentives to distort or suppress some of this critical information. Monitoring universality and nondiscrimination in health care will, therefore, be influenced by policy choices: fragmentation and internal competition in the provider system promote inconsistency and incompleteness in the data sets assembled from providers' reports. Consequently, a fragmented and stressed provider system will generally be harder to monitor accurately, offering greater protection to inferior providers. These providers, to the extent that they realize who they are, will have an incentive to resist system improvements which would benefit everyone else. In a country with multiple, competing payment sources, such as the U.S., the same concerns apply to payment sources.

In addition, since data are collected primarily through some sort of interaction with the health care system, we will generally have the worst data about the groups with the poorest access to health care and about the medical conditions for which access to care is most limited. Thus despite likely improvements in data quality and coverage, monitoring progress toward universality in access to health care will be complex and difficult.

While these obstacles are discouraging, we must also remember that the definition and acceptance of other human rights has usually both preceded and stimulated the development of good methods to monitor compliance with those rights. We do not deny a new medical treatment to everyone until it is available to all; similarly, we do not serve society best by refusing to enact rights to access and nondiscrimination in health care, or by refusing to monitor such rights, until we can monitor perfectly (if that were possible!) Statisticians make their living criticizing the available data, and then finding ways to extract valuable information from the inadequate data sets; there is no reason to suppose this subject will be different. Our conclusion is not that monitoring is impossible, but that its difficulty and complexity must be understood, and that adoption of human rights in this area will imply the commitment of significant cost and effort to improve the health information system in general and the monitoring methods in particular.

Summary and Conclusions

We have seen that outcomes data and analysis can provide a vital component of the information one would need in order to monitor universality and nondiscrimination in access to health care. The data available do not make such monitoring easy, however, and the data will generally be worse for exactly those groups and conditions we are most concerned about. Outcomes data collection and analysis also create opportunities for direct harm, as well as for misleading conclusions which may harm individuals and society in more subtle ways. Much additional work will be required to improve data collection and reporting sufficiently to support widely credible monitoring of human rights to universality and nondiscrimination in health care, no matter how those rights are eventually defined; and to implement the appropriate balance between promotion of public health and protection of privacy and confidentiality. Despite the difficulties, however, monitoring would be even more difficult without relying on the outcomes data we can obtain and utilize.

Part Three

Privacy,
Nondiscrimination and Consent

CHAPTER TEN

Introduction and Overview: Privacy, Nondiscrimination and Consent

Paula J. Bruening

Integral to the changes currently taking place in the United States' health care industry is the application of computer technology to the development of a health care information system. While a computerized health care information system is believed to offer opportunities to collect, store and link data in ways beneficial to the health care consumer and the health care delivery system as a whole, implementation of such a system is not without significant challenges and risks. This inquiry explores the potential to establish and employ a universally inclusive health information system that would collect and systematize more and better health data and, at the same time, optimize human rights standards of privacy, nondiscrimination and consent. The first half of this book discusses the challenges posed in designing and using an information system which would monitor the extent to which the goal of universal access to medical care has been attained. The extent to which access to health care is universal; the incidence of discrimination in access to health care; and the quality of health care people receive are considerations essential to this inquiry. The second half of this volume, which this introduction overviews, explores the potential risks of such a health care information system to the fundamental human rights of privacy, nondiscrimination and consent.

The advent of the "information age," bringing with it revolutionary changes in the way information is collected, disseminated, stored, linked, and used, has crucial implications for the evolution of the health care system. Faced with spiraling costs, a strained reimbursement system, and a growing population lacking access to medical care, the health care industry is looking to information technology and its ability to collect, store, transfer and link data, to offer new sources of information to address these problems. Yet even as these capabilities are recognized, it also is clear that computerization of this information poses challenges to human rights of privacy and traditional concepts of consent.

The vision of a computerized system of medical records is not new. Indeed, over the past 30 years, academic, commercial and government research has produced successful pilot programs and commercial implementations of parts of comprehensive digital health information systems. A report of the Institute of Medicine, released in 1991, entitled *The Computer-based Patient Record: An Essential Technology for Health Care,* explores in detail the potential benefits of a system of computerized medical information on health care, while also outlining the fundamental components of such an information system.[1] In 1994, a system of electronic medical records was a linchpin of the Clinton administration's proposal for health care reform.[2]

A high performance computing network would allow linkage of hospitals, doctors' offices, and community clinics. Patient records, including medical and biological data, would be available to authorized health care professionals anytime, anywhere over these networks, allowing health care providers to access immediately, from any location, the most up-to-date patient data. Data could in the future include not only textual records but would also incorporate medical images from clinical or laboratory tests. From an administrative standpoint, such a system could provide efficiency gains and cost savings. Most often cited is the projected savings in administrative costs involved in processing an estimated five million health care claims per day. It is believed that a network would allow improved management of and access to health care-related information, and reduce costs for processing insurance claims through electronic payment and reimbursement. High-speed networks could also enable medical collaboration through use of interactive, multimedia telemedicine technologies over distances.[3]

1.   See Institute of Medicine, *The Computer-Based Patient Record: An Essential Technology for Health Care*, eds. Richard S. Dick and Elaine B. Steen (Washington, D.C.: National Academy Press, 1991).

2.   *Health Security Act of 1993*, 103rd Cong., 1st sess., S. 2357.

3.   Office of Technology Assessment, *Protecting Privacy in Computerized Medical Information,* OTA-TCT-576 (Washington, D.C.: U.S. Government Printing Office, September 1993), 16.

Many hospitals have computerized their administrative or clinical records; many insurance claims and orders for supplies are submitted electronically; many research materials are distributed over computer networks; and electronic distribution of consumer health information has begun. However, there is still no system that comprehensively facilitates the flow of all types of health information and systematically addresses the needs of clinicians, administrators, policymakers, human rights advocates, patients, consumers, and most importantly for purposes of this volume, researchers.[4]

Thus far the application of computer technology in the health care industry has been limited to its use in discrete departments within hospitals. Computers are widely deployed, but not widely connected. Data is still stored and conveyed primarily in paper form. Health information is rarely converted to digital form and shared among the clinics, primary care offices, hospitals and critical care units, nor among the population-based health services that address community-wide health issues. Computers are typically used to administer specific, limited types of health information, but are not linked into an infrastructure that might allow broader efficiencies or higher quality health care.[5]

This stage in the establishment of health information is important to the interests of human rights, as it presents technical experts with the opportunity to design systems that will protect human rights. But design of such safeguards is only possible to the extent that protective guidelines and protocols have been considered and developed by policymakers.[6]

The human rights issues of privacy, nondiscrimination and consent spotlighted by computerization of health information are not new; these issues have long been pertinent to information maintained on paper records systems as well. The ethical obligations of health care workers to protect the confidentiality of sensitive medical information have been the subject of discussion since the Hippocratic Oath. Issues of appropriate use of medical information by parties both inside and outside of the health system have formed the basis of proposed U.S. legislation intended to protect individuals from discrimination.[7] The question of informed consent long

---

4. Office of Technology Assessment, *Telemedicine: Bringing Healthcare On-line*, OTA-ITC-624 (Washington, D.C.: U.S. Government Printing Office, September 1995), 9.

5. *Ibid.*

6. Office of Technology Assessment, *Protecting Privacy*, 16.

has been debated in the context of medical research and treatment.[8] Rather than create these issues, computerization sharpens their focus, prompts reconsideration of their resolution and provides, at least in part, the potential for technological solutions.

Privacy

Implicit in much of the discussion of human rights is a tension between a traditional concept of privacy and the perceived need of the health care system and society at large for access to certain kinds of individual and aggregate health care data. As described by Samuel Warren and Louis Brandeis in an 1890 article that first enunciated the concept of privacy as a legal interest deserving independent protection, privacy is "the right to be let alone."[9] In spite of its breadth, this view has been influential for nearly a century. However, in the 1960s, 1970s and 1980s, the evolution of the common law pertaining to reproductive and sexual liberties[10] inspired further and more sophisticated inquiry into the meaning of privacy. Recognizing the proliferation of information technology, in 1973 the Department of Health, Education and Welfare commissioned a report entitled *Records, Computers and the Rights of Citizens,*[11] which recommended enactment of the legislation, which became the *Privacy Act of 1974,*[12] and the establishment of the Privacy Protection Study Commission.

Historically, the health care provider's obligation to protect the confidentiality of patient information is traced to the Oath of Hippocrates, written between the Sixth Century B.C.E. and the First Century A.C.E., which states:

---

7.   *The Americans with Disabilities Act, U.S. Code*, vol 42, sec. 12101 (1989).

8.   See *Principles of Biomedical Ethics,* 2nd ed., eds. Tom L. Beauchamp and James F. Childress (New York, NY: Oxford University Press, 1983).

9.   Warren & Brandeis, "The Right to Privacy," *Harvard Law Review*, 4 (1890): 193.

10.   See, for example, *Griswold v. Connecticut*, 381 US 479 (1965) and *Roe v. Wade*, 410 US 113 (1973).

11.   Advisory Committee on Automated Personal Data Systems, Department of Health and Human Services, *Computers and Citizens Rights* (Washington, D.C.: U.S. Government Printing Office, 1973).

12.   Public Law 93-579, 93rd Cong., 2nd sess., *Privacy Act of 1974.*

What I may see or hear in the course of the treatment or even outside of the treatment in regard to the life of men, which on no account one must spread abroad, I will keep to myself. . . .

Confidentiality requirements for physicians were formulated differently in later ethical codes. First adopted in 1847, the American Medical Association's Code of Ethics in 1980 required that:

A physician shall respect the rights of patients, colleagues and of other health professionals, and shall safeguard patient confidences within the constraints of the law.[13]

Recent policy statements of the AMA more clearly detail the responsibilities of physicians to protect patient rights to confidentiality in the medical record, setting forth particular instances when the obligation to safeguard patient confidences is subject to exceptions for legal and ethical reasons.[14]

The American Hospital Association's Patient's Bill of Rights frames this responsibility within the framework of the need to share certain kinds of information. The patient has the right: ". . .to expect that all communications and records pertaining to his/her care will be treated as confidential by the hospital and any other parties entitled to review certain information in these records."

These policies underscore the reality that a patient's right to privacy in his or her information is not absolute. Information has always been shared among many professionals – physicians, nurses, therapist, and laboratory technologists – who are involved in delivery of health care. Administrators and managers of health care institutions require information to develop budgets, measure productivity and costs, assess market position, monitor quality of care and allocate resources. Increased federal involvement in health care has resulted in greater need by the government for medical information; government programs to control quality and limit fraud, abuse, and waste have needs for medical records. In addition to these health care-related demands, employers, insurers, and others wish to use health care information for non-health-related purposes.[15]

---

13. *Code of Medical Ethics* (Washington, D.C.: The American Medical Association, 1980).

14. *Code of Medical Ethics,* Current Opinions (Washington, D.C.: The American Medical Association, 1992).

15. Office of Technology Assessment, *Protecting Privacy,* 10.

Nondiscrimination

Among the human rights potentially affected by the establishment of health information systems is universality, which is based on the recognition of the intrinsic value and worth of all human beings. More comprehensive and better quality information collected could enable researchers to better understand current impediments to access to health care, facilitating inclusion of populations who do not have full access to the health care system.

Yet these vulnerable populations are often those who wish to hide from the health information system and who may decide to "opt out" by misrepresenting their identity or status. The reason is that the very information, which, if collected, might aid in making health care available to underserved or vulnerable groups, can also be the basis for discrimination. Medical information can affect such basic life activities as getting married, securing employment, obtaining insurance or driving a car.[16] Medical conditions have long served as the basis for discriminatory practices, making it difficult to participate in these activities. Patients with AIDS, cancer, epilepsy and other diseases have been subjected to discrimination by employers, landlords and mortgage lenders.[17] Because of its highly sensitive nature, improper disclosure of medical information can result in loss of business opportunities, compromise to financial status, damage to reputation, harassment and personal humiliation.

The nonuniversal nature of the health care delivery and reimbursement system in the United States adds to the concern about discrimination. Health insurers, pressured by economic concerns, may exclude high risk patients from coverage, rendering an increasing number of persons "medically uninsurable."[18] This problem is exacerbated by the new capabilities of genetic testing, which not only reveal information about the patient as he or she is, but about his of her potential future condition. Without policy guidelines, a more comprehensive databank of health information could worsen this situation.[19]

---

16. Alan Westin, *Computers, Health Records, and Citizen Rights* (Washington, D.C.: U.S. Government Printing Office, 1976), 9.

17. S. Rept. 101-116 on *The Americans With Disabilities Act, U.S. Code*, vol. 42, sec. 12101 (1989).

18. Mary Ann Bailey, "Guidelines and Mechanisms for Regulating Access to Data: Private Health Insurance Issues," in this volume.

19. *Ibid.*

Consent

The patient's ability to exercise rights in their health information have traditionally been founded on principles of informed consent. Physicians generally must obtain patient consent before disclosing patient records to third persons. Medical and research codes, as well as federal regulations, have traditionally emphasized the elements of disclosure, voluntariness, comprehension and competence to consent. For there to be informed consent to medical treatment, the act of consent must be genuinely voluntary, and there must be adequate disclosure of information to the patient about what is to be done. Patients must comprehend what they are being told about the procedure or treatment, and be competent to consent to the procedure.

This model of informed consent requires communication of information and comprehension by the patient of what he or she is being told, so that informed consent to disclosure of medical information arguably is possible only when patients are familiar with the data contained in their records and understand what they are consenting to disclose. Because many patients are neither granted access to their medical records nor apprised of which portions of the record are accessible to others, most patients are ill-equipped to make intelligent choices about authorizing disclosures, and in emergency situations, patients often are not competent to consent. The high cost of health care generally leaves patients little choice about relinquishing health information to health insurers, rendering the "voluntary" aspect of informed consent a fiction. Further, such an approach to release of information fails to recognize the intrinsic role of health care information in the health care system – for insurance claims reimbursement, for medical research, for outcomes studies, and for public health analysis.

Alternative approaches to the informed consent model most often proposed for protection of personal health data have been based on a system of fair information practices. The basic principles of fair information practices were originally set forth in *Computers and the Rights of Citizens*.[20] The report identified five key principles:

1. There must be no secret personal data record-keeping system;

2. There must be a way for individuals to discover what personal information is recorded and how it is used;

---

20. See Alan Westin, *Computers, Health Records, and Citizen Rights.*

3. There must be a way for individuals to prevent information from being used or made available for other purposes without their consent;

4. There must be a way for individuals to correct or amend a record of information about themselves;

5. An organization creating, maintaining, using or disseminating records of identifiable personal data must assure the reliability of the data for its intended use and must take reasonable precautions to prevent misuses of the data.

Among the benefits of such an approach cited are increased patient awareness of what is in the medical record, as well as increased involvement in health care decisions.[21] But a fair information practices approach also codifies a fundamental shift in thinking about protection of medical information from the traditional notions of *informed consent* by the patient to release of information to one of *patient notification* of the collection and storage of his or her information and the potential uses for that information.

The chapters in this section explore ways in which more and better health information can be systematized, while promoting privacy, nondiscriminatory practices and the patient's ability to exercise control over use of his or her data. At the same time, they recognize a tension inherent in these coincident goals, and suggest that their resolution exists in the notion that an individual gains access to the health care system in exchange for reasonable use of certain medical information by the system for prescribed purposes. The chapters seek resolution of these tensions in a variety of different ways.

The chapter by Fritz Scheuren discusses the recognized capability of electronic health record systems to link records. It examines the potential role of record linkages in a new health information system and how those linkage applications may affect both the rights of individuals to privacy and their rights to access to health care services. Moving beyond the issues within the health system, the chapter examines the implications of linkages between health and other record systems for research and to more problematic and possibly threatening linkages of these records for nonresearch purposes. As an overall approach, the author recommends that attempts at data linkages be undertaken incrementally so that the vulnerabilities of the

---

21. Office of Technology Assessment, *Protecting Privacy*, 3.

linkage system can be thoroughly understood and that inadvertent compromise of human rights can be avoided.

The work of Eleanor Singer, Robert Y. Shapiro and Lawrence R. Jacobs addresses the question of privacy through *public education and awareness*. Their chapter discusses public knowledge, beliefs and attitudes about the privacy of health care information, and considers how people might best be informed with respect to their rights and responsibilities in this regard. The chapter accomplishes this by analyzing the results of surveys of the American public on privacy dating from 1978, and through the specific survey on health information privacy carried out in July 1993. It also examines public response to the numerous questions concerning privacy of information pertaining to HIV-status, health information in the workplace, and genetic testing. The chapter explores the implications of these results about informing the public of their rights and responsibilities in their health care information.

Singer, Shapiro and Jacobs propose strategies for educating the public, among them a general information campaign, education of the patient by his or her health provider, and a system by which at regular intervals patients sign an informed consent or a notification statement and are offered an opportunity to inspect his or her medical record.

Other chapters propose systems of *guidelines and standards* to address the privacy question. This approach may be of particular interest to policymakers, as presently medical information is afforded no protection under federal law, and there is significant variation in the nature and quality of state laws regarding privacy in health care information. Among the states that have regulations, statutes, or case law recognizing medical records as confidential and limiting access to them, these are not consistent in recognizing computerized medical records as legitimate documents under the law, and generally do not address the questions raised by such computerization. Commentators have noted that guidelines and/or legislation would provide health care professionals with a more consistent sense of their responsibilities for maintaining privacy.

George T. Duncan adopts a standards setting approach, examining the general question of health data privacy in considerable detail. He raises issues surrounding an electronic medical record, and explores the ethical standards historically relied upon to protect privacy in medical information. Specific issues of access to medical records are addressed, and the current legislative environment is surveyed. He then discusses previous efforts at establishing standards, and assesses proposed recommendations.

Robert Ellis Smith's work addresses the more specific question of treatment of research data, outlining the need to safeguard medical information used in this manner, while recognizing that individually identifiable information is often essential to effective research. Using the framework of a national health-care information network, he proposes specific guidelines for providing confidentiality in research projects that use medical records, and provides mechanisms implementing those standards. The guidelines proposed by Smith are developed from a variety of sources, and each guideline is accompanied by suggested specific mechanisms for its execution.

Vincent Branigan and Bernd Beier suggest an integrated approach to the protection of privacy, examining public policies and legal structures historically addressing the privacy question, and exploring the role that *technology* may take in furthering human rights norms. They argue that recent developments in computer technology provide some mechanisms for protecting privacy and implementing policy decisions about rights in medical information systems, but require substantial changes in both the technological approach and organizational controls. To shift the traditional paradigm for thinking about the nature of the privacy problem in information systems, they propose the use of new technology. Technology that would allow depersonalization of information for which personal identification is not relevant is one important component of this shift. Their article describes the inherent security advantages that flow from this change.[22]

Finally, Mary Ann Baily suggests that *structural reforms* to the broader health care delivery system are required to allow collection, storage, and use of medical information in a manner consistent with human rights norms. Baily examines the human rights issues that arise in regulating access to private health insurance data, and reviews basic facts about the structure of health insurance, the changing role of data as insurers and employers respond to the pressure to control expenditures on health care, and current legal and ethical constraints on data collection and use. She then considers

---

22. The Appendix to this volume includes an excerpt from a 1993 report of the Office of Technology Assessment, *Protecting Privacy in Computerized Medical Information.* Entitled "Selected Topics in Computer Security," it describes various security measures which can provide clinical access and utility for personnel and still maintain the security and confidentiality of patient information.

the distinction between appropriate and inappropriate use of insurance-related health information, and discusses policies for preventing inappropriate use. The author argues that the current system of health care delivery is at odds with the protection of confidentiality and privacy. She argues that economic incentives to make inappropriate use of personal health information are inherent in the present health care delivery system, and believes that guidelines for appropriate use will not be effective because of the cost involved in their observance and in imposing sanctions. Thus she concludes that structural changes in the system are required to diminish the incentive and/or opportunity to use data in ways that endanger human rights, and thus reduce the need for regulation.

CHAPTER ELEVEN

Linking Health Records: Human Rights Concerns

Sets forth propositions w/o any analysis or support; then offers very reasonable cautions recommendations [handwritten annotation]

Fritz Scheuren

1. Purpose

The purpose of this paper is to provide an introduction or "starter set" for reflecting on human rights issues that arise when bringing together or linking the health records of individuals. In particular, the paper will discuss the potential role of record linkages in the proposed new United States health information system; specifically, how linkage applications may affect both the rights of individuals to privacy and their rights of access to health care services.

Four potential types of record linkages will be covered (see Figure 1 below). The primary concern will be with linkages of health records, such as the computerized enrollment and encounter records proposed to be created under the Health Security Act or other health care reform legislation.[1] As the columns of Figure 1 indicate, linkages for both statistical and administrative purposes will be considered. As the rows of Figure 1 imply, there will be a discussion of record linkage within the health system, e.g., records of individuals may be linked to records of providers or insurers. The paper will also consider linkages of health care records with records from other systems, such as vital records or Social Security, income tax and welfare program records.

In all, the paper is organized into seven sections: the present introduction and statement of purpose (section 1); a background section on what is

---

1. *Health Security Act of 1993*, 103rd Cong., 1st sess., S. 2357. See also, for example, Committee on Regional Health Data Networks, Institute of Medicine, *Health Data in the Information Age: Use Disclosure, and Privacy,* M. S. Donaldson, and K. N. Lohr, eds. (Washington, D.C.: National Academy Press, 1994).

meant by record linkage – both in general and with respect to health record systems (section 2); then there are four short sections, each devoted to a cell in Figure 1 (sections 3 to 6); and, finally, a brief overall summary with recommendations (section 7). The main questions to be addressed throughout are the extent to which linkages should be permitted, for what purposes and under what conditions.

Figure 1. **Potential Types of Health Record Linkages** **(Cell entries reference paper section where topic is covered)**		
Linkage	Purposes	
	Administrative	Statistical
Within health record system	Section 3	Section 4
With other record systems	Section 6	Section 5

2. Background

This section is a review of automated record linkage techniques, the nature of record linkage errors, and some overall system concerns in a world where multiple opportunities exist to carry out record linkages.

a. Types of Record Linkages

It seems fairly safe to speculate that once human beings began to keep records there were efforts to link them together. Until well into this century, though, such work was done manually and often only with great difficulty and expense; however, there now exist four broad types of automated record linkage (see Figure 2) – each of which will be described below by means of an example.

Figure 2. **Examples of Linkage Types and System Structures**		
Type of Record Linkage	Record System Structure	
	Intended for Linkage	Incidental to Linkage
Deterministic	Social Security and Medicare systems	National Death Index (NDI)
Probabilistic	1990 Census Post Enumeration Survey	NDI Links to the Current Population Survey

In the United States, the first national experience with automated record linkage systems was the assignment, beginning in 1935, of social security numbers (SSN's) to most wage workers. Initially this system was based on a single punch card for each worker; these cards were updated, using the SSN as an account identifier, and a cumulative total kept of taxable wages received under covered employment. Record linkages at the Social Security Administration were computerized in the 1950s, and SSN's are issued now to virtually all Americans.

From its inception, the intended use of the Social Security number was to carry out record linkage. Efforts, not always successful, were made so that SSN's, when assigned, would be unique and each person would have just one.[2] Further, the wage reporting system was designed so that updates by SSN would be conducted in a manner relatively free of error. Put another way, the Social Security system was designed or *intended* all along for automated record linkage, and a straightforward, so-called *deterministic* linkage rule of *exact matching* on SSN's was to be the basic approach.

Birth and death registration in the U.S. offers a useful contrast to Social Security. These vital registers, which became complete only in the 1930s, were not intended for automated linkage operations.[3] Identifying items, like names, are on these records, of course, and could be used as matching keys but would not always be unique alone – common surnames, like Smith or Johnson or Williams, being notable cases where linkage problems might be particularly severe. Automated linkages to U.S. death records did not begin nationally until the inception in the 1970s of the National Death Index or NDI. The NDI in its original operations relied on *multiple exact matches* as a way to locate potential linkages;[4] hence, as shown in Figure 2, the NDI may serve as an example of a deterministic automated linkage approach that was *added on* to a system not initially designed for such a use.

Deterministic match rules are easy to automate but do not adequately reflect the uncertainty that may exist for some potential links. They can

---

2. See R. Herriot and F. Scheuren, "The Role of the Social Security Number in Matching Administrative and Survey Records," *Studies from Interagency Linkages* (Washington, D.C.: U.S. Social Security Administration, 1975).

3. Despite early advocates, such as H. L. Dunn, "Record Linkage," *American Journal of Public Health* 36 (1946): 1412-16.

4. J. E. Patterson and R. Bilgrad, "The National Death Index Experience: 1981-1985," *Record Linkage Techniques-1985*, proceedings of the Workshop on Exact Matching Methodologies, Arlington, VA, 9-10 May 1985 (Washington, D.C.: U.S. Department of Treasury, 1985), 245-54.

also require costly manual intervention when errors occur in the matching keys. More complicated methods were needed that weighed the linkage information, allowing for errors and incompleteness, and minimizing the clerical intervention required to select the best link from all those possible. Such techniques are called *probabilistic*. The main theoretical underpinnings for probabilistic matching methods were firmly established by the late 1960s with the papers of Tepping[5] and, especially, Fellegi and Sunter.[6] Sound practice dates back even earlier, at least to the nineteen 1950s and the work of Newcombe and his collaborators.[7]

The Fellegi-Sunter approach is basically a direct extension of the classical theory of hypothesis testing to the problem of record linkage. A mathematical model is developed for recognizing records in two files which represent identical units (said to be matched). As part of the process, there is a comparison between all possible pairs of records (one from each file) and a decision made as to whether or not the members of the comparison-pair represent the same units, or whether there is insufficient evidence to justify either of these decisions. The three outcomes from this process can be referred to as a "link," "nonlink" or "potential link."

In point of fact, Fellegi and Sunter contributed the underlying theory to the methods already being used by Newcombe, and showed how to develop and optimally employ probability weights to the results of the comparisons made. They also dealt with the implications of restricting the comparison pairs to be looked at, that is of "blocking" the files, something that generally has had to be done when linking files that are large.

Many of the major public health research advances made in recent decades have benefitted at least in part from probabilistic linkage techniques. Included are such well-known epidemiological findings as the effects of smoking, risks from radiation exposure, asbestos and many other

---

5.   B. Tepping, "A Model for Optimum Linkage of Records," *Journal of the American Statistical Association* 63 (1968): 1321-32.

6.   I. P. Fellegi and A. Sunter, "A Theory of Record Linkage," *Journal of the American Statistical Association* 64 (1969): 1183-10.

7.   H. B. Newcombe, "Record Linking: The Design of Efficient Systems for Linking Records into Individual and Family Histories," *American Journal of Human Genetics* 19 (1967): 335-59. H. B. Newcombe, J. M. Kennedy, S. J. Axford, and A. P. James, "Automatic Linkage of Vital Records," *Science* 130, no. 3381 (1959): 954-59. H. B. Newcombe and J. M. Kennedy, "Record Linking: Making Maximum Use of the Discriminating Power of Identifying Information," *Communications of the Association for Computing Machinery* 5 (1962): 563-66.

carcinogens arising in the workplace, through diet or other exposures – increasingly in populations with genetic predispositions.[8] These benefits have to be considered when exploring record linkage impacts on privacy and other rights. We will return to this point at the end of this paper, where trade-offs are explicitly considered.

Most of these automated linkages, like Newcombe's studies of radiation exposure at Chalk River (and elsewhere), were not envisioned when the records were originally created. Some probabilistic linkage systems were intended, however – notably for "post-enumeration" surveys (PES's), carried out to evaluate U.S. decennial census coverage. For example, the PES for 1990 was particularly well-designed for carrying out probabilistic linkages.[9] Another good example of a continuing probabilistic linkage that has been a real success for statistical purposes is the bringing together of the NDI and Current Population Survey.[10] This linkage, though, was not planned into the design of either of the data sets being employed.

b. Nature of Linkage Errors and Identifying Information

All linkage operations are subject to two main types of errors: matching records together that belong to different entities (false matches), and failing to put records together that belong to the same entity (false nonmatches). These errors can have different human rights implications, depending on what the linkages are used for (see Figure 3).

If the linkage is to assemble data about an individual so an administrative or diagnostic determination can be made about that individual, then the consequences of any error could be grave indeed. Potentially, a different (lower) standard of accuracy could be tolerated, provided a suitable adjustment is made when analyzing the results of linkage operations whose

---

8. See, for example, G. W. Beebe, "Why Are Epidemiologists Interested in Matching Algorithms?" *Record Linkage Techniques-1985*, proceedings of the Workshop on Exact Matching Methodologies, Arlington, VA, 9-10 May 1985 (Washington, D.C.: U.S. Department of Treasury, 1985), 139-44. See also endnote 57.

9. See, for example, W. Winkler and Y. Thibaudeau, "An Application of the Fellegi-Sunter Model of Record Linkage to the 1990 U.S. Census," *Statistical Division Report Series,* CENSUS/SRD/RR -91/09 (Washington, D.C.: U.S. Bureau of the Census, 1991). See also T. Belin and D. Rubin, "A Method of Calibrating False-Match Rates in Record Linkages," *Journal of the American Statistical Association* 90 (1995): 694-707.

10. See E. Rogot, P. D. Sorlie, N. J. Johnson, C. S. Glover, and D. W. Treasure, *A Mortality Study of One Million Persons: First Data Book*, NIH Publication No. 88-2896 (Bethesda, MD: Public Health Service, National Institutes of Health, 1988).

purpose is to obtain information about a group.[11] More will be said about these issues in later sections, particularly how this distinction affords an opportunity to both preserve individual privacy rights – through group matches – but still attain societal information needs.

Figure 3. Linkage Error Implications on Human Rights		
Types of Linkage Error	Linkages Used For	
	Data About that Individual	Information About a Class of Individuals
False Matches	Potentially very serious	May be less serious
False Nonmatches		

If an efficient (low-cost, essentially error-free) health care linkage system is a goal, then consideration needs to be given to the establishment of a health identification "number." In ideal circumstances, personal identifying information on a medical record should satisfy the following requirements:[12]

- The identifying information should be *permanent*; that is, it should exist at the birth of a person to whom it relates or be allocated to him/her at birth, and it should remain unchanged throughout life;

- The identifying information should be *universal*; that is, similar information should exist for every member of the population;

- The identifying information should be *reasonable*; that is, the person to whom it relates and others should have no objection to its disclosure for medical purposes;

- The identifying information should be *economical*; that is, it should not consist of more alphabetic, digits and other characters than necessary;

- The identifying information should be *simple*; that is, it should be capable of being handled easily by a clerk and a computer;

---

11. See H. L. Oh and F. Scheuren, "Fiddling Around with Matches and Nonmatches," *Proceedings of American Statistical Association, Social Statistics Section* (Washington, D.C.: ASA, 1975). F. Scheuren and W. E. Winkler, "Regression Analysis of Data Files that Are Computer Matched," *Survey Methodology* 19, no. 1 (1993): 39-58. See also W. E. Winkler and F. Scheuren, "Linking Data to Create Information," (delivered at the Statistics Canada, XII Methodology Symposium, Ottawa, Canada, 1 November 1995).

12. See M. Fair, "An Overview of Record Linkage in Canada," (presented at the American Statistical Association annual meeting in Orlando, FL, August 1995).

- The identifying information should be *available*;

- The identifying information should be *known*; that is, either the person to whom it relates or an informant acting on his/her behalf should be able to provide it on demand;

- The identifying information should be *accurate*; that is, it should not contain errors that could result in a discrepancy between two records relating to the same person;

- The identifying information should be *unique*; that is, each member of the population should be identified differently.

The Social Security number, incidentally, fails several of these tests. Only now is it beginning to be issued at birth; also it is far from being accurately reported. In practice, too, because of incentives created by the SSN's use in the tax system, the number is not always unique. Some people use more than one SSN, even in the same year, and more often over longer periods of time. Multiple uses of the same SSN by different people have been common, as well.

Concerns about the risks to health records from unauthorized disclosures are greater with an identifier like the SSN, which is widely available on many large private data bases, like credit files, and of course many nonhealth-related federal, state, and other government files.[13] In the Office of Technology Assessment's 1993 report[14] on privacy, the following recommendation is made with regard to the SSN.

The use of the Social Security number as a unique patient identifier has far-reaching ramifications for individual health care information privacy that should be carefully considered before it is used for that purpose.

Elsewhere[15] the stronger recommendation has been made *not* to use the SSN as a health identifier. Its use could lead to matching errors and might

---

13. K. Davis, "Guarding Your Financial Privacy," *Kiplinger's Personal Finance Magazine*, 1995, 49.

14. See Office of Technology Assessment, *Protecting Privacy in Computerized Medical Information* (Washington, D.C.: U.S. Government Printing Office, 1993).

15. See F. Scheuren, "Correspondence with Dr. Elmer Gabrieli on a Health Identification Number," in *Guide for Unique Healthcare Identifier Model,* (Philadelphia: ASTM, May 1993, draft). Ironically, public opinion poll data suggest that the American people favor the adaptation of the SSN, rather than the introduction of a new health identifier. See endnote 33 for details.

greatly increase the potential for unregulated linkages between health and nonhealth data sets.

c. *Some Proposed Health Record Linkage Systems*

The proposed Health Security Act[16] calls for the establishment of a National Health Board to oversee the creation of an electronic data network. The types of information collected would include: enrollment and disenrollment in health plans; clinical encounters and other items and services from health care providers; administrative and financial transactions and activities of participating states, regional alliances, corporate alliances, health plans, health care providers, employers, and individuals; number and demographic characteristics of eligible individuals residing in each alliance area; payment of benefits; utilization management; quality management; grievances, and fraud or misrepresentation in claims or benefits.[17]

The Health Security Act specifies, among other things, the use of uniform paper forms containing standard data elements, definitions, and instructions for completion; requirements for use of uniform health data sets with common definitions to standardize the collection and transmission of data in electronic form; uniform presentation requirements for data in electronic form; and electronic data interchange requirements for the exchange of data among automated health information systems.

A prototype health care record linkage system may be worth considering as well, since it spells out an initial schematic of a person-level health or patient record. Data could come from an array of health care settings, linked together using a "linkage processor." This processor would determine the linkage and also assign the unique patient identifier in the actual patient record. Record types would differ by the type of provider from which they are derived. The functions of the record linkage software program are outlined in Figure 4. It is anticipated that the patient-identifying information would be housed in a person's primary care unit. The linkage processor stores the patient-identifying data and generates the unique identifier. It processes records from other providers and links the record as shown. Some initial data categories and identifying information are outlined in Figure 5.[18]

16. *Health Security Act of 1993*, 103rd Cong., 1st sess., S. 2357.

17. See Institute of Medicine, *Health Data in the Information Age*.

18. See H. Schwartz, S. Kunitz, and R. Kozloff, "Building Data Research Resources from Existing Data Sets: a Model for Integrating Patient Data to Form a Core Data Set,"

d. Additional System Concerns

In all data capture systems, of course, it is important to explicitly build in the means to address privacy rights, the degree to which confidentiality promises are required (and kept), and the means used to make individual data physically secure. While such concerns are general, record linkage systems have some unique aspects that may bear discussion – particularly the systems described above. Figure 6 summarizes these, emphasizing the additional complexity introduced by the linkage environment and the degree to which linkage systems are or should be "auditable." By "auditable" it is meant that, at a minimum, each access to identifiable data is controlled and a log kept of the individuals who obtained the data and of all transactions that occurred (in other words, an *audit trail* is kept so that outside monitoring is possible).

Tore Dalenius has provided a good review of privacy, confidentiality and security goals in statistical settings.[19] His work may afford a point of departure for the discussion here. In common speech, the words privacy, confidentiality and security partially overlap in usage, and often have meanings that depend greatly on context. Each can also have an emotional content, which makes precise definitions difficult, even contentious. For example, Dalenius quotes Westin (1967) as saying about privacy, "Few values so fundamental to society as privacy have been left so undefined in social theory or have been the subject of such vague and confused writing by social scientists."

A good start on giving meaning to the word "privacy," or "information privacy" (our context here), might be the definition first articulated by Justice Brandeis as the "right to be let alone . . . the most comprehensive of rights and the right most valued by civilized man."[20] Attempts to update this definition have been many and will undoubtedly continue. All afford the individual or data subject some, sometimes sole, rights over what matters they want to keep private and what matters they are willing – or want – to reveal.

Record linkage settings pose a particular challenge to an individual's ability to exercise his or her privacy rights. The sheer complexity of the setting makes it hard to clarify for the subject what the potential benefit or

---

(presented at the American Statistical Association annual meeting in Orlando, FL, August 1995).

19. See T. Dalenius, *Controlling Invasion of Privacy in Surveys*, Continuing Education Series (Stockholm, Sweden: Statistics Sweden, 1988).

20. *Olmstead v. United States*, 277 U.S. 438, 478 (1928). (Justice Brandeis dissenting.)

harm may be to permitting access. Consider the linkage of just two files, say, of "n" and "m" variables respectively. Cognitively for the individual involved, the linkage decision may seem like one of no particular moment. The combined file will consist of data already given out earlier – a single file of "n + m" – rather than two separate files. But a deeper look – at relationships, for example, between variables – shows that a combinatorial explosion of facts about an individual has taken place – from $2^n + 2^m$ to 2^{n+m}. (Incidentally, to illustrate what this means, assume just that n=m=11; then the combined file has over 1000 times more information about the relationships between variables than the two files separately.)

Ready examples come to mind where individuals present themselves in one way (to get Medicaid or Medicare), but in another setting (perhaps a job interview) give a different, even contradictory set of "facts." When records from these two encounters are linked, obviously the implications may be many, since these differences would be revealed.[21]

Obtaining data at different points in time and for different primary purposes is a difficulty that is peculiar to linkage settings. The privacy decision an individual may wish to make could, therefore, change over time and might depend on the particular data items as well as the purposes for which a release from their privacy rights is being sought. Singer et al.,[22] for example, advocate that patients sign an informed consent or a notification statement at regular intervals, not simply the first time a patient visits the provider's office.

---

21. Some implications are obvious. For example, "Information in medical records can conceivably affect you for the rest of your life if revealed to an employer or insurance company" (*Washington Post,* Health Section, 8 February 1994). The obvious cases are not the only ones to be worried about, though. The combinatorial possibilities are so great that they may not only impair full consent to linkage by patients but also access decisions by data stewards.

22. E. Singer, R. Shapiro, and L. Jacobs, "Privacy of Health Care Data: What Does the Public Know? How Much Do They Care?" in this volume.

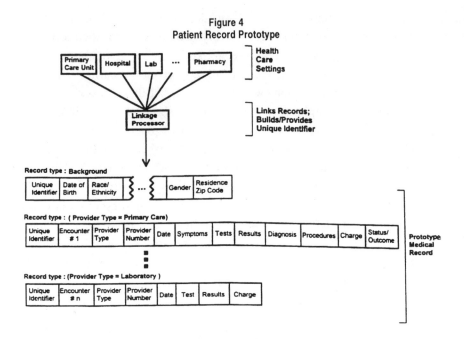

Figure 4
Patient Record Prototype

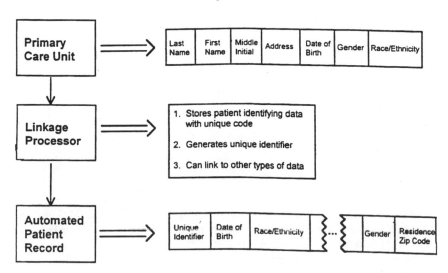

Figure 5
Record Linkage Architecture

Figure 6 Some Overall Record Linkage System Concerns		
Linkage Issues	Complexity	Auditability
Privacy Confidentiality Security	Extremely high, may be beyond our current understanding, without training and experience	May be very difficult to establish, maintain, or use in monitoring access

They then go on to recommend that the consent or notification statement spell out to whom the information about the patient may be disseminated, for what purposes, and what the patient's rights are with respect to this information. Such an approach, especially as it relates to secondary uses of data and the time period for which the informed consent is valid, seems clearly required in a linkage setting where patient-specific information may accumulate over time and from many sources (not just one provider). It may be necessary for a regulatory body to develop regulations standardizing the contents of informed consent and disclosure policies. These regulations could definitely state what constitutes an "informed consent" and legitimate nonconsented disclosure. Even then, only experience will tell whether true informed consent will be possible for most individuals.

Indeed, without wishing to jump to conclusions, it may be reasonable to conjecture that, for some kinds of data linkage at least and certain individuals, our technological abilities to electronically merge data sets may have outstripped our sense of what a data subject would have to "consent to in an *informed* way" for the systems to be built on an entirely voluntary basis. If this is so, then simply creating the health linkage system envisioned might in and of itself take away the privacy rights of some people.

The problem of complexity in record linkage systems may warrant the attention being given to complexity in general systems.[23] Linear thinking alone may, in any case, be insufficient to address what will happen not only to the individual's ability to manage his or her own data but to the system's integrity overall. What confidentiality promises can be made and kept in such a world? How can one even speculate realistically about the risks to data corruption or unauthorized disclosure? Recent experiences else-

---

23. J. Horgan, "From Complexity to Perplexity," *Scientific American* 272 (June 1995): 104-109. See also, M. M. Waldrop, *Complexity* (New York: Simon and Schuster, 1992).

where[24] do not encourage belief that reasonable ways exist of being clear about even what the threats are.

Among the crucial "fail safes" is to provide an audit trail for every query against a record and any retention of a data subset. Such systems already exist for some real time settings, although not necessarily in a way that would allow a simple scale-up. A crucial step is the maintenance of these systems so they operate properly.[25] While beyond the scope of this paper, it might be noted that the expense of this maintenance step and a mechanism to "monitor the monitoring" needs a lot of attention, too. Arguments in favor of doing record linkages for efficiency reasons have not fully weighed these costs. In Brannigan and Beier,[26] other sound system architecture issues and recommendations are made that would be needed to implement essential confidentiality and security procedures, especially if large scale record linkages are to be employed.

3. Administrative Data Linkages within the Health System

By an administrative data linkage we mean a linkage of data about an entity done with the intention of taking some direct action regarding that entity. In a health setting, the most obvious example would be to assemble (link) data about a patient from multiple sources in order to improve the diagnosis or treatment of that individual. We will start with this case and then go on to discuss administrative health linkages more generally.

---

24. "Superhack," *Scientific American,* 271 (July 1994): 17. This is a story of a group of about 600 computer "hacks," collaborating over the Internet, who broke a computer security encryption algorithm. About 17 years earlier, it was predicted that this feat would take 40 quadrillion years. Once the effort started, it took 8 months! For more on this, see also *Science,* May 1994, 776-77.

25. In contrast, consider a recent story in the *Washington Post* about how, despite an existing monitoring system, inadequate controls were used for access to sensitive information. See Stephen Barr, "1,300 IRS Workers Accused of Snooping at Tax Returns: Employees Used Computers to Peek at Friends' Files," *Washington Post,* 18 July 1994, Section A, p. 1.

26. See Vincent M. Brannigan and Bernd Beier, "Medical Data Protection and Privacy in the United States: Theory and Reality," in this volume.

a. Linkages for Direct Patient Care

Figure 7 lays out some of the dimensions in administrative record linkages aimed at improving the health of a patient. Each row covers a broad area dealing with, respectively, overall issues, technical (and administrative) aspects, legal matters, the perception of the public and of experts. The primary focus of the figure is to directly address under what conditions linkages should be permitted (column 1) and areas for future study (column 2). Since the goal of this paper is to be a "starter set," only illustrative suggestions have been made in the cells, both here and elsewhere.

Among the general conditions for linkage, a signed notification statement seems needed.[27] In this context, a "notification statement" might tell the patient who will have access, for what purposes and with what oversight. Hoffman in a recent paper makes the observation that "too many people may already have insufficiently monitored access to hospital patient records." He seconds Mark Siegler's thesis that "medical confidentiality, as it has been traditionally understood by patients and doctors, no longer exists." Siegler, after a patient expressed concern about the confidentiality of his hospital record, scanned his medical chart and enumerated "at least 25 and possibly as many as 100 health professionals and administrative personnel . . . [who] had access to the patient's record," all with legitimate reasons to examine the chart.[28]

Secure physical access is essential, and any linkage stipulated as done for diagnosis and treatment of a patient should be available only for the use of the patient and his or her caregivers. Concerns exist about the patient data requested for such encounters, and whether the demands and burdens on the patient are reasonable. The collection of uniform patient data has clear advantages; the specific data required, though, will need external review, possibly by a regulatory body – similar to that discussed earlier on consent standards. After all there are privacy rights given up by patients to their caregivers, and these should be limited to an essential minimum.

Patient and primary caregiver controlled access might involve encryption techniques or other measures designed to prevent or at least reduce the risks of unauthorized (unmonitored) use. Linkages might be time-limited

---

27. See Singer, Shapiro, and Jacobs, "Privacy of Health Care Data."

28. B. Hoffman, "Patient Confidentiality and Access to Medical Records: A Physician's Perspective," *Health Law in Canada* 10 (1990): 210-12. N. Cummings, "Patient Confidentiality," summary of "Confidentiality in Medicine – A Decrepit Concept," by M. Siegler, *Second Opinion*, 1993, 112-16.

to reduce exposure further. As noted, Brannigen and Beier[29] have made numerous other important suggestions. System administrative issues are extensive, and concerns about monitoring operations deserve continued study.

Figure 7 Administrative Data Linkages Conducted for the Health of Patients		
Broad Areas	Possible Response	
	Under what conditions (Column 1)	For future study (Column 2)
Overall Recommendations	Just notification needed; if for use of patient and patient caregivers only.	Concerns about coercive aspects of government "monopoly" in health care.
Technical Aspects	Encryption to prevent unauthorized access and reduce risks of reidentification.	Concerns about how to monitor operation.
Legal Questions	For federal records, subject to the Privacy Act; use seemingly fully permitted now.	Electronic data linkages across governmental jurisdictions deserve more study; also roles of intermediaries (e.g., Health Information Trustee – HR 4077).
Public Views	Direct evidence lacking but indirect evidence suggests that health uses to aid patients would be seen very positively.	Concerns about public view of risks associated with system need to be better understood.
Expert Opinion	An obvious use, seemingly favored by all.	Need to continue research on uniform reporting issues so as to obtain promised benefits of electronic linkages without an undue burden.

Fair information practices must be adhered to – as required in the Privacy Act and reinforced by pending legislation.[30] Continuing study of state and local restrictions[31] should be pursued to find good working models and to anticipate areas where weaknesses may arise in the National System, if litigation occurs. The *Privacy Journal* has regularly compiled state and federal privacy laws, and is a useful resource here.[32]

---

29. See Brannigan and Beier, "Medical Data Protection and Privacy."

30. Introduced by Condit as HR 4077 in the 103rd Congress; also reintroduced (again by Condit) in the 104th Congress as HR 435.

31. As recommended by OTA, *Protecting Privacy.*

32. For example, see Robert E. Smith, *Compilation of State and Federal Privacy Laws,* (Providence, RI: *Privacy Journal*, 1992).

Direct evidence of public reaction is lacking on linkages used solely to aid the patient. Such use is presumed to be very positively received. There is a large segment of the public,[33] though, that is concerned about any electronic record linkage system of the scope envisioned, mainly because of general mistrust of the government and other large institutions. These individuals, or some of them at least, might not think the benefits to be derived warrant the risks they perceive for abuse inherent in such a large-scale record linkage effort.

Virtually all "experts" take the position that notification of the use envisioned here is enough. One exception is Goldman,[34] who states,

> Personally identifiable health records must be in the control of the individual. Personal information should only be disclosed with the knowing, meaningful consent of the individual.

The distinction between consent and notification may not be as important here as elsewhere. With notification there is always a "quid pro quo" – give these data about yourself if you want to participate. In this setting patients are often asked to give what amounts to "coerced" consent; therefore, the distinction may be in name only. Logically, however, it seems inconsistent to withhold information about yourself that could be used to aid you. Unquestionably, though, a refusal to comply could mean denial of access to health care services.

---

33. Inferred from Harris-Equifax, *Health Care Information Privacy: A Survey of the Public and Leaders.* (New York: Louis Harris and Associates, 1993). See also J. Blair, "Ancillary Uses of Government Administrative Data on Individuals: Public Perceptions and Attitudes," (unpublished Working Paper, Committee on National Statistics, National Academy of Sciences, Washington, D.C., 1995). As Blair points out (and this author confirmed by calling Harris and Associates), the Harris-Equifax survey has important limitations on its interpretability; nonetheless, its main conclusions are in essential agreement with other research on privacy concerns. Blair summarizes these as well. Almost no matter how you ask the question, there are roughly about one-sixth to one-fifth of the population who oppose electronic record linkages on privacy grounds. Conversely, again almost no matter how you ask the question, about the same fraction will favor beneficial sounding linkages on efficiency grounds. The two-thirds or so in the middle will differ in their opinions, depending on the specifics. See also footnote 55.

34. House Committee on Post Office and Civil Service, Subcommittee on Census, Statistics and Postal Personnel, statement by Janlori Goldman regarding H.R. 3137: Data Needs and Related Issues for Implementing Health Care Reform, 103rd Cong. 2nd sess. (16 March 1994). For an excellent expression of an alternative view, see Newcombe, "When Privacy Threatens Public Health," *Canadian Journal of Public Health* 86 (1995): 188-92.

b. Other Health Administrative Linkages

Many other health linkages are possible besides those directly involved with patient care. These could range from linking treatments received by a patient to the costs of those treatments, to associating outcome measures (e.g., death or survival) to the types of medical procedures employed, and even to linkages whose intent was to detect fraud or malpractice. Data about a hospital or other health facility might be sought by looking at all the records of the patients that can be linked to that hospital. The number of possibilities, in fact, is very large – too large to cover in any depth here. Some observations may be helpful, nonetheless, to fix a few of the ideas about what the privacy dimensions are:

- First, in administrative linkages such as these, the patient may become just a data point in an endeavor focused elsewhere.[35] The dehumanizing aspect of this change of focus is inherently unsettling. Provisions like those in Figure 7 seem insufficient when the person looking at the data is not the primary caregiver but an administrator concerned about financial results, the efficiency of a medical technique, etc. (i.e., someone without any personal relationship to the patient).

- Second, to handle the changed circumstances, among other things a "need to know" principle[36] might be applied to limit the routine availability of detailed health and demographic data. To illustrate: if data about a hospital's performance are needed, only hospital-level patient aggregates might be provided, rather than complete individually identifiable patient detail.

Clearly much greater safeguards seem needed once there is no longer a personal bond between the patient and the individual using the data about that patient. Arguably, establishing a convincing system that would warrant the patient and public trust required here may be exceedingly difficult.

An important issue that may deserve comment is the "final" disposition of a patient's health (and related financial) records when the patient dies. Even for federal record systems, the Privacy Act no longer offers any protection, for example. We are learning more and more about the genetic

---

35. E. H. Kluge, "Advanced Patient Records: Some Ethical and Legal Considerations Touching Medical Information Space," *Methods of Information in Medicine*, 1993, 95-103.

36. See Brannigan and Beier, "Medical Data Protection and Privacy."

causes of some illnesses. Matching records from deceased patients could put their descendants (or other relatives) at risk for possible differential treatment. If the view is taken, as quoted above in Goldman, that the patient "owns" his or her records then, by inference, upon death the estate of the patient owns that patient's records, and their disposition is a matter to be settled by the heirs. In any event, inter- or intra-generational record linkage needs careful consideration and might be done, as a rule, only with the consent of individuals so linked.

4. Research Data Linkages Within the Health System

It can be argued that some research uses of data linkages within the health system are administrative and so are already covered by the discussion in Section 3, especially the subsection: Other Health Administrative Linkages. There can be a fine line between applied research (intending to serve a permissible administrative purpose) and basic research (involving possibly an unanticipated analysis of variables originally obtained for another purpose).

Rather than try to draw the line, however, we will confine our attention to "basic research," since this involves some potentially new issues. In particular, our discussion will focus on researchers who are in some sense outside the Health Care System – i.e., individuals who do not already have access to the patient data. Such a decision has consequences, of course. For example, important issues, like what research doctors do when using data about their own patients, go undiscussed. On the other hand, there is already an extensive body of practice on this topic, and record linkage issues do not seem primary.

In any event, for the basic research setting we have confined attention to, Figure 8 attempts to set out a summary of the main issues. As in Figure 7 earlier, included are some overall recommendations, legal and procedural questions addressed, as well as perceptions concerns (both by the public and among the experts). These are further elaborated below.

Notification of patients about basic research uses may be sufficient in some settings, while a specific consent may be needed in others. All basic research should be authorized by a review board mechanism of some sort, with an annual public report, perhaps, to an outside citizens' body. Requirements for securing consent pose difficult logistical and statistical problems that need extensive study. Anonymous group matching offers a potentially promising middle ground that could allow individual consent decisions to be honored, yet may not greatly sacrifice approved scientific ends.[37] However, as Figure 8 states, an extensive development and evaluation period is needed before this approach will prove its value.

The elimination of all identifying items about a patient would seem to be a necessary prerequisite for broad access to the health system data base by outside researchers. The risks of potential reidentification[38] are an ongoing concern, especially as nonhealth electronic systems grow in size and potentially have common variables which overlap those in health data bases. Research access through contractual arrangements, as proposed by Herriot,[39] has already begun in some settings (where it might be evaluated) and deserves study in others (where it has yet to be applied). The development of wholly synthetic data sets[40] also warrants work and may be potentially promising because of the public assurances that can be given which might satisfy even those who greatly distrust government. As noted earlier, there are a significant minority of individuals who oppose linkages, and this group grows larger when there is no clear and compelling purpose for such linkage, except an ill-defined one – like "basic research."[41] Lifelong patient linkage projects, which are particularly attractive basic research tools, may be subject to potentially severe public reaction if done without continuing consent (as occurred in Sweden[42]).

---

37. N. Spruill and J. Gastwirth, "On the Estimation of the Correlation Coefficient from Grouped Data," *Journal of the American Statistical Association* 77 (1982): 614-20. J. Gastwirth and W. O. Johnson, "Screening With Cost-Effective Quality Control: Potential Applications to HIV and Drug Testing," *Journal of the American Statistical Association* 89 (1994): 972-81. Contrast J. Gastwirth, "Ethical Issues in Access to and Linkage of Data Collected by Government Agencies," *Proceedings of the American Statistical Association, Social Statistics Section* (Washington, D.C.: ASA, 1986), 6-13.

38. See, for example, T. B. Jabine and F. Scheuren, "Goals for Statistical Uses of Administrative Records: The Next Ten Years," *Journal of Business and Economic Statistics*, 1985.

39. See D. Wright and S. Ahmed, "Implementing NCES's New Confidentiality Protections," *Proceedings of the American Statistical Association, Section on Survey Research Methods*, (Alexandria, VA: American Statistical Association, 1990).

40. D. B. Rubin, "Comments on Confidentiality: A Proposal for Satisfying All Confidentiality Constraints Through the Use of Multiple-imputed Synthetic Microdata," *Journal of Official Statistics* 9 (1993): 461-68.

41. See Harris-Equifax, *Health Care Information Privacy*. See also Blair, "Ancillary Uses of Government Administrative Data." See endnote 33. Clearly, though, we do not know enough to be sure.

Figure 8. Basic Research Data Linkages within the Health System		
Broad Areas	Possible Response	
	Under what conditions (Column 1)	For future study (Column 2)
Overall Recommendations	Notification and even maybe consent required for individual linkages, plus research review board authorization.	Statistical properties of group linkages and their use need extensive study when consent not given.
Technical Aspects	Elimination of all obvious (and not so obvious) identifiers. Access to data also limited by reidentification risks and "need to know."	Research on use of synthetic data. Continuous study of (ever) changing reidentification risks.
Legal Questions	Laws often unreasonably require *no* risk of redisclosure.	Research on "proof of harm" issue. Legislative and litigation research on contract-based research access.
Public Views	Significant negative sentiment tied to distrust of government and lack of a specific clear purpose.	Study reactions to long-term (lifelong) record linkage.
Expert Opinion	For the most part strongly favor broad basic research uses requiring only notification.	Nonmedical uses of health system records need more study.

In general, even the strongest human rights advocates make an exception for research uses of individual data, stating[43] that "Information that is not personally identifiable may be provided for research and statistical purposes." Given the growing power of probabilistic matching, though, we may not be far from the day when the only way to remove personally identifiable information about some individuals is to remove all direct data concerning such individuals from a research file. Additionally, there may be some concerns about the appropriateness of nonmedical uses of health care records (e.g., for the decennial census[44]), a point more appropriately covered in the next section.

42. See Dalenius, *Controlling Invasion of Privacy in Surveys.*

43. See House Subcommittee on Census, Statistics and Postal Personnel, statement by Janlori Goldman, "Data Needs and Related Issues."

44. See Singer, Shapiro, and Jacobs, "Privacy of Health Care Data."

5. Research Linkages between Health and Other Record Systems

Our discussion of basic research issues within the health system (Section 4) forms a bridge to a discussion of research data linkages between health and other record systems. Many parallels exist, as may be seen by comparing Figure 8 with Figure 9 below. There are, however, some new elements too.

- First, deterministic matching algorithms should be possible within the health system, assuming some form of health identifier is settled on. Generally, though, unless the SSN is used as the health identifier, only probabilistic matching methods will be available between health and nonhealth record systems; hence greater uncertainty about linkage quality will exist.

- Second, these nonhealth systems were clearly intended for nonhealth purposes; thus, their use in health record linkage research, through the simple expedient of health legislation, seems problematic. In fact, a strong case might be made for "consent-only access" to at least some of them. Also any retroactivity in this expanded use should not be taken lightly either.

- Third, there seems to be a wide range of record linkage options, spanning matches to vital records at one end of the spectrum[45] (a traditional epidemiological tool) with tax records at the other[46] (something seldom done). The views of experts and the public appear to move predictably along this continuum, from some acceptance to almost none.[47]

---

45. See Fair, "An Overview of Record Linkage in Canada."

46. But see, for example, F. Scheuren, "Historical Perspectives on the Estate Multiplier Technique," *Statistics of Income, Estate Tax Wealth Compendium* (Washington, D.C.: U.S. Internal Revenue Service, 1994).

47. F. Scheuren, "Methodological Issues in Linkage of Multiple Data Bases," *Record Linkage Techniques-1985*, proceedings of the Workshop on Exact Matching Methodologies, Arlington, VA, 9-10 May 1985 (Washington, D.C.: U.S. Department of Treasury, 1985), 155-78. F. Scheuren, review of *Private Lives and Public Policies: Confidentiality and Accessibility of Government Services,* by Duncan, Jabine, and de Wolf, *Journal of the American Statistical Association* 90, no. 429 (March 1995): 386-87.

Figure 9. Research Data Linkages between Health and Other Record Systems		
Broad Areas	Possible Response	
	Under what conditions (Column 1)	For future study (Column 2)
Overall Recommendations	Generally, consent should be required, plus research review board authorization.	Same as Figure 8.
Technical Aspects	Same as Figure 8.	Same as Figure 8.
Legal Questions	Conforming legislation needed to Tax Code, Social Security Act, etc.	Research on "proof of harm" issue. Legislative and litigation research on contract-based research access.
Public Views	Significant minority would not consent to individual linkages.	Research on reactions to group linkages for statistical purposes. Study parallel to HIV testing.
Expert Opinion	For the most part, strongly favor health research uses only requiring notification.	Nonmedical uses of any linkages need more study.

- Fourth, even anonymous group-matching methods need more study in this setting, and not just their statistical efficiency, as noted in Figure 8, but their public acceptability. Black males seem particularly opposed to some linkages. Concerns like those in Fisher et al.[48] merit examination here too.

As already noted, some experts are concerned about proposals using health records to improve the accuracy of the decennial census population count.[49] In fact, except in cases where explicit consent is obtained, it may make sense to confine all matches of health records to nonhealth records solely to those research purposes related to health. The control of any linkages between health and nonhealth records, say with Census Bureau data, needs careful study too.[50] Most federal statistical agencies, for example, currently *lack* auditable record linkage systems[51] and would have to

---

48. James Fisher et al., "Gaining Respondent Participation: Issues of Trust, Honesty and Reliability," in this volume.

49. See Singer, Shapiro, and Jacobs, "Privacy of Health Care Data."

50. One joint control option that may be of interest arose in the project described in Rogot et al., "A Mortality Study of One Million Persons."

51. See Scheuren, review of *Private Lives and Public Policy*.

greatly increase internal controls to meet what should be stringent electronic access (and audit) standards.[52]

6. Nonresearch Linkages between Health and Other Record Systems

As may be apparent by now, in this paper there has been a progression from linkage opportunities that might be viewed by most individuals as beneficial, even to be encouraged, to linkages that are more problematic. This section discusses linkages that, in the view of many, may be dangerous and should generally be discouraged.

Figure 10 sets out a summary of possible issues in nonresearch linkages between health and nonhealth systems. Some overall observations on this figure might be worth making too – highlighting what is new or controversial.

Figure 10. Nonresearch Administrative Data Linkages between Health and Nonhealth Record Systems		
Broad Areas	Possible Response	
	Under what conditions (Column 1)	For future study (Column 2)
Overall Recommendations	For nonhealth reasons only with a court order. For health reasons only to directly aid patients.	Continuing research on (changing?) understanding of all consent or notification statements.
Technical Aspects	Minimizing redisclosure risks, especially to open or decentralized systems like vital records.	Continuing research on record keeping practices in nonhealth record systems, government and private.
Legal Questions	Ban any use of a new health identifier in nonhealth record systems.	Study conforming legislative needs.
Public and Expert Opinion	In generally close agreement, with a majority favoring restrictions on nonhealth uses.	Continuous routine monitoring.

With the exception of a court order in a criminal case, all nonresearch linkages for nonhealth reasons should be prohibited. Even health administrative linkages (say, to use IRS address information to locate a person for health reasons) should be carefully limited (as is the case now). Areas for future study might include research on notification issues and consent-

---

52. See Brannigan and Beier, "Medical Data Protection and Privacy."

based exceptions. After all, new health needs keyed to helping individuals may arise over time, and hence notification statements might need to be changed or at least their understanding reviewed periodically.

Existing systems, especially vital records, have many variables in common with health care record systems. Vital records are also quite open and hence they pose a significant risk of redisclosure, especially in public use (or other widely available) research files. If an independent health identifier is not used, then perhaps the SSN, for example, should be removed, or access to it restricted on birth and death records.

A legal ban, of course as generally advocated, should be imposed on the use of any new health identifier created, *except in health systems*. Research on other obvious and not so obvious identifiers (e.g., geographic details), should be ongoing to be sure that (legislated?) health record practices keep up with technology and the changing nature of unauthorized disclosure risks.

Public and expert opinion both appear to strongly oppose nonhealth administrative use of health record systems.[53] Additional public opinion research, though, seems needed on this point and others. For example, what are the public's views on the risks to any *new* health system from the *existing* centralized federal record systems (at IRS and SSA, for instance)? What about their views on the real danger of probabilistic matches to private data bases or to open or decentralized government systems, like vital records?

7. Summary Recommendations

Throughout this paper, recommendations have been made that address aspects of privacy concerns in any large scale record linkage activity involving the proposed new health system or between that system and others. Figure 11 below provides a brief summary of these.

The overall treatment of linkage opportunities in this paper has gone from situations that simply called for a signed notification statement, preferably at regular intervals (Section 3), to suggested (Section 4) or required (Section 5) informed consent – for linkage research in the health

---

53. This might be inferred from the 1993 Harris-Equifax Questions on access to patient health data by insurance companies and employers. Also from Blair (1995) and the other research started by Scheuren (1985). See endnotes 33 and 47.

system or linked record research more generally. Finally (in Section 6), there was a brief discussion of how to *prevent* matching for nonhealth administrative purposes, except in rare instances. In all of these discussions, recommendations have been given along with the views of others; also areas for future study have been highlighted.

Figure 11. Selected Permissible Record Data Linkages by Purpose and Under What Conditions	
Type of Data Linkage	Permissible and Under What Conditions
Administrative Data Linkages for the health of the patient.	Just notification needed (if for use of patient and patient caregivers only).
Other Administrative Data Linkages of Patient Records within the health system.	Greater safeguards seem needed once there is no longer a personal bond between patient and service provider (caregiver).
Basic Research Data Linkages within the Health System.	Notification and even maybe consent required for individual linkages, research review board authorization.
Research Data Linkages between Health and Other Record systems.	Generally consent should be required plus research review board authorization.
Nonresearch Administrative Data Linkages between Health and Nonhealth Record Systems.	For nonhealth reasons, only with a court order. For health reasons, only to directly aid patients.

Frankly, this paper advocates a "go slow," careful approach to any attempt at data linkages undertaken as part of health care reform. It is unlikely that all the potential vulnerabilities of the new linkage system will be learned by anything other than experience – hopefully not too hard won. Prototyping linkage experiments are key.[54] Patient consent and notification experiments will also be needed, as well as continuous study of public and patient opinion. An evolutionary rather than revolutionary strategy seems to represent the kind of humility and listening needed to avoid major blunders, especially in any advertent or inadvertent "takings" of privacy rights.

Much of the motivation around health reform speaks to efficiencies that can be gained with standardization of reporting and electronic data networking. These arguments seem to have merit; however, even if true, such changes will require a great many people to learn to do things in new ways and, potentially, paper records may need to continue to be employed for a long time (even if all new encounters are captured electronically).

---

54. See Schwartz et al. "Building Data Research Resources."

Because the job is so big, it is important to begin *now, but incrementally*. If structured properly, an orderly transition could be conducted, leaving ample time for human rights impacts to be respected.

An Afterword

An afterword may be worth making concerning the recommendations about "rights" in this paper; in particular, the rights to privacy and consent need to be set alongside the rights to universality and nondiscriminatory treatment.[55]

Record linkage can aid a society in achieving advances in the well-being of its citizens. This point may have been lost in the detailed discussion of privacy and consent concerns. For example, the epidemiological literature is full of health studies that use record linkage techniques to advance knowledge.[56]

The benefit side of record linkage can be oversold, however. A recent *Science* article may be worth quoting in this regard.[57]

> Over the past 50 years, epidemiologists have succeeded in identifying the more conspicuous determinants of noninfectious diseases – smoking, for instance, which can increase the risk of developing lung cancer by as much as 3000%. Now they are left to search for subtler links between diseases and environment causes or lifestyles. And that leads to the Catch-22 of modern epidemiology. On the one hand, these subtle risks – say, the 30% increase in the risk of breast cancer from alcohol consumption that some studies suggest – may affect such a large segment of the population that they have potentially huge impacts on public health. On the other, many epidemiologists concede that their studies are so plagued with biases, uncertainties, and methodo-

---

55. As elaborated in Audrey R. Chapman, "Introduction: Developing Health Information Systems Consistent with Human Rights Criteria," in this volume.

56. Cited earlier were Beebe, "Why Are Epidemiologists Interested in Matching Algorithms?"; Fair, "An Overview of Record Linkage in Canada"; and Newcombe, "When Privacy Threatens Public Health"; among others. In particular, see endnotes 7-8, 10, 12, and 34. Also of note in this context is the paper by Jonathan Sugarman et al., "Improving Health Data among American Indians and Alaska Natives: An Approach from the Pacific Northwest," in this volume.

57. G. Taubes, "Epidemiology Faces its Limits," *Science,* 14 July 1995, 164-69.

logical weaknesses that they may be inherently incapable of accurately discerning such weak associations. As Michael Thun, the
director of analytic epidemiology for the American Cancer Society, puts it, "With epidemiology you can tell a little thing from a
big thing. What's very hard to do is to tell a little thing from
nothing at all." Agrees Ken Rothman, editor of the journal
Epidemiology: "We're pushing the edge of what can be done with
epidemiology." With epidemiology stretched to its limits or beyond, says Dimitios Trichopoulos, head of the epidemiology department at the Harvard School of Public Health, studies will
inevitably generate false positive and false negative results "with
disturbing frequency."

Where does all of this leave things? The claim that this paper is just a
"starter set" is believed mainly to be true; but, in some places, even that
may exceed current knowledge. What, in fact, many of the recommendations call for is simply more empirical work and hard thinking. Particularly
crucial are two of these:

- Establishing ongoing programs of experimentation (e.g., on consent
  and notification statements), plus public opinion research on privacy
  issues, both in general and with a particular focus on record linkage.[58]
- Institute statistical work on group matching or other techniques that
  would lessen the tradeoff between the competing values of furthering
  scientific research *and* safeguarding personal privacy.[59]

In the end, of course, the recommendations made here are simply the
author's weighing of the evidence from the perspective of nearly 25 years
of experience working on record linkage.

58. As advocated in Scheuren, "Methodological Issues in Linkage," and as pursued by
him over the past 10 years through the sponsorship of numerous public opinion polls,
asking various questions about linkage. Most of these are discussed in Blair, "Ancillary
Uses of Government Administrative Data." Work at the Bureau of Labor Statistics, with
focus groups and other cognitive research techniques, has also been sponsored. At this
point the summary given already in endnote 33 represents the limited state of knowledge.
59. Certainly the seminal work of Spruill and Gastwirth, "On the Estimation of the
Correlation Coefficient from Grouped Data," needs to be followed up. One strategy is
to employ multiple group matches – combined with Gibbs sampling, for example.

CHAPTER TWELVE

Guidelines and Mechanisms for Protecting Privacy in Medical Data Used for Research

Robert Ellis Smith[1]

Introduction

This paper is intended:

1. To demonstrate the need for safeguards to protect medical information in the hands of researchers;

2. To recognize that individual identifying information is often an essential part of research data;

3. To recommend standards or guidelines for providing confidentiality in research projects; and

4. To provide mechanisms for doing so.

These guidelines are offered in the context of a national health care information network, either through some sort of health care financing reform or through an extensive system of computerized patient records.

Medical Confidentiality

In recognizing a *constitutional right to privacy*, the U.S. Supreme Court has more than once said that at the core of this right is control over one's

---

1. Robert Ellis Smith is an attorney and journalist who has published *Privacy Journal* newsletter since 1974. He is the author of *Our Vanishing Privacy*, *The Law of Privacy Explained*, and other books on privacy.

body and, with that, an expectation of confidentiality in medical treatment. In its 1973 opinion upholding the right to an abortion, *Roe v. Wade*, the Supreme Court cited one of the earliest recognitions of a "right to be let alone," an 1891 case upholding the refusal of a plaintiff in a lawsuit to be compelled to submit to an involuntary medical exam.[2]

In a companion case to *Roe*, Justice William O. Douglas wrote, "The right to privacy has no more conspicuous place than in the physician-patient relationship unless it be in the priest-penitent relationship. The right to seek advice on one's health and the right to place reliance on the physician of one's choice are basic to Fourteenth Amendment values."[3]

This "right" often seems more rhetorical than actual. There are many occasions when one's medical history is not confidential. This is especially true in a time when virtually all payments for medical treatment are handled by a third party, whether a private insurer or a governmental insurer. Employers keep extensive medical information, and it is often shared within the workplace. Hospitals and clinics provide medical information to the press, and some facilities are now using patient records to market their services. In addition, there is a constant demand for medical records for peer review and for medical and non-medical research.

U.S. Representative Nydia M. Velazquez of New York is correct in saying, "In some states it is easier to access a person's medical history than it is to obtain the records of a person's video rentals."[4]

All states but Rhode Island, South Carolina, Texas, and Vermont recognize a "doctor-patient" privilege.[5] That means that doctors may not be *compelled to testify in court* about medical facts received in confidence. The privilege does not directly affect disclosures voluntarily made by a physician nor does it affect disclosures made out of court. It does not protect medical information in the hands of those who are not doctors.

Doctors are also bound by ethical restrictions on patient confidentiality, stemming from the ancient oath of Hippocrates, the Greek physician regarded as a father of medicine.[6] The rationale of this code – that total candor

---

2. *Union Pacific Railway Co. v. Botsford*, 141 US 250 (1891).

3. *Doe v. Bolton*, 410 US 179 (1973).

4. Testimony before U.S. House Committee on Government Operations, Subcommittee on Information, 103rd Cong., 2nd sess., 20 April 1994.

5. *Compilation of State and Federal Privacy Laws* (Providence, RI: *Privacy Journal,* 1992).

6. As a physician, Hippocrates apparently engaged in longitudinal studies himself.

is essential for quality medical care – was articulated best by a federal court in Ohio, in 1965:

> Since the layman is unfamiliar with the road to recovery, he cannot sift the circumstances of his life and habits to determine what is information pertinent to his health. As a consequence, he must disclose all information . . . even that which is disgraceful or incriminating. To promote full disclosure, the medical profession extends the promise of secrecy. . . . The candor which this promise elicits is necessary to the effective pursuit of health; there can be no reticence, no reservations, no reluctance. . . .[7]

Once again, this ethical code does not cover non-medical professionals who handle medical information – like academic researchers – except to the extent that they impose it upon themselves.

Fewer than a dozen states – notably California, Colorado, Illinois, Massachusetts, Minnesota, Rhode Island, and Wisconsin – have sought to codify doctor-patient confidentiality with laws requiring medical information to be kept confidential.[8] There is no federal law.

In those states where there is no statute, courts have declared that there exists a *fiduciary duty* on the part of medical professionals to keep patient information confidential. For instance, the Supreme Court of Alabama has stated,

> It must be concluded that a medical doctor is under a general duty not to make extra-judicial disclosures of information acquired in the course of the doctor-patient relationship and that a breach of that duty will give rise to a cause of action. It is, of course, recognized that this duty is subject to exceptions prompted by the supervening interests of society, as well as the private interests of the patient himself.[9]

The court said further,

> Unauthorized disclosure of intimate details of a patient's health may amount to unwarranted publicization of one's private affairs with which the public has no legitimate concern such as to cause

---

See L. S. King, *A History of Medicine* (Middlesex, England: Penguin, 1971); and cited in Boruch and Cecil (see note 11).

7. *Hammonds v. Aetna Casualty & Surety Co.,* 243 F Supp 793 (N D Ohio 1965).

8. See note 4.

9. *Horne v. Patton,* 291 Ala 701, 287 So 2d 824 (Alabama 1973).

outrage, mental suffering, shame or humiliation to a person of ordinary sensibilities. Nor can it be said that an employer is necessarily a person who has a legitimate interest in knowing each and every detail of an employee's health. Certainly, there are many ailments about which a patient might consult his private physician which have no bearing or effect on one's employment.

An important exception to the general rule of non-disclosure is an instance when a professional is obligated to prevent harm to another and *should,* therefore, release information gained in a patient consultation.[10]

The AIDS epidemic has created special concerns about the disclosure of individual medical information because of the stigma that has been associated with the disease. Disclosure of the results of an individual's HIV test or of the status of a person with AIDS is prohibited by many state laws enacted in the last 10 years. In the past seven years, courts have held that disclosure of information about AIDS is an invasion of privacy, whether or not a law is on the books.[11]

An absolute defense to a common-law claim of privacy invasion is that the victim *consented* to a release of information. In a medical context, a knowing, informed authorization to release medical data provides consent. This means that the language and the circumstances of an authorization form that a patient is asked to sign are crucial.

Confidentiality in a Research Context

Just as medical professionals rely on the patient's expectation of confidentiality, so do researchers. Candor on the part of research subjects is important in medical and social research. Research subjects tend to cooperate more fully when there is an assurance of confidentiality,[12] although findings are split on whether an assurance of confidentiality at the time data are gathered helps or hurts responses, or does not matter.[13]

10. *Tarasoff v. Regents,* 13 Cal 3d 177, 118 Cal Rptr 129, 529 P 2d 553 (California 1974).

11. Robert Ellis Smith, *War Stories: Accounts of Persons Victimized by Invasions of Privacy,* (Providence, RI: *Privacy Journal,* 1993), 3-6.

12. Robert F. Boruch and Joe S. Cecil, *Assuring the Confidentiality of Social Research Data* (Philadelphia: University of Pennsylvania Press, 1979), 67 et seq.; also National Research Council, *Private Lives and Public Policies* (Washington, D.C.: National Academy Press, 1993), 8, 54.

The outcomes of some studies have more credibility if it can be said that the information was gathered in strict confidence, with complete candor and without any expectation that research subjects could gain or lose by how they responded.

The Vulnerability of Medical Information

There is no federal protection for medical records generally.[14] (Federal laws and regulations provide specific protection for drug-abuse, alcohol-abuse, Veterans Affairs, and AIDS information in some contexts.) Fewer than 12 states have laws protecting medical records generally.[15] For that reason and because medical information is shared with several non-medical entities, this information is subject to abuse – intentional or unintentional disclosures, use in misleading contexts, or use in ways that discriminate against the individual or exploit him or her commercially. A few anecdotes (not all of them involving medical information) show the different possibilities for breaches of confidentiality.[16]

- With a National Science Foundation grant, J. Steven Picou, a sociologist at the University of South Alabama, studied about 200 persons in Alaska to determine the social and psychological impact of the 1989 *Exxon Valdez* oil spill in Prince William Sound. In his interviews he discussed drug and alcohol use and family problems. Some of the persons in the survey were plaintiffs in spill-related

---

13. National Research Council, *Privacy and Confidentiality as Factors in Survey Response* (Washington, D.C.: National Academy Press, 1979).

14. The Privacy Protection Study Commission in its 1977 report defined a medical record as "a record, file, document, or other written materials relating to an individual's medical history, diagnosis, condition, treatment or evaluation which is created or maintained by a medical-care provider." *Personal Privacy in an Information Society* (Washington, D.C.: U.S. Government Printing Office, 1977), p 278n. For purposes of discussing privacy protection, information in the sole custody of an individual medical-care provider, like a doctor, is not a *medical record* unless and until it is shared with others (for instance, those who work with the individual provider). The Commission distinguished *medical-record information*, which it defined as "information obtained from a medical record or from the individual patient, his spouse, parent, or guardian, for the purpose of making a non-medical decision about him" (for instance, for insurance, employment, public assistance, or research).

15. See *State and Federal Privacy Laws*. (See note 4.)

16. For more medical examples outside of the research context, see Smith, *War Stories*. (See note 10.)

lawsuits against Exxon. A federal magistrate in Mobile, Alabama, ruled in 1993 that Exxon was entitled to his data, with identities of the respondents deleted. Still, many feared that their identities could be gleaned from the data, some of which concerned medical conditions. Although Picou protected the identities of his research subjects, the litigation suspended his research for nearly a year, and he viewed the result as "intolerable for survey research."[17]

- John Petterson conducted similar surveys about the *Exxon Valdez* spill aftermath for the Alaska towns that were affected. He gathered information reflecting on drug use, alcohol use, mental stress, and other factors in families. Petterson, an anthropologist in La Jolla, California, was unsuccessful in 1991 in preventing his raw findings from being turned over to Exxon. He said the material included "deductive identifications." A state court in Alaska said that only lawyers on both sides of the litigation could see the data, but Petterson was forced to take precautions for the possible next time.[18]

- Rik Scarce spent 159 days in jail in 1993 rather than comply with a grand jury order to answer questions about a radical group he was studying for his Ph.D thesis in sociology at Washington State University. Author of the definitive guide to radical environmentalists, Scarce interviewed a member of the Animal Liberation Front, a group charged with vandalizing an animal research lab at the university in 1991.[19]

- Staff members of Everywoman's Health Centre in Vancouver, British Columbia, were alarmed in August 1994 after receiving phone calls or mail at home from anti-abortion activists. They had made a point of not disclosing their home addresses and phone numbers. They discovered that the motor-vehicle records of at least three of the staff members had been accessed – and the access originated in the police department of the neighboring town of Delta, apparently through the Royal Canadian Mounted Police's computerized system.[20]

17. *Privacy Journal* 20, no. 1 (November 1993): 5.

18. *Ibid.*

19. *Ibid.*

20. *Privacy Journal* 21, no. 3 (January 1995): 4.

- When pupils at the Covenant Christian School in Morgantown, West Virginia, drew pictures and brought their works of art home, one parent was shocked to discover information on the reverse side. The school uses scrap paper from the nearby University of West Virginia. On the paper, the parent discovered a printout alphabetically listing names, Social Security numbers, and payment information for students who owe tuition bills. A university official, acknowledging that the disclosure probably violated federal and state laws on student records, said the disclosure occurred because of an "oversight."[21] This is one of several instances in which sensitive personal data have appeared in materials abandoned as trash and later discovered.

- Dr. Irving Selikoff, a New York City researcher conducting two studies on tobacco and cancer, assured his research subjects that the information they provided would remain confidential. In a lawsuit not involving Dr. Selikoff or two institutions where the information is stored, American Tobacco Company and two other companies (with a subpoena) compelled Dr. Selikoff to provide the data. A court held him in contempt for failing to comply, though it noted that it would take more than 1000 hours to delete data identifying the study subjects.[22]

- In 1988, several news organizations, including "60 Minutes," reported that Roy Cohn, the unpopular New York City attorney, was on the AIDS-treatment list of the National Institutes of Health. *Harper's* magazine reprinted the complete NIH medical record on Cohn.[23]

- Public health officials in Washington, D.C. said in 1987 that they lost a confidential book listing the names of 500 people testing positive for the AIDS virus.[24]

- A speculator bid $4000 for the patient records accumulated in more than 12 years of Dr. Donald Miller's family practice in the Greenville suburb of Taylor, South Carolina. The businessman said, "I'll buy anything that looks like I can make some money off of it." For $25

---

21. *Privacy Journal* 20, no. 4 (February 1994): 7.

22. *Mount Sinai School of Medicine v. American Tobacco Company*, 866 F2d 552 (2d Cir 1989).

23. *Harper's*, November 1986; *Privacy Journal* 14, no. 11 (September 1988): 3.

24. *Washington Times*, quoted in *New York Times*, 23 April 1987, p. A-21.

each he sold photocopies to former patients. The man eventually sold the records at a profit to a doctor in Jacksonville, Florida.[25]

- The Food and Drug Administration sponsored a raid of Dr. Jonathan Wright's alternative-medicine clinic in Kent, Washington, claiming he was distributing illegally manufactured vitamins and remedies. The physician had to petition a court for return of his patients' records; some patients were worried that they would be subpoenaed to testify.[26]

- In 1991 an epidemiologist at the Missouri Department of Health and a surveillance officer from the city AIDS program in St. Louis showed up at the offices of private physicians expecting names, addresses, ages, phone numbers, and Social Security numbers of all patients with the HIV virus or AIDS. They wanted to inspect individual patient records.[27]

- Objections to the federal census in West Germany in the 1980s led to a decision by the Federal Constitutional Court to postpone the survey because certain disclosures of personal data from the census were found to be unconstitutional.[28]

- Thousands of nude photographs taken of male and female students at major Northeastern universities for most of the first half of this century showed up in storage at the Smithsonian Institution in Washington in 1995. The frontal and profile "posture" photos were taken as part of a now generally discredited research project linking body shape and intelligence.[29]

- In 1992, copies of the medical file and the written account of her emergency treatment at St. Clare's Hospital in New York City were disseminated, mostly by facsimile transmissions, to several newspapers and television stations during the election campaign of Nydia Velazquez for Congress. She had been treated for depression after a suicide attempt in 1991.[30]

---

25. *New York Times,* 14 August 1991.

26. *Seattle Times,* 5 May 1993, p. E1.

27. *Riverfront Times,* weekly newspaper in St. Louis, MO, 26 June - 2 July 1991, p. 1.

28. David H. Flaherty, *Protecting Privacy in Surveillance Societies* (Chapel Hill: University of North Carolina Press, 1989), 81.

29. Article by Associated Press, *New York Times,* 21 January 1995; and the *New York Times Magazine,* 15 January 1995.

The Need for Identifiers in Research Projects

If all research projects used anonymous or cumulative data that had no identifiers, there would not be a major privacy problem. In fact, the first safeguard for privacy in research ought to be to do without identifiers linked to named individuals. (Still, it is possible to discern the identities of and cause embarrassment to the subjects of research using only anonymous or cumulative data. For that reason, all research projects using personal data, whether or not they identify the subjects directly, should include some degree of confidentiality safeguards.)

But, of course, many researchers insist, correctly, that the effectiveness and validity of their work can be assured only by means of identifying their research subjects. Valuable longitudinal studies are impossible without identifying individuals for follow-up in some way. In *Assuring the Confidentiality of Social Research Data*, psychologist Robert F. Boruch, now at the University of Pennsylvania, and attorney-researcher Joe S. Cecil, now at the Federal Judicial Center, make the point:

> [Longitudinal research][31] requires that an observation on a person at a particular time be linked with observations made on that person at subsequent times, for each person in a sample. The vehicle for linkage is typically, though not always, the individual's identification. The linkage implies some degradation of privacy, and so it behooves us to ask why such research is justified: to ask what we can learn or have learned from such research. . . .[32]
>
> [In addition] correlational research refers here to the process of establishing how two characteristics of an individual are related to one another. The average relation, for a large sample of individuals, may be represented in statistical form by a simple correlation coefficient, by a probability in an actuarial table, and so forth. For example, to identify the relation between level of health status and level of physical activity during work, one might obtain measures of both variables from each member of a suitable sample of individuals, link the two elements of information on each individual, and then compute an index of the relation based on that linkage. The correlation may be of descriptive interest alone,

---

30. *Velazquez v. St. Clare's Hospital,* 15737/94 (New York Sup. Ct., Kings County).

31. See also the term "epidemiologic follow-up study," used in National Research Council, *Survey Responses,* 171, and elsewhere. (See note 12.)

32. Boruch and Cecil, *Assuring the Confidentiality,* 31. (See note 11.)

in that it reflects the existence and strength of a relation between two variables. It may be more important to an individual, in that the correlation helps to predict future health status from current physical-exertion levels.[33]

Here are some examples of the value of longitudinal studies that required the identity of the research subjects:[34]

- The renowned Framingham Study, tracking the lives of 9,000 men, documented risks of heart disease, including the significance of cholesterol levels and other factors.

- Longitudinal studies have shown how patients comply with medical regimes, including those requiring prescriptions for drugs.

- A study in Denmark of 4000 adopted children showed how schizophrenia among them varied with its occurrence in their biological and their adoptive parents.

- Many studies have documented landmarks in child development and the link between nutrition and intelligence.

- The link between a rare type of vaginal cancer and the patient's mother having taken diethylstilbestrol (DES) was discovered in a Boston study that required linking medical data not only about the same individual over time but also about mothers and daughters.

- An epidemiological study at Johns Hopkins linked heart attacks with the administering of anticoagulants many years earlier

- The harmful side effects of taking oral contraceptives were discovered through epidemiologic studies of masses of medical records without patient consent.

Clearly, then, it is essential in some research to be able to identify individuals. It is rarely necessary, however, that the identity of the individuals and the data about the individuals be stored in the same place or

---

33. Boruch and Cecil, *Assuring the Confidentiality,* 31, 47. (See note 11.)

34. Examples 1 through 4 are from Boruch and Cecil, *Assuring the Confidentiality,* chapter 2. (See note 11.) Examples 4 through 7 are from U.S. House Committee on Government Operations, *Report of the U.S. House Committee on Government Operations on Health Security Act,* 103rd Cong., 2nd sess., (report 103-601, part 5), 121-24, from the testimony of Dr. Leon Gordis, chair of the Department of Epidemiology, Johns Hopkins School of Hygiene and Public Health. For other examples, see Leon Gordis and Ellen Gold, "Privacy Confidentiality, and the Use of Medical Records in Research," *Science* 207 (11 January 1980): 4427.

even be under the control of the same individual or institution. When identities are stored in the same place, the chances increase for unauthorized access and use.

By the same token, to facilitate necessary medical research, researchers need access to the results of previous research, including, in many cases, access to the identities of individuals involved. "Health research is an integral and necessary part of the modern health care system, and access to health care records is vital to the conduct of some health research projects," said the House of Representatives Committee on Government Operations, in its 1994 report on proposed legislation to protect confidentiality in the proposed national health care system.[35]

Guidelines for Privacy Protection

Thus, the need for using personally identifiable medical information in research must be reconciled with the need to protect the information from breaches of confidentiality. This is possible by abiding by guidelines for protecting confidentiality within a research context. These guidelines can be a part of any research project that uses medical records. The author has developed them from a variety of sources, notably:

1. The report of the Privacy Protection Study Commission, a federal study commission that completed its work in 1977 with recommendations for federal legislation;

2. *Assuring the Confidentiality of Social Research Data* (1979) by Robert F. Boruch and Joe S. Cecil;

3. A proposed "Health Information Privacy Code 1994" issued by the Privacy Commissioner in New Zealand;

4. The 1994 report of the House Committee on Government Operations, the *Health Security Act,* a proposal for protecting confidentiality in the Clinton Administration health care plan; and

5. The author's own experience.

Following the guidelines are suggested mechanisms for implementing each guideline.

---

35. U.S. House Committee on Government Operations, *Report on Health Security Act,* 120-21. (See note 33.)

a. Guideline One

There should be no release of personal information for research purposes if that violates the terms under which the information was originally gathered.[36] If data were gathered with a promise of confidentiality or a clear promise that it would be used only for specific purposes, then the data custodian ought to secure the informed consent of the individual before releasing it for research purposes.

b. Guideline Two

The research project should have been determined to be of sufficient importance and usefulness to warrant the possible threat to personal privacy.[37] When any kind of personally identifiable information is involved, there must be a means for screening out marginal projects, ill-considered research that "would be nice to do" or research to be conducted by inexperienced principals. When *medical information* (or other especially sensitive personal information) is involved, the undertaking should be an approved systemic and objective biomedical, epidemiological, or health services research or statistics project.[38] Special precautions must be taken when medical information is used in projects not directly related to the medical sciences, like the social sciences, where information is likely to be handled by non-medical personnel. If the possibility of a threat to privacy is high and the value of the project is not clear, then release of the personal information ought to be denied.

c. Guideline Three

When medical information is involved, a written protocol should describe the disclosure, use, and disposition of the medical records.[39] Writing one's plans requires a person to think in advance about them and to justify any deviation from them afterward. This assists in implementing Guideline Two.

---

36. This is adapted from Recommendation (7) of the Privacy Protection Study Commission, *Personal Privacy in an Information Society*, 591. (See note 13.)

37. This is adapted from Section 5136 of the proposed *Health Security Act*. See U.S. House Committee on Government Operations, *Report on Health Security Act*, 36. (See note 33.)

38. The language is from U.S. House Committee on Government Operations, *Report on Health Security Act*, 125. (See note 33.)

39. Original with the author.

d. Guideline Four

The research project or the organization of which it is a part should be bound (by existing law, contract, or commitment) to abide by the Code of Fair Information Practices. The code, first published by the HEW Advisory Committee on Automated Personal Data Systems,[40] has received general acceptance in the privacy field over the past 20 years. It is now the core of laws like the federal Privacy Act, the Family Educational Rights and Privacy Act, and fair information practices laws in 15 states.[41] The code requires that:

1. There must be no personal-information systems whose very existence is secret.

2. There must be a way for a person to find out what information about him or her is in a record and how it is used.

3. There must be a way for a person to prevent personal information that was obtained for one purpose from being used or made available for other purposes without the consent of the person.

4. There must be a way for a person to correct or amend a record of identifiable information about the person.

5. Any organization creating, maintaining, using, or disseminating records of identifiable personal data must assure the reliability of the information for its intended use and must take precautions to prevent misuse of the data.

e. Guideline Five

No individual should be required to divulge medical information about himself or herself for a research or statistical purpose.[42] This means that providing medical information expressly for research should be voluntary (except in specially approved studies where voluntary participation would skew outcomes).

---

40. U.S. Department of Health, Education and Welfare, *Records, Computers and the Rights of Citizens* (Washington, D.C.: U.S. Government Printing Office and Cambridge: MIT Press, 1973), p. xx.

41. See *State and Federal Privacy Laws.* (See note 4.)

42. This is adapted from Recommendation (4) of the Privacy Protection Study Commission, *Personal Privacy in an Information Society,* 602. (See note 13.)

In many cases, of course, the medical data would have been previously collected, as in the case of outcomes research relying on existing medical records. In those cases, researchers should comply with Guideline One, using only data where the individual has not expressly said that he or she does not want the data used for other purposes.

Special precautions must be taken when data are requested voluntarily from individuals who are vulnerable because they are incompetent, infirm, incarcerated, institutionalized, of minor age, or in subordinate positions to the research investigator (like students or employees).[43]

f. Guideline Six

Researchers should show that they are aware of applicable federal, state, and local laws concerning confidentiality and have a means for complying with them.[44] There are a plethora of privacy laws affecting certain kinds of records:

1. state government files (including, in some cases, records in state universities) in 15 states;

2. records held by federal agencies, as well as federal contractors operating data systems for the federal government (the federal Privacy Act);

3. patient records in Veterans Affairs facilities;

4. records of *students* in federally assisted universities and school systems;

5. occupational health records;

6. computer files protected by state and federal laws punishing computer-related crimes;

7. files in drug and alcohol treatment facilities and community mental health centers; and

8. HIV and AIDS-related information in federal programs and in most states.[45]

---

43. Privacy Commissioner of New Zealand, *Health Information Privacy Code 1994 with Commentary* (Auckland: Office of the Privacy Commissioner, 1994), Part 4, Sec. 18(2), p. 49.

44. This is adapted from Recommendation (5C) of the Privacy Protection Study Commission, *Personal Privacy in an Information Society,* 585. (See note 13.)

45. *State and Federal Privacy Laws,* 32-37. (See note 4.)

Before accepting medical information, researchers *in government agencies* should become aware of disclosure requirements under the applicable federal or state Freedom of Information or Open Meetings laws and adapt their protocol or notice to individuals accordingly. Because a Freedom of Information law may mandate disclosure of a researcher's materials ultimately, it is possible that a researcher may have to secure the consent of an individual data subject, or to refrain from using certain information, or to destroy individually identifiable information sooner than he or she otherwise would.

g. Guideline Seven

A research project involving medical information should employ, as necessary, techniques for preserving anonymity, preventing the linkage of data and personal identifiers, assuring accuracy and timeliness, securing the data, and wisely destroying or preserving the data after the project is completed.[46] Special precautions should be taken when data from one source are merged with data from other sources. Prompt destruction of study data or identifiers may seem to be one way to guarantee privacy protection, but it may not be in the best interests of future research or of the data subjects themselves. Nonetheless, when data is destroyed or disposed of, it must be in such a way as to obliterate individual identifiers.

h. Guideline Eight

Individually identifiable medical data used in research should not be used for any decision or action directly affecting the individual.[47] This principle goes to the essence of the customary "research" exemption from most nondisclosure requirements: researchers are permitted access to personal

---

46. This is a consolidation of Recommendation (7) of the Privacy Protection Study Commission, *Personal Privacy in an Information Society,* 584; and U.S. House Committee on Government Operations, *Report on Health Security Act,* 36. (See notes 13 and 33.) See also New Zealand, *Health Information Privacy Code,* Part 2, Rule 8: "A health agency that holds health information *must* not use that information without taking such steps (if any) as are, under the circumstances, reasonable to ensure that, having regard to the purpose for which the information is proposed to be used, the information is accurate, up to date, relevant, and not misleading." (See note 42.)

47. This is adapted from Recommendation (1) of the Privacy Protection Study Commission, *Personal Privacy in an Information Society,* 574. (See note 13.) See also U.S. House Committee on Government Operations, *Report on Health Security Act,* sec. 5135, p. 35. (See note 33.)

data (often without consent) precisely because the individual is not vulnerable to negative consequences from this use of their data.

The purpose of research is to reach conclusions about groups of individuals or about phenomena, not to make decisions about individuals. Because of this, researchers are permitted access to sensitive personal information they might otherwise be denied. To preserve that privileged access, researchers must use the data only for the original purpose, unless they further get the consent of the individual.

It would be inappropriate for a researcher or anyone else to identify one or more data subjects for discipline, medical treatment, insurance rating, or anything else based on research categorizations or findings. If in the course of research, this appears to be advisable, the matter should be referred to the individual data subject or to the entity that provided the data. This is true even if the disclosure would seem to be in the interests of the individual; a researcher cannot predict with certainty the consequences of making even well-intended disclosures.

The sole exception to this guideline is to prevent imminent harm to an individual (in which case many professionals are *obligated* to disclose information to the proper authorities).[48] This exception would justify a researcher disclosing to police authorities that a research subject had homicidal intentions (even though clearly this disclosure would have consequences to the individual). Likewise, it would justify disclosing that a medical record shows that an individual has a contagious disease not previously known to the medical provider. Often in clinical research, the provider and the researcher are the same person.

i. Guideline Nine

An entity regularly engaged in research with medical information should develop an unequivocal reputation for confidentiality and fairness in its information practices.[49] This can be done by impressing upon staff the importance of confidentiality, by publicly resisting improper demands for information, and by providing timely notices to data subjects, as appropriate, about the nature of its work. The public may be more permissive in approving the use of sensitive medical information if it is persuaded of the benefits of the work conducted by a research entity.

---

48. The standards are described in *Tarasoff v. Regents*. (See note 9.)

49. Original with the author.

j. Guideline Ten

Researchers should not invoke incorrect notions of "privacy" for their own interests.[50] Boruch and Cecil call this "institutional self-protection . . . under false colors of privacy."[51] For instance, a researcher should not refuse to disclose truly *cumulative* data or findings, saying to do so would violate personal privacy, unless this is true.

The right to privacy does not protect corporations, organizations or other "artificial persons" or "legal persons." Courts agree that privacy, by definition, is uniquely a personal right.[52] While promises of confidentiality or considerations of trade secrets may prevent a researcher from sharing nonpersonal data, the concept of "privacy" ought not be invoked as a shield.

Further, it is improper for a researcher to invoke "privacy" as a reason for declining to release details about methodology or outcomes or truly anonymous or cumulative data that, for other reasons, he or she wishes not to disclose. To do so devalues the concept of privacy and dilutes its valid protections.

Similarly, "privacy" ought not be invoked to prevent the disclosure of information about deceased persons. An individual's right to privacy virtually expires upon death. Considerations for the privacy of and emotional distress to surviving friends and relatives may affect whether a researcher discloses certain individually identifiable information, and the law recognizes their rights. But the supposed right to privacy of the deceased is not a consideration, according to court decisions.[53]

k. Guideline Eleven

Before releasing cumulative data, a researcher should make sure that sensitive microdata cannot be discovered about individuals by inference or otherwise.[54] This is called "inferential disclosure" by one of the giants in this field, Tore Dalenius.[55]

---

50. Original with the author.

51. Boruch and Cecil, *Assuring the Confidentiality,* 83. (See note 11.)

52. Robert Ellis Smith, "The Law of Privacy Explained" *Privacy Journal,* 1993, sec. 1.15.

53. *Ibid.,* sec. 1.15.

54. Original with the author.

55. Quoted in National Research Council, *Private Lives,* 144. Boruch and Cecil use the term "deductive disclosure." (See note 11.)

To disclose seemingly anonymous statistics about medical diagnoses, family makeup, and ages in a data set of, say, 80,000 households could easily reveal the identity of the presence of leukemia in a family known to have two girls of certain ages, a boy of a certain age, a father of a certain age, and a mother of a certain age. Only one family among the 80,000 may fit that description.[56] Releasing cumulative data about car ownership, family income, and the presence of cancer in all families in a census bloc of 200 households would have the same effect.

Especially with computer-assisted analyses, a person could infer or deduce additional amounts of individually identifiable information from a seemingly anonymous data set.

l. Guideline Twelve

There should be no disclosure of individually identifiable medical information by a researcher, except (1) to an auditor who is bound by the same confidentiality restrictions as the researcher and who does not preserve the data himself or herself; (2) in rare cases, to prevent imminent physical injury, harm, or death to an individual or imminent serious criminal property damage, when the information is not available from the original source; or (3) to comply with a judicial order, when the researcher's organization has exhausted all alternatives to disclosure and when the individual data subject(s) have had an opportunity to contest the validity of the demand.[57] It may not be possible for a researcher to resist totally a judicial demand for individually identifiable information, but the researcher must be diligent in determining the legal sufficiency and legitimacy of the demand and must explore all possibilities for conditional disclosure, for protected (*in camera*) disclosure, or for simultaneous notice to the research subjects.

An individual whose identity and medical information is wrongfully disclosed should have a legal right of action against the researcher and/or organization that discloses the information and against the individual receiving the information, in accord with legal principles established by privacy case law in the jurisdiction.

---

56. Example used in National Research Council, *Private Lives,* 145. (See note 11.)

57. Adapted from Privacy Protection Study Commission, *Personal Privacy in an Information Society,* 583. (See note 13.)

Mechanisms for Implementing the Guidelines

To implement the foregoing guidelines, there are a variety of techniques and mechanisms available. Researchers should adopt these mechanisms as much as possible. Some may be duplicative; others may be unnecessary if the sensitivity of the information, the risk of disclosure, or the level of harm that could be caused by disclosure is not high.

The following mechanisms for protecting privacy are grouped so as to correspond to the numbered guidelines.

a. Group One Mechanisms – to Implement Guideline One

There should be no release of personal information for research purposes if that violates the terms under which the information was originally gathered.

A. A researcher can protect himself or herself and provide the best protection for data subjects by procuring informed consent. Still, securing the consent of an individual may skew results, or be impractical or too expensive, and so it is not a prerequisite for research use.

B. If a researcher has an ongoing relationship with an organization that is the source of medical information, that organization may secure the consent of the individual for research uses when the data are originally collected.

b. Group Two Mechanisms – to Implement Guideline Two

The research project should have been determined to be of sufficient importance and usefulness to warrant the possible threat to personal privacy.

A. Researchers should document the importance of their project, especially if it requires the gathering or handling of sensitive personal data. *Who* determines whether research is of "sufficient importance" is less crucial than documenting that *someone* has made that determination and on what grounds.
    This documentation could include a "balancing" test, weighing the intrusion against the value of the information to be discovered.

B. Researchers should be prepared to say that the outcome of a research project may simply not warrant the intrusions.

If anecdotal evidence shows that many impoverished persons rely on pet food for sustenance, does that warrant an extensive research project that will only increase the humiliation of the respondents, especially when the study is unlikely to be used to alter social policy? A medical sociologist at Virginia Commonwealth University in the 1970s wisely declined to conduct the study.[58] "Some research is not worth the cost, both in terms of privacy invasion and dollars," said Edward H. Peoples, Jr.[59]

Is it ethical to subject thousands of Los Angeles school children to the discomfort of skin tests, then not notify or follow-up the hundreds of children who showed positive signs of exposure to tuberculosis? This was done in 1976.

"Most government statistics are great for professors to analyze after the fact but are of little value in making operating decisions," said John T. Dunlop, then professor at Harvard University.[60]

c. Group Three Mechanisms – to Implement Guideline Three

When medical information is involved, a written protocol should describe the disclosure, use, and disposition of the medical records.

   A. Written protocols must make clear who has access to sensitive information and under what circumstances. Provisions for confidentiality and for disposition of personally identifiable information should be a part of the research protocol.

   B. "Research protocols must be developed prior to undertaking health research, specifying the personal information to be collected, why this information is necessary for the research, and the use to which this information will be put."[61] While many researchers will see this as needlessly time-consuming and costly, they will probably discover that the exercise, besides protecting the rights of individuals, serves to sharpen their ideas about the goals of the project and streamlines their demands for data.

---

58. *Privacy Journal* 2, no. 3 (January 1976): 5-6.

59. *Community Nutrition Institute Weekly Report* 45 (13 November 1975): 4. Quoted in *Privacy Journal*. (See note 53.)

60. *Ibid.*

61. New Zealand, *Health Information Privacy Code,* Part 4, Sec. 15(1), p. 48. (See note 42.)

C. A paper trail helps the researcher document good-faith efforts to protect privacy. It is also the means for imposing sanctions on untrustworthy researchers who deviate from their written protocol. It establishes the legitimacy of the project, irrespective of privacy considerations.

d. Group Four Mechanisms – to Implement Guideline Four

The research project or the organization of which it is a part should be bound (by existing law, contract, or commitment) to abide by the Code of Fair Information Practices.

A. Researchers should subscribe to the ethical standards in their profession concerning confidentiality. Thus, non-medical personnel involved in the project commit themselves to be bound by the confidentiality strictures of their own disciplines. This will bolster their case if at a later time they must invoke a researcher's "privilege" to prevent the disclosure of individually identifiable information.

B. If the discipline or professional association of which a project staff person is a member does not have an ethical standard concerning confidentiality, that person's access to sensitive individually identifiable information should be denied – and the denial should be documented. At the same time, the staff person and the principal researcher should work within that discipline or professional association to implement confidentiality standards.

C. Asking all project personnel to read the *Code of Fair Information Practices* and to agree in writing to abide by it makes clear to them the importance of confidentiality. It also uncovers at an early stage any aspects of the research plans that are inconsistent with the code and therefore must in some way be reconciled.

D. Public advisories about the nature of research being conducted reduces the secrecy attached to a project. In addition, publicity may lead data subjects to believe that they are being "compensated" for the use of their data by the benefits to be derived from their participation. As a by-product, of course, publicity alerts other researchers about ongoing projects.

E. By the same token, sending a progress report or summary of research findings to data subjects provides a form of "compensation" for the use of their data. (Using personal data for commercial profit without compensating the individual or securing his or her consent is recognized as a privacy tort.[62] Providing information about the project to the data subject may serve as this "compensation." It may also comply with the public-notice requirement in the first element of the *Code of Fair Information Practices.*)

F. Asking research subjects to scrutinize and correct information about themselves, while not required in the research context, is the best assurance of data quality.[63] It may have the added effect of bringing to the attention of the researcher relevant variables that had previously been overlooked. In the context of medical records, "correcting" means amending, adding to, or rebutting information in the file, not erasing it or changing it (unless the medical provider agrees that the information should be erased or changed).

G. In any case, the research project must be equipped to respond to inquiries from data subjects about the content and accuracy of information about themselves.

H. All accesses to personal data, whether the access is manual or automated, should be logged and identified. Passwords should be required.

I. Sensitive medical information ought not be maintained in computer systems linked to other systems by modems or other means, unless absolutely necessary. If it is linked, computer hackers and others may have unauthorized access or viruses may corrupt the data. Techniques

---

62. Smith, "The Law of Privacy Explained," sec. 1.11. (See note 51.)

63. There is a contrary view: "If information is to be used only for statistical purposes, and the safeguards to prevent identification are sufficient, we see no need for data subjects to be given access. Great efforts should, of course, be devoted by those responsible to ensuring the accuracy of statistical data, but we accept that it is not always essential, and often not cost-effective for statistical purposes, to attempt to ensure absolute accuracy. In consequence, we see no need for individuals to have a general right to correct errors in data held about them for statistical purposes alone. It is difficult to see how an individual can be harmed by the use of inaccurate data about him in a statistical analysis in which he cannot be identified," said the United Kingdom Data Protection Committee in 1978. Martin Bulmer, ed., *Censuses, Surveys and Privacy*, (New York: Holmes & Meier Publishers Inc., 1979), 222. But imagine the trauma if research data incorrectly lists a person as having the HIV virus and, years later, a research staff person, with the best of intentions, recommends a treatment to that person. Or what if the data are later published in such a way that the person can identify himself or herself?

for assuring computer security – available from several trade associations – should be used.

J. When the sensitivity of the data and the size of the project warrants it, a researcher should implement a *security management plan*. Prototypes are available from computer-security consultants and trade associations.

K. To insure against possible conflicts of interest, each project should appoint a privacy officer, or disclosure officer, who monitors the project for privacy compliance and acts as an advocate for the interests of data subjects in internal discussions. This need not be the individual's exclusive responsibility, but this responsibility should be distinct from the goals of the research itself.[64]

An ethics committee or oversight committee could serve this function, so long as the responsibility does not rest with someone who has a stake in the outcome of the project. It is this person (or committee) who should monitor the project for compliance with these guidelines.

L. As privacy problems become more acute, there are two prototypes that researchers could use as enforcement mechanisms. One is the ethics committee in each state bar association, which will render an opinion upon request as to whether a certain course of conduct meets the ethical standards of the legal profession. The ethics committee also rules on complaints of unprofessional conduct. The other is the National Commission for the Protection of Human Subjects in Biomedical and Behavioral Science Research, established by the National Research Act of 1974. In the 1970s, it defined ethical principles, recommended policies, and answered specific inquiries about the propriety of a course of conduct.

A third method of enforcement is simply to use compliance with the guidelines as evidence of "reasonable care" in any legal challenge or disciplinary proceeding concerning a course of conduct. By the same token, failure to abide by the guidelines would be evidence of a failure to take "reasonable care."

---

64. European "data protection laws" require an organization that operates a database to have a data protection officer, to whom complaints are directed and who serves as a liaison with the regulator.

e. Group Five Mechanisms – to Implement Guideline Five

No individual should be required to divulge medical information about himself or herself for a research or statistical purpose.

A. In gathering information by interview, a technique of "randomized response," or variations on it, may be used. "In a simple variant of that approach, the researcher presents each member of a sample with two questions, one innocuous and one sensitive, each answerable with a Yes or No response. The respondent is asked to roll a die and to answer the first question if (say) a one turns up on the die, and the second if two, three, etc. show up. Given the proper sampling scheme and the odds on answering each question, it takes only a little algebra to estimate the proportions in the population who answered Yes to each question," according to Boruch and Cecil.[65] This presumably provides protection even in a group interview, in which other members of the group do not know whether an individual is answering question one ("Have you ever wet the bed?") or two ("Do you like broccoli?").

B. Researchers should assure data subjects that refusal to provide all or part of requested information will not affect the provision of health care to the individual in any way.[66] If this is not workable, the researcher should collect the information a second time in another manner.

f. Group Six Mechanisms – to Implement Guideline Six

Researchers should show that they are aware of applicable federal, state, and local laws concerning confidentiality and have a means for complying with them.

A. Research staff must be reminded that state or federal confidentiality laws not specifically covering medical information may affect their work. This is true, for instance, if students are research subjects or if drug-abuse information is used or if there is unauthorized access by computer.

---

65. Boruch and Cecil, *Assuring the Confidentiality*, 7. (See note 11.)

66. Adapted from New Zealand, *Health Information Privacy Code*, Part 4, Sec. 17(2), p. 49. (See note 42.)

B. It may be possible for a government researcher who will ultimately be compelled to release certain data (under a Freedom of Information law) simply to have the data stored outside of his or her agency. A researcher would then have periodic access to the individually identifiable information he or she needs in the hands of a nongovernment entity, like a private hospital, but not have it stored in his or her agency. Only anonymous data would be stored in the government agency.

g. Group Seven Mechanisms – to Implement Guideline Seven

A research project involving medical information should employ, as necessary, techniques for preserving anonymity, preventing the linkage of data and personal identifiers, assuring accuracy and timeliness, securing the data, and wisely destroying or preserving the data after the project is completed.

A. Data subjects may be assigned an alias, or asked to select one.

B. Personal data may be encrypted (scrambled) to assure confidentiality. The decryption key (unscrambling device) should be stored elsewhere and made available only to authorized persons.

C. Even elementary encryption may be used to prevent a direct link between medical data and the name of the individual. For instance, the data file may be assigned a sequential number, like 546. The name of the patient (stored elsewhere) to whom that data pertain may be retrieved by a formula (multiply the file number by 3 and subtract 5). The number 1633 is assigned to the patient's name. The formula (a x 3 - 5) is known only to selected personnel and is stored in a secure place. Or the original custodian of the records (a private psychiatrist, for instance) may hold the formula. To guard against unwarranted law enforcement access to medical data, the researcher may want to have the patient name file or the formula (or both) stored outside of the state jurisdiction or outside of the U.S. (This may or may not provide protection from legal process in the state.) Or the whereabouts of the formula (key) could be known only to someone outside of the jurisdiction of American courts (and possibly not even known to the researcher).

This is a variation on the link file system used by the American Council on Education.[67]

D. In gathering data on individuals from a second source, a researcher should avoid indirectly disclosing characteristics of those individuals. "Even being a member of a list may constitute sensitive information," observe Boruch and Cecil.[68] A researcher known to be studying a correlation between drug addicts and violent crimes, for instance, would be neglecting privacy by taking a list of data subjects to the local police and asking for conviction records. Instead, the researcher should have an intermediary do this or disguise his or her list of addicts by adding dummy names to the list.

E. In general, a researcher may use a broker or an intermediary to gather information from additional sources. For instance, in the direct-mail business, an organization often rents its membership or customer list to a second organization on the condition that the list is disclosed only to a "neutral" mailing shop (which has no interest in the addresses on the list), which performs the mailing for the requesting organization.

F. A project should keep a log of all disclosures of individually identifiable information.[69]

G. If a researcher has made preliminary assessments based on very sensitive data used without the individual's knowledge, he or she could collect the data from the individuals a second time, this time anonymously.

H. A researcher should have a careful plan for disposing of obsolete personal data – shredding, obliterating, or burning all materials that contain personal information. Back-up computer files must be erased (with assurance) as well as the principal documents. Materials with personal data should not be recycled or given away for other purposes.

h. Group Eight Mechanisms – to Implement Guideline Eight

Individually identifiable medical data used in research should not be used for any decision or action directly affecting the individual.

---

67. Described in Boruch and Cecil, *Assuring the Confidentiality,* 109. (See note 11.)

68. Boruch and Cecil, *Assuring the Confidentiality,* 121. (See note 11.)

69. This is required of government agencies by the *Privacy Act* and of credit bureaus by the *Fair Credit Reporting Act.*

A. Researchers should establish what has been called "functional separation,"[70] so that data collected and maintained for research or statistical use cannot be used or disclosed for any other purpose. This requires keeping research data segregated in distinct data files. Files maintained only for research purposes should be identified as such.

i. Group Nine Mechanisms – to Implement Guideline Nine

An entity regularly engaged in research with medical information should develop an unequivocal reputation for confidentiality and fairness in its information practices.

A. Researchers who regularly conduct research with medical information may choose to make a highly visible resistance to a demand for information. This will establish their reputation – and the reputation of those in their field – for preserving confidentiality.[71] Many journalists, members of Alcoholics Anonymous, staff of the Bureau of the Census, and some medical practitioners and lawyers have dramatically resisted demands for personal information, even risking incarceration. They have not always been successful, but they have succeeded in providing the public with a notion that AA, census, journalists, doctors, and lawyers are serious about protecting confidences.

j. Group Ten Mechanisms – to Implement Guideline Ten

Researchers should not invoke incorrect notions of "privacy" for their own interests.

A. Researchers should make clear to outsiders that concerns about "privacy" involve (1) only personal information, (2) only personal information that is sensitive, and (3) only personal information that is identifiable with a named individual or retrievable by that person's name or other identifier. When protecting nonpersonal information (about corporations, for instance) or protecting cumulative data,

70. Privacy Protection Study Commission, *Personal Privacy in an Information Society,* 572. (See note 13.)

71. Bulmer stresses the importance of maintaining public confidence, *Censuses, Surveys, and Privacy,* 207-209. (See note 63.)

researchers should refer to "trade secrets" or "confidential information," but not to "privacy."

B. Researchers may want to track and record the deaths of research subjects. They have additional leeway in using this data, because of the diminished right to privacy.

k. *Group Eleven Mechanisms – to Implement Guideline Eleven*

Before releasing cumulative data, a researcher should make sure that sensitive microdata cannot be discovered about individuals by inference or otherwise.

A. Instead of releasing a complete cumulative data set that may disclose individually identifiable microdata, a researcher may release only a sample of the data, showing the same outcomes.[72]

B. A researcher may *mask* the cumulative data by including "simulated data"; by using "cell suppression," "random error," "topcoding," or "blurring";[73] or by excluding certain variables, to the extent that this does not distort the outcomes.[74]

C. If "inferential disclosure"[75] is possible, the researcher should reconsider where and when the cumulative data are released. He or she must also weigh the sensitivity of the data. Inferential disclosure that is possible by reading an academic journal 10 years after the data were collected raises far fewer privacy concerns than inferential disclosure from data released to the community newspaper contemporaneously with its collection.

l. *Group Twelve Mechanisms – to Implement Guideline Twelve*

There should be no disclosure of individually identifiable medical information by a researcher, except (1) to an auditor who is bound by the same confidentiality restrictions as the researcher and who does not preserve the data himself or herself; (2) in rare cases, to prevent imminent physical injury, harm, or death to an individual or imminent serious criminal

---

72. National Research Council, *Private Lives,* 146. (See note 11.)

73. *Ibid.,* 10.

74. *Ibid.,* 146.

75. See Dalenius, at note 54 above.

property damage, when the information is not available from the original source; or (3) to comply with a judicial order, when the researcher's organization has exhausted all alternatives to disclosure and when the individual data subject(s) have had an opportunity to contest the validity of the demand.

A. A research team should "role play" how they will respond to outside demands for individually identifiable information in the future. This is much like having a contingency emergency plan. This would include consulting with the entity that provided the information, with the entity of which they are a part, with legal counsel, and possibly with the data subject.

B. Any communications to data subjects (or to others if the identity of the data subjects may be revealed) should be sealed and confidential. It is unwise to mail *postcards* to research subjects; it is unwise to leave telephone messages with family or friends if the nature of the research can become known; it is unwise to send facsimile messages containing sensitive personal information. Some facsimile machines have encryption capability and may be accessed by a key possessed by the addressee only. Medical researchers should use these devices. But there is no guarantee against dialing wrong numbers. Sensitive personal medical data should not be faxed.

Conclusion

The law and our society recognize a legitimate expectation of privacy in one's medical records. At the same time, there is a need to access and use medical records for legitimate research projects. And many of those projects require identifying individuals with the records, at least within the confines of the research project. Researchers are expected to reconcile these two interests.

The 1990s are a time of increased sharing of medical data for insurance reimbursement, government payments, administration, and even marketing. Within the decade there may well be created a major national or regional system for processing health care payments. This decade is also a time of gossip journalism, computerization of patient records, computer "hacking," and the marketing of personal information. In this decade there have been an unacceptable number of abuses of medical confidentiality.

This is the environment in which medical researchers must work. The major obstacle seems to be getting the researcher and his or her colleagues to recognize this reality and to accept the idea that adding privacy safeguards will not seriously deter their work. Once they have accepted that idea, implementing necessary precautions is not overly difficult or expensive. Implementing fair information practices will provide side benefits: increased public awareness of the role of research, closer ties with data subjects, better information management, improved accuracy rates, reduced demands for marginal data.

Principles developed over the past two decades provide guidance. Techniques for complying with the principles are numerous and readily available.

CHAPTER THIRTEEN

Data for Health: Privacy and Access Standards for a Health Care Information Infrastructure

George T. Duncan

1. Introduction

People seek both privacy and care. This tension between what is held privately and what is sought publicly is evident when people undergo medical treatment. Their sense of what is private is challenged and probed: to get data for health, physicians and nurses ask personal questions about bodily functions, embarrassing thoughts and sexual behavior. If patients are to get reimbursed, business offices, insurers and government agencies want to know about finances. If they are to resume their job, employers want details of their health status. If medical progress is to be made, researchers need data on patients and their treatment. On both the privacy side and the data access side, this tension is heightened by technological developments, especially in computer systems and telecommunication networks.

Emphasizing the privacy side, Nick Gallo writes for a popular audience, "Even as you read this, your personal medical history is just a few computer keystrokes away from an expanding army of bureaucrats."[1] This kind of journalistic coverage either reflects or has had an impact on public opinion. According to the Harris (now sponsored by Equifax) Health Information Privacy Surveys, the percentage of respondents that were "very concerned" about threats to their personal privacy jumped 20 percentage points, from 31% in 1978 to 51% in 1994.[2] Further, in the 1993 survey,

---

1. Nick Gallo, "Safeguarding Your Medical Records," *Better Homes and Gardens* (September 1994): 42.

27% believed health care providers and others had improperly disclosed information from their medical records.

In counterpoint on the access side, Fitzmaurice offers a vivid vision of a healthier future:[3]

- A sick child in a rural area gets sophisticated medical attention because of information transmitted by telecommunications;

- A state public health official who is alerted by an information system to a high incidence of children treated for respiratory disorders in a community diverts supplies of vaccine to where they are needed;

- A surgeon practices for prostate surgery using a virtual reality representation based on clinical measurements from the patient who will actually undergo the surgery.

Further, as emphasized by Gordis and Gold, major health studies have required the use of medical records.[4] These studies have demonstrated important health links, such as the relationship of cigarette smoking to lung cancer, coronary heart disease, and bladder cancer. Other studies have shown how concentrations of oxygen to premature infants results in blindness.

Reconciling these competing demands for privacy and data access is not easy, and has been the subject of much public debate and many legislative initiatives. This paper explores the human rights implications of privacy, confidentiality and data access standards for a national health information infrastructure. Based on a review of relevant studies by various groups and scholars, it recommends standards that seek to resolve the tension between information needs and privacy concerns. The basic thrust of this paper is that privacy and confidentiality need not be sacrificed to obtain the benefits of health information. Both can be achieved through

---

2.   Eleanor Singer, Robert Y. Shapiro, and Lawrence R. Jacobs, "Privacy of Health Care Data: What Does the Public Know? How Much Do They Care?" Paper presented at the 1995 Annual Meeting of the American Statistical Association in Orlando, FL (Washington, D.C.: American Statistical Association, 14 August 1995), 4. Most of this increase occurred between 1978 and 1983. Singer, Shapiro, and Jacobs discuss the 1993 Harris survey in detail.

3.   J. Michael Fitzmaurice, "Health Care and the NII," *Putting the Information Infrastructure to Work: A Report of the Information Infrastructure Task Force Committee on Application and Technology* (Washington, D.C.: U.S. Government Printing Office, May 1994), 41-56.

4.   Gordis, Leon, and Gold, "Privacy, Confidentiality, and the Use of Medical Records in Research," *Science* 207 (11 January 1980): 153-56.

standards that ensure responsible access to data and effective privacy and confidentiality controls.

The following questions are addressed:

1. Are there certain types of data that should not be collected?

2. What is a violation of health care information privacy?

3. What would deter potential violators of privacy?

4. What are appropriate requirements for informed consent and notification that protect the confidentiality of patients' records, while maximizing research access to data?

5. How can patients better access their own information?

6. How should an oversight body be instituted to oversee privacy in health care information?

First, it is necessary to establish a context for these questions that makes sense in the immediate future environment. Technological, medical, economic, and social considerations point to the increased use of electronic medical records that are linked via telecommunications in large-scale networks. Data users comprise those individuals and organizations involved in primary patient care, supporting activities, and social uses of health data. They can better serve patients and society generally by having a rich record that includes a broad range of information about individual patients and their institutional and caregiver interactions. Such information includes demographic, environmental, clinical, financial, employment, family history, and health history data. Juster notes that it is through such record linkage that most administrative data obtain research value.[5] Most often administrative data are linked with survey data. The administrative data include interesting outcomes variables, and the survey data provide valuable explanatory variables.

Issues revolving around an electronic medical record are raised in Section 2. It is necessary to lay out the enduring ethical concepts that undergird any attempt to establish standards. These ethical standards are explored in Section 3. With the grounding provided by the analysis of the electronic medical record environment of Section 2 and the discussion of

---

5. House Committee on Post Office and Civil Service, Subcommittee on Census, Statistics and Postal Personnel, testimony prepared by F. Thomas Juster, 103rd Cong., 2nd sess. (16 March 1994), 1-5.

ethical concepts of Section 3, specific issues of access to medical records are addressed in Section 4. The current legislative context is surveyed in Section 5. Previous standards activity is noted in Section 6 and a range of recommendations are assessed in Section 7. Conclusions are laid out in Section 8.

2. An Electronic Health Care Information Infrastructure

A patient's medical record is seen by an average of 77 people.[6] This factoid would clearly surprise, perhaps shock, most individuals who are not familiar with the scope of information flow in modern health care. This scope, as illustrated in Figure 1, certainly underscores concerns for confidentiality. But it also underscores the apparent benefits of access to medical data by a wide range of people and organizations. To keep pace with technology and the demands of today's world, adequate accessibility of medical data

Figure 1
The Flow of Personal Medical Data

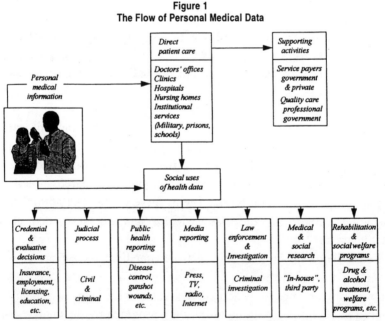

Adapted from: Alan F. Westin, Computers, Health Records, and Citizens Rights, report prepared for the U.S. Department of Commerce, National Bureau of Standards, Monograph 157, December 1976, p. 10.

---

6. Gallo, "Safeguarding Your Medical Records," 42. This is based on a survey of a large hospital and attributed by Nick Gallo to Patricia Thierry of the American Health Information Management Association (AHIMA).

requires implementation of an electronic health care information infrastructure. Further heightening the tension between privacy and data access, such an electronic implementation raises new concerns about protecting privacy and confidentiality.

An electronic medical record (a.k.a. computer-based patient record or CPR) is an "electronic patient record that resides in a system specifically designed to support users through availability of complete and accurate data, practitioner reminders and alerts, clinical decision support systems, links to bodies of medical knowledge and other aids."[7] Data are on individual participants, and include identifiers such as name, Social Security number, address; demographic data such as age, sex, and race; and encounter data such as diagnosis or DRG, providers, services, medical outcomes, insurer, and charges.

As Fitzmaurice and Simborg emphasize, just putting a paper medical record in electronic form is not sufficient for patient care, administration, or improvement of medical practice.[8] Electronic medical records must be implemented in a wide-area, comprehensive, integrated, networked information system. Such an interconnected communication network links all participants in a health care system. The scale can be large. The Office of Management and Budget states, "Our national health care system expects to become an intensive participant in the NII [National Information Infrastructure]."[9] As noted by Schwartz, Kunitz, and Kozloff, the purpose of a health information network is to reduce cost and improve the quality of patient care.[10] The information infrastructure, therefore, would include decision-support applications.[11] The networked aspect of this information

---

7. Institute of Medicine, *The Computer-Based Patient Record: An Essential Technology for Health Care,* eds. Richard S. Dick and Elaine B. Steen (Washington, D.C.: National Academy Press, 1991), 3.

8. Fitzmaurice, "Health Care and the NII," 42-43. D. W. Simborg and J. M. Gabler, "Reengineering the Traditional Medical Record: The View from Industry," *M. D. Computing* 9, no. 4, (1992): 198-200.

9. Office of Management and Budget, "National Information Infrastructure: Draft Principles for Providing and Using Personal Information and Commentary," *Federal Register* 60 (1995): 4366.

10. Harvey A. Schwartz, Selma C. Kunitz, and Rene Kozloff, "Building Data Research Resources from Existing Data Sets: A Model for Integrating Patient Data to Form a Core Data Set," draft manuscript, 1995, 1-24.

11. Nancy McCauley and Mohammad Ala, "The Use of Expert Systems in the Healthcare Industry," *Information and Management* 22 (1992): 227-35.

infrastructure is critical in determining the nature of privacy protection that can be afforded. As the Office of Technology Assessment (OTA) notes,

> Existing models for data protection, which place responsibility for privacy on individual institutions, will no longer be workable for new systems of computer linkage and exchange of information across high-performance, interactive networks. New approaches to data protection must track the flow of the data itself.[12]

Additionally, there is a range of health care information that is collected, stored, and transmitted about individuals. This information goes well beyond the content of the traditional medical record.[13] With electronic record linkage capabilities, this additional information supports educational, regulatory, research, public policy, and commercial uses. This wide range of application and the potential for abuse suggest that the health care information infrastructure requires effective data protection.

a. Motivation for Implementation of an Electronic Medical Record

Schwartz, Kunitz, and Kozloff remark,

> Although there is uncertainty as to the extent of restructuring of this country's health care system, there is considerable agreement regarding the need for uniform automated longitudinal patient data that link care across providers and sites and over time. Computer-based patient record systems, intersystem linkages, and appropriate privacy and security safeguards are necessary to achieve the cost, quality, access, and choice goals that are characteristic of the various health care reform plans.[14]

Here are five reasons for moving to an electronic medical record:

1. The uses of and legitimate demands for patient data are growing.

2. More powerful, affordable technologies to support computer-based patient records are now available.

---

12. Office of Technology Assessment, *Protecting Privacy in Computerized Medical Information,* OTA-TCT-576 (Washington, D.C.: U.S. Government Printing Office, September 1993), 9.

13. *Ibid.,* 75.

14. Schwartz, Kunitz, and Kozloff, "Building Data Research Resources from Existing Data Sets," 1.

3. Increasingly, computers are being accepted as a tool for enhancing efficiency in virtually all facets of everyday life.

4. Demographic factors, such as an aging population (which results in a growth in chronic diseases) and the continued mobility of Americans, create greater pressures for patient records that can manage large amounts of information and are easily transferable among health care providers.

5. Pressures for reform in health care are growing, and automation of patient records is crucial to achievement of such reform.[15]

Updating from 1991 to present, we find these reasons are perhaps even more salient. Indeed, even Reason 5 remains because health care reform continues unabated in spite of the recent failure of comprehensive federal health care legislation.

Information is needed to make informed choices about treatments, providers, institutions, and health plans.[16] Appropriate standards for defining, collecting, communicating, and storing administrative and clinical patient care data permit the potential of information to be realized.

- Scientific studies could point the way to medically effective and cost-effective care.
- Physicians could access most recent information about medical technologies, clinical treatments, and provider performance.
- Patient outcome information could be linked to medical treatment data.
- Administrative processes could be speeded and duplication of paperwork eliminated.
- Administrative costs could be lowered.

This is not just pie-in-the-sky speculation. Studies have shown a considerable variation in medical treatment patterns and their associated treatment costs without concomitant variation in patient outcome.[17] Other studies have pointed to limitations of the current status of patient records and patient level data.[18] Practitioners' vocabularies and documentation are not

15. Institute of Medicine, *The Computer-Based Patient Record*, 1-7.

16. Fitzmaurice, "Health Care and the NII," 41-56.

17. J. E. Wennberg, "Variations in Medical Practice and Hospital Costs," *Connecticut Medicine* 49 (1985): 444-53.

standardized and do not have consistent operational definitions and associated codes for data elements. Patient outcome data are limited and do not encompass functional status, satisfaction, and quality of life. Further, there are no accepted measures of these descriptors. Hospital measures of performance and other health care facilities measures are not defined.

b. Current Status of Information Technology for Medical Records

Appropriate information technology exists.

> Other areas already center operations around computerized systems. Notable in this are banks, airlines, stock markets, and even salvage yards.[19]

Much of this information technology could be adapted rather easily to the health care field.

Existing information technology is not fully implemented in health care.
According to an Institute of Medicine report,

> The current paper patient record is fragmented, located in numerous health care settings, poorly documented, variable across providers, and often illegible. Information about a single episode of care may reside in a physician record (history and symptoms); in the hospital (laboratory, surgical procedures); and in a rehabilitation or nursing home setting. Even within a single provider institution such as a hospital, information, if computerized, is likely to be contained in different, discrete departmental systems that are not integrated.

and

> While technology exists that could be used to automate the patient record and create health data systems, such as DBMS, optical storage technology, and record linkage software, these technologies have not been widely applied within the health care area. Thus, there are not systems in place that can support the CPR or that only need to be linked to provide a health data network.[20]

---

18. See M. L. Grady and H. A. Schwartz, eds., *Automated Data Sources for Ambulatory Care Effectiveness Research*, AHCPR Publication No. 93-0042 (Washington, D.C., 1993).

19. Fitzmaurice, "Health Care and the NII," 41-56.

20. R. S. Dick and E. B. Steen, eds., *The Computer-Based Patient Record: An Essential Technology for Health Care,* (Washington, D.C.: Institute of Medicine, National Academy Press, 1991), 5.

Fitzmaurice notes,

> The health sector, however, has lagged far behind the other sectors of our economy in applying information and communication technologies. Most hospitals and clinics have computers but relegate them to perform isolated, relatively small segments in the organizations.[21]

Value of Electronic Technology in Health Care.
Electronic technology has suggested its value in health care in a variety of ways:

- Electronic filing of medical claim information means more patient mobility and so cost saving and more competition, argues Alpert.[22] The Workgroup for Electronic Data Interchange (WEDI) believes "the cumulative net savings over the next six years (to the year 2000) is estimated to total over $42 billion."[23]

- Electronic databases can speed access to medical histories.

- Electronic technology can also reduce administrative costs. It is said that in Australia costs are 9 cents per claim versus 29 cents in the United States.

- Easy access to information via electronic technology can help a patient be a more informed consumer.[24]

- For the important specific case of the National Information Infrastructure (NII): The NII "can support research into cost containment efforts and payment initiatives to lower costs. . . . Further, the NII can provide information that increases knowledge about the medical effectiveness of alternative treatments and make it available to the providers and consumers of health care."[25]

---

21. Fitzmaurice, "Health Care and the NII," 42-44.

22. Sheri Alpert, "Smart Cards, Smarter Policy: Medical Records, Privacy, and Health Care Reform," *Hastings Center Report* 23 (1993): 16-17.

23. Workgroup for Electronic Data Interchange, report to the Secretary of the U.S. Department of Health and Human Services (Washington, D.C., October 1993), Executive Summary, iii.

24. Fitzmaurice, "Health Care and the NII," 43.

25. *Ibid.*

c. Threats to Security, Integrity, and Confidentiality

The development of a health care information infrastructure raises new concerns about privacy and security, as was empirically noted by Rind and Safran.[26]

> "It worries the hell out of me," says Frank Borgmann, a director of Florida's mental health services agency, who has tried unsuccessfully to keep pharmacies from selling their prescription files. "Data is like a whore. It gets passed around from hand to hand, in spite of the rules."[27]

Threats to security of an information system come from unauthorized access, computer viruses, and other forms of computer sabotage. They also come from unauthorized actions of persons within the system.[28]

> Stringent security protocols may make it more difficult for intruders to access patient-identifiable data. If the security measures are overcome and access is attained, however, the electronic medium will potentially allow for remote and unauthorized review of unlimited health information. It will greatly increase the dimension of inadvertent and unintentional breaches of confidentiality.[29]

> While resources can be directed toward minimizing risk of abuse of information by insiders, no system can be made totally secure through technology, and the greatest perceived threat to privacy in medical information exists in the potential for abuse of authorized internal access to information by persons within the systems, whether paper or computer based.[30]

Threats to integrity of an information system come if access is not reliable and timely, if updating is not properly done or if modifications are made that are not authorized. Threats to confidentiality come as we try to

---

26. D. M. Rind and C. Safran, "Real and Imagined Barriers to an Electronic Medical Record," *Proceedings of the Annual Symposium on Computer Applications to Medical Care* (Washington, D.C., 1993): 74-78.

27. Michael W. Miller, "Data Tap: Patients' Records Are Treasure Trove for Budding Industry," *Wall Street Journal,* 27 February 1992, sec. A1.

28. Francis H. Roger, "Security Threats and Trends in Society," *Medical Informatics* 14 (1989): 219-25.

29. Workgroup for Electronic Data Interchange, report to the Secretary of the U. S. Department of Health and Human Services (Washington, D.C., July 1992), Appendix 4, 3-4.

30. Office of Technology Assessment, *Protecting Privacy,* 12.

ensure that only what is necessary and authorized is revealed and that the information will go no farther than the authorized person. The enhanced capability of the computer, in concert with a network of worldwide telecommunications, intensifies privacy concerns. As noted by OTA, computerization of health care information raises confidentiality concerns:

- Data capture and creation of new databases is easy;
- Large amounts of data can be stored and easily retrieved;
- Theft of information can be invisible;
- Record linkage to other databases is easy;
- Large numbers of people can have access.[31]

We would add:

- Certain types of data are especially sensitive, e.g., records of psychiatric, drug and alcohol abuse patients and human immunodeficiency virus test results.[32]

3. Ethical Concepts

Technological and social change demand recurrent reference to a coherent ethical framework. In a society that espouses democratic and multicultural ideals, an ethics of information can be constructed on the three pillars of autonomy, empowerment, and accountability.[33] It is generally accepted in the United States and a number of other countries that ethics for dealing with personal records, including health care records, should have as its core respect for the individual.[34] The person is entitled to a degree of autonomy

---

31. *Ibid.,* 37.

32. Lowell C. Brown and Shirley J. Paine, "CPR and the Law: Plan now," *Health Systems Review* 25 (November/December 1992): 28-30.

33. George T. Duncan, Thomas R. Jabine, and Virginia A. de Wolf, eds., *Private Lives and Public Policies: Confidentiality and Accessibility of Government Services* (Washington, D.C.: National Academy Press, 1993), xiii-274.

34. See O. F. Van der Leer, "The Use of Personal Data for Medical Research: How to Deal with New European Privacy Standards," *International Journal of Biomedical Computing* 35 (1994): 87-95. Also see K. R. Iversen, "Security Requirements for Electronic Patients Records: the Norwegian View," *International Journal of Biomedical Computing* 35 (1994): 51-56. Also see K. Yamamoto et al., "Necessity to Improve Common Understanding about the Security Issues Among Hospitals in Japan and Some

and is expected to extend that shield to others. The individual cannot function without adequate empowerment. The individual must demand accountability from others. Both individuals and organizations are subject to accountability.

a. What are Privacy and Confidentiality?

Informational privacy is the question of what personal information should be collected or stored at all for a given social function. It involves issues concerning the legitimacy and legality of organizational demands for disclosure from individuals and groups, and setting of balances between the individual's control over the disclosure of personal information and the needs of society for the data on which to base decisions about individual situations and formulate policies. Confidentiality is the question of how personal data collected for approved social purposes shall be held and used by the organization that originally collected it, what other secondary or further uses may be made of it, and when consent by the individual will be required for such uses. It is to further the patient's willing disclosure of confidential information to doctors that the law of privileged communications developed. In this perspective, security of data involves an organization's ability to keep its promises of confidentiality.[35]

Kluge proposes an intriguing and useful shift in paradigm for personal information. Rather than viewing packets of personal information as property to be afforded confidentiality, we are to consider them as person-analogs.[36] Wherever they may travel in cyberspace, these electronic analogs inherit the privacy rights of their subject and so are to be afforded appropriate confidentiality. Apparently the closer the electronic analog approximates sensitive aspects of the patient, the more critical is the provision of confidentiality protection. This conception has some appeal because it provides an integrative perception for confidentiality issues. Concerns about record linkage, for example, are justifiable, as linked files are like a

---

Feasible Approaches," *International Journal of Biomedical Computing* 35 (1994): 205-12.

35. Alan F. Westin, *Computers, Health Records, and Citizen Rights* (New York: Petrocelli, 1976), viii-xviii.

36. Eike-Henner W. Kluge, "Health Information, Privacy, Confidentiality and Ethics," *International Journal of Bio-Medical Computing* 35, Suppl. 1 (1994): 27.

jigsaw puzzle assemblage of an image of a person. A linked file is a more complete image.

Is it the doctor-patient relationship that should be afforded confidentiality? Consider two different perspectives on medical confidentiality.

1. Protected information transfer between physician and patient. [Confidentiality involves a] sacred relationship between physician and patient [that] must be protected from third parties.[37]

2. Autonomy and respect for the individual patient.

Basing confidentiality analysis on the doctor/patient relationship is overly restrictive in current medical practice. Care, which was once delivered by a single medical provider, is now delivered in a variety of settings by numerous providers. Indeed, at a minimum this dyadic relationship needs to be expanded to a triadic one that would include the insurer.[38] Focus on the individual patient, on the other hand, retains its analytic validity regardless of the complexity of ways the patient interacts with the medical system. Hence the second perspective is preferred.

b. Why Privacy and Confidentiality Matter

The 1993 OTA report lays out well the need for privacy in health care information.

> Health information and the medical record include sensitive personal information that reveals some of the most intimate aspects of an individual's life. In addition to diagnostic and testing information, the medical record includes the details of a person's family history, genetic testing, history of diseases and treatments, history of drug use, sexual orientation and practices, and testing for sexually transmitted disease. Subjective remarks about a patient's demeanor, character, and mental state are sometimes part of the record.

---

37. Randall Oates, "Confidentiality and Privacy from the Physician Perspective," (presented at the First Annual Confidentiality Symposium of the American Health Information Management Association, Washington, D.C., 15 July 1992), 4. Also see Alfred M. Freedman, "The Erosion of the Hippocratic Tradition: A Voluntary National Commission Tackles Health Records Confidentiality," *Connecticut Medicine* 44 (1980): 43-46. Freedman emphasizes the Hippocratic tradition of "holy secrets" between practitioners and patients.

38. Harry Schwartz, "Don't Panic over Privacy," *USA Today,* 27 March 1992, 10A.

The medical record is the primary source for much of the health care information sought by parties outside the direct health care delivery relationship, such as prescription drug use, treatment outcomes, and reason for and length of hospital stay. These data are important because health care information can influence decisions about an individual's access to credit, admission to educational institutions, and his or her ability to secure employment and obtain insurance. Inaccuracies in the information, or its improper disclosure, can deny an individual access to these basic necessities of life, and can threaten an individual's personal and financial well-being.

Yet at the same time, accurate and comprehensive health care information is critical to the quality of health care delivery, and to the physician-patient relationship. Many believe that the efficacy of the healthcare relationship depends on the patient's understanding that the information recorded by a physician will not be disclosed. Many patients might refuse to provide physicians with certain types of information needed to render appropriate care if patients do not believe that information would remain confidential.[39]

Further, OTA cites a number of specific instances of what it deemed "health care information abuse."[40] Emphasizing another aspect of this issue, Gabrieli argues that in order to receive the best medical advice, the patient is, in effect, under duress to provide confidential information.[41] Finally, the Office of Management and Budget notes, "A critical characteristic of privacy is that once it is lost, it can rarely be restored. Consider, for example, the extent to which the inappropriate release of medical information could ever be rectified by a public apology."[42]

---

39. Office of Technology Assessment, *Protecting Privacy*, 5-6.

40. *Ibid.*, 27-29.

41. Elmer R. Gabrieli, *Guide for Unique Healthcare Identifier Model*, ASTM Committee E-31 on Computerized Systems, second draft (Philadelphia: ASTM, 26 May 1993), 1-45.

42. Office of Management and Budget, "National Information Infrastructure," 4362-70.

4. Access to Medical Records

a. Who Has Access to the Data?

Medical records may be seen by hospital staff, health insurers, government workers, researchers, employers, reporters, police, lawyers, and possibly marketers and family members. How about yourself as a patient? The Federal Privacy Act and other federal laws grant you the right to review your medical records if you are a federal government employee, live in a long-term care facility that accepts Medicare or Medicaid payment, or have received care in a federal medical care facility (such as Public Health Service facilities or Veterans Administration hospitals). This right is not necessarily absolute. Eighteen states have laws that give you access, within limits, to records. Regardless of legal requirements, some organizations like the AMA recommend that their members open records to patients. *Medical Records: Getting Yours* lists state-by-state laws governing patient access and advises how to obtain and interpret your own medical records.[43]

As noted by Alpert, Gallo, and OTA,[44] the various actors in the health care information system include:

- Employers, because of medical insurance and interest in medical status of employees;
- Marketers (such as Merck who, in purchasing Medco, plans to use pharmacy purchase data base);
- Insurers, especially as serviced by the Medical Information Bureau (MIB), who has about 700 life insurance companies as members. It provides medical summaries on over 12 million American and Canadian policy holders, including information on adverse driving record, participation in hazardous sports, and aviation activities;[45]
- Physicians, especially as linked to others by the Physician Computer Network, Inc. PCN operates a communications network of some 2000 office-based physician members in 1992, linked to various hospitals,

---

43. Bruce Samuels and Sidney M. Wolfe, *Medical Records: Getting Yours (A Consumer's Guide to Obtaining and Understanding the Medical Record)* (Washington, D.C.: Public Citizen's Health Research Group, 1992), 10.

44. Alpert, "Smart Cards, Smarter Policy," 13-23. Gallo, "Safeguarding Your Medical Records," 42-46. Office of Technology Assessment, *Protecting Privacy*, 3-4.

45. Detailed information on MIB is provided in Office of Technology Assessment, *Protecting Privacy*, 32-33.

clinical laboratories, Medicare/Medicaid intermediaries, Blue Cross/Blue Shield providers, managed care providers, insurance carriers, and pharmaceutical companies.[46]

b. Who Owns the Data?

Ownership lacks relevance because so many individuals and organizations have copies and claims. A court may subpoena records. Researchers seek to use aggregated data.[47] Conceptually, it is the connection with the patient, not the data per se, that is the important referent for confidentiality issues.

With a paper record it is generally acknowledged that the owner of the paper on which the record is maintained is the "owner" of the record.[48] For example, the American Medical Association has stated that the "notes made in treating a patient are primarily for the physician's own use and constitute his personal property."[49] Gallo claims, "Your patient record is the property of the doctor or health care facility that compiles it."[50] These two near-identical positions may, however, not be operationally meaningful for material entered electronically. As an extreme case of such electronic entry, consider posting data to the Internet and the attendant opportunities for multiplying data dissemination. A more unusual view, yet highly workable, is this: "Reified information-packages contained in advanced patient records should be considered as patient-analogues in information space."[51]

According to Schwartz, Kunitz, and Kozloff, current standards are ambiguous and create opportunities for data to be shared, sold, and linked without express consent from the patient.[52] Several levels of ownership

---

46. Detailed information on PCN is provided in Office of Technology Assessment, *Protecting Privacy*, 33-35. Also see Miller, "Data Tap."

47. Thomas L. Lincoln, "Privacy: a Real-World Problem with Fuzzy Boundaries," *Methods of Information in Medicine* 32 (1993): 104-107. J. R. Moehr, "Privacy and Security Requirements of Distributed Computer-based Patient Records," *International Journal of Biomedical Computing* 35 (1994): 57-64.

48. Office of Technology Assessment, *Protecting Privacy*, 82.

49. Samuels and Wolfe, *Medical Records*, 10.

50. Gallo, "Safeguarding Your Medical Records," 42.

51. Kluge, "Health Information, Privacy, Confidentiality and Ethics," 24. See also Eike-Henner W. Kluge, "Advanced Patient Records: Some Ethical and Legal Considerations Touching Medical Information Space," *Methods In Medicine* 32 (1993): 95-103.

52. Schwartz, Kunitz, and Kozloff, "Building Data Research Resources from Existing Data Sets," 1-24.

have been considered: ownership as the data subject, ownership as the data collector and coder, and ownership as the possessor and holder of data. The patient, as data subject, "owns" the data contained in a record, but does not own the record itself. Generally, record ownership is often state-determined, with most states agreeing that the facility or provider owns the physical media in which the data reside, and that it is subject to the patient's interest in the information contained in the record.[53] However, the legal concept of ownership is not considered to be relevant where technology makes the creation of a record and its dissemination instantaneous. Instead, the rights and responsibilities of both the record subject and the record keeper with respect to the information must be delineated. In addition, protection of individually identifiable health information must safeguard the data as it moves within the health care system and to the various entities that will use it for care, policy-making and research.

According to a 1994 report from the Committee on Regional Health Data Networks of the Institute of Medicine, Health Database Organizations (HDOs) are entities that have access to (and possibly control of) databases and that have as their chief mission the public release of data and results of analyses done on the databases under their control.[54] Characteristics include:

- single, common authority;

- authority to acquire and maintain information from a variety of sources in the health sector, as well as from other sources not directly connected with personal health care;

- files that have person-identified or person-identifiable data;

- service for a specific geographic area;

- population files that will include all members of a defined population (denominators) to calculate population-based rates of service utilization and health outcomes;

- data that are to be comprehensive regarding individuals and that will include administrative, clinical, health status, and satisfaction with care information;

---

53. American Medical Record Association, *Confidentiality of Patient Health Information* (Chicago: American Medical Record Association, 1985), 12.

54. Institute of Medicine, Committee on Regional Health Data Networks, *Health Database Organizations (HDOs),* (Washington, D.C.: National Academy Press, 1994).

- HDOs that will process, store, analyze and otherwise manipulate data electronically;

- files that can be designed for interactive access to assist with patient care when primary records are unavailable to treating physician;

- not being typically viewed as primary patient records and not meant to be passive warehouses for health information.

c. Why are Disclosures Damaging?

According to Lincoln, disclosures of confidential information result in damage to "personhood."[55] Data users have an ethical and fiduciary responsibility to avoid inflicting such harm. There are particular problems in psychiatry because it:

> . . . deals primarily with personality of the patient and where trust between patient and physician stands at the core of treatment. Abuse of this trust often makes psychotherapy impossible. Loss of confidentiality is not only embarrassing to the patient – it can lead to serious disruption of family and social life, and even to career and economic damage when confidential information is improperly used to make hiring or promotion decisions, to deny insurance benefits, or to refuse occupational licensing or admission to school.[56]

Some other types of data are particularly sensitive:

> One of the most disturbing failures to maintain research confidentiality occurred when the New York State Health Department disclosed the names of some 28 abortion patients in a publicly available report to the National Institutes of Health.[57]

Some classes of people may need special consideration:

- Minors have very real privacy interests that do not always coincide with the interests of parents;[58]

- Those with a genetic predisposition to medical problems, such as breast cancer or heart disease.

---

55. Lincoln, "Privacy: A Real-World Problem with Fuzzy Boundaries," 104-107.

56. Freedman, "The Erosion of the Hippocratic Tradition," 44.

57. *Ibid.*, 45.

58. *Ibid.*

d. Moral Obligation to Disseminate Personal Information?

In cases of sexually transmitted diseases, Bayer and Toomey discuss the obligation to notify sexual and/or needle-sharing partners of possible risk.[59] In a balanced fashion, they examine a "moral duty to warn" and the value of contact tracing.

e. Record Access

Kluge argues that a basic ethical concept, the adequate self-knowledge principle, rejects withholding medical information from the patient.[60] Taking this step further, Freedman questions, "How can patients authorize access to their records by third parties if they themselves do not know what the records contain?"[61]

f. Record Linkage

As noted by Schwartz, Kunitz, and Kozloff, record linkage techniques utilize names, date of birth, Social Security number, gender, address, and other demographic characteristics to "match" an individual's discrete records.[62] If all characteristics were maintained on all records, matching would be a routine process. However, different characteristics are housed in different records, and these characteristics may be maintained accurately or inaccurately.

It is important to note that the characteristics used to match an individual's records do not need to be housed in the automated patient record file. Instead, a unique patient identifier can be used that does not disclose an individual's identity. The unique patient identifier can be an encrypted number or a random number that is tied, in a separate, perhaps local file, to protect an individual's privacy. Access to this file of personally identifiable information and the unique patient identifier must be determined and appropriate policy developed.

In August 1993, the American Health Information Management Association recommended use of the Social Security number, with the addition

---

59. R. Bayer and K. E. Toomey, "HIV Prevention and the Two Faces of Partner Notification," *American Journal of Public Health* 82, no. 8 (1992): 1158-64.

60. Kluge, "Health Information, Privacy, Confidentiality and Ethics," 25.

61. Freedman, "The Erosion of the Hippocratic Tradition," 45-46.

62. Schwartz, Kunitz, and Kozloff, "Building Data Research Resources from Existing Data Sets," 1-24.

of an encrypted confidentiality code, for use initially to link a patient's records across the health care system. Access to a patient's records would require use of both the Social Security number and the confidentiality code. Providers would be free to use their own system of patient identification, but the records of different providers would be linked via use of the Social Security number with an encrypted confidentiality code. For the longer term, AHIMA believes a nationwide system of biometric identifiers must be implemented. To further protect an individual's privacy for data that are transmitted from the health care setting to a regional or national health data system, age can be substituted for date of birth, and a location code that indicates a person's socioeconomic status as derived from zip codes can be utilized.[63]

5. Legislative Perspectives

This section is intended to provide some perspective on various legislative initiatives regarding privacy, confidentiality, and data access issues in health care. No treatment of these issues could be complete without examining this ever-evolving legal framework. On the other hand, because the extent of legislation is voluminous, case law is immense, and the situation is dynamic, this brief section can hardly be comprehensive. Instead it will survey the current system and point to a few current legislative initiatives.[64]

The legislative foundation in this area is the *Privacy Act* of 1974.[65] It protects the confidentiality of health information in the patient record systems maintained by federal agencies, including federal hospitals and those maintaining a record system under a contract with a federal agency. The *Privacy Act* implemented a code of five fair information practices:

1. There must be no personal data record-keeping systems whose very existence is secret;

2. There must be a way for individuals to find out what information about them is in a record and how it is used;

63. Office of Technology Assessment, *Protecting Privacy,* 87.

64. Yvette Debow, "The Technology of Reform," *Insurance and Technology Health Insurance and Technology Supplement* (April 1994): 19-22.

65. *Privacy Act,* U.S. Code, vol. 5, sec. 552a (1974).

3. There must be a way for individuals to prevent information about them that was obtained for one purpose from being used or made available for other purposes without their consent;

4. There must be a way for individuals to correct or amend a record of identifiable information;

5. Any organization creating, maintaining, using, or disseminating records of identifiable personal data must assure the reliability of the data for their intended use and must take reasonable precautions to prevent misuse of the data.

The *Privacy Act* covers only the federal government, not other state or local government entities (except in certain aspects for those using the Social Security number) or private sector entities. In addition, it allows other uses of these records, if the purpose of the use is consistent with the reason the information was collected. As implemented, the *Privacy Act* has three major deficiencies in protecting patient confidentiality:

1. It places the burden on individuals to protect their own interests;

2. Its enforcement scheme provides remedies only after misuses have occurred;

3. It is not sensitive to the existing power imbalance between individuals and the federal government.[66]

From the information access perspective, the *Act* also creates some unnecessary barriers on access for research and statistical uses. As argued in Duncan, Jabine, and de Wolf, in restricting access to individually identifiable records, the *Privacy Act* fails to recognize the importance of research and statistical uses, and the fact that such uses do not directly result in actions regarding individuals, such as award or termination of benefits.[67]

Further, the *Privacy Act* does not protect data in the private sector.[68] Even as supplemented with other federal and state legislation, it is insufficient to deal with privacy and information issues in health care. Indeed, the OTA notes that the current system of protecting patient confidentiality has been built on a patchwork of codes and state and federal laws that are

---

66. Priscilla Regan, "Privacy, Government Information, and Technology," *Public Administration Review* 46 (1986): 633.

67. Duncan, Jabine, and de Wolf, *Private Lives and Public Policies*, 111-15.

68. William H. Roach, Jr., Susan N. Chernoff, and Carol Lange Esley, eds., *Medical Records and the Law* (Rockville, MD: Aspen Systems Corp., 1985), 87.

"inadequate to guide the health care industry with respect to obligations to protect the privacy of medical information in a computerized environment."[69]

There is no consistent confidentiality protection across states. Only California, Washington and Montana have general laws dealing with access to health information. Federal legislation is not comprehensive. "With the exception of records relating to substance abuse or records in the custody of the federal government, federal law does not protect the confidentiality of medical information. . . . Under current law, restrictions on the matching and aggregating of data bases apply mostly to records maintained by the federal government."[70] Forty states recognize doctor-patient privilege, but "Federal Rules of Evidence, which govern practice in federal courts, provide only a psychotherapist-patient privilege, not a general doctor-patient privilege. It is not recognized at common law (as is the attorney-client privilege)."[71]

Alpert well summarizes deficiencies in current legislation:

> Legal recognition of the status of the information is needed, along with a delineation of an individual's rights vis-á-vis that information. To date there has not been a consistent public policy formulated, much less articulated, with equal applicability to all Americans, that protects the patient's and society's interest in privacy or in the confidentiality of an individual's medical information.[72]

Case law is also sketchy in this area. The major U.S. Supreme Court case addressing medical information privacy is Whalen v. Roe.[73] In Whalen, a unanimous Court determined that a New York state data base of lawful users of abusable drugs was allowable because the prohibitions on public disclosure of the information in the data base were adequate to prevent any constitutional harm to the persons listed in the registry . . . the stringent physical and administrative procedures protecting the patient's interest in privacy played an important role in the Court's finding. The Third Circuit

---

69. Office of Technology Assessment, *Protecting Privacy*, 15.

70. Alpert, "Smart Cards, Smarter Policy," 13, 15.

71. *Ibid.*, 19.

72. *Ibid.*

73. *Whalen v. Roe*, 429 U.S. 589 (1977).

Court of Appeals, in its 1980 decision in United States of America v. Westinghouse Electric, held:

> The factors which should be considered in deciding whether an intrusion into an individual's privacy is justified are the type of record requested, the information it does or might contain, the potential for harm in any subsequent nonconsensual disclosure, the injury from disclosure to the relationship in which the record was generated, the adequacy of safeguards to prevent unauthorized disclosure, the degree of need for access, and whether there is an express statutory mandate, articulated public policy or other recognizable public interest militating toward access.[74]

a. Themes of Proposed Legislation

In her March 16, 1994 statement to the Subcommittee on Census, Statistics and Postal Personnel of the U.S. House of Representatives, Nan D. Hunter, Deputy General Counsel of the U.S. Department of Health and Human Services, sketched the privacy protections of President Clinton's *Health Security Act:*

- Within two years, the National Health Board will promulgate detailed standards for confidentiality of the information in the new system, based on principles in the new bill;
- There will be controls, with criminal and civil sanctions, on improper use of the Health Security Card of the unique identifying number chosen for the system;
- Within three years, the Board will propose comprehensive federal legislation to protect health information. This will cover, for example, all pre-existing records of physicians and hospitals;
- There will be ongoing monitoring and advice from people outside the federal government to assure that privacy concerns are carefully considered. The National Health Board will have an advisory council on privacy and health data that will include members distinguished in data protection and privacy, ethics, civil liberties, and patient advocacy.

---

74. *United States v. Westinghouse Electric*, 638 F7 2d 578 (1980).

Given criticism that these provisions are vague and ex post,[75] recent legislative proposals have been more specific in the area of data protection. The major themes that have been recently addressed in legislative proposals are as follows:

- Health care data panel. Sen. Christopher Bond's *Health Care Information Modernization and Security Act* of 1993 (H.R. 3137)

- Standards for electronic exchange of health care information (H.R. 3137) Sen. Daschle's *Family Health Insurance Protection Act* (S. 7)

- State standards for electronic exchange of health care information. Rep. McDemott's *American Health Security Act* of 1995 (H.R. 1200)

- Disclosure guidelines. Rep. Gary Condit's *Fair Health Information Practices Act* of 1995 (H.R. 435), based on model legislative language of the American Health Information Management Association (AHIMA)

- Penalties for privacy and confidentiality violations (H.R. 435) Bond bill (H.R. 3137)

- Patient inspection of health information about themselves (H.R. 435)

- Essentially abolish state "quill and pen" laws. Rep. William Thomas's *Basic Health Care Reform Act* of 1995 (H.R. 1234)

- Unique health identifier (S. 7)

- Health research (S. 7) specifies conditions under which an information trustee may disclose protected health information to a health researcher.

6. Standards Activity

A variety of health care industry groups are developing standards for an information infrastructure. These groups include the ASTM E31.17 Standards Subcommittee on Access, Privacy and Confidentiality of Medical Records. A wide range of issues are being addressed, including digital

---

75. John Morrissey, "Privacy Fears Place Another Hurdle in the Path of Reform," *Modern Healthcare* 24 (22 November 1993), 24. See also House Committee on Post Office and Civil Service, Subcommittee on Census, Statistics and Postal Personnel, "Census, Statistics and Postal Personnel," statement by Janlori Goldman regarding H.R. 3137: *Data Needs and Related Issues for Implementing Health Care Reform.* 103rd Cong., 2nd sess. (16 March 1994), 1-13.

signatures and encryption in health care: secret key and public key encryption, digital signatures, key management, public key certificates, authorization mechanisms, anonymity mechanisms, cryptographic APIs, and government cryptographic initiatives. Additional activity is taking place in Europe.[76]

As Fitzmaurice notes, "In the private sector of the United States, the development of medical information standards is coordinated through the American National Standards Institute (ANSI) Healthcare Informatics Standards Planning Panel (HISPP)."[77] This panel was formed in 1992 with a mission of:

- coordinating the development of standards for health care models and electronic health care records;

- interchange of health care data, images, sounds and signals;

- health care codes and terminology;

- communication with diagnostic instruments and health care devices;

- representation and communication of health care protocols, knowledge, and statistical databases;

- privacy, confidentiality, security;

- patient data definitions – codes, terminology, intersystem communication;

- uniform patient, provider, payer identifiers.

  Administrative health data standards are being developed by the ANSI-accredited standards committee X12, through its subcommittee X12N. The Workgroup for Electronic Data Interchange (WEDI) is a private sector advisory board that has provided leadership for these standards. Created in 1991, the Computer-based Patient Record Institute (CPRI) promotes and coordinates the development of CPR systems in the United States. The CPRI is composed of representatives from physician, hospital, computer system, vendor, managed care, university, and other national groups. The CPRI is working for the ubiquitous use of CPR systems in medical care, with work groups in four areas: Codes

---

76. John Mantas, "The Application of Advanced Information Technology in Medicine and Health Care: A European Approach," *International Journal of Technological Management* 7 (1992): 560-571.

77. Fitzmaurice, "Health Care and the NII," 46.

and Structure; CPR Systems Evaluation; Confidentiality, Privacy, and Legislation; and Professional and Public Education.[78]

One concern that has been raised is about the process of standard setting by industry groups. These groups require membership – and membership fees are sufficiently high that they may exclude participation by many interested individuals or groups. Current membership in WEDI, for example, ranges from $300 for individuals to $2,000 for government and not-for-profit organizations.

"The Unified Medical Language System (UMLS) Project sponsored by the National Library of Medicine focuses on linking terms and codes in patient records to evidence-based knowledge such as that in practice guidelines and the scientific literature."[79] The UMLS is developing a translator among existing coding structures, such as the ICD9 and SNOMED, and terms found in the literature for use with patient record systems. However, Bishop and Ewing argue that these structures are inadequate because they were developed for specific purposes, contain a great deal of overlap, and do not easily accommodate to the ongoing expansion that reflects change in and growth of knowledge.[80] The authors argue, instead, for a common language structure and codes, based on natural language associations, that can serve common purposes.[81]

"Through its Office of Science and Data Development, AHCPR promotes the coordination of the developers of patient care data standards and the analysis of confidentiality and privacy issues concerning researcher access to patient care data."[82]

The Institute of Medicine suggests standards for content, data-exchange and vocabulary, patient data confidentiality, and data and system security:

- Content standards are to provide a description of the data elements that will be included in automated medical records, with the intent

---

78. *Ibid.*

79. *Ibid.,* 48.

80. C. W. Bishop and P. Ewing, "Representing Medical Knowledge: Reconciling the Present of Creating the Future," *M. D. Computing* 9, no. 4 (1992): 218-225.

81. Schwartz, Kunitz, and Kozloff, "Building Data Research Resources from Existing Data Sets," 1-24.

82. Fitzmaurice, "Health Care and the NII," 49.

that uniform records will be produced, no matter where or in what type of health care setting the patient is treated;

• Data-exchange standards are formats for uniform and predictable electronic transmission of data, establishing the order and sequence of data during transmission;

• Vocabulary standards establish common definitions for medical terms and determine how information will be represented in medical records;

• Data and system security standards are to ensure that patient data are protected from unauthorized or inadvertent disclosure, modification, or destruction.[83]

7. Analysis of Recommendations Made in Previous Studies

To analyze previous recommendations regarding health care information, we build on the framework for an ethics of information, as outlined in Section 3. The three pillars of this framework are autonomy, empowerment and accountability. In Section 4 we laid out the some fundamental issues involving access to medical records. In Section 5 we gave some perspectives on the state of current and pending legislation in the medical record information infrastructure field. In Section 6 we sketched some of the activity in the medical record standards area. With the background of these last three sections, we examine how previous recommendations for health care privacy and access might build on this ethical framework. Some key sets of recommendations are given in the appendix, and reference will be made to them in this discussion.

a. Patient Autonomy

Fair information principles.

A common theme in promoting the autonomy of individuals, especially patients, who interact in the health care environment is a set of quite general "fair information principles." In the general setting they were laid out by Alan Westin.[84] In the medical and health management setting they have

---

83. Institute of Medicine, *Automated Medical Records: Leadership Needed to Expedite Standards Development,* report to the Chairman, U.S. Senate Committee on Governmental Affairs, GAO IMTEC-93-17 (Gaithersburg, MD: U.S. General Accounting Office, 1993), 37.

been endorsed in one way or another by Alpert, the Institute of Medicine, Jones, Schwartz, Kunitz, and Kozloff, and Westin.[85] As originally laid out, the five key elements of these fair information principles are:

1. There must be no secret personal data record-keeping system.

2. There must be a way for individuals to discover what personal information is recorded and how it is used.

3. There must be a way for individuals to prevent information about them, obtained for one purpose, from being used or made available for other purposes without their consent.

4. There must be a way for individuals to correct or amend a record of information about themselves.

5. An organization creating, maintaining, using or disseminating records of identifiable personal data must assure the reliability of the data for its intended use and must take reasonable precautions to prevent misuses of the data.

These fair information principles were the basis of the federal *Privacy Act* of 1974. In the health care area, specifically, they have been the basis of state law (Chapter 1751 of the Massachusetts State Code and the *Uniform Health Care Information Act,* as enacted in Montana and Washington) and the American Health Information Management Association's Health Information Model Legislation Language.

While essentially endorsing these principles, the 1993 OTA report joins with a 1986 report, *Electronic Record Systems and Individual Privacy,* in pointing out that in an era of complex computer networks, additional issues of data access, security of information flows, and notifying individuals of use of their personal data need to be addressed. The 1993 OTA report also

---

84. Alan F. Westin, *Privacy and Freedom* (New York: Atheneum, 1967).

85. Alpert, "Smart Cards, Smarter Policy," 13-23. Institute of Medicine, *Health Data in the Information Age: Use, Disclosure and Privacy*, eds. Molla S. Donaldson and Kathleen N. Lohr (Washington, D.C.: National Academy Press, 1994), 17. Mary Gardiner Jones, "Privacy Issues in Health Care Reform: The Consumer Perspective," (presented at the Privacy and American Business First Annual Conference: Managing the Privacy Revolution, New York, 4 October 1994). Schwartz, Kunitz, and Kozloff, "Building Data Research Resources from Existing Data Sets," 1-24. Westin, *Computers, Health Records, and Citizen Rights*, 1-24.

explicitly recognizes the importance of education of personnel involved in implementing these principles.[86]

These fair information principles are well-grounded in ethics. Further, they have stood the test of experience as guides for legislation over a range of fields, including health care information. Advances in technology, as well as social and economic developments, require that they be constantly reinterpreted in new settings.

Informed consent.

The importance of informed consent was affirmed by Westin.[87] Whether this basic ethical concept is adequately implemented can be tested by several criteria.

- Adequacy of information about content of data stored and disseminated, safeguards employed, and rights and obligations of data subjects and data users.[88]

- No coercion of subjects to provide data or agree to access, including not making agreement a precondition of service (If it is a precondition, then the appropriate concept is notification rather than informed consent).[89]

- The patient's consent must be affirmatively given (If affirmative action is not required, the appropriate concept is passive consent).[90]

- Clarity of communication to data subject.[91]

- A rational adult is making the decision.[92]

---

86. Office of Technology Assessment, *Protecting Privacy,* 76. Office of Technology Assessment, *Electronic Record Systems and Individual Privacy,* OTA-TCT-296 (Washington, D.C.: U.S. Government Printing Office, June 1986), 25-30.

87. Westin, *Computers, Health Records, and Citizen Rights,* viii-xviii.

88. Office of Technology Assessment, *Protecting Privacy,* 79. P. D. Reynolds, "Privacy and Advances in Social and Policy Science: Balancing Present Costs and Future Gains," *Journal of Official Statistics* 9, no. 2 (1993): 275-312. Schwartz, Kunitz, and Kozloff, "Building Data Research Resources from Existing Data Sets," 1-24.

89. P. D. Reynolds, "Privacy and Advances in Social and Policy Science," 294. Jones, "Privacy Issues in Health Care Reform," 1-8.

90. Jones, "Privacy Issues in Health Care Reform," 1-8.

91. Office of Technology Assessment, *Protecting Privacy,* 70.

92. P. D. Reynolds, "Privacy and Advances in Social and Policy Science," 275-312.

Notification.

Informed consent is appropriate when data providers have a clear choice, which they do not when they may be subject to penalties if they fail to participate. The term notification is more appropriate when the data provider cannot receive service without agreeing. Goldman and Westin have argued that the patient should be clearly notified of how their personal data are to be used and by whom.[93] Nonetheless, notification is not an ethical substitute for informed consent. Under notification there is, therefore, a heightened concern that the data provider be treated justly. Concern is manifest if the data provider can be considered to be in a weak position because of age, mental status or social/economic status. It is also heightened if the intended use for the data is beyond the mission of the collector, or if questions could be raised about the adequacy of confidentiality controls. One reason for such concern is the current lack of any mechanism, independent of the data collector and data user, to protect the interests of the data provider.[94]

Intercessory and oversight body.

Various writers and groups have proposed the formation of a legislatively-mandated intercessory body to deal with privacy and information issues. For example, Jones and Schwartz, Kunitz, and Kozloff recommend that Congress establish a quasi-independent National Medical Data Protection Board (term used by Jones).[95] These specific proposals for an institutional mandate can be thought of as implementing the functional recommendations of Westin.[96] The National Academy of Sciences Panel on Confidentiality and Data Access recommended the formation of an independent federal advisory board that would be responsible for promoting enhanced protection for federal data about persons, generally, and responsible data dissemination for statistical and research purposes.[97] With

---

93. House Committee on Post Office and Civil Service, "Census, Statistics and Postal Personnel," statement by Janlori Goldman, 12. Westin, *Computers, Health Records, and Citizen Rights*, 1-24.

94. Duncan, Jabine, and de Wolf, *Private Lives and Public Policies*, 61-89.

95. Jones, "Privacy Issues in Health Care Reform," 1-8. Schwartz, Kunitz, and Kozloff, "Building Data Research Resources from Existing Data Sets," 1-24.

96. Westin, *Computers, Health Records, and Citizen Rights*, viii-xviii.

97. Duncan, Jabine, and de Wolf, *Private Lives and Public Policies*, 203-18.

such an intercessory body in place, there would be some assurance that the interests of both data providers and data users would be protected.

Sanctions.

Establish sanctions for violations of data access privilege. Possible violations include improper possession, brokering, disclosure, or sale of health care information. Possible sanctions include denial of future access, forfeiture of posted bond, civil and criminal penalties, and allowing patients to collect damages.[98] Aside from the apparent deterrent effect of the sanctions themselves, a more significant deterrent may come from the evident signal that the sanction provides about what behavior is deemed wrong.

Restrictions on data collection.

Westin in his Recommendation 2 essentially argues for some public mechanism for deciding on the relevance and propriety of proposed schemes for collecting personal data.[99] There would seem to be considerable danger both in establishing restrictions free of context and of any blanket permission for data collection. Thus Westin's recommendation is worthy of implementation. One mechanism for doing this is through an independent data advisory board that would have a mandate for public discussion of particular cases. (See Intercessory and Oversight Body above)

Restrictions on data access.

Alpert suggests that legitimate data access be defined through legislation.[100] The Institute of Medicine lays out classes of users that may receive data.[101] Jones asserts the need for strict security measures.[102] Office of Technology Assessment argues for protocols for access of information by secondary users.[103] Goldman and Institute of Medicine argue that em-

---

98. Alpert, "Smart Cards, Smarter Policy," 21. Office of Technology Assessment, *Protecting Privacy,* 105.

99. Westin, *Computers, Health Records, and Citizen Rights,* viii-xviii.

100. See Recommendation 2 in Alpert, "Smart Cards, Smarter Policy," 21.

101. See Recommendation 7 in Institute of Medicine, *Health Data in the Information Age,* 7.

102. See Recommendations 1-3, 7, and 8 in Jones, "Privacy Issues in Health Care Reform," 1-8.

103. See Recommendation 5 in Office of Technology Assessment, *Protecting Privacy,* 108.

340 \ *Privacy, Nondiscrimination and Consent*

ployers should be denied personally-identifiable health records on their employees.[104] As with the previously discussed restrictions on data collection, there are real dangers here of broadly drawn measures. Proposals that establish a process for review of requests for access have more appeal than do recommendations for specific prohibitions.

Restrictions on data usage.

A variety of restrictions on data usage are contained in the several sets of recommendations:

- Jones would restrict the capability of data users to alter data – essentially a data integrity constraint.[105] This is consistent with an ethical principle that personal data should, as much as possible, be an accurate representation of its subject. *when? whether?* (s)

- Alpert and Schwartz, Kunitz, and Kozloff would impose data retention schedules.[106] This raises issues of timetable should be imposed, what value in terms of confidentiality is achieved through the restriction, and what loss in future, perhaps now unanticipated, data use might be sustained. Without addressing such considerations, a blanket imposition of data retention schedules is excessively restrictive.

- Marketing restrictions on personal data would be imposed by Alpert and Jones.[107] This recommendation has appeal in the abstract, but would alter substantially some current practices that can be argued to benefit the health care consumer. It requires public debate on a more disaggregated basis.

- Patient control of data is affirmed by Alpert and Goldman.[108] This proposal, although appealing in the abstract (as with other proposals discussed above), must be subject to some practical and ethical

---

104. See Recommendation 5 in House Committee on Post Office and Civil Service, "Census, Statistics and Postal Personnel," statement by Janlori Goldman, 12. Also see Recommendation 8 in Institute of Medicine, *Health Data in the Information Age,* 7.

105. See Recommendation 4 in Jones, "Privacy Issues in Health Care Reform," 4.

106. Alpert, "Smart Cards, Smarter Policy," 21. Schwartz, Kunitz, and Kozloff, "Building Data Research Resources from Existing Data Sets," 1-24.

107. Alpert, "Smart Cards, Smarter Policy," 21. Jones, "Privacy Issues in Health Care Reform," 1-8.

108. Alpert, "Smart Cards, Smarter Policy," 21. House Committee on Post Office and Civil Service, "Census, Statistics and Postal Personnel," statement by Janlori Goldman, 11-12.

limitation. Otherwise the patient could be at medical risk, appropriate administrative uses might be denied, and the benefits of medical research might be lost.

- Goldman also argues that no distinction should be made between paper and electronic records in terms of the protection they are afforded.[109] This position ignores the overwhelmingly lower cost of access and dissemination of records in electronic form, a fact which increases disclosure risk.

- Jones asserts that confidentiality obligations should transfer with any personal data.[110] This is quite consistent with the ethical concerns grounded in personal data as a representation of their subject.

Monitoring of data usage.

Audit trails of requests for personal medical information are recommended by Alpert, Jones, and OTA.[111] This would permit administrative actions to assure accountability of data users.

b. Empowerment

Patient access and control.

In the past, physicians have been accorded broad discretion to withhold from the patient information contained in a medical record if the physician felt that was medically desirable. Recent thinking, and the position of the American Health Information Management Association, supports greater patient access to their own data. This is also a recommendation of Alpert, Goldman, and Westin.[112] Office of Technology Assessment advocates education of patients about information practices.[113] These recommendations are consistent with an ethical principle of respect for the individual to make their own decisions and assessments.

---

109. House Committee on Post Office and Civil Service, "Census, Statistics and Postal Personnel," statement by Janlori Goldman, 12.

110. Jones, "Privacy Issues in Health Care Reform," 5.

111. Alpert, "Smart Cards, Smarter Policy," 21. Jones, "Privacy Issues in Health Care Reform," 3. Office of Technology Assessment, *Protecting Privacy,* 7.

112. Alpert, "Smart Cards, Smarter Policy," 21. House Committee on Post Office and Civil Service, "Census, Statistics and Postal Personnel," statement by Janlori Goldman, 12. Westin, *Computers, Health Records, and Citizen Rights*, viii-xviii.

113. Office of Technology Assessment, *Protecting Privacy,* 7.

Efficiency and effectiveness of care.

A variety of mechanisms on the information front have been recommended to improve the efficiency and effectiveness of health care.

- A unique patient identifier is supported by Alpert and Fitzmaurice.[114] The basic motivation is to provide appropriate and accurate information among concerned parties and to prevent fraud in reimbursement. To obtain research benefits, Schwartz, Kunitz, and Kozloff argue that health records from many sources need to be linked, and in some cases linked to other data, such as income and participation in various government programs.[115] They note that such linked data sets can be structured so that individuals would not be identified. From an efficiency and effectiveness perspective, having a unique patient identifier has obvious advantages. Concerns remain about the use of the Social Security number as this unique patient identifier, both because the SSN is not truly unique and that its use would allow linkage to large amounts of non-medical information. Goldman advocates an identifier restricted to the health care context.[116] Because so many extant medical records presumably already include a Social Security number, it is practical to have it as the patient identifier. With the Social Security number as an identifier, linkage to a variety of other databases that include personal information on the patient is possible. On the negative side, this possibility raises confidentiality concerns. On the positive side, it can permit health care research that better accounts for the broader context within which the patient lives.

- Medical information standards for database structure, content, and electronic data interchange are advocated by Fitzmaurice.[117] Schwartz, Kunitz, and Kozloff ask that legislation be developed for comprehensive data standards.[118] Establishing uniform standards fa-

---

114. Alpert, "Smart Cards, Smarter Policy," 21. Fitzmaurice, "Health Care and the NII," 52-53.

115. Schwartz, Kunitz, and Kozloff, "Building Data Research Resources from Existing Data Sets," 1-24.

116. House Committee on Post Office and Civil Service, "Census, Statistics and Postal Personnel," statement by Janlori Goldman, 12.

117. Fitzmaurice, "Health Care and the NII," 46.

118. See Recommendation 1 in Schwartz, Kunitz, and Kozloff, "Building Data Research Resources from Existing Data Sets," 1-24.

cilitates data access and can substantially improve the quality of medical care.

c. Accountability

Organizational accountability.

The Institute of Medicine stresses the need for health database organizations to be forthcoming with accurate data on provider-specific evaluations.[119] As health care consumer and payers become increasing conscious of quality and cost differentials among providers, this kind of information should be provided.

No excuses.

Westin asks that confidentiality not be used as a cover to block public oversight of government activity (see Appendix).[120] This argument would largely extend to other organizations, such as health care providers, that are licensed to act in the public interest.

Data sharing and value of research.

Alpert recommends that standards be developed for legitimate access.[121] Institute of Medicine recommends the release of non-person-identified data to qualified entities.[122] Goldman recommends that information that is not personally identifiable may be provided for research and statistical purposes.[123] Westin notes the importance of healthcare evaluation and medical research.[124] It is essential that any consideration of privacy and confidentiality issues not miss the value of personal data to both the patient's immediate health care and to medical research generally.

---

119. See Recommendations 2-4 in Institute of Medicine, *Automated Medical Records*, 7.

120. See Recommendation 11 in Westin, *Computers, Health Records, and Citizen Rights*, viii-xviii.

121. Alpert, "Smart Cards, Smarter Policy," 21.

122. See Recommendation 5 in Institute of Medicine, *Health Data in the Information Age*, 8.

123. House Committee on Post Office and Civil Service, "Census, Statistics and Postal Personnel," statement by Janlori Goldman, 12.

124. See Recommendation 12 in Westin, *Computers, Health Records, and Citizen Rights*, viii-xviii.

8. Conclusions

To be fully functional in supporting the delivery of high quality medical
care, an electronic medical record system must contain a broad range of
information that goes well beyond current diagnosis, health status, and
medical protocol initiated. It must include basic demographic information,
environmental facts about living and working conditions, longitudinal
clinical data, family history, and general health history. Given the reality
of a complex system of third-party payers, the electronic record must also
contain financial information. Thus – as recognized by the various studies
reviewed in this paper – purely from the standpoint of the patient's medical
and financial well-being, content standards should not be proscribed nar-
rowly. Further, research – whether directly related to patient outcomes in
the managerial practice of a particular provider, devoted to public policy
analysis of government initiatives, or attempts to obtain an empirical
understanding of health care in our society – requires data on more than
just medical outcomes. On the other hand, both the limited set of medical
information and the broader set of medical information contain highly
sensitive personal information that require data protection. In reconciling
the need for data access and the desire to maintain privacy and confidentiality, a variety of mechanisms have been proposed and are endorsed here.
Most importantly, there is a need for legislation that establishes standards
on privacy and data access for the health care information infrastructure.
A valuable component of such legislation would be the enabling of an
appropriate oversight body to ensure both privacy and data access in the
health care context.

In the introduction, a number of questions were laid out regarding
privacy standards. With the analysis of the previous sections, a response to
each of them can now be provided.

1. Are there certain types of data that should not be collected?

Clearly data should not be collected if it serves no discernible legitimate purpose, whether in the present or the future. In health care, legitimate
purposes for collecting individual patient data include determining a proper
course of treatment for the patient and contributing to a research base for
future medical treatment of other patients. Data are also legitimately collected for administrative purposes – insurance reimbursement, for example.
Further, data are legitimately collected to improve administrative functions, for example, the administration of the Medicare system. It is also
important to realize that health care data can have legitimate research uses

in areas that are outside the boundaries of health care studies. For example, individual-level data on health care utilization and financing can be essential for learning about how well people are prepared for retirement and in research on tax policy.

While "... it is inappropriate to collect volumes of personal information simply because some of the information may, in the future, prove to be of some unanticipated value," important future research uses for data can easily be missed if explicit thought is not devoted to them at the time of data collection.[125]

Data, even with a legitimate purpose, should not be collected if it seriously violates other ethical principles. It is well-established that any investigation that subjects a human research subject to risk must be justified to an independent authority. The National Research Act (P. L. 93-948) required justification to an IRB. Risk includes invasion of privacy, so unless it is significant to the well-being of the patient or to society, data should not be collected if it invades a patient's privacy. This principle would, in particular, proscribe medical experimentation where each arm (an arm is one of the treatments or controls) of the experiment is not deemed to potentially benefit the patient. It also argues for obtaining a patient's informed consent in most cases involving medical experimentation. Arguments for experimentation that are based on benefit to society, but not necessarily the patient, deserve careful independent scrutiny.

On the other hand, many observational studies that are based on medical data could not be carried out if patient consent were required. Here the data are already obtained so there is no question of invasion of privacy. Instead it is a question of appropriate confidentiality standards. In general, research and statistical uses that do not reveal an individual's identity are appropriate, while administrative actions, except those of clear benefit to the patient, such as contacting those whom it is later learned may require further treatment, would not be appropriate. Again, unless it is significant to the patient's medical well-being, data should not be collected unless it can be afforded confidentiality. This said, it should not be forgotten that highly personal information must, for the patient's well-being, be an integral part of the medical record.

---

125. Office of Management and Budget, "National Information Infrastructure," 4365.

2. What is a violation of health care information privacy?

Let's broaden this question to include, as well, confidentiality of health care information. It would be a violation for data about an individual that are collected or maintained for research and other statistical uses to be employed in an administrative or enforcement action affecting that individual. This would implement the principle of functional separation that was put forth by the Privacy Protection Study Commission in 1977. The commission recommended:

> . . . that the Congress provide by statute that no record or information contained therein collected or maintained for a research or statistical purpose under federal authority or with federal funds may be used in individually identifiable form to make any decision or take any action directly affecting the individual to whom the record pertains, except within the context of the research plan or protocol, or with the specific authorization of such individual.[126]

The same principle should apply to data collected for an administrative program and transferred to another agency of organization for research or statistical purposes. One of the key recommendations in Duncan, Jabine, and de Wolf is that statistical records across all federal agencies should be governed by the principle of functional separation.[127] Further, it would be a violation if a reasonable person would conclude that identifiable data about individuals were made available to any who have no legitimate need to know.

In fully answering this question, it is also useful to examine what is not a violation of health care information privacy. Some have argued that if data collected for one purpose were used for another purpose, confidentiality would be violated and so should be prohibited by law. As is argued by Bradburn,

> Such a blanket prohibition would be very harmful to society by denying it the benefits of legitimate research and statistical uses of data. No one can foresee all potential uses of data that would

---

126. *Personal Privacy in an Information Society* (Washington, D.C.: U.S. Government Printing Office, 1977), 8.

127. See Recommendation 5.1 in Duncan, Jabine, and de Wolf, *Private Lives and Public Policies,* 132-137. See also House Committee on Post Office and Civil Service, Subcommittee on Census, Statistics and Postal Personnel, testimony prepared by F. Thomas Juster, 1-5.

benefit society. If such prohibitions were enacted and enforced, society would lack important information that it could obtain only at greater cost through new data collection activities that might intrude further on individual privacy.[128]

Also, respect for the individual suggests that there is no violation of health care information privacy if the individual freely and with full information consents to specified access to their health care information. Thus respondents to voluntary surveys may reasonably be asked to consent to certain types of dissemination of the data they provide.

3. What would deter potential violators of privacy?

Potential violators of privacy and confidentiality can be deterred by providing sanctions against unauthorized disclosures by any data seeker or user. Confidentiality protection should be extended to identifiable data about individuals, wherever the data are maintained. Thus legislation is needed that would provide this data protection to all who are entrusted with identifiable health care data. In particular, data about an individual that are collected or maintained for research and other statistical uses, should not be used in any administrative or enforcement action affecting that individual. This principle of functional separation should be implemented in legislation. Further, social controls can be strengthened by promulgating codes of ethics and organizing discussions at appropriate meetings of data seekers and users. This educational process needs to engage all the various participants involved with health care information.[129] Data users can be required to submit to administrative arrangements, such as licensing procedures, that clearly specify their duties and responsibilities, as well as sanctions for noncompliance. For example, medical staff members might lose staff membership (Gardner 1989).

---

128. Norman M. Bradburn, letter to Rep. Thomas C. Sawyer on behalf of the Committee on National Statistics, National Research Council, 28 March 1994.

129. For an ethical framework directed toward nurses, see D. K. Milholland, "Privacy and Confidentiality of Patient Information: Challenges for Nursing," *Journal of Nursing Administration* 24 (1994): 19-24. For a discussion of responsibilities of social workers involved with AIDS patients, see Frederic G. Reamer, "AIDS and Social Work: The Ethics and Civil Liberties Agenda," *Social Work* 38 (1993): 412-419. For concerns for researchers, see Mary T. Koska, "Outcomes Research: Hospitals Face Confidentiality Concerns," *Hospitals* 66 (1992): 32-34. For recommendations to employers, see Christine Woolsey, "Employers Risk Lawsuits If Access to Medical Data Is Not Restricted," *Business Insurance* 26 (1992): 24, 26.

4. What are appropriate requirements for informed consent and notification that protect the confidentiality of patients' records while maximizing research access to data?

Patients and others who respond to health care surveys or who complete administrative forms should be informed about planned or expected uses of their data, as well as the possibility of unanticipated future uses for research or statistical purposes.[130] Further, respondents to voluntary surveys should be able, with informed consent, to permit selective access to their health care information.[131]

An ethical question of serious practical importance is, "When is patient consent to data access really informed?" Essentially this is an empirical question that must be addressed on a case-by-case basis. In particular, just as with other forms of informed consent in the medical context, informed consent procedures must take into account patient characteristics. Evidently, establishing informed consent is different for a psychiatric patient than it is for a comatose patient than it is for a prostate cancer patient at an early stage.

Another ethical question involves data subjects who may be deemed to be in an especially vulnerable situation. This might include patients who would not receive certain kinds of treatment unless they agree to access. It might also include children, who may require additional protection, especially the consent of a parent or guardian.[132] These are issues that need to be considered in particular cases. Some have gone so far as to argue that in some cases community consent should be required to minimize group harms.[133] These arguments pose significant practical problems in research and in patient care. Additionally, they are not generally accepted as ethical imperatives.

As pointed out by OTA, this issue of informed consent is linked to patient access to their own information.[134] Can consent be truly informed

---

130. See Recommendation 3.2 in Duncan, Jabine, and de Wolf, *Private Lives and Public Policies*, 75-77.

131. See Recommendation 3.3 in Duncan, Jabine, and de Wolf, *Private Lives and Public Policies*, 77-80.

132. OPPR Reports, "Protection of Human Subjects," code of Federal Regulations, Title 45, Part 46, Subpart D, Additional Protections for Children Involved as Subjects in Research. Revised as of 8 March 1983, pp.15-18.

133. Charles R. McCarthy and Joan P. Porter, "Confidentiality: The Protection of Personal Data in Epidemiological and Clinical Research Trials," *Law, Medicine and Health Care* 19 (1991): 238-241.

134. Office of Technology Assessment, *Protecting Privacy,* 118.

if the patient does not know what personal information about them is contained in the medical record?

5. How best can a patient's access to their own information be promoted?

It is a generally accepted fair information principle that individuals should have the means to obtain their personal information and the opportunity to correct information that could harm them.[135] Legislative action is needed to ensure that a patient can have reasonable access to their own personal medical information. Reasonable access might, for example, delineate timing and circumstances of access so as not to unduly interfere with ongoing medical procedures. They might also make special provisions for many children. Legislation should be reinforced by institutional policy guidelines. These guidelines should provide for independent review.

6. How should an oversight body be instituted to oversee privacy in health care information?

An independent federal advisory body should be created that is charged with fostering a climate of enhanced protection for all federal data about persons and responsible data dissemination for research and statistical purposes.[136] Correspondingly, state-level advisory boards should also be created with parallel responsibilities. Such a body cannot and should not rule on each request for health care information. These decisions are best made by the institutions that hold the data. Instead the advisory bodies would provide clear policy guidance to agencies, institutional review boards, and potential data users on privacy, confidentiality, and data access issues.

The federal body could advise Congress on the effects of legislation in this area. The state bodies could similarly advise their state legislatures. The advisory bodies could communicate to the public how confidentiality is protected, while allowing for legitimate medical and research use of their information. It is important that an advisory body reflects in its name, composition, and staff, as well as in its charge, its dual purpose: protecting the confidentiality of health care information and fostering responsible

---

135. See Office of Management and Budget, "National Information Infrastructure," 4363.

136. See Recommendation 8.5 in Duncan, Jabine, and de Wolf, *Private Lives and Public Policies*, 217-218.

access to that information, both for administrative purposes and for research and statistical purposes.

In summary, with adequate attention to privacy, confidentiality and data access issues, it is possible to develop an effective health care information infrastructure. Technological developments increase the tension between privacy demands and information needs, but also provide the tools for resolving this tension. An effective health care information infrastructure will serve patients in their medical needs, providing effective clinical decision support. It will ensure that privacy and confidentiality of health care information is adequately protected. It will serve the financial and administrative needs of insurers and the government. It will help realize benefits to the health care system, patients, and the public as a whole by providing data for research and other statistical purposes. In building a quality medical care system, there is no tradeoff between privacy and confidentiality on the one hand and data access on the other. Both are required if high quality data is to serve health care needs.

CHAPTER FOURTEEN

Medical Data Protection and Privacy in the United States: Theory and Reality

Vincent M. Brannigan and Bernd Beier

Introduction

This paper assumes that data privacy in complex medical information systems is technologically feasible – but often expensive, inconvenient, and conflicts with other goals of the health care system. The key question is how much effort we should expend on protection of patient data.

In most cases the problem of privacy is much worse with clinical information systems than with paper records. Paper records are difficult to find, often impossible to sort, and the record thief must go directly to the custodian. As a result, the security systems for such records are often very limited. When computer systems were developed, the same low security was carried over and implemented without any significant analysis of patient privacy protection. Patient privacy was viewed as just one of many factors to be balanced in system design. Networked information systems increase both the number of users and the number of patient records. Arguably, the risk of invasion of privacy increases exponentially with an increasing number of participants.

In many hospital information systems, all health care providers have access to data on all patients. Many hospitals rely on a kind of "paper" privacy, such as requiring all employees to sign documents that they will not reveal medical data on patients, and declaring the problem solved.[1]

---

1. France FHR Gaunt PN, "The Need for Security – A Clinical View," *International Journal of Biomedical Computing* 35, Suppl. 1 (1994): 189-94.

351

Courts have not been willing to accept such a "paper" approach, especially in an environment of HIV and other sensitive issues.

Privacy in medical information systems has been analyzed in a number of different articles, mostly focusing on either specific legal problems in medical privacy,[2] or on the particular technical difficulties in ensuring privacy.[3] There has been relatively less attention paid to the underlying demand for medical privacy and how that affects the law and the technology. This paper will analyze the legal structure of medical data privacy and propose a theory of privacy as it relates to medical information systems. This theory can then be used to categorize specific patient data and determine what level of protection might be available.

Finding a Right to Privacy

The right to privacy is one of the most elusive in American law. Courts hold that it exists, even as they disagree on where to find it, what it protects, who is protected and from whom. This section gives a small outline of the debate.

Privacy is not a unitary concept in American law. The legal status of privacy depends both on what is being protected and from whom. The key distinction is between the "public" right of privacy against government interference with an individual's personal life and the "private" right of action designed to prevent other private parties from interfering with the individual's personal life. These two concepts are not legally the same. One effect of this differentiation is that the individual right of medical data privacy depends very heavily on the public or private nature of the health care system that treats the patient, and the nature of the redress that the person seeks. As we move towards social funding of health care, the problem of privacy grows ever more complex.

---

2.   V. Brannigan, "Remote Telephone Access: The Critical Issue in Patient Privacy Protection," *Proceedings of the Eighth Symposium on Computer Applications in Medical Care* (Washington, D.C.: IEEE, 1984), 575-78.

3.   V. Brannigan and R. Dayhoff, "Medical Informatics: The Revolution in Law, Technology and Medicine," *Journal of Legal Medicine*, March 1986, 1-53. See also L. O. Gostin, J. Turek-Brezina, M. Powers, R. Kozloff, R. Faden, and E. D. Steinauer, "Privacy and Security of Personal Information in a New Health Care System," *JAMA* 270 (1993): 2487-93.

This paper concerns privacy as a legal right. In the legal system, the term "privacy" has been used in a number of different ways. To simplify the discussion, the following terms may be defined:

- *Locational* privacy protects a specific place against intrusion. This space was traditionally a home, but might be any place that we think of as private, such as a bathroom or telephone booth. The essence of the intrusion is to observe what is happening in the private space. Recording the literal intrusion, such as with a photograph or tape recorder, would be included in this category.

- *Behavioral* privacy protects the individual's right to engage in specific actions, and limits the ability of others to prohibit the behavior. Some writers use the term autonomy to describe this type of privacy, others relate it to a concept of the "private sphere" of actions. The protected behavior tends to relate to sex, child-rearing and bodily integrity. For example, *Roe v. Wade* protects behavioral privacy in the area of abortions.

- *Informational* privacy protects the individual's interest in data about that individual. Most medical records privacy issues are related to informational privacy.

Defining the three types of privacy is important because the legal protection of privacy in the public and private spheres depends very heavily on which type of privacy is involved.

a. Constitutional Law

Most constitutional and civil rights prohibit the government from doing specific acts. They do not guarantee the individual any positive benefit. For example, individuals in the United States generally have no constitutional rights to food, clothing, shelter, employment, education or medical care. Those rights, if they exist at all, are determined by the political process and are set out in specific statutes.

Privacy is treated much the same way. The United States Constitution does not guarantee privacy, but only prevents the government from interfering with a person's privacy. In addition, the explicit constitutional right of privacy is oriented towards locational rather than behavioral or informational privacy. The Fourth Amendment is clearly locational in nature, and has been so interpreted by the courts. Locational privacy, especially in homes, has been protected since the Constitution was adopted. On the other hand, locations other than homes, such as cars, have been given lesser protection. Since only locational privacy is mentioned in the Constitution, behavioral and informational privacy have had to be inferred.

The first case to define a specific federal concept of behavioral privacy in the medical area was a case that involved the right of a physician to import contraceptives to treat patients, despite a contrary federal law. This case interpreted a statute, but later cases put the right of behavioral privacy on a constitutional footing. In recent years, courts have created behavioral protection for "matters relating to marriage, procreation, contraception, family relationships, and child rearing and education."[4]

To this date, the Supreme Court has not created specific informational privacy rights. In the *Olmstead* case,[5] the court allowed wire-tapping of private telephone conversations, and it was not until 1957 that the Supreme Court recognized a privacy interest in a telephone conversation. But even that case involved privacy in a telephone booth. Properly analyzed, the privacy issue was related to the location, not to the information.

The leading Supreme Court decisions on pure informational privacy found no real right to privacy. *Laird v. Tatum*[6] dealt with the videorecording of the faces of anti-Vietnam War protestors by the government. The court refused to limit the ability of the government to create records of public acts, despite the suggested "chill" on First Amendment freedoms.

In the medical area, the pivotal case in public informational privacy was *Whalen v. Roe,* which allowed the state to create a database of lawful users of abusable drugs, on the grounds that the prohibitions on disclosure to the public were adequate to prevent any constitutional damage.[7] The court was unwilling to concede that compiling the information was itself a violation of privacy.

> [Disclosures] of private medical information to doctors, to hospital personnel, to insurance companies, and to public health agencies are often an essential part of modern medical practice even when the disclosure may reflect unfavorably on the character of the patient. Requiring such disclosures to representatives of the

---

4. *Paul v. Davis*, 424 US 693, 713 (1976).

5. *Olmstead v. United States*, 277 US 438 (1928).

6. *Laird v. Tatum*, 408 US 1, 92 Sup. Ct. 2318, 1972 U.S. LEXIS 25, 33 L. Ed. 2d. 154 (1972).

7. *Whalen v. Roe*, 429 US 589, 97 Sup. Ct. 869, 1977 U.S. LEXIS 42, 51 L. Ed. 2d. 64 (1977).

State having responsibility for the health of the community, does not automatically amount to an impermissible invasion of privacy.[8]

The Supreme Court has not taken any further steps to define any constitutional right to informational privacy, but a series of legal decisions in the lower courts have helped to define protection for patient's privacy rights. The most important recent decision on medical privacy is *Doe v. New York*, where the United States Court of Appeals found that individuals have a *constitutional* right of privacy in data concerning HIV status.

Individuals who are infected with the HIV virus clearly possess a constitutional right to privacy regarding their condition. . . . There is, therefore, a recognized constitutional right to privacy in personal information.[9]

While the Court of Appeals cited *Whalen*, it clearly went beyond *Whalen* in defining the constitutional right of privacy. More recently, another Federal Court of Appeals also found a constitutional right of privacy in medical records.

An individual using prescription drugs has a right to expect that such information will customarily remain private. The district court, therefore, committed no error in its holding that there is a constitutional right to privacy in one's prescription records.[10]

Finding privacy to be a constitutional right does not automatically protect individuals from injury. As noted above, any constitutional right to privacy is limited to governmental infringement on rights. In addition to this limitation, any assertion is subject to balancing tests widely used in constitutional law. In particular, society may demand some compromise with privacy to protect public health. Further, a reasonable court might find that few patients would run substantial health risks to protect medical privacy.

Disagree

not getting treatment for HIV?

b. Federal Statutory Protection of Privacy

Because of the limitation on constitutional rights, virtually all the informational privacy provided by federal law is statutory in nature. Congress

---

8. *Whalen v. Roe*, 429 US at 602 (footnote omitted).

9. *Doe v. New York*, 15 F3d 264 (2nd Cir 28 January 1994).

10. *John Doe, a SEPTA employee v. Southeastern Pennsylvania Transportation Authority (SEPTA)*, US Ct. of App. (3rd Cir 28 December 1995).

reacted to the *Olmstead* decision by prohibiting wiretapping, and then to the development of surveillance and recording systems by enacting the *Privacy Act*.[11] In *Westinghouse*, the federal court of appeals has set out the specific standards to be used by a court interpreting the *Privacy Act* in weighing privacy rights in medical records against the needs for reporting to public agencies.

Thus, as in most other areas of the law, we must engage in the delicate task of weighing competing interests. The factors which should be considered in deciding whether an intrusion into an individual's privacy is justified are:

- the type of record requested,

- the information it does or might contain,

- the potential for harm in any subsequent nonconsensual disclosure,

- the injury from disclosure to the relationship in which the record was generated,

- the adequacy of safeguards to prevent unauthorized disclosure, the degree of need for access, and

- whether there is an express statutory mandate, articulated public policy, or other recognizable public interest militating toward access.[12]

The *Privacy Act* has been the subject of substantial litigation and academic commentary.

At the state level, privacy is protected by statute in a limited number of circumstances. The most common are statutes protecting the privacy of patients with mental illness. In other cases states have passed privacy protection statutes in response to specific invasions of privacy. Many states protect library records, and Maryland passed a statute making disclosure of videotape rentals a violation of law after such disclosures were made about Supreme Court nominee Robert Bork.

This social concern can be seen as a risk for health care information systems. In the event of a privacy disaster, courts, Congress, or state legislatures can respond with statutes that profoundly affect how the health care system operates. On the other hand, governments often find it inevi-

---

11. *Privacy Act of 1974*, 5 U.S. Code 552a(a)-(q) (1976).

12. *United States of America v. Westinghouse Electric*, 638 F2d 570 (3rd Cir 1980).

table that they incorporate public constitutional rights into laws regulating private conduct, and state courts might be encouraged to expand the common law right of privacy. Even though the *Privacy Act* applies only to the federal government, it demonstrates the widespread public concern with privacy in relation to computer systems. Thus to simply be in compliance with current law is not enough to avoid legal problems in the future. Systems must be developed which are secure and flexible enough to cope with foreseeable changes in the law.

c. State Common Law Rights

The lack of specific constitutional and statutory protection should not be taken to mean there is no legal protection at all.[13] The courts are clearly concerned with the problem of computerized data banks, and condition their acceptance of data gathering on what are perceived to be adequate safeguards. The concept of a legal right to damages from those who invade privacy is generally traced to an early law review article by Brandeis and Holmes. Over the years their formulation was adopted in the restatement of torts as four distinct rights, only two of which are relevant here. The first is the right of seclusion, or the right to avoid those who would intrude into the private sphere, and the second is the right to avoid publication of private facts.

These rights would seemingly apply to medical data; however, the courts have created so many exceptions to the right of medical privacy that it is legitimate to question whether they truly recognize an effective right of privacy.

The first exception is that some courts require "publication" in the sense of a widespread distribution of the information. The distribution of confidential information to a few persons is not publication. In the case of medical privacy, it is arguable that it is not the number of persons given the information, but their relationship to the patient that determines the scope of concern; there may only be a small number of persons interested in the particular patient, but disclosure to any one of them could be devastating.

Second, virtually all states allow courts to subpoena medical records, at least if the plaintiff makes the state of health an issue in the case. Since

---

13. *Office of Technology Assessment, Protecting Privacy in Computerized Medical Information* (Washington, D.C.: Government Printing Office, 1993).

subpoenas are typically issued by the clerk of the court, after a request by a lawyer, hospitals may be ordered to disclose records that have little or no significance to a given claim.

Third, many states have a wide circle of persons who are considered to be "legitimately interested" in a person's health, such as spouses or employers. The concept of "legitimately interested" can effectively destroy any right of privacy. For example, are co-workers "legitimately interested" in a person's diagnosis of AIDS? Isn't that interest precisely why privacy is important?

Fourth, public figures may not be accorded privacy protection, as the public is considered "legitimately interested" in their conditions.

Fifth, some commentators have held that the First Amendment prohibits a state from imposing liability for truthful speech about a person, even if it invades their privacy, because of the constitutional protection of freedom of speech and press.

Sixth, even the courts that have imposed liability for intentional release of medical information have not imposed liability for negligent release of medical information. This raises the possibility that it is not privacy that is protected, but the intentional invasion of privacy which is punished. In such a situation, the invasion of privacy becomes equivalent to the intentional infliction of emotional distress.

One of the most striking decisions detailing a lack of medical privacy was the Kansas court that allowed an insurance company that obtained medical data under a specific release to transmit the data to an insurance industry data bank, called the medical information bureau.

As this limited summary indicates, medical information privacy in the past did not receive a great deal of protection in the law. As a practical matter, the great change in privacy law has been as a result of AIDS. Hospitals have had the inadequacy of the privacy protection in their paper records declared by the courts. In the *Behringer* case, the court was dealing with the inadequacy of the hospital protection of a patient chart containing an AIDS diagnosis:

> While there is some dispute as to the propriety of charting as an acceptable medical practice, the Medical Center felt there were safeguards in the general confidentiality guidelines set forth in its by-laws and employee manuals. According to stated policy, charts were limited to those persons having patient care responsibility, but in practical terms, the charts were available to any doctor,

nurse or other hospital personnel. Despite the CDC's recommendation that access to HIV results be limited, the Medical Center
had no policy physically restricting access to the HIV test results
or the charts containing the results to those involved with the
particular patient's care. In addition, the broad confidentiality
policies of the Medical Center specifically restrict HCWs from
discussing patient's charts with other HCWs. . . .

It is not the charting per se that generates the issue; it is the easy
accessibility to the charts and the lack of any meaningful Medical
Center policy or procedure to limit access that causes the breach
to occur. Where the impact of such accessibility is so clearly
foreseeable, it is incumbent on the Medical Center, as the custodian of the charts, to take such reasonable measures as are necessary to insure that confidentiality. Failure to take such steps is
negligence. . . .

Insuring confidentiality even by Medical Center employees required more,
in the present case, than simply instructing employees that medical records
are confidential. The charts are kept under the control of the Medical Center
with full knowledge of the accessibility of such charts to virtually all
Medical Center personnel, whether authorized or not. Little, if any, action
was taken to establish any policy or procedure for dealing with a chart such
as plaintiff's.[14]

The holding of *Behringer* is that "paper" protection of privacy is
insufficient. Real protection must be built into any system. Adequate
regulation of privacy protection may be a formal prerequisite for deciding
information systems can be implemented. The *Behringer* case supports a
policy goal of a high, though not absolute, protection of privacy. Acceptable privacy risks arise from the inherent needs of medical practice, not the
administrative needs of the information handler. All the cases cited make
it clear that holding someone responsible for a data release is not sufficient,
actual protection of the data is required.

Hospitals often have a very casual attitude towards patient privacy
protection. In *Doe v. Shady Grove Adventist Hospital* a patient's diagnosis
of AIDS was reportedly disclosed by hospital staff members. When the
patient sued under the name John Doe, the hospital tried to force the patient

14. *Estate of William Behringer, M.D., Plaintiff, v. The Medical Center at Princeton,
Dennis, Doody, and Leung Lee, M.D.*, 249 N.J. Super. 597, 592 A2d 1251, 1991 N.J.
Super. LEXIS 165 (25 April 1991).

to reveal his true name to the press and public.[15] The hospital gave no explanation why it was insisting on this violation of any shreds of privacy the patient had left. The Maryland Court of Special Appeals suggested that the hospital was attempting to minimize the damages the hospital might have to pay.

" Widespread dissemination of appellant's identity in this litigation would . . . exacerbate the injury he alleges that he has already suffered at the hands of appellees. Appellees [the hospital] will then be able to argue that appellant suffered no damages as a result of their actions, because the information later became public. "

Alternatively the court was concerned that the hospital was trying to intimidate potential plaintiffs.

Potential plaintiffs, who believe that their rights may have been violated, will be loath to bring their complaints to court if the end result will be further and even more widespread violation of those rights.

If a single message can be extracted from the legal opinions, it is that reasonable protection of patient privacy is a compelling state interest.

Medical Privacy

The right of privacy was unknown to the common law prior to the Holmes/Brandeis formulation. To properly analyze privacy in medical care, it is necessary to understand the historical development of the concept of medical privacy. We add to that development a theoretical structure to help the analysis.

a. History of Medical Privacy

The principle of medical privacy is commonly thought to arise from the oath of Hippocrates:

> What I may see or hear in the course of treatment or even outside
> of the treatment in regard to the life of men, which on no account
> one must spread abroad, I will keep to myself, holding such things
> to be shameful to be spoken about.[16]

---

15. *John Doe v. Shady Grove Adventist Hospital et al.,* 1991 Court of Special Appeals of Maryland 1991 MD App. LEXIS 221.

16. Areen et al., *Law, Science, and Medicine,* (Mineola, NY: Foundation Press).

However, on closer examination, medical privacy was much more limited than the oath would suggest. The oath prescribed a professional obligation for the physician not to reveal secrets, it created no obligation that the patient's secrets not be revealed by others. In other words, it limited the physician, rather than creating a right for the patient.

This raises the interesting legal possibility that there is no fundamental legal right of medical privacy. Instead, what we think of as medical privacy may simply be a combination of professional responsibility on the part of the physician and an extension of the locational privacy of the household.

This possibility rests on the different classical treatment of physicians and hospitals. From ancient times to the 20th century, most patients were attended by physicians in their homes. Households, from at least the time of the Romans, have been treated as special places for the purpose of privacy. The Constitution specifically mentions the privacy of houses. The patient's privacy was secured by the possibility of obtaining care in the privacy of their own homes, coupled with a limitation on the physician's disclosure of what was observed in the home.

In comparison, even in the Middle Ages the poor were often treated in public charitable hospitals. There does not appear to be a great deal of evidence of a tradition of medical secrecy connected with these hospitals. The poor were often several to a bed, and many beds to a room. Physicians attended the patients in public, often accompanied by students. Even outside the hospital, persons who were afflicted with infectious disease or mental illness were often required to broadcast that fact, and wore special clothing for the purpose.

A certain division can thus be established. Among those who were householders, and could invite physicians into their homes, medical privacy rested on the locational privacy of the household. For the poor treated in the charity hospital, privacy did not exist.

In the 19th century, at least in advanced urban areas, paying patients began visiting physicians in their offices, rather than the physicians visiting the patients in their homes. This did not change the nature of the privacy problem substantially. The locational privacy of the household was simply transferred to the physician's office. The professional responsibility of the physician became a contractual matter, with privacy part of the professional contract.

The revolutionary change came with the increased treatment of even paying patients in hospitals, resulting from the development of modern surgical and medical treatment. The needs of a modern hospital created a demand for medical record-keeping and produced a conflict between the two models of medical privacy: the paying office patient model, that includes privacy, and the poor hospital patient model that does not.

Since medical privacy arose only from the professional contract, and was not a traditional obligation of the hospital, it may not have become part of the original contract between the patient and the hospital. Patients, however, continued to believe that their affairs received the same confidential treatment they would have received in the physician's office.

In reality the data was protected more by accidents of hospital structure than deliberate intent. Locational privacy was secured by the separation of wards into private and semiprivate rooms, and informational privacy was accomplished by the chaotic manner of keeping hospital records. Medical records in hospitals were, as a practical matter, inaccessible to all but the most determined record thief. Records were cryptic, handwritten in a single copy, and often could not be reconstructed, even for legitimate purposes.

However, changes in medical therapy, health insurance and cost control are demanding more detailed and exact medical records, and computerized information systems have made provision of those records to both authorized and unauthorized observers easier.[17]

b. A Theory of Privacy in Medicine

The existence of separate concepts of locational, behavioral, and informational privacy in the law indicates a lack of an overall concept of what privacy is trying to accomplish. While some legal authors have attempted to integrate the concepts, most have limited the issues to libertarian concepts of the interaction of individual and state. However, when analyzed functionally, medical informational privacy relates to the context in which information might be used or perceived by others.

Clearly not all medical information is equally "private." That a woman delivered a baby, that a leg has been broken or that glasses are worn are events which are often, though not always informationally public. Developing technology creates both loss of privacy and the potential for new types of privacy. Lineless lenses conceal the use of bifocals and breast implants can conceal surgery.

---

17. E.H.W. Kluge, "Health Information, Privacy, Confidentiality, and Ethics," *International Journal of Biomedical Computing* 35, Suppl. 1 (1994): 23-27.

What remains constant is that people have some types of data which they wish to keep concealed from others. We believe that the key element that determines whether individuals desire to keep data private is the context to which the data relates. For example, the marital status and age of the mother, or the identity of the father may make a substantial difference in the desire for privacy.

Consequences of disclosure of medical information are very complex. They can range from embarrassment, loss of self-esteem, financial loss, loss of employment, divorce or even the triggering of homicidal or suicidal impulses. Therefore the goal of individuals in the area of information privacy is to preserve themselves from real or perceived adverse consequences of the data becoming known.

Our approach is that the difference in individual concern for disclosure of medical information depends on how the receiver of the information might act or react towards the patient. To put it another way, the critical issue is not the type of data but the consequence to the patient of the information being known.

The group of people who receive the information will be described as the reference group. They can include family, friends, coworkers, employers or the public at large. Disclosure of certain types of data would not generally result in adverse consequences from the reference group. This data can be defined as indicating *Normality*. A person who would not be subject to adverse consequences can be defined as *Normal*. Normal in this sense does not mean physically or mentally fit or able, it merely means within the group who would not suffer adverse consequences.

Our theory is that the purpose of informational privacy is to allow individuals to project themselves as falling within the definition of normality for their reference group and thus avoid adverse consequences, even if in reality they are outside the normal range.

Under this concept, privacy is "operative" or functional in terms of allowing the individual to project themselves in a certain way. An individual's concern with privacy depends very much on whether the particular medical information is indicative of a state that the reference group would think of as Normal. For example, medical information indicating that an individual has had an appendectomy would rarely put an individual outside any group's definition of Normal. On the other hand, a report of electroconvulsive therapy was sufficient to deprive Senator Eagleton of his vice presidential nomination. Normality is obviously a cultural phenomenon.

[handwritten: (ie. post- violation) — These are all remedially-oriented, rather than preventive]

The legal debates over obscenity have created a deference to contemporary community standards in determining obscenity, within broad constitutional guidelines. The same could be done with normality.

As a functional or operative approach, the concentration is not on a right of privacy but instead on the social question of whether this is the type of data that the society considers should be kept private, and at what cost. In other words, is the social interest in allowing people to project themselves as "normal" high enough to justify the cost and inconvenience of protecting the data? To put it another way, is the administrative convenience worth the invasion of privacy?

This functional approach to privacy is very different from the European approach, that keeps data private to protect the individual's right of self-determination or self-development.[18] As an operative right, privacy in the area of medical care is not an absolute right, but a policy goal to be explicitly balanced against other social goals. In particular, if there are effective laws against certain actions based on the data, it may make less difference that the data becomes known. For example, if the *Americans with Disabilities Act* provided adequate protection against discrimination, there might be much less concern with the adequacy of the data protection. Certain areas of concern clearly cause more problems than others. Heightened areas of legal concern include:

1. Data related to sexual privacy,

2. Data related to individual determinations of life expectancy,

3. Data related to personality and mental illness,

4. Data related to use of controlled substances, and

5. Data related to genetic conditions or predispositions.

It is interesting that most of the earlier cases dealing with constitutional privacy rights involved contraception and abortion. In more recent cases, AIDS/HIV has become the centerpiece of privacy litigation. Both issues involve several of these factors.

[handwritten: Future: Genetic testing]

There are social concerns with privacy that may be considered in addition to the administrative convenience issues. For example,

---

18. B. Beier and V. Brannigan, "Principles for Patient Privacy Protection: USA and Germany," *Proceedings of the Fourth World Conference on Medical Informatics*, Amsterdam, 1983, 967-70.

1. Disclosure of positive drug tests has been defended on the grounds that the social condemnation resulting from the lack of privacy is part of the deterrent effect of the antidrug policy;

2. Disclosure of infectious disease can be part of a policy of limiting spread of the disease;

3. For treatable disease, disclosure can be part of a social strategy of encouraging openness and testing and treatment. Arguably, an emphasis on privacy can result in stigmatizing the individuals whose data is revealed.

Clearly, in the United States a balance is called for between an unrealistic desire to protect all data and the callous ignoring of the consequences of release of data.[19] Prompt and technologically sophisticated responses to legitimate needs are most likely to prevent the type of privacy disaster that severely impacts on system development.

Two different issues must be resolved in any balancing. The first is the range of interests which are considered worthy of protection, and the second is who should do the balancing.

To accomplish these results we must define a system for producing the socio/political judgements. The most obvious consideration is that the developers and users of the data are not the only parties who have a stake in the social decision. Their interests are clearly in the area of administrative convenience. It has been in their interest to treat privacy as essentially a technical problem to be resolved by system developers. This is wrong. Privacy and security are political, not technical decisions, and the society as a whole has to determine its priorities.

Saying a problem is political does not make it any easier to rationally solve. The problem with political determination is a lack of technological sophistication in the political process and the creation of legal straitjackets for new technology. The German data protection laws, for example, are designed for computer centers that do batch processing of data. The use of remote terminals for time-shared data processing was only accommodated by stretching the principles of the law. The emergence of networked microprocessors threatens to make the legal structure unworkable.

19. V. Brannigan and B. Beier, "Informational Self-Determination: A Choice-Based Analysis," *Datenshutz und Datensicherung* 4 (1985): 281-86.

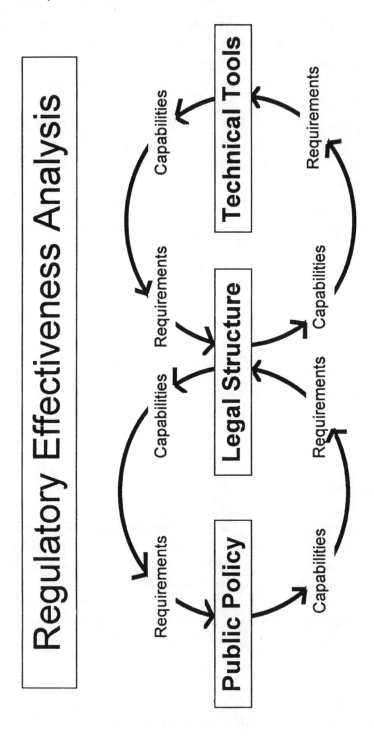

Regulatory Effectiveness Analysis

Protection of Medical Privacy

The technical protection of privacy requires an integrated analysis of the various players and parties involved in the privacy decisions. In this section we will use a research technique developed for the study of privacy in the hospital environment. A case study and a comparison study of medical privacy show some of the problems involved in providing adequate protection.

a. Regulatory Effectiveness Analysis

Regulatory Effectiveness Analysis (REA) is a method for evaluating the success of an existing or proposed regulatory program. It is under development at the University of Maryland. REA is designed to measure separately and together three key components of a technical regulatory system.

The first component is the set of *Public Policies*. Public policy is a narrative statement of the goals to be achieved by the regulatory program. These statements can be either concrete or abstract.

The second component is the set of *Legal Structures* used to implement the regulation. Regulation requires a legal mechanism to enforce the social will on individuals who would not otherwise comply.

The third component is the set of *Technical Tools* available for regulation. Every technology has a distinct and often limited set of technical tools available. Technical tools are not limited to machines or laboratories. Encryption, ID cards, IQ tests, statistical quality assurance and double-entry bookkeeping are all technical tools.

The theory of Regulatory Effectiveness Analysis is that all three of these components must be properly designed to achieve a working regulatory system. Public policies must be coherent, legal structures must contain all necessary elements, and technical tools must be available and produce the needed results. Further, the components interact. Public policy, legal structures and technical tools have interlocking sets of requirements and capabilities. *Requirements* are the preconditions which must be satisfied by other components before a given component can function. *Capabilities* reflect the ability of a tool to satisfy a requirement of another component.

Figure 1 shows the interaction of the three components and their respective capabilities and requirements. For example, each specific public policy requires certain capabilities in the legal structure. Similarly, each legal structure has capabilities that can satisfy the needs of public policy.

Regulatory Effectiveness Analysis is a study of 1) whether the components of a system are clearly defined, and 2) whether the capabilities and requirements of a given set of components are properly matched. If a component is ill-defined or there is a mismatch between policy goals, structure and tools, a *Discontinuity* exists. For example, the Food and Drug Administration was supposed to regulate software under the 1976 Medical Device Amendments. The legal structures established under the 1976 amendments were premarket approval or product standards. However, both of these legal structures require a technical tool which can test a given piece of software and determine how safe it is. Such a tool did not exist. This created a discontinuity, which required changing one of the components.[20]

Under the Medical Device Amendments of 1990, the FDA was given the authority to allow software on the market with minimal testing, but was given strengthened authority to pull it from the market after an injury. The FDA thus had a new legal structure, which required a different, but available technical tool. It is much easier to show that a given piece of software is defective than that a piece of software is not defective. However, using the legal structure of post-market removal of defective products meant that the policy goal of preventing all defective products from reaching the market had to be adjusted.

Discontinuities can exist among the components, even when the individual component is properly designed. To use a computer analogy, a perfectly good parallel printer will not work if connected to a serial port.

b. Public Policies

Public policies in all areas of technical regulation tend to be stated in very vague terms. As a result, it is usually more effective to look first at the legal structure and the technical tools, since they will more clearly indicate exactly what public policy is being supported. It is then possible to compare it to the nominal public policy and determine whether a discontinuity exists.

c. Legal Structures

While an infinite variety of legal structures might be considered if REA is used to generate a regulatory program, for the purpose of evaluating an

---

20. V. Brannigan, "The Regulation of Medical Software as a Device under the Food, Drug and Cosmetic Act," *Jurimetrics Journal of Law, Science and Technology*, 27, 370-82.

existing system it is only necessary to look at the structures actually used. Prior research indicates that in regulatory law a small number of legal terms accurately describes the basic legal structures available. Two of the most common types of legal structures can be described as *Precautions* and *Responsibility*. These terms are used in the analysis to avoid the use of legal jargon. They represent a complex combination of specific legal tools. The *Precaution* approach can be described as a legal structure where the policy maker has determined in advance which technical tools must be implemented, and where the individual has the obligation of carrying out the specific acts. Under the Precaution approach, the individual is supposed to implement the tool, but is not expected to determine whether the tool will perform the intended function satisfactorily. For the Precaution structure to function, a defined individual must carry out the action, the action to be carried out must be specified, and a method for determining the action has been carried out must be specified.

In the *Responsibility* structure, a defined person is assigned the obligation to prevent an injury from occurring, with potential penalties if they do not. For the Responsibility structure to function, it requires a defined individual who will be sanctioned for the default, the default, the injury, and the sanction must all occur in a reasonably short time, the sanction must be sufficient to deter the unwanted conduct, the responsible individual must have actual control over the default, and the injury must be traceable to the defined default.

The two structures have different requirements and possibilities. Under Responsibility, the person has discretion to choose the methods of avoiding the injury. The sanction is imposed for failure to choose an adequate method. Under the Precaution approach, the discretion has been exercised by the individual who defined the precaution.

d. Technical Tools

The regulatory effectiveness analysis asks two questions:

1. Do legal structures exist which properly implement the technical tools?

2. Do the legal structures and technical tools, acting together, correspond to the policy statements contained in the public policy?

REA is fundamentally a paper audit, which points out discontinuities or unfulfilled possibilities in a system. A REA does not necessarily indicate what level of privacy is afforded by the hospital. It indicates what level of privacy is being mandated by compliance with the regulatory program.

Case Study:
The Privacy Act and the Veterans Health Administration

To conduct the REA, it is necessary to determine the policy goals, legal structures and technical tools. In the case of the VHA, the relevant materials are found in the *Privacy Act*, the *Federal Register*, and internal VHA documentation. The *Privacy Act* includes specific requirements. For example, agencies must:

> . . . establish appropriate administrative, technical, and physical safeguards to insure the security and confidentiality of records and to protect against any anticipated threats or hazards to their security or integrity.[21]

Congress ordered, as a matter of national policy, that agencies develop, implement and disclose to the public systems for protecting data from disclosure. In accordance with the *Privacy Act*, in 1991 the VHA published its safeguards in the *Federal Register:*

1. . . . Access to patient medical records is restricted to VHA employees who have a need for the information in the performance of their official duties.

2. Access to the . . . computer rooms within the health care facilities is generally limited by appropriate locking devices and restricted to authorized VHA employees and vendor personnel. ADP peripheral devices are generally placed in secure areas (areas that are locked or have limited access) or are otherwise protected.[22]

Access to file information is controlled at two levels: the system recognizes authorized employees by a series of individually unique passwords/codes as a part of each data message, and the employees are limited to only that information in the file which is needed in the performance of their official duties. Information that is downloaded and maintained on personal computers is afforded similar storage and access protections as the data that is maintained in the original files.

---

21. *Privacy Act of 1974.*
22. *Federal Register* 56, 1054.

The *Federal Register* notice does not clearly indicate the legal structure used to carry out the statutory policy. However, the *Federal Register* notice does promise the citizen that the VHA has implemented at least the following three types of technical security tools:

1. passwords for access to the data in the system,

2. a system of classifying and restricting users based on their need to know, and

3. protection of downloaded data on personal computers.

It is necessary to determine which legal structures have been chosen to implement the technical tools. The implementation of the required security procedures is governed by the 1991 draft, *Manual for VHA Computer Operations.*[23] For example, the manual states:

> there shall be no local modification of the . . . security software
> features . . . codes shall be changed at least once every 90 days
> . . . all . . . user access shall be through the kernel security system.

Despite these individual instances of Precautions, it is clear from reading the manual that the VHA is relying primarily on the Responsibility tool for staff compliance with the act. Numerous passages assign responsibility. However, as noted above, there are specific criteria for a functioning responsibility system. The first criteria is a defined individual who will be sanctioned. However, responsibility in the VHA is not clearly defined as resting on a specific individual.

Even more serious, there is no definition whatsoever for one of the key technical tools, the "need-to-know" system. The *Federal Register* notice states that the VHA actually controls access to data on a "need-to-know" basis. However, the entire implementation of the "need-to-know" concept is indicated by a single line in the manual:

> 16.08 (a) Use of VHA information assets . . . is restricted to those
> with a need for them in the performance of their duties.

The operations manual defines no standards or requirements for the need-to-know system, and identifies no individual who is to ensure that one exists. It is unclear why the VHA, which felt it necessary to specify how long a password must be, does not feel it necessary to establish a "need-to-

---

23. Department of Veterans Affairs, *Information Resources Management Manual* (Washington, D.C., 30 July 1991).

know" policy and enforce it on local facilities, or even establish a requirement for a local policy.

a. Agency Responsibility versus Local Control

The *Privacy Act* makes it an *agency* responsibility to determine "the policies and practices of the agency regarding storage, retrievability, access controls, retention, and disposal of the records." The *Federal Register* notice states that the VHA has made the policy decisions and set out requirements for the systems. However, the actual security policy appears to be determined by the local facility manager, not the agency. With very few exceptions, there are no limitations on their freedom of action. *Each VHA facility is responsible for designating the sensitivity of the data/information under its administrative control.*

b. Personal Computers

The *Federal Register* notice also requires that personal computers meet the same level of security. *Information that is downloaded...and maintained on personal computers is afforded similar storage and access protections as the data that is maintained in the original files.* There is simply nothing in the manual which provides a legal structure or technical tool to carry out this policy.

c. Results

The movement of patients into hospitals has created a conflict between different traditions of privacy. Based on experience in other areas, if the health care industry does not show adequate concern for patient privacy, legislation will be adopted that could produce very negative effects. One solution is to recognize a functional definition of privacy and create representative consensus committees to articulate standards for privacy.

Regulatory effectiveness analysis has uncovered a number of discontinuities:

1. The policy stated in the *Privacy Act* is *precaution*-oriented; however, the legal structure adopted by the VHA is *responsibility*-oriented. However, the responsibility is diffused among several different places, and the audit system does not "close the loop."

2. The actual security system is under the jurisdiction of local officials, who are authorized to make the decision that a certain privacy risk is acceptable.

3. The statute requires a statement of the safeguards in the system. The *Federal Register* notice promises a "need-to-know" system. However, the *Operations Manual* does not define a "need-to-know" system.

4. There are no technical tools or legal structures to guarantee that the downloaded information on personal computers is actually afforded the level of protection stated in the *Federal Register* notice.

Regulatory Effectiveness Analysis appears to be an effective means of pinpointing discontinuities within a regulatory compliance program. However, it should not be assumed that a discontinuity indicates a failure of will in complying with a statute. As the FDA example shows, avoiding discontinuity may require adjustment of the policy goals, as well as refinement of the technical tools.

Comparison Study:
Physician Records in the National Practitioner Data Bank

The National Practitioner Data Bank (NPDB) is a large computer system located in Camarillo, California. It is operated by the UNISYS corporation as a contractor to the U.S. Public Health Service. The NPDB is a product of the *Health Care Quality Improvement Act of 1986*. Congress granted antitrust immunity for medical practitioners engaged in "peer review" activities, but mandated the creation of a national reporting system for medical practitioners who had been disciplined, successfully sued for malpractice, or whose hospital privileges had been curtailed. Hospitals, medical societies, malpractice insurance companies and state licensing boards are required to report data to the NPDB. Hospitals are required to get reports from the NPDB when granting privileges to physicians, and every two years thereafter.

The NPDB operates by collecting reports on physicians submitted by authorized reporters, consolidating the reports together, and sending the consolidated reports, upon request, to authorized institutions. The NPDB process would be analogous to a single request for a patient's entire computer-based medical record, as opposed to a clinical inquiry on a specific visit. As such, it makes a reasonable technical analogy to the proposed interinstitutional transmission of computer-based medical records.

Even though the information put into the data bank is often public or semi-public, and there is a clear public interest in collecting the data, the confidentiality of the data was a major concern of organized medicine. Physicians and other practitioners did not want the public to have access to the data. In a compromise, the release of the data is extremely restricted. Neither patients nor malpractice insurance carriers can get access to the data. The AMA still expresses doubts as to whether the precautions taken are adequate.

a. Why Is the NPDB Relevant to Patient Privacy Protection?

The data bank was developed to protect patient safety, as well as the integrity of the health care system. Prompt access to the data bank may be life-critical; and data subjects feel that the data is highly sensitive, and demand protection. Patients often have to rely on physicians for protection from the health care system. Physicians have defined in this data bank what privacy expectations they have for their own sensitive medically related data, and using this data bank to define the standard of privacy would help ensure uniform treatment of physicians and patients. The nature of the data involved, the types of transfers, and the prominent role played by organized medicine in setting the privacy requirements are an excellent rationale for using the data bank as a standard for patients' "reasonable expectations of privacy."

b. Technical Data Protection Tools in the NPDB

To ensure the confidentiality of the data, the PHS took a series of precautions. The computer is physically on the premises of a secure defense contractor, and the system is run in an off-line configuration. All persons with access to the computer system must have security clearances. Requests for information can be made electronically, through the same secure COMPUSERVE/INFOPLEX system used by the Internal Revenue Service. This is a high-security electronic mail system, where the system managers cannot get access to the data. The requester deposits the inquiry in a mailbox, where it is retrieved by the system computer. No direct electronic connection to the data bank computer is permitted. Requests can only be made electronically from authorized users, who have been furnished with special software provided by the data bank. Although the inquiries are not encrypted, the packet switching system is considered protected against interception.

All requests must be made in a format specified by the data bank, and requests can only be made for a report under the name of the data subject, with appropriate identifying information. No searching of the data bank is permitted. All requests for information are logged, and the log is made available to the practitioner. A copy of any adverse report sent to the data bank is sent to the practitioner. Provisions for disputing the report are available to the physician. No telephone inquiries are allowed, and requests from practitioners for their own records must be notarized. All reports are sent by mail. No electronic responses are currently permitted, although such responses are being explored. The author was advised that any reply would be encrypted, and sent only to the e-mail address of the entity which made the inquiry.

The data bank is wholly self-supporting, with an access charge of $6 per hospital inquiry. More than a million inquiries were made in the most recent year. Persons reporting data, and physicians requesting copies of their own files are not charged. The entire privacy system is enforced by civil penalties of up to $10,000 per violation, which can be collected by the DHHS inspector general.

c. Discontinuities

Three discontinuities in the NPDB are apparent. First, while each inquiry must be made by an authorized entity, there is no requirement that the individual practitioner authorize the inquiry. The second discontinuity is that there is no technical tool to control the purpose for which data is requested, although the applicable regulation appears to limit the lawful purposes for getting the data. These discontinuities appear to be an administrative oversight, not a deliberate decision. The problem exists because the applicable regulation says that a health care entity may request a report from the data bank if they "may be entering employment or affiliation relationships" with the practitioner. This language would be broad enough for a hospital to obtain data on any practitioner in the community, without their consent or advance knowledge. Of course the practitioner would have knowledge later if a personal request was filed, since the other request would appear on the log.

The third discontinuity is that there is no limitation on how long the inquiring hospital may keep the information. Once the data has been received from the NPDB, the only restriction is that it not be disclosed. There is obviously a risk of stale data, but that relates more to accuracy than confidentiality. The indiscriminate retention of records poses a real risk of disclosure that may not be counterbalanced by a need for the data. Unless there is a demonstrated need for a permanent record, either the data could be purged, or the data object itself could be programmed to self-destruct after a period of time, unless consent for a permanent record had been granted. None of these problems is especially difficult. Consent forms, need-to-know certification, and data purging can be required to obtain access – without substantial change in the data bank operation.

Data Protection Standards

Using *Behringer* and *Whalen* to set public policy and legal structures, and using the NPDB as a source for technical tools permits definition of a "reasonable expectation of privacy" for patient records. After correcting the discontinuities noted above, the NPDB appears to provide a reference standard for the technical requirements for a reasonably secure multi-institutional system for transfer of patient records. Even in its present form, such a system would have the following capabilities:

- Restriction to authorized requesters by a requirement of possession of the restricted requesting software,
- Password protection to identify individual requesters,
- All requests come through a secure e-mail system, no direct electronic connection to the data bank,
- Data search only by patient name, no random browsing of the data bank,
- Audit trail available to the data subject,
- Secure data facility, separate from the treating institution,
- Responses sent in a secure manner, only to pre-approved addresses, and
- Possibility of disputing incorrect or unneeded data.

  The system could easily have the following additional capabilities:

- Electronic responses, sent encrypted through secure e-mail to a mailbox accessible only to user with authorized decryption software (under study),
- Search only for an authorized purpose (possible), and
- Search only with request of patient (possible).

It is not clear that there exists any workable combination of tools, structures and policies which would afford patients the privacy contemplated by the *Privacy Act*. The open nature of hospitals, the life-critical nature of access to data, the huge number of employees and the need for 24-hour access make the technical job extremely difficult. Third, nothing in this paper describes the actual level of patient privacy protection in the VHA. Actions which are not mandated by regulation will not be captured by this type of analysis.

Possible Paradigm Shifts

The protection of medical privacy in the United States will be difficult under the current assumptions about access to medical data, rights of patients, administrative convenience, and the level of technological protection available. However, none of these concepts are fixed. It may be possible that "paradigm shifts" will allow substantial improvement in patient privacy protection. Three examples of such shifts are provided, including organizational change, technological developments, and shifts in the legal structure of privacy.

a. "Need-to-Know" Authorizations in Medical Computer Systems

"Need-to-know" systems which restrict access to computerized data to those with a specified need for the data have been described as part of the solution to the problem of privacy in health care information systems. However, no operational "need-to-know" system is described in the medical literature. Recent legal developments in constitutional privacy protection make a "need-to-know" system mandatory, not optional. In sophisticated information systems, users can utilize the unique characteristics of the system itself to implement a high level "need-to-know" system, based on the institution's own patient treatment pattern.

Regulators of medical information systems often state that medical data is or should be restricted on a "need-to-know" basis. Ethics scholars have indicated that any use of patient data without consent must be based on some substantial need for the information, and clinicians have recognized "need-to-know" as the proper automated implementation of the Hippocratic oath.

Obviously, agreement on the desirability or inevitability of a "need-to-know" system does not answer the question, "Who truly 'needs to know' which pieces of data?"

b. Need-to-Know: Definitions

Developing a "need-to-know" system requires a sophisticated under-standing of medical, social, legal, and technological requirements for both privacy and the provision of health care. Some medical users believe that if data would be useful to a medical professional, then that user has a need to know. Under this thinking a medical researcher has a "need" for any data that might help in research. But in constitutional analysis, even a socially desirable activity can only be carried out in a manner which minimizes the intrusion on the protected right. For example, researchers would rarely, if ever, "need" the patient's identity. As a result, privacy protection often requires changes in otherwise convenient methods of administration. It is critical to understand that cost and administrative convenience have rarely been allowed to be balanced against constitutional rights. For example, patient identifiers are often used to simplify administrative tasks. Human names are easily remembered and may contribute to preventing mistakes in the administration of health care. However, use of names is simply a custom, not a necessity. Distinguishing between those privacy risks which are necessary and those which simply represent administrative convenience is one of the most important tasks in privacy analysis. For this paper, the legal criteria for a "Need-to-Know" is defined as *the smallest intrusion on the patient's privacy which will permit completion of a well-defined, so-cially desired task.*

c. Need-to-Know: Privacy Protection

In the field of computer science, there is a rich literature of methods of implementing privacy protection systems; however it is normally assumed that the job of deciding who should have access to the data has already been done. Few, if any, medical models of "need-to-know" have been published, and there is no literature examining the special hazards and opportunities of information systems to create a functional "need-to-know" system.

A substantial gap exists between the information specialists and the medical community over privacy protection. Information specialists often do not know who needs the information and for what purpose, and the medical community has no idea what privacy protection system might be available. As a result, privacy protection tends to be sacrificed to administrative convenience in the turf battles among the various medical specialties and the administrative and information communities.[24] As networked systems and telemedicine develop and hospitals forge computer links with other health care providers, the problems will get worse. Many patients have several physicians or other sources of health care. Health plans involve multiple institutions. Who decides which provider gets access to what data?

The special privacy disclosure hazards of information systems have been widely documented, but information systems also have special privacy protection advantages. Access to data can be controlled dynamically, the data can be easily subdivided and segregated, and real time alerts of security violations can be provided. Basing access to computerized information systems on the historical system of access to paper records both ignores the increased risk of computer systems and the possibility of introducing novel privacy protections.

d. Need-to-Know: Dimensions

Normally, data access rights have been structured as "layers," where privileges are greatest on the inside and lowest on the outside. Developments in health care and information systems have rendered such a model obsolete. A consultant, for example, might have a high need to know, but only for a limited time. Others might have a longer durational need to know, but only of limited information. Some medical information might be needed by some, but not all clinicians. A pharmacist, for example, rarely needs to know the name of the patient for whom a prescription is being filled. The pharmacist only needs to know that the prescription is authorized, will be delivered to the correct patient and that it does not conflict with other medications for the patient. None of this requires the patient's identity.

"Need-to-know" should therefore be classified along a series of *Dimensions*. Dimensions are used to categorize the relationship between the data and the person making the request. Dimensions describe the type of patient data, the type of health care provider, the type of data action, and so forth.

---

24. V. Brannigan, "Remote Telephone Access," 575-78.

These dimensions can be articulated and classified independently, but interact dynamically. Each dimension affects data access authorization. The core assumption is that each health care worker stands in a definable relationship with each portion of a patient data file.

Using these dimensions, computer systems can provide customized "need-to-know" functionality. Such systems are a product of the examination of the individual institutional health care environment. However, a proper dimensional framework assures that key decisions about access are made by policy makers in a deliberate manner. A series of dimensions can be created.

Patient file dimension

Each patient file is composed of least five dimensions:
1. *Identifier information*: information which can be used to discover the patient's identity but is not needed for treatment, such as name, birth date, Social Security number or universal identifier.

2. *Identifiable information*: any information which might be used to generate an identifier, but is otherwise relevant to treatment, such as the date of an auto accident.

3. *Coded identifier*: alphanumeric linking tool used to ensure that all data on a patient is linked together. It can be generated for each admission.

4. *Standard medical data*: clinically significant medical data which is not "restricted data," as defined below.

5. *Restricted data*: data is "restricted" because of its unusual sensitivity and lack of broad medical significance. The classification of restricted data is a social determination, and might include categories such as elective abortions, some mental health data, and some pharmaceutical data.

Under either standard or restricted data there might be further subdivisions, such as free text or patient codes. Since free text is inherently more capable of creating a security violation, greater access limitations might be justified.

Health care worker dimension

Health care workers are divided by their status in relation to the patient:

- *Treating team:* Health care practitioners directly engaged in regular care of the patient. These would be the people who are routinely allowed to write or execute orders on a patient, and normally have a legitimate knowledge of the patient's identity. The treating team includes several subcategories:

  Category 1 members can add members of the treating team and set access. This might be the responsible health care provider.

  Category 2 members need general access to patient files. This would include anyone with direct patient responsibility.

  Category 3 members need limited access. These are support staff who perform limited functions.

- *Consultants:* Health care practitioners who need contact with the patient's data but are not part of the treating team. Consultants usually do not routinely need identifier information or permanent access. Second opinions are treated as a consultation. Usually consultations are addressed to specific individuals, but may be addressed to departments, who then designate the individuals.

- *Clinical supervision:* This category defines the medical authority to review care on specific patients and initiate changes (e.g., chief of service, and direct clinical quality assurance).

- *Referral:* Authority to transfer a patient to a new treating team, at the same or another institution.

- *Medical support services* (e.g., tests, procedures, pharmacy, transcription): These can be distinguished from consultations when they do not require transmission of the patient file and are addressed to departments. Support services can use coded identifiers. If identified information is needed, the service is normally a consultation.

File access duration dimension

Duration of access to the patient file is an independent dimension. For example, even a treating physician may not need access when a patient has left the hospital. Support staff rarely need access when they are not on duty.

Some only need access when a specific procedure is being performed. Possible limited dimensions include access during specific hospitalization, treatment, consultation or referral, timed access (night coverage, shift assignments), and access to archive data only (prevents access to live data on patients currently being treated).

Data file transaction dimension

This dimension specifies what transactions are permitted in the file. Some examples include:

- *Read authority:* Authority to read the file.

- *Write authority:* Authority to write entries to a file.

- *Copy authority:* The right to make copies of a file, for example by downloading to a remote system.

- *Change authority:* Authority to determine that an earlier entry should be overruled, either to correct an error or change the record. This is not an edit authority; in medical records, all entries must be preserved.

Data base authority dimension

This dimension defines the ability of the user to scan or browse the data base, rather than get information on specific identified patients. Because patient identity can be generated, data base authority represents one of the most significant threats to privacy. Users with data base authority can be classified into several groups:

- *Quality Assurance, Cost Control, Long-Term Planning, and Research:* These categories of users review the data base for purposes other than clinical care for a given patient. As just one example, these persons might be given access to archived data without identifiers.

- *Administration, bed control, and staff scheduling:* These and similar tasks require access to current treatment and prognosis data, but not identifiers. An expert system or trusted intermediary might be used to stratify nonarchived data for immediate administration purposes. Insurance reimbursement can normally use coded identifiers, after an authorization is obtained from the insurer.

- *System staff:* The question of data base access to confidential data by the system staff raises special security problems. However, they normally should have no "need-to-know" identified data.

Emergency access dimension

The system must be arranged to allow temporary emergency access by any health care worker, for example, in a typical "code" situation. However, the use of emergency access would trigger an immediate quality review, to determine why no authorized user was present, and a security review to assure that no *security breach was involved.*

Implementation

Each institution has to implement the system by examining its own operations and assigning access dimensions. Certain principles should govern this assignment:

- *No one should have access based simply on a speculative need which would only occur under rare circumstances.*
  Loopholes in security systems are often justified on "what if" scenarios of very low probability. The emergency override provides an adequate response to any true need, and system authorizations can be altered through experience with the system.

- *Routine access to identifier data should be based solely on the patient's clinical needs.*
  The key evaluation is whether the patient needs the health care worker to have the identifier data.

- *Outside access to identified patient data should be strictly limited.*
  Special security precautions are needed before passing data outside the secure system. This means that telemedicine and other extended access to records demands special analysis. System operators can expect detailed scrutiny of their decisions on who gets access to medical data.

A "need-to-know" system appears to be a constitutional requirement. Administrative convenience will not be accepted as a substitute. Determining who "needs to know" patient information is a special task totally apart from technical "security" analysis. The introduction of information systems initially replicates existing information access environments. However privacy protection often requires confronting traditional methods of operation.

The proposed structure for "need-to-know" systems does not attempt to define who needs to know; rather it sets up a framework to ask the appropriate questions which will allow a system to be created. This framework can be used to develop prototype "need-to-know" systems by examining the information flow in a variety of specific environments. The framework can then be used to produce a wide variety of "need-to-know" systems suited to the special needs of divergent communities and institutions.

Proper concern for patient privacy is not merely a design criterion for multi-institutional clinical networks. The concern for privacy may determine whether such networks are created at all. Paper protection of privacy will not be acceptable to courts, and prompt and technologically sophisticated responses to privacy concerns will be necessary to establish wide area networks. The computer system used for the National Practitioner Data Bank provides a model for protecting patient privacy in bulk transfer of records on multi-institutional wide area networks. With simple upgrades, such a system would provide a substantial level of privacy protection for transfers of computer-based patient records.

New Information Technology: Depersonalized Records

The development of medical networks has made more obvious the failure of traditional data protection legislation, such as the German hospital data protection laws. An entirely new paradigm of information security may be required to accomplish the social goal of protecting personal autonomy in the face of ever-larger collections of automated data.

The problem arises because the legal system is still responding to an outmoded traditional data bank paradigm. The traditional data bank was a large computer holding millions of data files sorted or sortable by individual names. Credit bureaus provided the best example. The term "data bank" conjures up a traditional bank, where the risk was bank robbery, and so the money was kept in a vault. Enormous efforts over the years went into building stronger and stronger vaults, until someone realized that modern bank robbery involves the manipulation of computerized data, and the cash in the bank was only the smallest part of the bank robbery problem.

The last 25 years have seen a similar dramatic shift in the fundamental nature of the computerized data bank. Data banks began as large mainframe computers, and have evolved into complex open networks over which vast quantities of data flow automatically. Instead of a single mainframe computer processing batches of information, now there is the Internet – a worldwide interconnection of a fantastic variety of computer systems. Just as the vault is no longer the centerpiece of banking security, the modern computer is simply a node on a network. Network security is the critical issue.

Medical information systems have been particularly active in these developments. Multi-institutional networks have developed in both the public and private sectors. Extension of local networks to physicians' offices and service providers is routine. Entire health care systems consist of a large network of small computers. In many cases it is difficult even to put the system into the terms used in the data protection laws.

The legal system is often in the position of chasing technology. Data protection laws were clearly written for the paradigm of the traditional data bank. Most traditional data protection laws have a concept of the data bank equivalent to the old credit bureau computer. The law assumes that there is a large building which houses the computer and the vulnerable data, and most traditional data protection approaches rely on building ever stronger and better walls around the data. In the beginning, this was expressed as physical controls. For example, the regulations in the German data protection law emphasized the importance of physical access control to the "storing place" or *Speichernde Stelle*. This storing place is defined as the "location" where the data is stored and processed. The data protection law did not provide for electronic access.

Even as systems and laws become more advanced, there is still the concept of an electronic "location" where the data is stored and processed. Passwords, encryption and audit trails are simply the electronic versions of the same Maginot Line mentality.

We can safely say, after 20 years of experience, that the traditional data protection approach does not work. In the U.S., the technical problems have meant that there is still no general data protection law, and the specific laws designed to cover narrow areas are poorly enforced. The European laws lag badly behind the technology. This conflict between the law and the technology has profound effects. Societies around the world have articulated a wide variety of legal rights to privacy, but as a practical matter the rights depend on the ability of the technology to protect those rights.

Conventional analysis is that we have to choose between two approaches. The first approach is to tightly restrict the technology and forego its advantages; the second is to adopt the technology and forego privacy. What is needed is a paradigm shift, to allow the legal system to adapt to the technology. The best result is where the legal system can use capacity inherent in the new technology to accomplish the social goal.

a. New Technology

Perhaps the best analogous paradigm shift is the revolution in credit cards and credit records that has taken place with the widespread adoption of "point of sale" terminals for verifying credit card eligibility. The problem of computer privacy was first recognized when credit bureaus automated their credit files to support the actions of credit card issuers. The vast mass of highly personal data contained in credit files was needed because credit cards were open-ended credit approvals, and there was no easy way to intercept a stolen card or cut off a customer over the limit. These highly personal records were often inaccurate and could be misused. However, further advances in technology have tended to reduce, rather than enhance the problem. "Point of sale" terminals have created a world in which instant verification of the particular transaction can be accomplished directly at the retailer. Stolen cards and over-limit accounts are easily blocked. As an interesting result, for many consumers credit ratings are no longer critical. By depositing an adequate sum in the card-issuing bank, credit card approvals up to that balance are given by the computer systems.

Such a revolution goes far beyond simply dispensing with the need for a credit report. Once approvals are based on the presence of funds in a designated account, there is no longer any need whatever to know the retail customer's name. A security code or photograph or personal identification number is used to verify the user of the card. In this environment, use of the customer's name is an anachronism. In the banking area, the technological development has allowed the individual to create an entirely new kind of privacy. As long as the consumer keeps the money deposited in the bank, their name, occupation, marital status, bankruptcy history, annual salary and lifestyle are of no importance.

This development can change fundamentally our view of the nature of the privacy problem in information systems. While the special privacy disclosure hazards of information systems have been widely documented, information systems have come to have special privacy protection possibilities which did not exist in paper systems. Data can be easily subdivided and segregated, and real time alerts of security violations can be provided. As a result, basing the structure of computerized information systems on the historical system of personally identified paper records both ignores the increased risk of computer systems and the possibility of introducing sophisticated privacy protection systems.[25]

---

25. Gostin et al., "Privacy and Security of Personal Information," 2487-93. See also

b. Depersonalizing Medical Information

In the health care system, the same technological development will allow the same paradigm shift to take place. Consider, for example, a patient in a hospital. Who exactly "needs" to know the patient's name? And why? A pharmacist, for example, rarely "needs" to know the name of the patient for whom a prescription is being filled. The pharmacist only needs to know that the prescription is authorized, will be delivered to the correct patient and that it does not conflict with other medications for the patient. None of this requires the patient's identity. Names are not automatically relevant to health care. Patients can be and are treated under assumed names. There is no fundamental need for personal identifiers in a hospital record. Patient names are used to simplify administrative tasks. Human names are easily remembered and may contribute to preventing mistakes in the administration of health care. However, use of names is simply a custom, not a necessity.

More importantly, the use of names or other personal identifiers is almost irrelevant in an information system. Names are an especially poor method of associating data together in a virtual file. The only obvious reason to use them is that most individuals are in the habit of remembering them. Putting all the patient's data into a single file under the patient's name is simply using the computer as an electronic file cabinet. These identified patient files do not take advantage of the special characteristics of the computer system. Permanent personal identifiers, such as Social Security numbers, addresses, birthdates or other identifiers are simply names under another format. Passwords are a form of changeable identifier which is used by many information systems to associate data together. Computers simply do not need names to associate disparate data elements into a useable file. All they need is a control facility that knows what separate data elements belong together. This separate facility does not have to be and is not normally incorporated into the data element itself.

Once names (or other specific personal identifiers) become optional, there can be dramatic changes in the entire information protection structure. It is our proposal that the rapid development of online technology has allowed the medical community to implement a widespread "depersonalizing" of medical data files. This depersonalizing will be coupled with an appropriate identifier control facility.

Paul v. Davis, 424 US 693, 713 (1976).

Depersonalized data would be stored anywhere on the network under a coded identifier. A *Coded identifier* is an alphanumeric linking tool used to ensure that all data on a patient can be linked together. It can be generated for each unit in the data file.

c. Identifier Control Facility

The core of the proposal is that each computer or network would be equipped with an Identifier Control Facility or ICF. The ICF would assign identifiers and keep track of the location of all patient data. Only the ICF would have the personal identifier file. Data would be stored in the various locations under coded identifiers issued by the ICF. The ICF would be able to reconstruct the scattered bits of record as they are needed. The patient record is then the output of a process by which the ICF assembles and transmits the file as needed. The ICF would keep the personal identifiers for the data collections in a segregated secure file.

The best analogy to the ICF is the way a File Access Table controls the access to data on a hard disk. Data on a disk is not stored in a single place. It is stored in whatever sectors are available. The File Access Table keeps track of these sectors and automatically assembles the file as needed by the user. There is no technical barrier to applying the same concept on an entire computer or a network.

d. Inherent Security Advantages of the Proposed System

1. The fragmentation of each record into small units inhibits unauthorized "deanonymization" of the data. For example, if the data fields reporting abortions simply are stored under coded identifiers, there are no other events in the file which one could cross-match to deanonymize the file.

2. Data integrity can be improved, because while names and other identifiers are inherently subject to duplication, the coded identifiers can be structured to be unique.

3. Local needs for partial record accumulations can be accommodated without the use of personal identifiers. It may be necessary to link together for some purpose two portions of the record, but no personal identifier would be needed.

4. Integrated complete records could be sorted in secure archives, controlled by the ICF. This would allow network machines to concentrate on currently needed data.

5. Authorized users (including researchers, administration, and quality control) could have access through the ICF to the data needed for their functions. For security, they would not be permitted to maintain data bases of such downloaded information. Transferred files would self-destruct after appropriate intervals. Further, these users would rarely need personal identifiers, so transfer of partial files would be appropriate. Insurance companies would have their own ICF, which could verify insurance coverage, and proceed from that point on a coded identifier basis.

6. Authorized transfers of entire records between ICFs can be easily encrypted for transmissions. This reduces the encryption burden, and would allow use of public networks for data transfer.

7. Local needs for records are satisfied by the records kept under the coded identifier.

8. Systematic rationalization of record sets which did not involve threats to privacy would be automatically performed. For example, the ICF can regularly compile an entire series of lab tests together and store it under a single new coded identifier.

9. In contrast to the current environment, every additional computer or record on the network increases the level of security. Data are distributed widely, but no data item can be linked to any other.

10. Telemedicine can be accommodated by the automatic transfer of the most parsimonious file adequate for the consultation. If the "need-to-know" analysis indicates that the file is a security risk, then only transfer to an appropriate trusted ICF would be allowed.

11. System staff at the individual computers would have no special capability to access private records. The ICF staff might have the capability, but could not do so without leaving audit trails at the remote storage computers.

Special Concerns

This approach requires a high level of system reliability, high speed network links, and sophisticated programming structures. None of these are in particularly short supply, but departments may resent the loss of control over information systems which occurs when patient identities are stored elsewhere. The cost of such elements may be offset by the reduction of security concerns on individual network computers. The adequacy of data privacy and security would obviously rest in the security of the Identifier Control Facility. However, this approach allows both regulatory and technical attention to be concentrated on a smaller number of highly secure ICF locations. This approach does not eliminate the need for "need-to-know" systems. It controls how data is stored, not who can access the data.

It is not clear what the optimum size would be for this type of system. It may be necessary to develop networks of ICFs, each controlling an optimum-sized network. However, the faster the network links and the more sophisticated the ICF, the larger the system which can be controlled. Environments which store raw text data may require special controls to avoid the use of personal identifiers in text data (e.g., entries should be "the patient" rather than "Mr. Jones").

The system would require an "info-notary," a special data control official who would authenticate ICFs and set up systems to authenticate personal requests for individual's own data. This person's function could be part of the German data protection controller function.

It is not often that a technology both creates a problem and later provides its own solution, but that appears to be the case in medical privacy. Under this proposal, the bigger the data base, the more patients, the more users, and the more locations involved, the more security exists for patient data in the overall system.

One can argue that humane medicine requires a personal relationship between the physician and patient, but this may be an illusion, or a result of romantization of a particular portion of the health care system. This desire for a personal relationship may not be universal. Some people prefer the personalized attention of a small town, and others the anonymity found in some large cities. In either case, the patient can choose personalization if they desire, but they do not have to have it forced by the computer system.

Medical Records Confidentiality Act of 1995

The most important recent reform proposal in the area of medical privacy is the *Medical Records Confidentiality Act of 1995.*[26] This act reflects a complex compromise among the various stakeholders in health care. Sponsored by both the Democratic and Republican leadership, if it is passed it will represent a significant advance in medical privacy protection.

The philosophy of the act might be described as the creation of a *cordon Sanitaire* around the medical data maintained by "health information trustees." The concept of health information trustees is novel to the *Act* since it includes anyone who receives or obtains protected health data. This tends to correct loopholes in state acts, which often apply only to health care providers. Health information trustees include essentially anyone who gets access to protected health data.

On its face the *Act* is rigorous and comprehensive. It makes the information trustee strictly liable for any unauthorized "disclosure" of protected information, gives patients the right to correct incorrect information, and provides for civil and criminal penalties against violators. Persons injured may sue for $5,000 in liquidated damages, or actual compensatory damages, plus attorney's fees. Punitive damages are also permitted.

The devil, of course, is in the details. The *Act* sets up the secretary of DHHS to make "regulations" to carry out some portions of the *Act,* but it is not clear how those regulations interact with the general responsibilities. The *Act* also seems to permit law enforcement access to medical files on a very limited showing of necessity.

Perhaps the most questionable portions of the *Act* deal with the ability of health information trustees to compile information together into comprehensive data bases. While the data bases would be protected under the statute, there would seem to be little balance between adminstrative convenience and the desire to keep data from being collected.

Conclusion: Data Privacy, Theory or Reality?

Privacy in medical information systems in the United States can only be described as loose or nonexistent. It is not merely a question of having the

---

26. S. R. 1360, 104th Cong., 1st sess.

will to protect privacy, it is not clear that any system using conventional privacy technology can provide the combination of access and security which is needed for modern medical care. As the Europeans have found out in trying to enforce data protection laws, privacy is not merely a question of passing laws. Providing meaningful protection to patient privacy will require a concentrated application of legal, technological and organizational reforms. In some cases it might mean that we have to make choices between lower cost health care and privacy protection. Such choices are not new, but it is important that they be made publicly as a matter of social policy, rather than privately by system administrators.

CHAPTER FIFTEEN

Privacy of Health Care Data: What Does the Public Know? How Much Do They Care?

Eleanor Singer, Robert Y. Shapiro,
and Lawrence R. Jacobs[1]

The purpose of this paper is to sketch out public knowledge, beliefs, and attitudes about the privacy of health care information, and then to consider how people might best be educated with respect to their rights and responsibilities in this area. The paper does four things:

1. First, we sketch out the changing general privacy concerns on the part of the American public, primarily as documented by a series of Harris surveys dating from 1978.

2. Second, we review the scanty findings on public knowledge and attitudes related specifically to the privacy of health care information. Most of these derive from a July 1993 Harris survey on health information privacy and from several other Harris surveys, but some questions have been asked by other survey organizations as well.

3. In this connection, we also comment on the much more numerous questions that have been put to the public concerning the privacy of information pertaining to HIV-status, and we do the same for questions that have been asked about the confidentiality of health information in workplace settings and for the handful of questions that have been asked about genetic testing. We then use these results to

1.   We would like to thank the Robert Wood Johnson Foundation for its Investigator's Award to Shapiro and Jacobs; Alan Westin, Claudia O'Grady, and Greg Shaw for assistance in assembling the data; and Mick Couper, as well as a number of anonymous reviewers, for helpful comments on an earlier draft.

393

formulate some general observations in the area of public opinion of health information privacy.

4. Finally, we review the findings for what they imply about informing the public about their rights and responsibilities.[2]

Introduction

In 1993, the Office of Technology Assessment (OTA), in response largely, but not entirely, to concerns raised by the Clinton administration's proposals for health care reform, published a report titled, "Protecting Privacy in Computerized Medical Information," now unfortunately out-of-print.[3] The report followed on two earlier examinations of privacy in electronic record systems,[4] which concluded that advances in information technology enable government agencies, the private sector, and individuals to process, store, transmit, merge, and access information with great speed, and that such information should be protected. The problem of protecting the privacy of medical information, increasingly stored in electronic records, is complicated by several considerations:

1. The definition of what constitutes health care information is vague. The OTA report points out that its core is the medical record, generated and maintained by health care provider(s) and the patient in the course of the patient's health care; but it also includes information collected by life and health insurers, pharmacies, educational institutions, rehabilitation and social welfare programs, public health agencies, and others. Hence, crafting adequate and effective protections is neither simple nor clear-cut.

---

2. The first three parts of the paper are based on Harris reports and electronic searches of several archives of poll data. We searched all health care items in the Roper Center's POLL (Public Opinion Location Library) data base and the Harris and State Poll survey archive data bases at the Institute for Research in Social Science (IRSS) at the University of North Carolina; a further search on the intersection of "rights" and "health" was also done in the Roper POLL.

3. Office of Technology Assessment, *Protecting Privacy in Computerized Medical Information,* OTA-TCT-576 (Washington, D.C.: U.S. Government Printing Office, 1993).

4. Office of Technology Assessment, *Electronic Record Systems and Individual Privacy,* OTA-CIT-296 (Washington, D.C.: U.S. Government Printing Office, June 1986). Office of Technology Assessment, *Defending Secrets, Sharing Data: New Locks and Keys for Electronic Information,* OTA-CIT-310 (Washington, D.C.: U.S. Government Printing Office, October 1987).

2. Health care records are increasingly created, stored, and manipulated electronically. This may not only make it more difficult to safeguard their confidentiality, but it increases the demand for them, as well as creating new demands.

3. There is a dearth of legal protections for the confidentiality of health care information. The OTA 1993 report summarizes the situation as follows: "The present system of protection for health care information offers a patchwork of codes; State laws of varying scope; and Federal laws applicable to only limited kinds of information, or information maintained specifically by the Federal Government. The present legal scheme does not provide consistent, comprehensive protection for privacy in health care information, whether it exists in a paper or computerized environment."[5] As of early 1997, there was still no federal law defining an individual's specific right to privacy in his or her personal health care information held in the private sector or by state or local governments. At the federal level, the provisions of the Privacy Act of 1974 apply to systems of health care records in the custody of the federal government; and federal regulations protect the confidentiality of patients who seek drug or alcohol treatment at federal facilities.

4. Requirements for informed consent for disclosure of medical information, where they exist, are undermined by several considerations:

    (a) Patients ordinarily don't know what is in their medical records, and laws governing patient access are neither universal nor uniform;

    (b) Disclosure of the information is required for certain purposes, including reimbursement of medical claims and receipt of life or health insurance. The "voluntary" nature of informed consent is limited by these requirements.

Despite the ambiguity surrounding health care information and the absence of legal or regulatory protections, privacy of health care information is a topic that engenders strong feelings. In its survey of public attitudes toward the privacy of health information, Harris (July 1993) classified 48% of its national sample of adults as falling into the "High Concern" group on medical privacy issues; about one-third of those asked say they are "very

---

5. Office of Technology Assessment, *Protecting Privacy*, 12-13.

concerned" about the protection of medical privacy in a national system of health insurance, and an equal number are very concerned that there may be one computerized data bank containing the medical records of all citizens (Harris, July 1993).[6] A 1995 survey by Princeton Survey Research Associates found that 59% of those asked were very (29%) or somewhat (30%) concerned that the "growing use of computers" threatens their privacy in the area of job and health records.

In all likelihood, the sentiments described above are not based on knowledge of what information exists in various kinds of data bases or on how such information might be used, nor are they based on knowledge of what laws or procedures currently exist to protect such data from intrusion. For example, although almost 90% of those who have a particular doctor or clinic they go to claim to know "everything" or to have a general idea about what is in their medical record, only 24% of these people have ever requested their medical record, and 8% of these requests were denied – one-third because the record couldn't be located, and another quarter for no reason (Harris, July 1993). And as far as legislation is concerned, current protections in the area of health care information exist on the state and local, rather than the national, level, and are in all likelihood not very well or widely known. We have, in any case, been unable to find any national survey questions that inquire into knowledge about these issues. Thus, general concerns about privacy undoubtedly influence more specific concerns about the privacy of health information.[7]

At the same time, the two sets of attitudes are not identical. High concern about health information privacy exists among both high- and low-income groups, as well as among high- and low-education groups, whereas groups high in socioeconomic status do not generally express great concern about privacy in other areas.[8] Furthermore, unlike other areas in which privacy attitudes have been investigated, Harris found that the

---

6.   Citations in parentheses refer to surveys containing the data discussed in the text. The surveys are listed with additional detail at the end of this report. For the Harris privacy surveys, we have drawn on reports published by Harris and containing interpretive essays by Alan F. Westin, as well as on the archived data.

7.   For a discussion of the relationship between general and specific attitudes, see H. Schuman and S. Presser, *Questions and Answers about Attitudes Surveys* (New York: Academic Press, 1981), chapter 4.

8.   For a discussion of this issue, see the "Interpretive Essay" by Alan F. Westin in *Health Information Privacy Survey*, ed. Harris-Equifax (New York: Louis Harris & Associates, 1993), 14-21.

sample of leaders in various health-related institutional sectors is at least as concerned about the privacy of health information as the general public – a sign that fears about data security may be well founded in this area.

Before we begin this discussion of public opinion in the area of health information privacy, some caveats are in order. As is true of many questions asked by researchers, few people in the general public are likely to have experienced a breach of privacy with respect to their health information, and even fewer are likely to have been harmed by such a violation.

As we point out below, between 3% and 15% of the public, depending on the person or organization asked about, believe that medical information about them was ever improperly disclosed, and about one-third of these believe that they were harmed by the disclosure (Harris, July 1993). And, as already noted above, very few people have ever actually inspected their medical record. For most people, therefore, these questions are highly abstract, and we know nothing about what they actually have in mind when they are asked questions about their concerns about the privacy of health care information. By the same token, the ability of most people to imagine the kinds of uses that might be made of health information about them is also likely to be quite limited. Under these circumstances, they are especially likely to extract what information they can from the survey instrument itself: from the context provided by other questions, from the response alternatives provided, from the words used to frame the question, and so on.[9] As a result, we should not be surprised to find that the marginal distribution of answers to questions about the uses and abuses of health information varies from one survey to another, depending on question wording and context, and we might even expect inconsistencies in responses to questions within the same survey.

---

9. See, for example, H.-J. Hippler and S. Sudman, eds., *Social Information Processing and Survey Methodology* (New York: Springer, 1987); H. Schuman and S. Presser, *Questions and Answers in Attitude Surveys* (New York: Academic Press, 1981); N. Schwarz and S. Sudman, eds., *Context Effects in Social and Psychological Research* (New York: Springer, 1992); N. Schwarz and S. Sudman, eds., *Answering Questions: Methodology for Determining Cognitive and Communicative Processes in Survey Research* (San Francisco: Jossey-Bass, 1996); and S. Sudman, N. Bradburn, and N. Schwarz, *Thinking about Answers: The Application of Cognitive Processes to Survey Research* (San Francisco: Jossey-Bass, 1996).

Trends in Concerns about Privacy

The series of Harris surveys on privacy, begun for the Sentry Insurance Company in 1978 and now sponsored by Equifax,[10] documents a large increase in public concern about privacy. In response to the question, "How concerned are you about threats to your personal privacy in America today . . . very concerned, somewhat concerned, not very concerned, or not concerned at all?," the percentage of those responding "very concerned" increased by some 20 percentage points, from 31% in 1978 to 51% in 1994. By far the largest proportion of this increase, however, occurred between 1978 and 1983, when the percentage of the population saying they were "very concerned" jumped from 31% to 48% (17 percentage points). And in fact, six percentage points of that increase occurred from January 1978 to December 1978 alone. In terms of events in the real world, it is not clear why this large increase should have taken place; however, the survey mode (and of course the sampling design) changed from personal interviewing in 1978 to telephone interviewing in 1983.

Paralleling the increase in reported concerns about privacy is an increase in what Westin refers to as the "distrust index," made up of responses to four questions, each answered with either agree or disagree: voting has no effect on what the government does; government can generally be trusted to look after our interests; business helps us more than it harms us; and technology is almost out of control. Those responding with three to four distrustful answers are classified as high in distrust; those with two such answers as moderately distrustful. In 1994, 69% of all adults were classified as high or medium in distrust, compared with 49% in 1978; 31% exhibited high distrust in 1994.[11] The increase in distrust also parallels a more general decline in confidence in institutions during this period.[12]

---

10. Equifax, an information marketing company, has commissioned a series of public opinion surveys about privacy-related issues, now conducted yearly by Louis Harris and Associates, with the consultation of Alan Westin, professor of public law and government at Columbia University. The samples vary in size from approximately 1,000 to 2,200, and are surveyed by telephone using random-digit dialing procedures that select numbers in the 48 contiguous states. Response rates are not given.

11. See the "Interpretive Essay" by Alan F. Westin in *Consumer Privacy Survey*, ed. Equifax-Harris (New York: Louis Harris & Associates, 1994), xi-xii.

12. See S. M. Lipset and W. Schneider, *The Confidence Gap,* rev. ed. (Baltimore: Johns Hopkins Press, 1987).

Public Beliefs and Attitudes
about the Uses of Health Care Information

Trust in Physicians and Hospitals

Generally speaking, the public is quite trusting of physicians to keep health care information confidential, and is only somewhat less trusting of hospitals, though the exact percentages vary, depending on the wording of the question. In response to a 1978 Harris survey, for example, 75% said private doctors were "doing enough" to keep the personal information they have on individuals confidential, and 66% gave the same response about hospitals. In the same survey, 84% said doctors "limit their personal information about individuals" to what is really necessary, but only 69% said the same about hospitals. And in 1993, only 7% of the public believed that their doctor had ever improperly disclosed information about them, while 11% believed the same about a hospital or clinic where they had been treated. Nevertheless, in 1984, a survey by Roper found that only 21% of their sample thought it would be "very difficult" for a government agency considering them for a job to get information from their own doctor without their permission, and a somewhat larger percentage (35%) thought it would be difficult for a prospective employer to get such information without permission. Still, although the exact percentage expressing trust in private physicians varies, depending on the question asked, it is clear that the public puts more trust in private physicians than in hospitals and clinics, and more trust in the latter than in health insurance companies or employers to keep health information about them confidential. What the implications of this are, as increasing numbers of Americans enroll in HMO's, is not clear. They may transfer their trust in their private physician to the HMO, or they may assimilate the HMO to clinics and hospitals, with a consequent decline in trust.

Attitudes Toward Proposed Uses of Health Information.

The July 1993 Harris survey asked about the acceptability of two kinds of medical information uses: first, the provision of identified information to pharmaceutical companies for purposes of drug advertising, and the use of patients' names for fund-raising by hospitals. In both cases, the question stipulates that patients have not been asked for their permission, and between 60% and 66% of respondents oppose these practices. However, the questions are long and complex, and it is not clear whether respondents oppose the release of names without prior consent, or whether they oppose the practices altogether.

Another question asked by Harris concerned the use of individual patient records for medical research into the causes of diseases or the value of specific drug treatments. Respondents were asked whether their permission should be required for use of the record, even if they were not personally identified in publications resulting from the research. Almost two-thirds said permission should be required, and 56% said such permission should be required each time the record was used (and that general advance consent would not be sufficient).

In 1994, Harris modified the question by stipulating (in addition to the absence of personally identifying information in publications) that "a Board in each health care institution ensures that researchers and hospitals follow proper procedures for assuring the confidentiality of all records used." Instead of asking whether permission should be required, the question now asked "how acceptable" respondents found this use of their medical records without being contacted in advance. Phrased this way, the question elicited a response of 41% saying they found it either "very acceptable" or "somewhat acceptable" for their records to be used in this way, without being contacted in advance; but 43% found it "not acceptable at all" and 15% were not sure. When those who said they were opposed were asked whether they would change their position if "a federal law made it illegal for any medical researcher to disclose the identity or any identifiable details of a person whose health record they had used for research," 28% of those who had been opposed said they would change their position, bringing acceptance to 58% (Harris, 1994). Just how seriously one should take these alleged changes of opinion is not clear, however; respondents may simply have felt pressured to change their responses by the persistent questioning. A similar question asked by Wirthlin in June of 1994, but worded to make agreement with the requirement for individual consent more likely, elicited 83% agreeing "a patient's approval should be required before any provider (that is, a doctor, hospital or laboratory) can send diagnosis or treatment data to another organization or individual for medical research purposes," and the same proportion agreed when the last part of the question was changed to read, "for any purpose whatsoever."

Concerns about Abuse and Expectations of Benefits

We consider three topics under this heading: the number of people who say they have experienced improper disclosure of medical information in the past, and the harm resulting from it; concerns about possible misuses of the data and the importance of confidentiality; and expectations about the impact of computers and the advent of health care reform on the quality of health care and the privacy of health care information.

Improper disclosure

Seven percent of the public say they have foregone medical treatment in order not to jeopardize job prospects or other life chances, and 11% say they have failed to file a health insurance claim in order to protect their privacy (Harris, July 1993). As many as 27% reported in 1993 that some person or organization had improperly disclosed personal medical information about them, with insurance companies cited by the greatest number (15%). Persons with incomes greater than $50,000 were most likely to say that such improper disclosure had occurred, although they were less likely than other groups to say they were harmed by the disclosure (Harris, July 1993).

Some reports of improper disclosure on the part of the public may be inaccurate, since people are not likely to become aware of such disclosure unless it has some consequences for them. However, Harris also surveyed a group of "leaders" in the health care industry – doctors, nurses, chief executive officers of hospitals or HMO's, state regulators, and so on. A quarter of this group claimed to know of confidentiality violations involving individual medical records that harmed or at least embarrassed the person whose information was disclosed. (It is not clear whether the question, or the responses, refer to personal or indirect knowledge.) Most frequently mentioned were test results and diagnostic reports (by 37% of those aware of any violations). Although the most frequently mentioned outcome was embarrassment (by 39% of those aware of violations), 12% said the person was denied health insurance and 13% said the person was denied a job or lost a job as a result.

A 1991 survey by Neil A. Holtzman, Ruth Faden, and others supports concerns about improper disclosure of confidential information by physicians.[13] The authors surveyed, by mail, physicians' and genetic professionals' knowledge of genetics and genetic testing, and also provided them with various scenarios, and then asked whether they would disclose confidential

---

13. See G. Geller, E. S. Tambor, B. A. Bernhardt, G. A. Chase, K. J. Hofman, R. R. Faden, and N. A. Holtzman, "Physicians' Attitudes toward Disclosure of Genetic Information to Third Parties," *The Journal of Law, Medicine, and Ethics,* 21 (1993): 238-40.

genetic information to family members and unrelated third parties. One of the scenarios involved a 35-year-old man with Huntington's disease. Providers were asked to whom they thought the patient's test results should be disclosed *without requiring his permission.* Five percent of physicians would disclose such information to the Drivers' License Bureau without permission; 3%, to a health insurance company; 29%, to healthy adult children; 20% to a spouse; and 16%, to a sibling. Medical geneticists were less likely to disclose such information, and genetic counselors least of all.

Importance of confidentiality

Both the public and the sample of leaders were asked by Harris about the importance of six factors for a good national health care program. The six were: controlling costs; detecting fraud; protecting record confidentiality; providing health insurance for those who do not have it; providing better data for research; and reducing paperwork burdens. Protecting confidentiality ranked third (after detecting fraud and controlling costs), rated as "absolutely essential" by a larger percentage than providing health insurance for those who don't have it (Harris, July 1993), a sequence perhaps attributable to the emphasis on privacy in the survey as a whole.

Expectations about computers

Some of the concerns about the misuse of medical information appear to be linked to the use of computers, though it is difficult to tell, because of the way questions are worded, whether people believe certain practices – disclosure of information to people who are not supposed to see it, and mistakes in health conditions or problems being entered into patients' files – happen often, or whether they believe the practices happen often because computers are involved.[14] The sample of leaders was divided as to whether increasing use of computers would strengthen or weaken confidentiality:

---

14. An instance where reference to computers clearly seems to make a difference in people's responses occurs with respect to opinions about the kinds of information life insurance companies are entitled to. In a November 1978 Harris survey, only 44% of a national sample said insurance companies should not have the right to obtain information about whether the applicant had been turned down or rated a bad risk for health or life insurance, but 68% said they should not be allowed to use a central computer file for that purpose!

doctors and nurses tended to think it would weaken confidentiality, whereas CEO's and state regulators tended to believe computers "could be managed to help strengthen the confidentiality" of medical records. The leaders, to a greater extent than the public, believed it to be very important that organizations hired to review medical records have detailed privacy and confidentiality policies in place (Harris, July 1993). (See also the section on Beliefs about the Need for Privacy Legislation, below.)

Leaders, but not the general public, were asked by Harris about potential benefits of easier access to medical information. Substantial majorities agreed that the quality of health care could be improved through "outcomes research," "practice pattern analysis," fraud reduction, and the development of "practice guidelines," and about the same proportions believed costs could be reduced as a result of these practices. However, 73% of the leaders did *not* believe that medical privacy would be better protected in a national health care system than it is at present (Harris, July 1993).

Beliefs about the Need for Privacy Legislation

In the belief that the desire for new legislation would reflect people's knowledge of, and confidence in, current arrangements, Harris asked, in July 1993: "If national health care reform is enacted, which one of these two approaches do you favor to safeguard the confidentiality of individual medical records in such a system?" Fifty-six percent of the general public, and 58% of the leaders favored enactment of "comprehensive federal legislation that spells out rules for confidentiality of individual medical records"; 39% of the public and 41% of the leaders said "continue with existing state and federal laws and professional standards on confidentiality, disclosure and security"; the rest did not know or refused (Harris, July 1993).[15] (In 1978, Harris had asked: "Although there are already some laws regulating what information private organizations can collect about individuals, Congress is currently considering passing additional privacy legislation. In which of the following areas do you think it is important that Congress pass legislation?" 65% thought it was important to do so in the area of medicine and health.)

---

15. The Information Infrastructure Task Force Privacy Working Group (IITF) recently proposed a set of "fair information practices" pertaining to personal information. See *Federal Register* 60, no. 13, (20 January 1995) 4362-70.

In fact, however, it is most unlikely that responses to this question reflected good information about the current system of safeguards, especially on the part of the public (See the discussion of existing legislation in the "Introduction," above).

The leaders, as well as the public, were also asked how important they considered each of several potential provisions of new legislation to be. Three of these were rated "extremely important" by 68%-76% of the leaders and the public: Rules defining who would have access to medical records and what information could be obtained; granting rights to people to inspect and correct or update their records; designating all personal medical information as sensitive, and imposing penalties for unauthorized disclosure. The fourth – creation of an independent National Medical Privacy Board – was considered extremely important by only 28% of the leaders and 46% of the public.

A series of questions by Yankelovich Clancy Shulman in October 1991 shows large majorities favoring regulation of companies collecting and selling personal information, including medical history information. Eighty-three percent of the sample said such companies should be prohibited by law from selling information about their medical history; 93% said they should be required by law to ask permission from individual citizens before making personal information, including medical history information, available; and 88% said such companies should be required by law to make records available to individual citizens to permit them to correct inaccuracies. Similar results were obtained in a May 1986 Roper survey: 80% of a national sample said organizations should be required to notify individuals of the kind of personal information, including medical records, they have in their files; 80% said that for a small service and handling charge, any individual should be able to get a copy of his/her file; 84% said anyone should be able to have criticisms and corrections included in the file; and 88% said organizations should be required by law to get the person's permission before passing the information on to others. These results were virtually identical to those obtained by Roper in June 1974 (83% said notify; 81% said get copy; 86% said include corrections; and 89% said get permission).

Privacy of Health Care Information: The Case of HIV Infection

So far, we have examined the attitudes of the public toward privacy of health care information in the abstract. We turn, now, to look at these attitudes with respect to three more specific situations: treatment of those infected with HIV; medical information in the workplace; and disclosure of the results of genetic screening. We use these as case studies to formulate some hypotheses about the determinants of public attitudes in this area.

Reporting on trends in public opinion about AIDS in 1987, Singer, Rogers, and Corcoran noted that opinion with respect to regulation was mixed: on some issues, opinion was apparently becoming more accepting of people with AIDS; on others, less accepting; but in all cases fairly substantial numbers of people – between 25% and 45% – were in favor of some kind of regulation (e.g., quarantine, identity cards, contact tracing), which of course implied some loss in individual privacy.[16] Summarizing trends in public opinion between 1987 and 1992, Rogers, Singer, and Imperio noted that the public has, from the beginning and by substantial margins, tended to see AIDS as a community health rather than as a civil rights issue, but that the percentage taking a restrictive stance varied from one topic to another and over time.[17] For example, opinions concerning who should be tested for AIDS ranged from 80% to 90% for immigrants, prisoners, and people applying for a marriage license to around 75% for people in high-risk groups, patients in hospitals, and food handlers to 35% for children entering school and 40-50% for employers testing their workers. (Nevertheless, about 75% of the public said in 1991 that workers testing positive for the AIDS virus should be allowed to continue to work – a right assured by the 1990 *Americans with Disabilities Act.*) Typical of the readiness to opt for presumed safety rather than protection of privacy were responses to two questions, both cited by Rogers, Singer and Imperio.[18] The first was asked by Harris in 1987: "It is more important to identify who has AIDS than to protect personal privacy (Agree/Disagree)," with which 74% of the respondents agreed. The second was asked by CBS/*New York Times* between June 3 and June 6, 1991: "Do you think the government

---

16. E. Singer, T. F. Rogers, and M. Corcoran, "The Polls: A Report – AIDS," *Public Opinion Quarterly* 51 (1987): 580-95.

17. T. F. Rogers, E. Singer, and J. Imperio, "Trends: AIDS – An Update," *Public Opinion Quarterly* 57 (1993): 92-114.

18. Singer, Rogers, and Imperio, "Trends," 105-9.

should require doctors, dentists, and other health care workers to be tested for exposure to the AIDS virus, or would that be an unfair invasion of privacy?" Eighty percent said the government should require testing; only 16% regarded this as an unfair invasion of privacy. Although the exact percentages may have been influenced by the controversy over Kimberly Bergalis' assertion that her dentist had infected her with the AIDS virus, percentages in other years indicate similar priorities.[19]

The public supports warning past and present sexual partners of someone who has tested positive to the AIDS virus (69%) vs. keeping the information confidential (24%), and by virtually the same margin supports contact tracing by public agencies (*Los Angeles Times,* 24-28 July 1987). However, a somewhat different asking of the question in 1992, by the Response Analysis Corporation for the American Civil Liberties Union Foundation, produced a somewhat larger proportion (36%) in favor of keeping test results confidential.

Misinformation about how AIDS is transmitted, and negative attitudes toward homosexuals, strongly predict support for restricting the rights of infected persons (e.g., requiring them to carry ID cards, or quarantining them). Level of education also plays an important role as a predictor of knowledge about AIDS and of attitudes toward those infected.[20]

Privacy of Medical Information in the Workplace

Paralleling expressed public concerns about the privacy of health information is a tendency to countenance disclosure of such information to others. For example, in 1987 a survey by the Roper Organization asked a series of questions about information "that a business corporation has a right or does not have a right to know about a person they are considering hiring." The table below shows the percentage saying the firm has a "right to know" about each type of information:

---

19. *Ibid.*

20. V. Price and M-L. Hsu, "Public Opinion about AIDS Policies: The Role of Misinformation and Attitudes toward Homosexuals," *Public Opinion Quarterly* 56 (1992): 29-52.

Type of Information	Right to Know
General health at present time	85%
History of serious illness in past (cancer, heart trouble, etc.)	71%
Medical or psychiatric care currently being received	69%
Exposure to the AIDS virus by giving you a blood test	68%
Any susceptibility to certain kinds of illnesses	64%
Any history of mental illness in past	59%

In 1982, 86% said the company had a right to know about general health, and 68% said it had a right to know about medical or psychiatric care currently being received. Even when Wirthlin reversed the question wording in 1994, asking, "Do you agree or disagree with the following statements: Employees should not be required to disclose their medical history to an employer, even if their medical condition may negatively impact their job performance?" 64% disagreed with the statement – i.e., agreed that the firm had a right to know.

Between 1974 and 1976, shortly after Watergate, Roper asked a series of questions about the kind of information it would be appropriate for the FBI to have on file "on you or someone like you." The table below shows the percentage agreeing it would be appropriate, by type of information and year:

> These days many different kinds of organizations have on computers information about you and people like you. For example, employers, credit companies, local police, the Internal Revenue Service, etc., may all have various kinds of information about you. Here is a list of different kinds of information that could exist on you or someone like you. For each one I'd like you to tell me whether you think it is information that is appropriate for the FBI (Federal Bureau of Investigation) to have on file or not.

Percent Agreeing It Is Appropriate				
	1974	1975	1976	1978
Any history of psychiatric care or treatment	51%	44%	49%	—
Health records	40%	33%	34%	31%

Similar questions asked by other organizations yield somewhat different distributions. For example, Harris asked, in 1978, whether it was justified to maintain a central file containing the names of all individuals who had been treated for mental health problems, for use by employers; 24% said it was.[21]

Believing it is appropriate to have information in an FBI file does not mean people are ready to see it released indiscriminately. For example, in 1978, Roper asked, "Assuming the FBI does have that kind of information on file about you, I'd like to ask you who you think should have access to it?" Whereas 48% said a company in private industry that was considering hiring them was entitled to their health records, only 14% said the information should be made available to a credit card company.

Although substantial numbers are apparently prepared to make health information available to prospective employers, people have generally been reluctant to grant employers the right to inquire into lifestyle habits off the job, such as smoking (Harris, March 1993; Response Analysis Corporation, 1992). Majorities also say that serious health problems, such as having had cancer or a heart attack or being HIV-positive, should not be grounds for refusing to hire someone (Harris, March 1993). At the same time, most people are willing to grant health and life insurance companies the right to inquire into actual health conditions, lifestyle issues, and prior health care costs (Harris, 1990; Harris, 1978; Opinion Research Corporation, 1970). When asked directly about genetic tests, 86% say that health insurance companies should not be allowed to *use* genetic test results in deciding to issue or refuse coverage, although 58% agree that the person's insurer deserves to *know* whether a person is "a carrier of a defective gene or has a genetic disease" (Harris, 1992).

Here, as with other topics, the way questions are worded has a great deal to do with the responses obtained. In 1984, for example, NORC asked: "Do you think that companies should be required to give not only employees and former employees, but also government officials and labor unions,

21. People apparently distinguish between the privacy that should be accorded different kinds of information. In 1977, Harris asked how long different kinds of information should be stored "in computers" before it was erased: one year, five years, 10 years, 25 years, or a whole lifetime, or whether it should never be stored at all. For medical records, the median response was a whole lifetime; for mental health records, six years; and for psychological tests, one year. We cannot, of course, discount the possible effects of question sequence or the response alternatives offered on the responses obtained to what is otherwise a very vague stimulus.

free and open access to employees' health records, including information regarding exposure to substances that pose a potential health risk but not including their personal medical files?" 77% respondent affirmatively, whereas 75% disapproved the disclosure of employees' personal medical files, asked about in the subsequent question. But what, exactly, are "health records" that do not include "personal medical files"?

Privacy of Genetic Information

The concept of genetic monitoring and screening antedates the discovery of DNA by Watson and Crick in 1953.[22] Ultimately, it is hoped that improved understanding of the genetic basis of disease will permit development of more effective therapies, but at present, genetic monitoring and screening are for the most part limited to detecting or predicting disease.

About 50 inherited genetic defects are currently known to increase an individual's susceptibility to toxic or carcinogenic effects of environmental agents.[23] However, in most cases the precise agents are unknown, and as a result prevention of disease among people with a known genetic disposition is likely to require avoidance of a whole class of harmful stimuli.

When such avoidance is voluntary, it arouses little controversy. But when it is enforced by others – for example, by an employer refusing to hire a worker on the basis of a pre-employment screening test – the policy raises practical and ethical concerns.[24] A set of interpretations of the

---

22. Office of Technology Assessment, *Genetic Monitoring and Screening in the Workplace,* OTA-BA-455 (Washington, D.C.: U.S. Government Printing Office, October 1990), 6.

23. *Ibid.,* 11.

24. See, for example, P. R. Billings, M. A. Kohn, M. de Cuervas, J. Beckwith, J. S. Alper, and M. R. Natowicz, "Discrimination as a Consequence of Genetic Testing," *American Journal of Human Genetics* 50 (1992): 476-82; E. Canter, "Employment Discrimination: Implications of Genetic Screening under Title VII and the Rehabilitation Act," *American Journal of Law and Medicine* 10 (1984): 323-47; E. Draper, "High-Risk Workers or High-Risk Work," *International Journal of Sociology and Social Policy* 6 (1986): 12-28; E. Draper, *Risky Business* (New York: Cambridge University Press, 1991); N. A. Holtzman, *Proceed with Caution* (Baltimore: Johns Hopkins Press, 1989); D. Nelkin and L. Tancredi, *Dangerous Diagnostics* (New York: Basic Books, 1989); M. Rothstein, *Medical Screening of Workers* (Washington, D.C.: Bureau of National Affairs, 1984); and L. Uzych, "Genetic Testing and Exclusionary Practices in the Workplace," *Journal of Public Health Policy* 7 (1986): 37-57.

Americans with Disabilities Act by the Equal Employment Opportunity Commission in 1995 for the first time includes protections for workers with genetic predispositions to disease, thus perhaps reducing some of these concerns.

An OTA assessment of genetic screening in the workplace in 1982 and again in 1989, which included a survey of such practices among the largest U.S. companies, public utilities, and labor unions, concluded that little change had taken place in the number of companies conducting genetic monitoring or screening during the seven-year period: Of the 330 companies responding to the 1989 survey, 20 health officers reported that their companies had conducted genetic monitoring or screening, either currently or in the past 19 years, compared with 18 health officers in the Fortune 500 1982 sample who said they had ever used such tests. However, 12 of the 20 were currently using such tests in 1989, compared with only 6 in 1982. Health officers were as likely to report changes in the workplace as a result of genetic screening or monitoring as they were to report negative actions affecting individual workers.[25]

Only 30% of the unions queried responded to the survey. Of those that did, four out of 10 reported having a formal policy related to the use of genetic screening. Many viewed it as a threat to the rights of employees and most were opposed to using such tests to link such predispositions to workplace hazards, exclude members from risk situations, or establish evidence of preemployment health status for liability purposes. The recent interpretation of the ADA by the EEOC is in line with this position.

The negative views about workplace genetic screening held by union leaders are largely mirrored by public attitudes. Four identical questions about workplace screening were asked on two national surveys. The first was a telephone survey by the Gallup organization, carried out in February 1990; the second was the General Social Survey, a personal interview survey carried out by the National Opinion Research Center in the spring of 1991.

The questions asked were as follows:

> Using techniques available today, it is possible to tell whether someone has inherited a tendency to develop certain cancers and certain forms of heart disease. These tests do not mean that a

25. Office of Technology Assessment, *Genetic Monitoring and Screening in the Workplace,* "Summary," p. 21.

person will always develop the disease, but only that he or she may do so, depending on other conditions. Should employers have the right to give these genetic tests to people who are applying for a job, or shouldn't they have that right?

Should employers have the right not to hire workers if tests show they have an inherited tendency to develop certain forms of cancer or heart disease, or should they not have that right?

Suppose workers will be exposed to some cancer-causing materials on the job. In that case, should employers have the right not to hire workers whose tests show they have an inherited tendency to develop certain forms of cancer, or
(Form 1): Should they be required to clean up the workplace so it is safe for everyone?
(Form 2): Should they not have that right?

(Asked on Gallup Survey only) Removing cancer-causing materials from the workplace can be expensive. How much more would you be willing to pay for a product to cover the cost of removing cancer-causing materials from the workplace: 1 or 2% more, up to 10% more, up to 25% more, more than 25% more, or would you not be willing to pay anything more?

Suppose a genetic screening test for certain forms of heart disease is made available by an employer to workers who want to take it. Who do you think should have control over access to the test results – the worker or the employer?

Responses on the two surveys were virtually identical. As measured by these questions, public opinion about genetic screening in the workplace was overwhelmingly negative in 1990-91. By a ratio of roughly nine to one, people rejected the proposition that employers should have the right to screen prospective employees for genetic defects before hiring them, or that they should have the right to refuse to hire someone whose test is positive. (A question asked by ABC in 1990 elicited only 12% agreeing that employers should have the right to make workers take tests "to find out if [people] are likely to come down with a genetic disease – as much as twenty years before it happens." Similar results were obtained by Harris in March 1993.) Even when the issue is posed in terms of possible health risks to the worker, roughly three out of five in both samples reject the employer's right not to hire. And when an alternate version of this question is posed, almost 20 times as many people say employers should "make the workplace safe for everyone" as assert the employer's right not to hire someone who might be adversely affected by current working conditions. (If the question is put so as to imply that the reason for genetic testing is to protect the worker, majorities favor employers using such tests: to the question [asked on the March 1993 Harris survey], "Should employers be able to use such tests to identify persons who would be at special risk in handling chemicals or other materials at the workplace, or not?," 63% responded affirmatively, although 72% of these said employers should be required to provide other, safe jobs to such employees.)

However, when, on the Gallup survey, a follow-up question was asked about "how much more" the respondent would be willing to pay for a product in order to make the working environment safe for everyone, there was no greater commitment to pay cleanup costs among those who thought employers should make the workplace safe for everyone than among those who thought employers should be free not to hire someone who might be harmed by working conditions. Though apparently paradoxical, this is by no means an unusual finding. For example, it is not at all unusual to find that people who want taxes reduced do not want a concomitant cut in services, but instead assume the shortfall can be reduced by eliminating waste and inefficiency, or by tradeoffs with spending in other areas.[26]

Several demographic characteristics were significantly related at the zero-order level to the tendency to grant employers leave to test prospective workers or refuse to hire those with positive test results. Though not every one of these characteristics is related to each of the four questions, the general trend is clear: lower education, lower income, nonwhite race, being unemployed, and being rated by the interviewer as low in interest or understanding are all related, on the Gallup survey, to approval of genetic screening in the workplace. A similar pattern of relationships obtains on the GSS. Union membership was unrelated to attitudes toward genetic screening in the workplace on either survey, but those with more favorable attitudes toward unions (measured only on the GSS) were much more likely to be opposed to genetic screening.

In 1992 Harris asked several questions directly relevant to privacy of genetic information. In answer to the question, "In your opinion, if someone is a carrier of a defective gene or has a genetic disease, does anyone else, besides that person, deserve to know that information?," 57% said yes;

---

26. See, for example, L. deHaven-Smith, "Ideology and the Tax Revolt," *Public Opinion Quarterly* 49 (1985): 300-309; and S. Welch, "The 'More for Less' Paradox: Public Attitudes on Taxing and Spending," *Public Opinion Quarterly* 49 (1985): 310-16.

41%, no. Those who said yes were asked who else deserved to know the information; responses agreeing with each of the categories mentioned are as follows: employer, 33%; insurer, 58%; spouse or fiancé, 98%; other immediate family, 70%. On this issue, there does not seem to be a well-defined position asserting the privacy of the information. As we shall see below, this pattern is characteristic of public opinion about privacy-related issues: support for privacy depends very much on whether people feel more threatened by the protection of privacy or by its loss.

Some Organizing Principles

Reflecting on the diverse poll results reported above suggests the following generalizations:

1. Despite the apparent evidence to the contrary, people are not concerned about the privacy of health care information in general; they are concerned about protecting the privacy of sensitive information about themselves. As in most controversial areas, privacy is not the only value engaged with respect to the disposition of health care information. Thus, for example, people are quite willing to agree to contact tracing in the case of AIDS patients, and they are ready to define AIDS as a community-health rather than a privacy issue, because most people are not HIV-positive and are more concerned about the risks of being infected than about the privacy interests of patients. At the same time, most people are unwilling to have medical information about *themselves* disclosed without their permission, even when the information does not identify them by name. In that situation, the privacy value of information about themselves outweighs the juxtaposed social value of "research." (Disclosure of medical information to employers and insurance companies appears to be an exception, but we don't know what public response would be if it were stipulated that this information would be made available without their explicit permission.)

2. People trust individuals they know personally to protect medical information about themselves; they have less trust in impersonal institutions. The operative sentiment here is "trust," since most people do not in fact know whether their physician has divulged information about them. Those people who claim to have had information

improperly divulged are much less trusting of the system of protections for health care information than those who have never had such an experience, and the sample of institutional leaders, who are more likely to have observed breaches of confidentiality than the general public, are likewise less trusting and more concerned.

3. Despite the growing anti-government climate in which some of these questions were asked, the public does appear to want government laws to protect confidential health information. A number of Roper and other items show this, and it is consistent with what we know about the public's suspicion of big government in the abstract but support for protective regulation in specific case after specific case.[27]

4. The public appears to have little knowledge and few convictions in the area of health care information, its uses and potential abuses. As a result, answers change dramatically depending on the context in which questions are asked, and public opinion can likewise be expected to change as more information and arguments are presented on one side of this issue or the other, and as the issue becomes more salient.

How Can the Public Be Educated?

There are many obstacles to educating the public in this area. Chief among them are the difficulties outlined at the beginning of this paper: (1) the absence of clarity concerning just what is comprised by the term, "health care information" – in other words, what kind of information is at risk; (2) the lack of consistent legislation or regulation in this area, and the locus of much legislation at the local or state level; (3) the risks to breaches of confidentiality posed by the increasing computerization of information processing, storage, and retrieval, which makes possible the linkage of many pieces of information about an individual and their instantaneous transmission to other recipients, and which increases the difficulty of obtaining informed consent to such dissemination. Furthermore, as noted earlier, most people are probably unaware of the potential consequences to them of disclosure of medical information, even if it is authorized – for

---

27. B. I. Page and R. Y. Shapiro, *The Rational Public: Fifty Years of Trends in Americans' Policy Preferences* (Chicago: The University of Chicago Press, 1992), chapter 4.

example, possible discrimination in employment or lack of eligibility for life or health insurance.

Given these obstacles, what strategies are available for educating the public?

It seems to us indispensable that a definition of what is intended by "health care information" be adopted that will be clearly understood by the public. That means spelling out what kinds of information are included under this definition, instead of relying on some vague general terms. Although the list can probably not be exhaustive, it can be much more specific than the kinds of terms currently in use, even if the last phrase of the definition would have to be, "and other similar kinds of information."

Second, it seems to us indispensable that a set of fair information practices, along the lines of those advocated by the Information Infrastructure Task Force Working Group,[28] be developed for this area at the federal level. So long as regulations vary by state and locality, it will be impossible to educate people about their rights and obligations; and in fact, it would be meaningless to talk about "rights." Since information is likely to be transmitted from one jurisdiction to another, which regulations would apply? To whom can an individual who believes his or her rights have been violated, appeal?

Assuming these two preconditions have been met – and it is not at all clear to us that they will be – there are three main avenues of education open to health care institutions and to privacy advocates. One is a general information campaign, mounted with high visibility through the mass media. Such campaigns are very expensive, and the evidence for their success is mixed at best.[29] They may succeed if there is a crisis; or if saturation coverage persists for a long time (as in the Mothers Against Drunk Driving Campaign); or if the message is also incorporated into entertainment programming. In general, public information campaigns will capture the public's attention only by way of major issues or problems focused on by the mass media. Furthermore, such campaigns must provide

---

28. IITF, "Fair Information Practices," *Federal Register* 60, no. 13 (20 January 1995): 4362-70.

29. See, for example, H. H. Hyman and P. B. Sheatsley, "Some Reasons Why Information Campaigns Fail," *Public Opinion Quarterly* 11 (1947): 412-23; C. T. Salmon, ed., *Information Campaigns: Balancing Social Values and Social Change* (Newbury Park, CA: Sage Publications, 1989); E. Singer, T. F. Rogers, and M. B. Glassman, "Public Opinion About AIDS Before and After the 1988 U.S. Government Public Information Campaign" *Public Opinion Quarterly* 55 (1991): 161-79.

information by credible sources, leaders and experts, and in a comprehensible fashion; the public needs information shortcuts, with experts and information campaigns highlighting the most important and interconnected facts. For an issue as complex as health information privacy, we suspect a public information campaign would not be very effective in educating the public, although a campaign based on some dramatic privacy violations with which many people identify might be successful in mobilizing public opinion.

A second, more promising avenue is education of the patient by his or her health provider. Such an educational campaign would target the patient at every visit. Additional materials could be disseminated to patients at home in order to reach those who do not often utilize health care services and in order to reinforce materials distributed at the provider's offices. These materials would inform patients about the uses made of health care information about them: what kinds of information are disseminated, to whom they are disseminated, whether or not their permission is required for dissemination, and what their rights are – e.g., right of access, right to correct inaccuracies, what is meant by confidentiality, rights in case confidentiality is breached, and so on.

Still a third avenue for educating the public is to have patients sign an informed consent or a notification statement at regular intervals, not simply the first time a patient visits the provider's office. Those consent or notification statements should include the essentials of the information described above: To whom information about the patient may be disclosed, for what purposes, and what the patient's rights are with respect to this information. For example, it has been proposed that if a national system of health insurance is instituted, the names and addresses of subscribers should be made available to the Census Bureau in order to improve the accuracy of the decennial count. People should either be free to decline such use of the information about them or, if Congress and the courts decide they do not have the right to decline, they should at least be notified of the use that is being made of the information.

Many of the consent forms in current use are so broad and general as to be virtually useless in providing either information or protection to patients, and one of the services that could be provided by the AAAS Program on Science and Human Rights is to draft model forms that would better perform these functions.[30]

Furthermore, the patient should be offered an opportunity, at regular intervals, to inspect his or her medical record and correct inaccuracies, and to see a log of people or institutions to whom information has been made available since the last inspection, and for what purposes. (If records have been merged, we assume that each provider with whom the patient has contact would have access to the complete record, and that the merged record would be made available regardless of the particular provider whom the patient consults.) Such a system would, it seems to us, make clear in a way no other system can what the nature of the information is that is being disclosed, and to whom and for what purposes the disclosures are being made. Furthermore, we believe the burden of offering such access should be on the provider rather than on the patient.[31] The patient should be free to decline the offer to inspect the record and the log, but it should be required that the offer be made. Until such a system is instituted, power over health care information will be disproportionately on the side of providers and institutions, rather than in the hands of the individuals whose information is being used.

Polls Cited

The survey results reported in this paper were obtained from published reports, the Roper Center's POLL database, and the Harris archive and State Poll archive at the Institute for Social Science at the University of North Carolina. All surveys are based on national samples. The list below gives the name of the survey, the starting date of interviewing, the mode of interviewing, and the sample size for each of the surveys drawn on in the paper:

---

30. For a discussion of issues related to consent forms, see Office of Technology Assessment, *Protecting Privacy,* 69-76.

31. Several reviewers have pointed out that this procedure would add greatly to the expense involved, to which we respond that there is no reason why such a valuable resource as health information should be provided at no cost.

Organization	Start of Interviewing	Interviewing Mode*	Sample Size
ABC TV	4/90	T	505
Gallup	2/90	T	1006
Louis Harris & Associates (Harris)	2/77	T	1522
Harris	11/78	P	1513
Harris	9/83	T	1256
Harris	1/90	T	2254
Harris	5/91	T	1254
Harris	4/92	T	1000
Harris	3/93	T	1000
Harris	7/93	T	1000 + 651 leaders
Harris	8/94	T	1005
National Opinion Research Center (NORC)	1/84	T	1006
NORC	2/91	P	1517
NORC	1/94	PR P	2992
Opinion Research Group	11/70		1950
Princeton Survey Research Associates	2/95	T P	753
Response Analysis Corp.	11/92	P	993
Roper Organization	2/74	P	1940
Roper Organization	6/74	P	1987
Roper Organization	2/76	P	2009
Roper Organization	2/78	P	2002
Roper Organization	8/82	P	2000
Roper Organization	5/86	P	1994
Roper Organization	8/87	T	1987
Wirthlin Group	6/94	T	1011
Yankelovich Clancy Shulman	10/91		500

*T=Telephone; P=In-Person

Guidelines and Mechanisms for Regulating Access to Data: Private Health Insurance Issues

Mary Ann Baily

True Stories

"A woman had a pregnancy test, and the charges were reported on a summary report to the employer . . . the nature of the charges was not reported. However, . . . the laboratory in question only performed a limited number of tests, and most of them were for pregnancy. Since the woman was trying to keep her possible pregnancy a secret at work, she was upset. She claimed that she was passed over for a promotion because of this." [1]

"Health Information Technologies, Inc., helps automate private physicians' insurance claims. When it transmits claims and payments between the insurance company and the physician, it retains electronic copies of these records, and it can later sell them (presumably *[emphasis added]* *without physician or patient names) for pharmaceutical and other related kinds of marketing."* [2]

"A manager at a large Boston company was being treated for depression when she was suddenly told by her insurer to see another doctor or forget coverage. "I was at a crucial point with a therapist I really trusted," she says. She considered appealing, but feared that would jeopardize her

---

1.   H. Jeff Smith, *Managing Privacy: Information Technology and Corporate America* (Chapel Hill and London: University of North Carolina Press, 1994) 110.

2.   In Institute of Medicine, *Health Data in the Information Age: Use, Disclosure, and Privacy*, eds. Molla S. Donaldson and Kathleen S. Lohr (Washington, D.C.: National Academy Press, 1994), 142, taken from M. Miller, "Patients' Records Are Treasure Trove for Budding Industry," *Wall Street Journal*, 27 February 1992.

career. "If you're an executive and making big decisions and they think you're depressed, they think you're incompetent. I was deathly afraid my bosses would find out."[3]

Little Timmy Dawkins' cancer treatment was successful, although he was left with health problems. Most of his medical expenses were paid by his schoolteacher father's employment-related family coverage. As Timmy was finishing his chemotherapy, however, his parents learned that to renew its policy, the school would have to pay premium increases of 200%. The school shopped for another plan, approaching 20 companies, but could not get a bid. The leader of the teacher's union said, "It was all laid off on Tim Dawkins. One agent told us, 'We'll write you insurance, but we can't take Tim.'" The school refused out of sympathy for the family, and finally found a plan with premiums 15% higher, but with large deductibles. Timmy's parents were upset that Mr. Dawkins' coworkers had to accept an inferior plan because of them, and also worried about the future.[4]

"After a bout with depression, Mr. X sought psychiatric help, was hired in a new job, and sought insurance benefits through his new employer. The sales unit he supervised was very successful, but one day his supervisor asked him why he saw a psychiatrist. The supervisor learned of this through a copy of an insurance claim in the personnel office. Mr. X deflected the inquiry. Three months later, the supervisor accused the man of failing to reach sales goals, and fired him."[5]

A health insurance executive described receiving a request from an employer: "He [the employer] said, 'I want you to pull me a list of all the people working for me who've filed anything for AIDS. I'm going to fire every one of those sons-of-bitches.' We told him no, so he canceled his account."[6]

3. Carol Hymowitz and Gabriella Stern, "Cutting Psychotherapy May Trim Productivity," *Wall Street Journal*, 10 August 1994, B1, 8.

4. "When Illness Strikes and Health Insurance Won't Pay," *Washington Post*, 26 June 1990.

5. Robert Ellis Smith, with Eric Siegel and James S. Sulanowski, *War Stories: Accounts of Person Victimized by Invasions of Privacy* (Providence, RI: publ. by *Privacy Journal*, 1990), 65.

6. Smith, *Managing Privacy*, 71.

Introduction

Managing personal health information in a manner that respects human rights is a difficult balancing act. To ensure that people are able to obtain basic health services without discrimination, extensive data must be gathered on the health status of individuals and the care they receive. At the same time, respect for individuals' rights to privacy and control over information about themselves requires limits on the collection and disclosure of personal health data.

This paper considers the balancing act in the context of private health insurance, especially employer-provided health insurance. The first section reviews the development of private health insurance and its response to national concern about rising health care expenditures. The second section explains how the role of private health insurance data is changing as insurers, employers and government struggle to control expenditure, and describes current constraints on the collection and use of data. The third section considers the definition of appropriate use of insurance-related health information, and the fourth section discusses policies for preventing inappropriate use.

The paper argues that currently Americans have the worst of both worlds. The privacy of personal health information is inadequately protected, yet our health care information systems are not able to provide the kind of information needed to run the health care system efficiently or monitor access to it. Information systems are evolving rapidly, however, in response to economic forces. There is an urgent need for action on a framework of ethical principles, law and regulation that can shape the process and indicate how balance among conflicting objectives should be achieved.

Given the limitations of law and regulation in shaping behavior, there is also an urgent need to consider structural reforms that would better align private incentives with the desired outcome. For example, it would be desirable to break the link between employment and private health insurance, or if that is impossible, create structures that limit employer access to health information at the level of individual employees. It would also be desirable to reduce the payoff to discrimination among insurance subscribers on the basis of risk. This can be done most easily in a financing system with a single national payer (or several large regional single payers); it can also be done in a multi-payer system but the task is more complex.

Background Information on Private Health Insurance

To understand the issues in managing information access in private health insurance, one must know something about the industry's development and structure.

a. The Evolution of Private Health Insurance

Private health insurance was originally introduced by hospitals as a way to ensure that patients would be able to pay their hospital bills. The first private health insurance companies were the non-profit Blue Cross and Blue Shield companies. Each company served its own geographical area and based premiums on average expenditure for its entire risk pool, without differentiating between low and high risk subscribers ("community rating").

As the health insurance market developed, for-profit insurance companies, called "commercial" insurers, began to offer health insurance products also, competing with Blue Cross/Blue Shield plans by offering lower premiums to the better risks. This, of course, meant that average expenditure in the Blue Cross/Blue Shield risk pools rose and premiums had to be increased, leading more lower-risk people to shift to commercial insurance. Eventually, many Blue Cross/Blue Shield companies were forced to abandon community rating and offer policies with risk-adjusted premiums also.

Health insurance was sold to individuals and to groups. Premiums for members of a group were usually lower than premiums for individual coverage; the cost of writing and marketing group policies was lower, and if the group was fairly large and had not been formed solely for the purpose of buying health insurance, the insurer could dispense with costly medical underwriting (assessment of the risk status of individual group members through detailed questionnaires and medical exams).

The usual insured group consisted of the employees of a particular firm or the members of a union, and often their dependents as well. Such groups had the advantage that at least the primary insureds were healthy enough to work. More important, employment-related group insurance got a tremendous boost from federal tax policy, since health insurance provided by employers as a fringe benefit was exempt from taxation. In effect, workers got their health insurance at a significant discount, i.e. the tax they would have paid on the money their employers spent for health insurance if the money had been paid in wages. This is a major reason why over 85% of

Americans below retirement age who have private health insurance obtain it through employment, as workers or the dependents of workers.[7]

Initially, premiums for employment-related group insurance were set without regard to differences in risk among groups. As with individual insurance, however, commercial insurers began offering lower premiums to firms with below-average expenditures on claims. Eventually, "experience rating" – adjusting a firm's payments in accord with its employees' previous claim experience – became a common practice in the market.

"Self-insurance" by large firms also became common. When a firm buys a group policy from an insurance company, it is buying a package of risk-bearing (the risk of large fluctuations in employee health care expenditures) and claims administration. A large firm has so many employees that health care expenditures become fairly predictable; such a firm may reasonably decide that bearing the risk directly is cheaper than paying another firm to do so, especially if the firm is being experience-rated anyway. The firm can use its own personnel to administer claims, or contract with an outside company for that function alone.

Government policy reinforces a firm's incentive to self-insure. Private health insurance companies are subject to state insurance regulation, which may include financial reserve requirements, premium taxes, and mandated coverage of specific services. By federal law, self-insured firms are exempt, since the Employee Retirement Income Security Act of 1975 (ERISA) preempts state regulation of employer-provided health benefits. ERISA thus increases the financial advantage of self-insurance over the purchase of outside insurance. As a result of this advantage, the majority of insured workers now work for firms that are to some extent self-insured.

Since most of the privately insured receive their coverage through their own or a family member's employment, a job change or a change in marital or dependency status often forces a change in health insurance coverage. Insurance plans vary tremendously in structure, differing in the types of services covered, the limits on service amounts, choice of provider, and cost-sharing (out-of-pocket payments required when services are used). Many plans temporarily or permanently omit coverage for preexisting conditions (health problems present at the time the policy coverage begins).

---

7. Employee Benefit Research Institute, *Sources of Health Insurance and Characteristics of the Uninsured: Analysis of the March 1994 Current Population Survey*, Special Report SR-28 and Issue Brief Number 158 (Washington, D.C.: EBRI, February 1995), 5.

Thus, a change in plan can result in disruption of care arrangements and unexpected expense. Moreover, given the limits on coverage, many of the insured would find themselves with inadequate protection against financial disaster in the event of a very serious illness or accident.

The private insurance system also leaves many people without health insurance altogether. People who are unemployed, outside the labor force, or in jobs that do not provide health benefits are likely to be uninsured. Unless they can obtain group coverage through another family member, they must be able to afford more costly and less comprehensive individual insurance; if they are in poor health, they face even higher premiums or may be unable to obtain coverage at all. Low income workers are especially likely to be in jobs without health benefits, yet have incomes too low to afford individual coverage.

Government programs exist, but fill in only some of the gaps.[8] The result is a complex and inadequate "safety net," which cannot reliably guarantee access to essential health care and protection from financially ruinous medical bills. This can mean personal tragedy for many Americans, and ongoing concern about the adequacy and permanence of their health coverage for many more.[9]

b. The Place of Cost Control in Private Health Insurance

Since private health insurance plans began as a means for health care providers to make sure of payment for their services, perhaps it is not surprising that insurers failed to take an activist role in restraining the use of health care resources. Insurers reimbursed for "medically necessary care," leaving it to the medical profession to define medical necessity. Physicians were generally paid their customary fees and hospitals their usual charges; both professional ethics and economic interest supported a generous definition of medically necessary care for the privately insured. Since insured patients did not pay the full cost of their care directly, they did not object to such a definition.

---

8.   More than 40 million people had no public or private insurance whatsoever in 1993. *Ibid.*

9.   For further discussion of the issues raised in this section, see Janet O'Keeffe, "The Right to Health Care and Health Care Reform," in *Health Care Reform: A Human Rights Approach*, ed. Audrey R. Chapman (Washington, D.C.: Georgetown University Press, 1994).

The result was a high rate of increase in health care expenditures for the privately insured. Premiums for individual insurance spiraled upward, as did business expenditures for group insurance for employees. At the same time, experts questioned whether all the expenditure was yielding health benefits that were worth the cost.

In such circumstances, an economist would expect insurers to begin to compete with one another in searching for acceptable ways to restrain the use of care and, therefore, the rate of increase in premiums. Given the predominance of employment-related insurance and its favored tax treatment, however, there was little incentive for them to do so. Employees received their insurance as a fringe benefit from their employers; many did not even know how much their employers were paying, let alone appreciate that the money was money that could have been distributed in wages. Even if they did, most wanted health insurance, and the tax subsidy allowed them to get it at a substantial discount. Businesses cared about total employee compensation, not how large a share went to fringe benefits. Moreover, if insurers or employers did attempt to constrain the decisions of patients and their physicians, employees were likely to see this as an undesirable intrusion into the patient-provider relationship rather than a consumer benefit.

Meanwhile, as the cost of employer-provided health insurance increased, the revenue loss to federal and state governments caused by its favorable tax treatment also increased. The tax code provisions did not come up for a vote each year, however, in contrast to appropriations for programs like Medicaid, the federal-state health program for certain categories of the poor.

An exception to the relative indifference to the efficiency of the standard of care can be found in the "health maintenance organization (HMO)." HMOs combine insurance with comprehensive service delivery; subscribers are served by a defined group of providers who practice in an organization with a financial incentive to be conservative in the use of resources. The HMO evolved from the prepaid group practice, an organizational form invented in California in 1929, and later adopted by the industrialist Henry Kaiser as a vehicle for the provision of cost-effective care to workers at the Grand Coulee Dam. In the late 1960s, the physician Paul Ellwood gave the prepaid group practice its new name (HMO), and he and others began to promote it as a remedy for rising health expenditures. HMOs are the exception that proves the rule, however; they faced physician opposition and patient suspicion and remained a small part of the health care market until the 1980s.

Eventually, health care expenditures rose so much that public officials were forced to pay attention. State insurance regulators became increasingly concerned about soaring private insurance premiums. State legislators found that the rising cost of health care made it more and more difficult to fund Medicaid and other programs for the medically indigent. Medicaid was a problem at the federal level as well; however, what really caught the federal government's attention was the growing budgetary impact of Medicare, the government health insurance program for people over 65 and over and people eligible for Social Security disability benefits. The government response to the cost problem was a range of cost containment policies implemented at the local, state and federal levels, some program-specific, others more general.

Meanwhile, the passive stance of employers toward rising health care expenditures also began to change. Employers found that total employee compensation had to increase significantly every year just to maintain health benefits at the same level. To workers, however, wages seemed to be stagnating, since the additional income could not be used to improve their everyday standard of living. Employers began to realize that if waste and inefficiency in the production and delivery of health care could be reduced, as well as expenditure on ineffective or only marginally beneficial services, employers and employees could be better off.

Finally, cost control had the attention of both the public and the private sectors. The result was an explosion of change in the health care system – change that began before the recent unsuccessful attempt by the Clinton administration to enact comprehensive health care reform, and that will continue in some form whether or not there are further federal reform initiatives.[10]

c. Cost Control Strategies

A private insurer or self-insured employer can choose from a wide range of strategies to hold down its expenditures on health care. The insurer or employer can manipulate the composition of its risk pool to avoid people who are likely to use a lot of care, set coverage limits on individual services in utilization or dollar amounts, exclude some types of services from coverage altogether, or impose cost-sharing on subscribers to induce them to limit their utilization. These strategies avoid direct intrusion of the insurer into the patient-provider relationship, and were the first line of defense against rising insurer costs.

Private insurers and self-insured employers can also select strategies that put the pressure on health care providers to reduce utilization and expenditure. As expenditures have continued to rise, this has become the second line of defense. Such strategies include seeking provider discounts on reimbursement for services and inducing providers to eliminate care that is ineffective or not worth what it costs. Providers can be induced to limit care through the provision of explicit guidelines and standards, direct review of physician and patient decisions for appropriateness, and the appointment of physician-gatekeepers charged with managing patient care in a cost-effective manner. The gatekeeping can be organized within an HMO framework or more loosely, through bureaucratic and financial incentives that encourage conservative use of resources.

The strategies are not mutually exclusive. For example, the "preferred provider organization (PPO)" uses incentives for patients and providers. The insurer identifies health care providers who are willing to offer discounted fees and/or practice cost-conscious medicine; insureds have free choice of provider, but have higher cost-sharing when their choice is not on the "preferred provider" list. Experimentation with such combination strategies has resulted in a host of new insurance product/health care delivery structures, referred to loosely as "managed care." The term is imprecise;[11] however, it usually implies an active stance of payers toward providers, in which payers use various methods to pressure providers to bring the benefits of health care into line with the costs. This contrasts sharply with the passive stance embodied in traditional insurance structures.

Managed care has significantly changed the landscape of private health insurance. By 1993, only one-third of the privately insured had traditional

11. The Congressional Budget Office defines managed care as "any type of intervention in delivery and reimbursement of health care services that is intended to reduce unnecessary or inappropriate care and to reduce costs," a definition so broad that it includes almost anything. Congressional Budget Office, "The Effects of Managed Care on Use and Costs of Health Services," CBO Staff Memorandum (Washington, D.C.: CBO, June 1992). Congressional Budget Office, "Effects of Managed Care: An Update," CBO Staff Memorandum (Washington, D.C.: CBO, March 1994).

insurance; more than 40% belonged to PPOs, and more than 20% belonged to HMOs. Moreover, over 95% of the traditional plans had some form of utilization review. By comparison, as recently as 1988, more than 70% of workers were in traditional plans; only 17% were in HMOs and only 10% in PPOs.[12]

The Changing Role of Data in Private Health Insurance

The pressures to control cost and the rise of managed care have changed the role of data in private health insurance, with important implications for human rights. Today, there are strong financial incentives to collect more data and to use it more extensively than in the past.

a. Past Role of Data

Traditionally, private insurance companies used data to decide whether to insure an applicant and at what premium, to pay the claims submitted, and to maintain oversight in case of fraud. To set the initial premium for large groups, companies needed only general information about the type of business and labor force. Medical underwriting of individual and small group policies required more detailed information. Applicants completed a form with questions on past and present health status; upon review, the company would make an immediate decision on coverage and premium, or ask for further information, such as medical records, a physical examination, screening test results, or a physician statement. To assist in the application review, many insurance companies had access to the Medical Information Bureau, a database of information provided by the Bureau's member companies about individuals who had previously applied for life, disability or health insurance.[13]

To pay claims and maintain oversight, indemnity insurers needed the names of providers, the types and amounts of services received, and an indication of the reason the services were prescribed. Generally, they did not need detailed medical information on individuals or groups once in-

---

12. Employee Benefit Research Institute, *Sources of Health Insurance and Characteristics of the Uninsured*, 6.

13. The Medical Information Bureau is explained in Office of Technology Assessment, *Protecting Privacy in Computerized Medical Information*, OTA-TCT-576 (Washington, D.C.: U.S. Government Printing Office, September 1993), 32-33.

sured, since they relied on the individual provider's assessment of medical necessity to justify payment, and were not aggressive in policing potential fraud. Insurers maintained administrative records, and providers maintained medical records, with the two linked only by the application and claims forms.

The picture was different in a health maintenance organization. The integration of insurance and service delivery, especially in staff or group model HMOs, placed medical records and administrative records within the same organization. In principle, HMOs had both the incentive and the ability to pay more attention to the management of resources, including the relationship between expenditures and patient outcomes. In practice, however, this incentive was muted by the prevailing indifference to cost control, and the fact that doing things very differently from the fee-for-service sector was likely to create resistance rather than market advantage.

b. Present and Future Role of Data

Today, in an environment in which the main concern is cost control,[14] the importance of data has changed dramatically. Suddenly, it is vital to know where the money is going, what health benefits it is yielding, and where expenditures can be reduced without sacrificing important benefits. At the same time, there has been an enormous increase in information processing capabilities, making possible comprehensive, computerized information systems linking medical and administrative records from multiple sources.

In today's private health insurance market, the competitive pressure to divide up the risk pool according to expected expenditures is intense. Insurers have a strong economic interest in data that can be used to discriminate on the basis of risk in decisions about whether to insure and at what premium.

Employers also have an economic interest in data on risk status. Given the potential influence of health status on productivity, absenteeism, and turnover and training costs, all employers, even those who do not offer health insurance, have an incentive to use health information to discriminate in hiring, retention and promotion decisions. The incentive is strengthened when the employer offers health benefits and is experience-rated or self-insured, because individual health status then has a direct effect on

---

14. Even those whose primary concern is increased access to care believe that significant improvement in access is possible only if costs can be brought under control.

benefit costs. Self-insured firms are particularly well-placed to respond to the incentive to discriminate, since they can have direct access to the information generated by their health insurance plans.

There is also increasing economic pressure to monitor the standard of care. Managed care strategies of cost control require insurers and self-insured employers to gather detailed data on the process of care so that they can, on the one hand, control service utilization and therefore total expenditures, and on the other hand, maintain a competitive level of quality.

To achieve a good balance between quality and cost, insurers need solid information on the relationship between resources used and health outcomes. Despite the enormous share of national resources the United States devotes to health services (almost one-seventh of total output), surprisingly little is known about the impact of these expenditures on health. Which treatments are effective and for which patients? How can effective treatments be most efficiently delivered? In other words, what does a cost-effective standard of care look like? These fundamental questions cannot be answered without empirical research, which in turn requires good data.

The private sector is not alone in its need for better information. As third-party payers themselves, federal and state governments have an interest in care management and research on the process of care.[15] They also need information to carry out their responsibilities as regulators of the private sector. For example, any federal or state health care reform plan that retains a role for competing private insurance plans must deal with risk selection, i.e., it must somehow remove the incentive insurers have to compete by manipulating the composition of the population they insure, rather than by providing high-quality coverage at low cost. Managing risk selection requires data on the composition of each insurer's risk pool and the factors that influence individual choice of health plan and use of services. Federal and state governments also need data to monitor the distribution of health care and its cost, so they can make sure that the needs of vulnerable groups entitled to health care are being met.

The new information needs are changing the ways in which data are collected and used. In the past, insurance company databases were of little use for purposes other than the determination of coverage and payment.[16]

---

15. For example, in recent years, the federal government's Agency for Health Care Policy and Research has begun an ambitious program of research on patient outcomes.
16. The AIDS epidemic highlighted this fact. In the epidemic's early years, there was intense interest in total annual expenditures on AIDS-related health care, the relative

Now insurance companies are developing the internal records needed to track the use of resources. Integrated insurance/delivery systems are beginning to produce data sets suitable for the study of the relationship between treatments and outcomes for the patients they serve.

Heightened awareness of the burden of administrative costs has resulted in efforts to standardize billing forms and diagnosis and procedure codes. The shift to managed care has highlighted the importance of developing better measures of quality, so meaningful comparisons of health care providers can be made. The new interest in outcomes research encourages the development of linked databases that enable individual patients to be tracked through the entire health care system.[17]

As the result of these incentives, the health care system is evolving into one in which far more information on a privately insured person's health status and medical treatment will be collected, stored and scrutinized by insurers, employers, and others outside the immediate patient-provider relationship. There are both risks and benefits inherent in this new situation.

c. Risks and Benefits in the Use of Personal Health Information

Individuals have much to gain from better health care information systems. Better record-keeping could lead to more efficient organization of care, resulting in fewer errors and lower costs. Improved understanding of the process of care, in both medical and managerial terms, could result in a higher yield from health care resources, with a composition and distribution of services that better reflects individual and societal priorities.[18]

---

shares paid by private insurance, Medicare, and Medicaid, the breakdown of expenditures by type of service, and so on. It was impossible to make accurate estimates of these numbers; individual third-party payers could not even measure what they themselves were spending on the disease. AIDS researchers found themselves reminding Americans over and over that, contrary to popular belief, little was known about health care expenditures for *any* specific disease or condition – lung cancer, breast cancer, diabetes, etc. In fact, by the early 1990s, there was probably better information on the cost of AIDS than on any other condition.

17. For a full discussion of the move to develop comprehensive and inclusive health databases, see Institute of Medicine, *Health Data in the Information Age.*

18. For concrete examples of the potential benefits from better data, see Leslie L. Roos, David S. Fedson, Janice D. Roberts, and James F. Blanchard, "Supporting the Delivery of Preventive Services Through Information Systems: A Manitoba Example." Also see Noralou Roos et al., "Designing an Information System to Monitor Population Access to Care, Health and Health Care Use," in this volume. Also, see Institute of Medicine, *Health Data in the Information Age.*

There is also much to lose, since disclosure of personal health information can result in harm. Insurers could use it to deny insurance coverage. Employers could use it in hiring, firing and promotion decisions, or to counter workers' compensation claims. Disclosure of health information could cause harm in personal lives; for example, it could adversely affect a campaign for public office, admission to an educational institution, access to credit, even an application for a driver's license. Disclosure of some kinds of information could cause social humiliation and damage personal relationships. Finally, even when disclosure has no specific adverse consequences, it represents a loss of privacy, which in itself may be considered a harm by someone who does not want the information revealed.

The harm does not depend on the amount of information disclosed. Revealing a diagnosis alone could be damaging in the case of alcoholism, drug abuse, mental illness, pregnancy, AIDS or other sexually transmitted disease. Sometimes, the disclosure of use of a good or service would be enough; for example, use of psychiatric services could lead to an inference of mental illness, and data on pharmaceutical prescriptions could reveal diagnoses of sexually transmitted diseases, mental illness, chronic conditions such as diabetes, and so on.

Concern about unwanted disclosure can adversely affect the way people use the health care system. People may censor what they say to their health care providers, get care outside of their insurance plan, or forego care altogether, in order to keep sensitive information from finding its way to their employers and coworkers. They may be reluctant to protest unfair gatekeeping decisions, particularly in the area of mental health treatment, fearing that a complaint will draw attention to personal matters. Employers and insurers may take advantage of these reactions, in effect using concern about loss of privacy as an implicit cost-control strategy. The result is a reduction in the quality and usefulness of private health insurance to enrollees, as well as distortion in the structure of cost-control and lower-quality data in databases.

d. Current Restrictions on the Use of Personal Health Information

The fact that physicians and hospitals recognize obligations of confidentiality sets some bounds on disclosure of information to persons outside the patient-provider relationship. The physical difficulty of gaining access to and copying bulky paper-based files without detection imposes some restraint on unauthorized use of medical records.[19] The narrow focus of traditional insurance records has limited the information available from that source. An assortment of federal and state laws and regulations restricts disclosure of some kinds of health information in some circumstances.

Nevertheless, given the potential for harm, the safeguards are surprisingly weak. There is no systematic legal or ethical framework to guide private insurers and self-insured employers in the management of personal health information so that human rights are respected. In an influential report on this issue, the Office of Technology Assessment concluded:[20]

> The present system of protection for health care information offers a patchwork of codes; State laws of varying scope; and Federal laws applicable to only limited kinds of information, or information maintained specifically by the Federal Government.[21]

> These [state] statutes, however, do not address the flow of medical information to secondary users outside the treatment process, who are deemed to legitimately have access to the information. They do not address the responsibilities of third-party payers in handling this information, nor do they impose rules about the use of medical information by secondary users of that data: parties that use medical records for nonmedical purposes.[22]

> Legal and ethical principles currently available to guide the health care industry with respect to obligations to protect the confidentiality of patient information are inadequate to address privacy issues in a computerized environment that allows for intra- and interstate exchange of information for research, insurance and patient care purposes. Lack of legislation in this area will leave the health care industry with little sense as to their responsibilities for maintaining confidentiality. It also allows for a proliferation of private sector computer databases and data exchanges without regulation, statutory guidance or recourse for persons wronged by abuse of data. . . .[23]

---

19. See Vincent M. Brannigan and Bernd Beier, "Medical Data Protection and Privacy in the United States: Theory and Reality," in this volume.

20. See Office of Technology Assessment, *Protecting Privacy.* See also Lawrence O. Gostin et al., "Privacy and Security of Personal Information in a New Health Care System," *JAMA* 270, no. 20 (24 November 1993): 2487-93.

21. Office of Technology Assessment, *Protecting Privacy*, 12-13.

22. *Ibid.,* 43-44.

23. *Ibid.,* 44.

The OTA Report notes that some business firms are already using their activities in health insurance claims processing, office management, prescription drug sales, or patient billing to develop and sell aggregate health information for profit, perfectly legally, without patient knowledge or consent.[24]

The changes occurring in the health care information field will greatly increase the potential for harm. Linked, computerized records will make it easier to gain undetected access to personal health information, as well as increase the amount of information that can be accessed.

The use of personal health information in the employment setting is an especially sensitive issue. The *Americans With Disabilities Act* imposes some restrictions in this area.[25] For example, employers may not make medical inquiries of job applicants before they make a conditional offer of employment, although they may ask if a person is physically and mentally able to perform the essential functions of a job.[26] After the offer has been made, the employer may require a prospective employee to answer questions about health and/or take a physical exam, but only if all prospective employees are asked to do so. At this point, a person who needs a reasonable accommodation to do the job must request the accommodation. These rules are designed to make it possible to demonstrate that discrimination on the basis of disability has occurred; if an employer makes an offer, requests medical information and then rejects the applicant, even though the employee's health does not interfere with the ability to perform the job, the applicant has potential evidence of discrimination.

The ADA also provides some protection to people with disabilities in the area of health insurance benefits, although some of its provisions are not clear and will ultimately have to be resolved by litigation. The health

24. Also, see George T. Duncan, "Data for Health: Privacy and Access Standards for a Health Care Information Infrastructure," in this volume.

25. The assistance of Janet O'Keeffe on the implications of the *Americans With Disabilities Act* is gratefully acknowledged. For further discussion, see Janet O'Keeffe, "Disability, Discrimination, and the Americans with Disabilities Act," *Implications of the Americans with Disabilities Act for Psychology*, eds. Susanne M. Bruyere and Janet O'Keeffe (New York: Springer Publ. Co., 1994), chapter 1. See also Institute of Medicine, *Employment and Health Benefits: A Connection at Risk*, eds. Marilyn J. Field and Harold T. Shapiro (Washington, D.C.: National Academy Press, 1993).

26. For example, an employer can ask, "Can you lift up to 50 pounds in weight, carry it 20 feet and put it on an eight-foot-high shelf, for eight hours a day?" The employer cannot ask, "Have you ever had back problems?"

insurance protections are derived from the ADA provision stating that an employer may not discriminate against an employee in the "terms or conditions of employment." Legislative reports accompanying the bill note that this phrase includes fringe benefits.

The ADA was not intended to revise health insurance industry policies and practices, however. The law and the Equal Employment Opportunity Commission regulations state that "The act shall not prohibit or restrict an insurer, HMO, or entity that administers employee benefit plans from underwriting risks, classifying risks, or administering such risks that are based on or not inconsistent with State law." The implementing regulations ensure that employees with physical and mental disabilities cannot be refused insurance *if* a health plan is offered, but they do not require an employer to offer a health plan, nor do they require that an employer's health plan contain benefits important to the person with the disability.[27]

Under the regulations, insurers can continue to engage in traditional insurance practices, such as the exclusion from coverage of preexisting conditions, even if these result in limitations on individuals with disabilities. Employers may not, however, set a lower level of benefits for a specific disability, such as AIDS, or for a discrete group of disabilities, such as cancers. In essence, exclusions applied to *all* employees are not discriminatory, whereas exclusions applied only to those with a particular disability are discriminatory.

Employers may not refuse to hire people who have disabilities (or who have dependents with disabilities) because of concerns about the effect on health insurance costs. Moreover, they have the legal burden of proving that their insurance practices are justified (for example, needed to prevent the insolvency of a health insurance plan) rather than merely a subterfuge[28] to evade the purposes of the ADA. The law applies in cases where the prospective employee (or the employee's dependent) meets the ADA definition of disabled; it is unclear to what extent it would protect persons not ordinarily considered disabled who are nevertheless expected to generate large insurance claims. One such category, people with a genetic predisposition to disease (for example, those who test positive for the gene for

---

27. For example, the plan's mental health benefits may be inadequate for a person with serious mental illness.

28. Proving insurance subterfuge may be difficult. The U.S. Supreme Court, when considering a similar provision in the Age Discrimination Act, ruled that a "subterfuge" requires a conscious intent by the insurer to evade the law.

Huntington's disease), caused enough concern to be explicitly included in the EEOC's clarification of the ADA term "disability" in March 1995.[29]

Finally, the law does not restrict employer access to the medical information required to implement cost-control strategies. The law does impose some confidentiality requirements; nevertheless, once the employer has the information, it may be easy to use it for other purposes, especially within the firm, without detection.[30]

Guidelines for Appropriate Use

What guidelines should be established for the collection and use of personal health information in the private insurance context? It is tempting to evade the issue by relying on consent. There could be a simple prohibition on revealing personal health information to anyone, for any purpose, without the person's explicit, informed consent. For example, a patient would have to consent to the release of information to his or her insurer so that reimbursement could occur; if the insurance company wished to use the information for another purpose, or release it to someone else, it would have to seek explicit consent for that, and so on. In principle, the individual would thus define appropriate use, and maximum control over privacy would be assured.

Unfortunately, this is not a satisfactory solution. People have responsibilities as well as rights. The health care system is a social entreprise; those who benefit from it have a duty to cooperate in the collection of the data needed to make it efficient and fair. Although individuals should not have to give up all privacy rights in exchange for health care access, it would be unreasonable to allow them complete authority over the definition of appropriate use of information about themselves.

Moreover, a legal requirement for explicit informed consent would not ensure protection of privacy anyway. Private insurers and employers could simply demand blanket consent as a condition for health coverage or employ-

---

29. The EEOC says that employers may not discriminate against someone in employment solely on the basis of genetic information about the individual. Kathy L. Hudson, Karen H. Rothenberg, Lori B. Andrews, Mary Jo Ellis Kahn, Francis S. Collins, "Genetic Discrimination and Health Insurance: An Urgent Need for Reform," *Science* 270 (20 October 1995): 393.

30. Institute of Medicine, *Employment and Health Benefits*, 246.

ment. People could find themselves coerced into agreement by their need for employment and health insurance, and by the lack of viable alternatives.

Thus, there is a strong case for a framework of law/regulation/ethical principles which includes privacy safeguards, but permits collection of data essential for administration, monitoring, and research. Other chapters in this volume discuss the concept of such a framework; Table 1 summarizes the essential elements it must include.[31]

The difficult policy work lies in infusing specific content into this general framework. In the case of insurance-related personal health information, there are four broad categories of use that demand attention: inclusion of data in comprehensive health databases; use for nonmedical purposes; use for medical underwriting; use for cost control.

Table 1. **Framework for Regulating Collection and Use of Personal Health Information**
A framework must:

DEFINE appropriate use of personal health information, distinguishing among uses that are
    appropriate with or without consent,
    inappropriate with or without consent, and
    appropriate only with informed consent,
  where appropriateness depends on
    the specific data to be used,
    the identity of the data user, and
    the purpose to which the data will be put;

DEFINE the rights of individuals to know about, inspect and correct the health information about themselves that is being collected and stored;
ESTABLISH security standards that ensure the integrity of the information and regulate access to it (this includes giving or withholding authorization for access, AND protecting against accidental and covert disclosure);
ESTABLISH procedures for determining whether violations of standards have occurred and what, if any, sanctions should be imposed on those responsible;
INCLUDE an ongoing process for interpreting, adjusting, and administering the standards and procedures (this process could be under the guidance of the courts, an established agency of the executive branch of government, a newly constituted entity such as a Data Protection Board, or some combination of these entities; it could also include private entities, such as associations of insurers, health care providers and information management specialists);
BE NATIONAL in scope (although some administrative functions could be located at the state and local level).

---

31. See especially Duncan, "Data for Health."

a. Inclusion of Insurance-Related Personal Health Information in Large Databases

Other chapters in this volume discuss the importance of comprehensive, inclusive databases to the promotion of equity and efficiency in the health care system.[32] Data are essential for monitoring the adequacy of access to care (especially for vulnerable populations), providing quality information so consumers can make informed choices among health plans and health care providers, and carrying out research on the effectiveness of care and the efficiency with which it is delivered.

Therefore, private insurers, employers and providers can and should be required to supply data on health status, utilization and financing of care, without explicit consent from each individual, to larger databases constructed to serve these social purposes. The specific data required should be tailored to the social purposes and, of course, privacy safeguards should be in place.[33]

b. Use of Insurance-Related Personal Health Information for Nonmedical Purposes

The justification for limiting privacy by requiring data to be supplied without consent is the responsibility of those within the system to cooperate in making it work, reinforced by the obligation of society to protect access to health care. This justification does not apply to nonmedical uses, especially uses such as the sale of personal health information to for-profit businesses for marketing use. Many people view the use of personal health information for such purposes as an unacceptable invasion of privacy. The review of public opinion polls by Singer, Shapiro and Jacobs reports that large majorities of people in surveys think companies that collect and sell personal information (including medical information) should be required to get permission from the individuals, or to refrain from selling the information at all.[34]

---

32. See especially Roos et al., "Designing an Information System."

33. For further discussion of these issues, see Fritz Scheuren, "Linking Health Records: Human Rights Concerns," and Robert Ellis Smith, "Guidelines and Mechanisms for Protecting Privacy in Medical Data Used for Research," in this volume. See also Institute of Medicine, *Health Data in the Information Age.*

34. Eleanor Singer, Robert Y. Shapiro and Lawrence R. Jacobs, "Privacy of Health Care Data: What Does the Public Know? How Much Do They Care?," in this volume.

Since some nonmedical uses of personal health information may not harm the individuals and may even benefit them, an across-the-board prohibition does not seem to be in order. It is reasonable, however, to require that informed consent be obtained, and where truly voluntary informed consent is impossible, to prohibit the use of the information altogether.[35]

c. *The Use of Personal Health Information by Insurers and Employers for Medical Underwriting*

This use raises a more difficult issue: the inherent contradiction in relying on a "catastrophe-based" private insurance model (designed to protect against financial loss from a relatively unlikely chance event) to accomplish a social insurance objective. The difference between catastrophe-based insurance and social insurance is illustrated in the controversy early in the AIDS epidemic over the screening of insurance applicants to assess their risk for AIDS. There was fierce debate about whether private health insurers should require HIV test results of applicants or use other personal characteristics[36] as indicators of risk status, and then make risk status the basis for refusing coverage, when the effect would be to make it very difficult for people at risk for AIDS to ensure access to medical care.

The insurance problems these people were facing were neither new nor unusual; they were very familiar to people with diabetes, a history of cancer, and many other health conditions.[37] The AIDS debate simply highlighted an essential feature of the catastrophe-based health insurance model. In such an insurance market, an insurer must make an actuarial forecast of an applicant's health expenditures and set premiums accordingly, or risk being driven out of business by adverse selection (the tendency of people with a greater-than-average probability of loss to disproportionately seek insurance). Moreover, in such a model, insuring

---

35. For example, releasing the names and addresses of parents of newborns to organizations marketing baby products is unlikely to result in actual harm, and many parents might even welcome the catalogs and free samples that result. Others, on the other hand, might consider it an invasion of privacy and would prefer to be able to refuse consent.

36. An example is use of an address in an area known to have a high proportion of gay residents, to exclude single male applicants.

37. For a discussion of the issue, see Office of Technology Assessment, *Medical Testing and Health Insurance*, OTA-H-384 (Washington, D.C.: U.S. Government Printing Office, August 1988).

someone who is known to be sick is absurd. As health insurers said during the AIDS insurance debate, "No one expects insurance companies to write fire insurance policies on burning houses!" Medical underwriting is the process of discriminating among applicants on the basis of risk.

The trouble is, universal access to health care requires a different model, that of social insurance: universal third-party coverage (public and/or private) for at least an adequate level of health care, with a fair distribution of cost so the poor and the sickly do not have to make overwhelming sacrifices to have coverage. An unregulated private health insurance market cannot achieve this social insurance goal, which is fundamentally incompatible with adjusting individual coverage and cost to actuarial risk.

Medical underwriting is most obvious in the individual insurance market. It is also a factor in the group market, however, although in a somewhat different way. Workers who refuse health insurance coverage when they first join a firm and change their minds later on often have to undergo medical underwriting. Many group insurance plans exclude coverage for care for conditions the person insured already had when the health insurance coverage began, usually on a temporary basis (the waiting period is usually 10 months to two years). Very small groups are required to supply health information about individual members to obtain group insurance.

For larger employment groups, it is the group that is underwritten rather than the individual members. The initial premium is based on the group's overall characteristics; after that, renewal and premium adjustment decisions are generally based on claims experience, in effect adjusting the premium to reflect the level of ill health in the firm's labor force. In a small-to-medium-sized firm, a single person with a serious illness may cause the firm's premium to be raised or its insurance to be cancelled altogether, as the example previously discussed of Timmy Dawkins illustrates.

In the Dawkins case, Timmy's father had the support of his employer and fellow employees. Others, not so fortunate, find their insurance access problem transformed into one of access to employment. Although the ADA prohibits discrimination to hold down health insurance costs, employers have a major incentive to evade the law. Also, a firm can avoid the discrimination issue altogether by simply failing to offer health benefits. In that case, not only the high-risk worker but the firm's entire labor force finds access to employment-related group insurance restricted.

At this time, private health insurance is the primary source of coverage for Americans under 65, yet the more likely someone is to need care and be unable to pay out-of-pocket, the less he or she can count on private health insurance to be there to pay.

Declaring medical underwriting to be inappropriate is no solution. Prohibiting the use of a specific type of information may be feasible when discrimination is based on perception of risk rather than reality (as has sometimes been the case).[38] When there *is* a real difference in risk, however, prohibition will have real financial effects on insurers, to which they will respond. When the District of Columbia prohibited insurers from requiring HIV tests, commercial insurers simply stopped writing individual insurance policies in the District. A similar prohibition in California led to the use of a less HIV-specific screening test, and some people were rejected for coverage who were actually of average risk.

It is reasonable to require insurers to have an evidentiary basis for their underwriting standards; beyond this, however, information management policy can do little. What is needed is a set of policies that either establishes a national health insurance program based on a social insurance model, or restructures and regulates the relationship between private and public insurance programs so that the social insurance objective can be met. We will return to this point in the next section.

d. The Use of Insurance-Related Information by Insurers and Employers to Control Costs

Insurers and employers play a central role in controlling health insurance costs; therefore, they have a legitimate need for access to insurance-related data. The result, however, may be insurer and employer knowledge of personal information the person would prefer to keep secret, or worse, the use of sensitive information for other purposes.

---

38. For example, some insurers have made assumptions about links between personal characteristics, sexual orientation, and risk of HIV infection for which there is no evidence. Some insurers have charged higher premiums to healthy people who happen to be blind or deaf, without any evidence that their expenditures on health care are likely to be higher than average. The ADA requires insurers to use sound actuarial data in its evaluation of risk, which will provide a basis for challenging coverage decisions made on the basis of stereotypes. Janet O'Keeffe, "Disability, Discrimination and the Americans with Disabilities Act."

Employer access to personal health information is particularly troublesome. Currently, employers collect employee health information in a variety of ways and use it for a variety of purposes. Many firms now screen new employees for health problems, to make sure they can do the job and to establish a benchmark for future Workers' Compensation claims of job-related adverse health effects. They test for illegal drug use, which leads them to collect information about use of legal drugs so that test results can be properly interpreted. They establish Employee Assistance Programs for employees with personal problems; the result is files with information on drug or alcohol use, mental illness, or sexual problems. They provide wellness programs, which generate information about health-related personal habits.[39]

It wouldn't be reasonable to declare all these activities inappropriate *a priori*;[40] however, where to draw the line on the collection and use of information and how to enforce it is unclear. Opinion polls reflect the uncertainty. On the one hand, majorities in several polls reviewed by Singer, Shapiro, and Jacobs believe that employers have a right to information about a prospective employee's health. On the other hand, they don't think employers should use the information in the obvious way; for example, majorities say that employers should not use serious health problems, such as a history of cancer or heart disease or infection with HIV, as grounds for refusing to hire someone.[41]

Although this paper cannot resolve all the issues raised by employer use of personal information about employees, some conclusions about use of insurance-related health information are in order. Many employers *do* have easy access to the information generated when employees use their health insurance benefits; for example, members of the Institute of Medicine's Committee on Regional Health Data Networks were repeatedly told that self-insured employers can obtain access to patient-identified claims

---

39. For anecdotal examples of how this information can be used, see Ellen E. Schultz, "Your Money Matters: If You Use Firm's Counselors, Remember Your Secrets Could Be Used Against You," *The Wall Street Journal*, 26 May 1994, p. C1. Ellen E. Schultz, "Open Secrets: Medical Data Gathered by Firms Can Prove Less than Confidential," *The Wall Street Journal*, 18 May 1994, p. A1, A5.

40. For example, it would be unreasonable to say airlines could not require physical examinations of pilots to make sure they really were fit to fly, or to say that companies should never offer wellness and employee assistance programs because information generated by the programs could someday be used against a worker.

41. Singer, Shapiro and Jacobs, "Privacy of Health Care Data."

information. Their report says, "Indeed, some third-party administrators (TPAs) provide human resources personnel with dial-in capability to perform their own analyses of data concerning a firm's employees and dependents."[42] The introductory examples and the discussion above show that such information can be and is used for purposes other than cost control.

Consistent with the previous discussion of other nonmedical uses of insurance-related information, employers should be required to get explicit consent from employees to collect and use personal health information for any purpose other than administering health benefits. Moreover, they should be required to segregate insurance-related personal health information from other information about employees, and establish strict privacy and confidentiality rules, allowing access only to those who must have it to run the benefit plan (sometimes referred to as "erecting a fire wall around the data").

These don't address problems of transfer, loss of ins. coverage, etc. employee selection based on health status,

Prevention of Inappropriate Use

Guidelines for appropriate use are of little value unless observed and enforced. Effective implementation of a framework designed to protect both privacy and access to health care depends on a number of factors. The cost of observing the guidelines is one; for example, it takes resources to control access to computerized databases or obtain informed consent. The cost of verifying compliance and imposing sanctions is another; this cost, in turn, depends on the incentives to violate the guidelines and the ease with which violations can be detected.

Enforcement cannot rely entirely on legal or administrative action after the fact, initiated by a person who has been harmed. Since there are subtle ways to collect and use information, many victims may not even know what has happened. Those who do must bring suit or make a complaint, which costs money, time, and emotional energy, and in some cases, increases harm by making a loss of privacy more complete. In these circumstances, the likelihood of successful litigation may be low enough so that it is cheaper for the data-user to pay the cost of occasionally being found responsible for harmful use or disclosure than to prevent it.

To avoid this, security measures must be specified, and sanctions imposed for violating them, whether or not harmful use or disclosure has

---

42. Institute of Medicine, *Health Data in the Information Age*, 159.

occurred. Unfortunately, this is just the type of regulation that is often considered intrusive and expensive by business and the public. Thus, one should also consider structural changes that remove the incentive and/or the opportunity to make inappropriate use of personal health information.

Designing a framework that takes all these factors into account is made especially difficult by the complexity of the American health care system and the increasing role that for-profit entreprises are playing within it. Since comprehensive reform of health care financing has failed, the health care system is likely to remain fragmented. To build the comprehensive, inclusive databases needed for administrative efficiency, access monitoring and research someone will have to coordinate the activities of multiple parties: private insurers, employers, health care providers, public insurers, and government employees at the local, state and federal levels.

Some insurers and employers will have strong economic incentives to refuse to provide data, or worse, to provide inaccurate data. They may view the data as proprietary – akin to "trade secrets" – and be reluctant to surrender something they believe gives them a market advantage. Alternatively, they may fear that the data will reveal discrimination or inferior quality, and expose them to administrative or market sanctions.

Insurers and employers will also have economic incentives to use data in ways that invade privacy and can cause harm, as described above. Linking databases promises significant social benefits, but if computerized databases are linked, and insurers and providers have ready access to patient information from multiple sources, the temptation to profit from it will be strong. Security measures are available.[43] At a cost, databases can be made reasonably secure (although never absolutely secure) against the outsider who "breaks in" and browses at will through files of sensitive personal information. More difficult is securing data against the unscrupulous authorized insider, who is actually a greater threat. Protecting against insiders is complicated by the great variety in the types and sizes of organizations that would need authorized access to insurance-related information. Some might take privacy and confidentiality very seriously; others might not care about it at all.

---

43. For examples of the benefits of linking datasets, see Roos et al., "Supporting the Delivery of Preventive Services"; Roos et al., "Designing an Information System"; "Population Access to Care, Health and Health Care Use." For discussion of benefits and privacy safeguards, see Scheuren, "Linking Health Records."

Imposing and enforcing a "fire wall" rule on employers is obviously difficult when a firm administers its own health insurance plan. There may be difficulties even when the plan is administered by an insurance company, however. Consider this quote from an insurance company employee speaking about monthly reports to employers:

> . . . First, we were only going to tell employers the total charges for their companies. Then, we decided it was okay to do it by division, but we would never put any [sensitive medical information] on the reports. But now we're giving out totals in small categories that sometimes only include a few claims, so employers can figure out which employees had which charges, even if we don't explicitly tell them. So, we say we don't give out diagnoses, but I think it could sometimes be figured out. . . .[44]

The strength of the financial incentive to use information in ways that adversely affect individuals varies from one organization to another. For example, some insurance companies have more market power than others. In the 1980s, New York's Empire State Blue Cross could be less concerned about testing for HIV infection than other Blue Cross companies because its very large share of the state market made adverse selection less of an issue. The impact of a single worker's serious illness on labor costs is felt much more by a small firm than by a large one. The ability to find out about and then complain or sue over violations of human rights, whether to health care or to privacy, also varies. People of low educational and socioeconomic status are at a disadvantage, as are people whose time and energy are consumed by coping with their health problems.

Perhaps the most important difficulty to be reckoned with is the current anti-tax, anti-regulatory mood of the country. At this time, it may be close to impossible to achieve consensus on the requirements that should be imposed on private entreprises *and* the appropriation of sufficient funds to enforce them. This makes it all the more important to explore whether there are structural changes in the system that can reduce the incentive and/or the opportunity to use data in ways that endanger human rights, and thus reduce the need for regulation.

An obvious step would be to *break the link between employment and health insurance.* There are many reasons to do this, as the literature on health care reform shows; this is another one.[45] Eliminating or at least

---

44. Smith, *Managing Privacy,* 70.

capping the special tax advantage given to health insurance would be one place to start. It would also be desirable to change the ERISA provisions that apply to health benefits, to reduce the incentive for firms to self-insure.

If fluctuations in the cost of health insurance no longer had a direct impact on an employer's labor costs, some (although not all) of the incentive for health-related employment discrimination would be removed. More important, employers would no longer be involved in the management of care and would not have routine access to insurance-generated health information.

An obvious remedy for the access problems caused by medical underwriting would be to *place the entire population into a single risk pool for health insurance purposes.* The most direct way to do this is to set up a national single payer system. Such a system does not need to discriminate on the basis of risk or refuse to share data. Again, there are other reasons advanced in favor of a government-regulated, single-payer system. For example, it has been argued that administrative costs would be far lower,[46] and that such a system could more easily achieve universal coverage for an adequate level of care and distribute the cost fairly.

People have not argued that a government-sponsored, single-payer system is desirable for the protection of privacy. In fact, a reduction in privacy has been assumed to be an inevitable and undesirable aspect of any single-payer system, both by those in favor and those opposed.

There are sound reasons to be wary of the "big brother" potential of national health care databases in such a system. Nevertheless, most Americans probably do not realize how little protection of privacy there is now, and how rapidly it is likely to erode, given the economic forces at work in health care. Practically speaking, it could well be easier to enforce effective privacy safeguards in a government-regulated, single-payer system than in a system that relies heavily on competing private for-profit health insurers. Given the lack of political support for regulating private companies, it is likely that people will be forced to accept whatever privacy the private

---

45. For a discussion of these issues, see Mary Ann Baily, "Policies for the 1990s: Rationing Health Care," in *Competitive Approaches to Health Care Reform*, eds. R.J. Arnould, R.F. Rich, W.D. White (Washington, D.C.: Urban Institute Press, 1993), and the references cited therein.

46. See, for example, United States General Accounting Office, *Canadian Health Insurance: Lessons for the United States,* GAO/HRD-91-90 (Washington, D.C., June 1991).

market offers voluntarily, and given the economic incentives, it may not be much.

Unfortunately, there is even less support for establishing a single-payer system, eliminating or capping the tax subsidies, reducing the role of employment-related insurance in the private insurance market, or for that matter, any other fundamental reform. More limited reforms may be feasible; they would have a limited impact, but would be better than nothing.

There is a long list of partial reforms that have been proposed at one time or another. From the human rights perspective, there are two key elements to look for in such proposals. The first is movement of the financing system in the direction of universal, continuous third-party coverage for at least a basic standard of care, with risk adjustment to reduce the incentive to insurers and employers to discriminate on the basis of health status, and premium subsidies to make coverage affordable for everyone. The second is separation of employers from person-identifiable insurance-related data.

Examples of limited reforms include development of state-subsidized private insurance risk pools for high-risk individuals,[47] restructuring of the small-group insurance market to create larger risk pools and to reduce administrative costs, elimination of arbitrary discrimination in medical underwriting, redesign of public insurance programs to protect people who through no fault of their own are unable to maintain private insurance coverage; and so on.

If employment-related insurance is to maintain its dominant role in the system, one reform that deserves a serious look is the "health insurance purchasing cooperative" or "health alliance" (as it was called in the Clinton Reform Plan). The health alliance, usually assumed to be independent and nonprofit, would act as an expert buyer of health insurance for businesses and individuals, offering a range of plans that have met standards of coverage, quality and cost-effectiveness. Employees would choose a plan, and insurers would be required to accept whoever applies, up to capacity. The alliance would collect premiums from employees and employers and transmit them to insurers, and would therefore be in position to administer a risk adjustment and premium subsidy policy. With such a policy, insurers

---

47. A number of states have already established such risk pools; however, the pools have not been very successful in reaching the target population, largely because covering a high-risk population is (naturally) expensive, and the premium subsidies have not been large enough to make the policies affordable.

and employers would have less of an incentive to discriminate on the basis of health. They would also have less opportunity, since the alliance (not the insurer) would manage the enrollment process, and the employer would be separated from person-identifiable data about employees. The alliance would have to have privacy and confidentiality standards, and they would have to be enforced; however, it would be easier to regulate a single regional alliance than a host of individual insurance companies and employers with financial incentives to break the rules.

Conclusion

The American health care system is rapidly evolving into one in which far more information on a privately insured person's health status and medical treatment will be collected, stored and scrutinized by insurers, employers, and others outside the immediate patient-provider relationship. This new health care system can be one that is more respectful of human rights, not less respectful, but only if we take action soon. Personal health information is much less protected than most people realize, and the changes under way will make things worse. It is time to establish a framework that provides for real protection of both privacy and access to health care, and to make the structural changes that can help make this framework effective.

CHAPTER SEVENTEEN

Conclusions

Thomas Jabine

Introduction

The final chapter of this report on health care information and human rights presents the conclusions of the Advisory Committee for the project. The chapter has four sections. The second and third sections correspond to the two major parts of this volume. The second section, which focuses mostly on statistical issues, is about how health information can be obtained and used to monitor access to basic health care services, with emphasis on underserved, vulnerable, and excluded populations. The third section has a broader scope, covering both statistical and nonstatistical uses of health information. It asks what uses of individual health data, by what organizations, for what purposes and under what conditions, are appropriate, taking into account the human rights norms of privacy, nondiscrimination, and consent that were described by Audrey Chapman in the first two chapters.

The fourth and final section of this chapter discusses the apparent conflicts that are encountered in trying to observe the four human rights norms that are relevant to the collection and use of health information. In order to obtain data needed to monitor the achievement of access to basic health care services by all persons, without discrimination, it may be necessary to permit some encroachments on individuals' privacy and their ability to control uses and disclosures of their own information. Such apparent conflicts are most evident in efforts to use patient information generated by the private health care sector to monitor access to and quality of health care; they are much easier to deal with in collecting health data in population-based surveys. Views on how the conflicts among human rights norms can best be resolved depend in part on the present structure of the U.S. health care system and on expectations about future changes in the system.

Several of the preceding chapters in this volume have included formal recommendations. The Advisory Committee decided, however, that it would be more appropriate to present its own views in the form of conclusions or findings, rather than formal recommendations. We hope that our statement of conclusions will be helpful to groups and individuals who are concerned about the human rights questions associated with the U.S. health care system and its information infrastructure.

Members of the Advisory Committee, who are listed in Appendix 1, brought a variety of experience and expertise to this project. Working mostly in two subcommittees corresponding to the two major parts of this volume, they met several times to formulate the scope of the project, discuss the issues, and discuss drafts of the commissioned papers, each of which had been reviewed by one or more committee members. As can be noted by comparing the list of committee members with the table of contents of this volume, several committee members were also authors or coauthors of commissioned papers.

When the time came to prepare this summary, committee members were asked to submit short statements outlining the major points that they thought should be included. Rather than asking each member to comment on the same specific set of issues, it was left to them to decide what topics to cover in their statements. Based on these inputs, a draft summary was prepared, reviewed by the committee members, and revised to produce this final version. Given the varied background of the committee members and the difficult nature of the questions addressed, it would have been surprising to find unanimity on all points. Nevertheless, only rarely were the conclusions submitted by individual committee members in direct disagreement. Where such differences did occur, we describe them.

On one basic conclusion there was no disagreement. Unlike many other countries, the United States is not presently committed, through its laws and international treaty commitments, to provide universal access to basic health care services. The Advisory Committee members all support the adoption of such a commitment.

Using Health Information to Monitor Access

a. What kinds of data are needed for monitoring?

The starting point for specifying data requirements on any topic is a precise statement of the concepts to be measured and the target populations for measurement. A comprehensive, detailed monitoring plan for the U.S. health care system will require definitions that are more precise than those that now exist for the concepts of universality, access and quality of care. It will also require the ability to translate these concepts and definitions into measurable statistics, whether the data are obtained from population-based surveys, records generated by the health care system, or other sources.

Particular care will be needed in identifying and defining vulnerable population groups, those that are at greatest risk of discrimination. Some of the chapters in Part I illustrate approaches to defining and collecting information for selected population groups. Bennett looks at national data for AFDC recipients and other poor women. Fisher *et al.* describe local area studies of drug users, using two different methods to find and locate members of the target population. Sugarman *et al.* describe the difficulties in obtaining health data at the tribal level for American Indians and Alaska Natives in the Pacific Northwest.

Basic concepts and definitions will have to be reviewed periodically and modified, when necessary, in response to changes in medical technology, the structure of the health care system, the composition of the population it serves, and the economic and social environment in which it operates. The importance of adapting to and tracking the effects of such changes is also illustrated by some of the papers in Part I. Bennett discusses the likely effects of welfare reform, both on the access to health care by poor women and on the sources of data needed to monitor changes. Sugarman et al. look at recent trends toward "self-governance," a process whereby individual tribes are being given more direct control over federal resources for Indian health programs. Data to evaluate the results of this trend will have to be obtained largely from the tribes themselves, rather than from federal agencies, such as the Bureau of Indian Affairs.

In general terms, data for monitoring access to basic health care services should:

- Include information about health status and use of health care services. As suggested by Fowler and Samuelson in the introduction to

Part I, the definition and indicators of access that were selected by the Institute of Medicine in its 1993 study provide a good starting point in developing a specific monitoring plan.

- Provide disaggregated data so that access and outcomes can be measured and evaluated for groups that are at high risk of discrimination. Such groups may include, but are not limited to: minority racial and ethnic groups, the poor, the homeless, migrant workers and their families, illegal immigrants, chronically ill or disabled persons, persons who are HIV-positive, and persons receiving treatment for mental illness. As noted below, many of these vulnerable groups are not adequately covered by existing data systems. Data for different geographic areas are also essential; many health care problems are local and need to be studied and dealt with at the local level.

- Provide comparable data over time (time-series data) so that progress in achieving universality can be monitored. However, as in any type of longitudinal analysis, target populations, concepts and definitions may have to be changed periodically to adapt to changing monitoring needs.

No one single statistic or indicator can be used to monitor and ensure universality of access to basic health care services. Low rates of use of health care services do not necessarily indicate inadequate access. A carefully selected set of statistical indicators can provide a basis for identifying possible problems. In-depth studies of specific population groups and types of health care services are necessary to understand the nature of the indicated problems and seek solutions to them.

b. What Are the Existing Sources of Data and What Are Their Strengths and Weaknesses?

Large-scale national surveys of households or persons, such as the ongoing National Health Interview Survey and periodic surveys of medical expenditures, Medicare beneficiaries, and persons in nursing homes are a continuing source of high-quality data with a reasonable degree of comparability over time. They will inevitably constitute an important element of any system for monitoring access and universality. However, some of the most vulnerable groups, such as migrant workers and the homeless, are not covered or inadequately covered by these surveys. Also, sample sizes for these national surveys are not large enough to provide usable data at state and local levels and for small population groups, such as specific Indian tribes or persons with relatively rare disabilities or chronic conditions.

Many health surveys with content similar to the national surveys, covering limited geographic areas and special populations, are undertaken by state and local health agencies and private organizations. Some of these surveys provide useful monitoring data for groups that are at high risk of discrimination. Frequently, however, availability of such information is sporadic over time, and the concepts, definitions and target populations may vary widely from one survey to another. The standard of data quality, on average, is probably below that achieved in the large, ongoing national surveys.

Vital records, such as birth and death certificates, used in conjunction with population counts or estimates, are also an important resource for health care monitoring. They have virtually complete coverage, and hence can provide data disaggregated by geographic area and other classification characteristics that are included on the birth and death certificates. Mortality differences across subgroups are not, in themselves, clear evidence of discrimination in access to health care services, but can indicate a need for more intensive analyses of specific groups and causes of death. Birth certificates for most states provide information on whether mothers have received prenatal care.

Administrative records developed by various components of the U.S. health care system for the purposes of treatment, health insurance, and payment of providers are likely to become more important for monitoring as they become more widely computerized and their content and format more standardized. Some of these data systems can provide important information on the use and quality of health care services among those receiving care, and can also serve as sampling frames for surveys to collect data that cannot be obtained from records. Records maintained at the federal level, especially for the Medicare program, are a particularly valuable source of data. As described in the chapter by Kurtzig, several states have made considerable progress in the development of systems containing comparable patient and encounter-level data from providers, especially hospitals, in their states.

The Medicare claim system provides an example of what having a single insurance system can do for monitoring access to health care. In recent years, substantial progress has been made in learning to use Medicare administrative data, supplemented by surveys of beneficiaries, to study how medical care is being delivered and how different subgroups of the elderly population use medical care.

However, administrative records have significant limitations. Because of the fragmented character of our health care system, coverage is limited to specific population groups (e.g., Medicare records cover only persons 65 and over, and some disabled persons) and to persons who are insured or have received health care services. The content of the records is dictated primarily by their administrative uses, rather than possible statistical and research uses. For nonfederal systems, especially those in the private sector, there are some ongoing efforts to achieve greater standardization, but progress has been slow. Finally, the comparability over time of information in administrative systems can be impaired by changes in coverage and content that are dictated by operational factors, such as new technology and changes in the structure of the health care system. Devolution of greater responsibility to the states or, as illustrated in the chapter by Sugarman et al., to individual Indian tribes will make standardization more difficult to achieve, with consequent difficulties in comparing the status of different population groups and localities.

c. Racial and Ethnic Classifications: A Special Problem

Clearly, some population groups defined by racial or ethnic origin can be identified as possible victims of discrimination when one looks at statistical indicators for topics like mortality, health insurance coverage, and use of health care services. However, as discussed in the chapter by Kurtzig, some difficult problems are associated with the collection and use of data about racial and ethnic groups for monitoring. There is no consensus on how best to define and measure the constructs of race and ethnicity. Federal standards have changed over time (and will soon change again), as have operational procedures for collecting race and ethnic data in various systems. How individuals report their own status may depend on the setting in which it is reported and on their current perceptions of their own best interests. Major federal administrative data systems, such as those maintained by the Social Security Administration, do not contain complete and accurate race-ethnic information. For mortality rates, studies have shown that biases, sometimes substantial, can be introduced by differences in classification of individuals in the numerator (death certificate) and the denominator (census report or birth certificate).

Monitoring access to health care by racial and ethnic groups ought not be abandoned because of these difficulties; rather, we should look for ways to improve the quality of racial and ethnic information in health records. However, analysts should be aware of the limitations of current data. Consideration of the problems that Kurtzig has described suggests that for some purposes it may be preferable to disaggregate health data on the basis of other demographic and socio-economic classifiers, such as income and education, and by geographic area.

d. Linking Data from Different Systems

Although much useful monitoring information can be obtained by the analysis of data from a single system, whether it be a survey or an administrative data set, the relevance and utility of statistical information can often be enhanced by linking data for the same persons from different systems. In national surveys of medical care expenditures, administrative data from providers are linked with data collected directly from sample persons, thus insuring availability of high quality information about the nature and costs of services used by different population groups. In longitudinal research on the effects of alternate forms of treatment or of exposures to environmental hazards, study populations are frequently matched against death certificates in order to determine outcomes. Because such linkages require at least temporary retention of data for identified persons and may be facilitated by the use of identification numbers, special consideration has to be given to privacy and confidentiality issues. These issues are addressed in the next section of this chapter.

e. Data for Monitoring: Summary

The Advisory Committee's main conclusions about monitoring universal access to basic health care services as a human right are as follows:

- Effective monitoring requires detailed specification of what is included in basic health care services and what is meant by access.

- There are many existing sources of statistical and research data, each with its own strengths and weaknesses, that are potentially useful for monitoring access. However, some of the groups that are most at risk – the homeless, illegal immigrants, and migratory workers – are not well-covered by existing data systems, and it will be difficult to develop high-quality monitoring data for them. Some of the resources of statistical agencies should be allocated to undertake special studies of these groups.

- Resource limitations preclude the development of detailed, high-quality monitoring data for every possible population subgroup. Effective monitoring will require deciding which population groups are most at risk of discrimination, and then using the limited resources that are available to obtain good monitoring data for those groups.

- Administrative records maintained to support provision of and payment for health care services are a potentially valuable source of data for monitoring, but their value is limited by the present fragmented nature of the U.S. health care delivery system. Further efforts at standardization by the government and private sectors, working together, could increase the value of data in these systems.

- The value of data for monitoring can be enhanced by linking data from different sources for the same persons.

Privacy, Nondiscrimination and Consent

a. Defining the Issues

The previous section gave our conclusions about the nature and sources of statistical information needed to monitor universality of access to basic health care services. In this section we address the other three fundamental human rights norms – privacy, nondiscrimination and consent – that have important implications for the collection and use of health care information about individuals.

Nondiscrimination was not a source of argument among the members of the Advisory Committee. We had no difficulty with the principle that access to an agreed-on set of basic health care services should be afforded to everyone ". . . without distinction of any kind, such as race, colour, language, religion, political or other opinion, national or social origin, property, birth or other status," as provided in the nondiscrimination provision (Article 2) of the *Universal Declaration of Human Rights.*[1] The

---

1.   *Universal Declaration of Human Rights*, adopted and proclaimed by United Nations General Assembly resolution 217 A (III) on 10 December 1948.

Committee did not attempt the difficult task of defining a set of basic services, but we have noted that doing so is a prerequisite for determining what specific data are needed to monitor universality and nondiscrimination.

This unanimity did not carry over, however, to the Committee's views about the human rights norms of "privacy" and "consent." The two terms are closely related. In the context of health care, they are associated with the following questions:

1. What kinds of information about themselves should individuals be asked to supply in connection with the receipt of health care services and payment for those services?

2. What uses of this information are appropriate?

3. Who should have access to the information that they provide or, to put it another way, what disclosures of their information should be allowed?

4. How much control should individuals have over uses and disclosures of their information? To what extent should informed consent be required for uses and disclosures?

If privacy is defined as the right to limit access to information about oneself, then it clearly cannot be an absolute right in the context of health care. At a minimum, individuals must provide some information about themselves in order to receive appropriate treatment. Unless payment is to be entirely out-of-pocket, some additional information may be required in order for them to receive insurance benefits. The question of privacy, then, becomes a question of the extent to which information provided for treatment and benefits should be protected from intentional disclosures for other purposes and from unintentional disclosures.

Standards of consent determine the extent to which individuals are informed about and given the opportunity to control what is done with the information they are asked to provide. At one end of the spectrum, a standard might require formal informed consent from an individual for each disclosure and use to be made of his or her information. An intermediate standard might call for notifying individuals of some of the disclosures and uses to be made, and requiring consent for others. A person objecting to some of the uses not requiring consent might have the option to decline to provide the information and to not obtain treatment or to seek it from another source, but in most instances these alternatives are likely to be unrealistic or unattractive. At the other end of the spectrum, patients might not receive any information about disclosures and uses of their data. Not surprisingly, none of the Advisory Committee members took this position; there was general agreement that persons should be informed of all of the uses to be made of the data they provide.

Many procedural and practical considerations are associated with consent procedures. For what persons and under what conditions can consent be truly informed and free of any coercion? Under what circumstances can proxies be used, and who are appropriate proxies? How can information about expected uses, and disclosures be presented clearly and accurately? If a blanket consent is given, for how long should it remain in force?

In thinking about what uses of individual health information should be permitted, it is helpful to distinguish between statistical and research uses, on the one hand, and administrative uses, on the other. For statistical and research uses, it may be necessary to use individually identifiable records at intermediate stages, for example to link data for the same individuals from different sources, but the end-product consists of tabulations and other aggregate statistics that relate to population groups rather than individuals. Administrative uses, however, affect specific individuals, determining, for example, what treatment they receive, how it is paid for, and perhaps even the nature of their future employment and health insurance coverage.

It should not be thought that all statistical and research uses of health information are benign. On balance, we can expect that findings from sound medical and epidemiological research can lead to improvements in the quality of health care, but poorly designed studies or misinterpretation of results may sometimes lead to incorrect conclusions about the relative benefits of alternative treatments. The large-scale national surveys discussed in the previous section are unlikely to cause harm to particular individuals or population subgroups. On the other hand, statistical analyses of the experience of a particular insurer or a health maintenance organization (sometimes referred to as "experience rating") may lead to changes in coverage that harm individuals who have certain types of disabilities or health conditions requiring treatment. If a self-insured employer finds, from a statistical analysis, that a certain class of conditions is accounting for a large proportion of benefit costs, the employer may use the medical records to identify individual employees and family members in that category and deny them continuing coverage, or perhaps even find reasons to terminate their employment.

b. The Current Situation

Even in the absence of a defined package of basic health care services that should be guaranteed to everyone, it is abundantly clear that universality has not been achieved in the United States, and that there is discrimination in access to adequate health care. For most persons, health insurance coverage is tied to their own employment or that of family members. There is wide variability in the adequacy of coverage of plans offered by different employers; many plans do not provide adequate care by any reasonable standard that might be developed. The *Americans with Disabilities Act* has provided some protection against discrimination, but access to employment and eligibility for health benefits can still be affected by existing conditions of applicants and their family members. Health problems of employed persons and their family members can threaten continued employment and health insurance coverage or, conversely, can lock a person into a particular job, with little real freedom of choice in seeking other employment.

Some of those whose health care is not linked to employment are covered by government programs – Medicare for older and some disabled persons, and Medicaid for some of those with low incomes – but many others are not covered by any program. The adequacy of the Medicare and Medicaid programs, (especially the latter), could, at least in some states, be diminished by some features of proposed reforms that are being considered by the Congress. Bennett argues that poor women are particularly threatened by proposed changes to the AFDC and Medicaid programs. Some of these changes, such as the transfer of responsibility for Medicaid to the states, might also adversely affect the scope, quality and, especially, the consistency across states of data for monitoring access to health care by the low-income population.

As described in the chapter by Baily, the present system which ties health care to employment has led to discrimination on the basis of health status, health services received and health-related behavior. Employers have incentives to use health information in hiring, promotion, and retention of workers, given real or perceived effects of health status on productivity, absenteeism and turnover and training costs. Because of the effect of benefit costs on a company's income, employers who offer health insurance, especially those who are self-insured, have an even stronger incentive to use individual health information. Employees, knowing that employers will have access to their health information, may be less truthful with their health care providers and thus fail to receive adequate care.

The greatest threats to privacy and control over disclosures and uses of one's own health information relate to information obtained and used by the private sector. Except for the limited protections afforded by the *Americans with Disabilities Act,* and by legislation that applies only to certain records about substance abuse, there is no federal law governing the use of health information by the private sector. Some states have relevant laws but, as noted by Duncan, these laws vary greatly in the type and amount of protection and control afforded to individuals. Only three states – California, Montana and Washington – have general laws dealing with access to health information. Robert E. Smith explains that most states recognize a "doctor-patient" privilege in the courts, but that this protection does not extend to medical information in the hands of those who are not doctors. Providers and insurers often require patients' written consent for a variety of disclosures and uses, but individuals who refuse to give their full consent to all uses incur the risk of not receiving the kind of care they need or the benefits to which they would normally be entitled.

Largely because of the requirements of the *Privacy Act,* individual health records maintained by the federal government receive somewhat better protection. The *Privacy Act* incorporates many, although not all, of the principles of fair information practices that were proposed for research and statistical uses of health data in the chapter by Robert E. Smith. When data are collected in national sample surveys, such as the National Health Interview Survey, persons asked to respond are informed of all uses that will be made of their information and told that their participation is voluntary. The confidentiality of data from the National Health Interview Survey is further protected by agency statutes that prohibit the use of the data for nonstatistical purposes. In terms of control over uses, the status of Medicare and other federal program records is different from that of data from the sample surveys; their use for a variety of statistical and research purposes does not require the specific consent of individual beneficiaries.

In the absence of federal law and regulation of health information in the private sector, increasing computerization of health records has facilitated uses of health information that many consider inappropriate, such as the sale of pharmacy purchase records to pharmaceutical companies for marketing use (Duncan, Chapter 13). On the other hand, computerization can make it easier for health providers to obtain the patient information they need in order to provide appropriate treatment, especially when multiple providers are involved or a patient has moved from one location to another. Technological developments in the collection, processing and dissemination of information have increased the tension between information needs of organizations and society at large and the desires of individuals for privacy and control over their own information. Yet, as explained by Brannigan and Beier, these developments also hold promise for improved control over access to individual health care information. There are practical steps that can be taken to make such information more secure, even in a world of computerized, linked databases, if we have the will to do it.

Many, perhaps most people are unaware of the extent to which their health information can be and is being disclosed, not just to providers and insurers, but to other organizations and individuals for a variety of purposes. In a democratic society, informed public opinion should play a role in the development of policy for appropriate access to and use of health information. Singer, Shapiro and Jacobs (Chapter 14) have made a useful contribution by summarizing findings from recent sample surveys about public knowledge and attitudes related specifically to the privacy of health care information. As the authors point out, most people have not given much thought to these issues, and therefore the results of opinion surveys are likely to be sensitive to the specific manner in which the issues are presented to them. The design and question wording for surveys on this topic should be carefully scrutinized, and the survey results used with caution.

Some Conclusions

a. Areas of General Agreement

Our review of the present situation with regard to privacy, nondiscrimination and consent leads us to the following conclusions:

- Individuals have relatively little control over the disclosures and uses of the information they supply to health providers and insurers. This is especially true in the private sector.

- Most people are not aware of the extent to which their individual health information is being disclosed and used for purposes other than providing and paying for their health care.

- Health information is being used to discriminate against individuals, adversely affecting their access to employment and adequate health care. Our fragmented health care system, with its links to employment, provides both incentives and opportunities for employers and insurers to discriminate. Because the United States does not have a health care system that assures universal, lifetime coverage, individuals are especially vulnerable to negative consequences as a result of both authorized and unauthorized uses of their health information.

- Existing federal laws place very few restrictions or controls on disclosures and uses of health care information in the private sector. New legislation, covering all kinds of individual health information, is needed to protect individuals against uses of their information that are discriminatory or violate reasonable standards of individual privacy. Such legislation will be more effective if it avoids elaborate and costly requirements that cannot be enforced. Subject to appropriate safeguards, statistical and research uses of information to monitor universality and nondiscrimination and to improve the effectiveness of the health care system should be allowed. Some examples of proposed guidelines for protecting the confidentiality of medical information used in research are provided in the chapters by Chapman (Chapter 2), Duncan, and Smith.[2]

- Computerization and the application of other new technologies to health records introduce new threats to privacy and to the confidentiality of these records. New technologies can also be used to make records more secure. Brannigan and Beier suggest several means by which better protection of individual data can be designed into a health information system, but this will happen only if a conscious effort is made and suitable incentives are created.

b. Unresolved Issues

There are two issues on which there were significant differences of opinion among the members of the Advisory Committee:

---

2. A bill covering these areas, S. 1360, the *Medical Records Confidentiality Act of 1995,* was introduced in the 104th Congress. This legislation is discussed briefly in the chapter by Brannigan and Beier. The Advisory Committee has not undertaken an analysis of the provisions of S. 1360, and did not take any positions concerning specific provisions.

1. What degree of control should individuals have over disclosures and uses of their own health information?

2. To what extent should linkages of health information from different record systems be permitted?

The two questions are closely related. Linkages of records from different systems, whether undertaken for administrative or statistical and research uses, often require disclosure of identifiable information and, in this sense, represent a subset of the disclosures and uses addressed by the first question.

As noted earlier in this section, one possible position on the issue of control is that written authorization should be required for all disclosures and uses of an individual's health information. It would not be correct to speak of informed consent in this context, because the possible consequences of refusal to provide authorization introduce an element of coercion. A somewhat less strict position would be simply to inform individuals about the nature of disclosures required for purposes of providing treatment or paying for patient care, and to require written authorization for other uses of their information, including statistical and research uses. Some members of the Advisory Committee supported this position.

Other members of the Committee, however, agreed with the position taken in the chapter by Baily: that as members of society and as beneficiaries of the health care system, individuals have a responsibility to make their data available for legitimate purposes, such as improving the effectiveness and efficiency of health care, and monitoring the extent to which the human rights goals of universality and nondiscrimination are being achieved. Allowing some individuals to opt out of such uses of their information might seriously distort some statistical data developed for these purposes. Those who took this position believed that such uses should be permitted only under specified enforceable conditions, including protection against improper uses and disclosures, and full notification of individuals about the kinds of uses to be made. Experimental research should, of course, always require fully informed consent of research subjects.

Another alternative to written authorization for all uses would be to have a review board which would evaluate proposed uses, including those involving linkages of records from different systems, and decide which ones were appropriate. As described by Duncan, such a board would ". . . oversee privacy and data access in health care information." It would be constructed to represent the interests of all groups concerned – patients, providers, insurers and others – and to evaluate objectively the trade-offs among the human rights norms of universality, nondiscrimination, privacy and consent.

The issues related to record linkages, as ably set out in the chapter by Scheuren, are complex. Advisory Committee members had varying views about the kinds of linkages that should be permitted, the kinds of identifiers that should be used to facilitate them, and the conditions under which informed consent by data subjects should be required. On the second point, some had strong objections to the use of the Social Security number.

Positions on these difficult issues are in part dependent on people's understanding of the present structure of the U.S. health care system and the directions in which it is likely to evolve. These considerations are reviewed in the next and final section of this chapter.

c. *Trade-offs and Strategies*

A major goal of this project was to examine how best to monitor health status and access to health care, especially for vulnerable and underserved populations, for the purpose of improving access to care and quality of care. However, in the absence of universality – guaranteed lifetime access to basic health care for all persons – increased data collection, computerization, and ready access to the data pose serious threats to people's economic security. Information about people's health is being used to deny access to employment and health insurance, discriminating against persons with conditions that are likely or thought to be likely to entail high costs of care.

There are two ways, not necessarily mutually exclusive, to confront this problem without losing the ability to obtain the data needed to monitor universality and nondiscrimination. One way would be to restructure the health care system to remove or substantially reduce incentives to discriminate against individuals on the basis of their health care information. The other would be to enact laws to regulate disclosures and uses of individual health care information and, in particular, prohibit its use by employers and insurers in ways that discriminate unfairly.

As explained by Baily, restructuring the system, especially by eliminating or weakening the links between employment and health insurance coverage, could have many beneficial effects. Employers would still have some incentives to use health information in hiring, promotion, and retention of workers, but the costs of health care for employees would no longer be an important factor in their decisions. Employees and members of their families might be less inclined to avoid seeking treatment for some health problems and to withhold relevant information from health care providers, for fear that it could influence their employment and insurance coverage. As a result, better quality data would be available for monitoring access and improving the quality of health care.

When this study began, policymakers at the federal level were trying to expand access to health care, and a universal right to care was at least a possibility. In that policy environment, the potential value of information to monitor and insure access was great, and one might have been willing to give some on privacy considerations in order to be sure of having the information. Midway through the study, however, the policy environment changed dramatically, and political and public support for expanding access to health care decreased markedly. Indeed, for some groups, especially the poor, less access has become a distinct possibility.

In this changed environment, where major restructuring of the system to expand access is no longer a real short-term option, there is a stronger need than ever for federal legislation, covering both the public and private sectors, to protect the privacy of individuals and to prevent use of their health information to discriminate against them. However, the legislative approach carries some risks. The need for monitoring data has not disappeared; in some respects it is greater. We will need to identify and track the population groups most seriously affected by discrimination and inadequate access to health care. Health information legislation, if not carefully drafted, could make it unnecessarily difficult to obtain the statistical information needed for this purpose. This is where it becomes necessary to strike a balance among the human rights norms that we have been examining.

We hope that those who are developing or attempting to influence legislation can do what we have tried to do in this project: engage in a dialogue among health statisticians, policy analysts, privacy advocates, and advocates of universal access to health care, and seek constructive ideas from all of these groups. Privacy advocates need to recognize that society can benefit from the availability of information about how the health care system is operating and that such information is essential in order to monitor the status of access to health care, especially at a time when reduced access to health care seems likely for the most vulnerable segments of the population. Policy analysts, researchers and statisticians must recognize that many people have well-founded concerns about their lack of control over the' uses that are being made of the information they are asked to provide in order to obtain adequate health care. Cooperation and understanding between data users and privacy advocates will be necessary to achieve the goal proposed by Duncan at the conclusion of his chapter: "In building a quality medical care system there is no tradeoff between privacy and confidentiality on the one hand and data access on the other. Both are required if high quality data is to serve health care needs."

Epilogue

The past four years have been a period of continuous change for the U.S. health care system and the environment in which it operates. New political forces, new laws, new technologies, economic and social pressures, and new organizational structures for providing health care are interacting in ways whose eventual outcome is hard to predict. Those of us who have a stake in the system – and that really means all of us – could not be blamed for feeling that we have been on a four-year roller coaster ride. We started 1992 excited (at least many of us were) about the possibility of fundamental reform of the system that would bring it closer to universal coverage. In 1993 our hopes began to fade as we descended the long slope that led to the abandonment of the Administration's health care reform initiative in the Fall of 1994.

But we had not necessarily reached bottom at that point. The shift in the control of Congress brought by the November elections led, in 1995, to numerous proposals to dismantle, reduce coverage, or devolve to the states many of the existing federal programs that provide health care coverage to disadvantaged sectors of the population.[1] All of these events were known to the contributors to this volume and, where relevant, were taken into account in their examination of human rights questions associated with health care information.

However, further important developments, in particular the passage of two major pieces of legislation, occurred in 1996, after the papers in this volume were completed. The roller coaster analogy is hard to maintain here, because although these new laws can result in improved access to health care for some, other groups of the population are likely to be placed at an even greater disadvantage. It's too early for a definitive evaluation of where we are headed, but we can identify provisions of the two laws that are relevant to the human rights norms that we have taken as our guideposts.

---

1. For a revealing account of the Clinton health care initiative and its aftermath, see H. Johnson and D. Broder, *The System* (Boston: Little, Brown & Co., 1996).

The Health Insurance Portability and Accountability Act of 1996, popularly known as Kennedy-Kassebaum, was signed into law by President Clinton on August 21. Its major goals were to increase access to health care benefits and to provide greater portability and security for existing benefits. The Act has the potential to mitigate some of the undesirable consequences of the link between health insurance coverage and employment. It places limitations on the exclusion of preexisting conditions from health insurance coverage and on arbitrary termination of coverage once a person is enrolled in a plan. It will be easier for a covered person who switches jobs to obtain coverage under his or her new employer. It is unlikely that the provisions of the Act can guarantee a complete end to employer discrimination against applicants and employees with high costs of health care, but some progress toward greater compliance with the human rights norms of universality and nondiscrimination can be expected.

Kennedy-Kassebaum also has implications for the human rights norms of privacy and informed consent as they apply to individuals' health data. A section of the Act entitled "Administrative Simplification" aims at improving the operation of the health care system and reducing administrative costs by requiring most federal and private health care providers and insurers to participate in a national network that would maintain computerized health records with standardized patient identifiers and data items. In addition to being used internally by providers and insurers, data could be transferred among health plans in the system as needed for coordination of treatment and processing of claims for persons with more than one health plan.

As pointed out in our "Conclusions" chapter, existing Federal law has little to say about disclosures and uses of health care information in the private sector. Legislation in this area was proposed and debated during 1996, but nothing was passed. Consequently, Kennedy-Kassebaum requires that the Secretary of the Department of Health and Human Services, in the absence of subsequent legislative action by the Congress, establish standards for transactions, the use of unique health identifiers, and the security of health information. Some privacy advocates have expressed concern that the timing requirements for standards are such that they will not necessarily be in place when the new computerized information system becomes operative.

At present, we can only guess at the effects of the "Administrative Simplification" provisions on the confidentiality of health care information. If carefully drafted, the security standards to be established by the Secretary of Health and Human Services could introduce some federal protection for the confidentiality of individual health information in the private sector. Depending on the extent to which the standards permit access to data in the system for statistical and research uses, standardization of identifiers and data elements may facilitate comparison of access and quality of care for different segments of the population who are covered by the system. On the other hand, it is unlikely that individuals will be given substantially more say over uses of their health data; at best, they may be better informed about who will have access to their data and for what purposes. The development of the new health care information network and the standards associated with it should be a matter of considerable interest to human rights advocates over the next few years.

After declining to approve earlier versions of welfare reform passed by the Congress, President Clinton signed the Personal Responsibility and Work Opportunity Reconciliation Act of 1996 on August 22, 1996. The effects of this welfare reform legislation on the U.S. health care system are less direct than those of the health insurance legislation, but are nevertheless likely to be substantial.

The legislation is complex, with implications for several welfare programs. The open-ended federal entitlement program of Aid to Families with Dependent Children (AFDC) is eliminated and will be replaced by a new program, Temporary Assistance for Needy Families (TANF), that provides block grants for states to offer temporary cash assistance. Considerable emphasis is given to work requirements and job training. Eligibility of legal and illegal immigrants for income-tested welfare assistance is severely curtailed. States will be given greater authority to establish eligibility requirements and benefits. Although initially proposed as part of welfare reform, comprehensive reform of the Medicaid program was not included in the 1996 legislation. However, changes in eligibility requirements for Medicaid, especially for legal and illegal immigrants, are likely to reduce the number of persons relying on Medicaid as their primary source of health care.

Looking at the cumulative affect of the complex provisions of the welfare legislation, it does not seem unreasonable to predict that they will lead to an increase in the number of persons lacking access to adequate basic health care, either through government programs like Medicare and Medicaid or through employment-related health insurance. This prospect underlines the need for special efforts to collect accurate and timely information to monitor the effects of both the health insurance and welfare legislation on access to basic health care, both in general terms and as it affects the most vulnerable groups of the population.

Some relevant efforts are, in fact, underway. The Census Bureau, in consultation and with support from the Departments of Health and Human Services and Agriculture, has initiated a Survey of Program Dynamics, in which a national sample of families from 1992 and 1993 Panels of the Survey of Income and Program Participation will be interviewed annually from 1997 through 2001.[2] A private organization, the Center for the Study of Health System Change, has launched a Community Tracking Study in 60 sample communities to track changes in the health care system and the effects of these changes on individuals and families.[3] These and other new initiatives will supplement existing sources of information such as national surveys, mortality records, and patient records that have been discussed in the papers in the section on Monitoring Underserved and Excluded Populations. However, for reasons that have been described in those papers, each of these sources of information has limitations associated with population coverage, sample size, and other factors. Data from national surveys may not be adequate by themselves to track the effects of the state variations in eligibility requirements and benefits that are now permitted.

In summary, the health insurance and welfare reform legislation passed in 1996 has significant implications for the establishment of health care information systems that are consistent with the human rights norms of universality, privacy, nondiscrimination, and consent. Nevertheless, if we look at the basic conclusions presented in our final chapter, we find that they are not greatly affected. With the implementation of welfare reform, there will be a greater need than ever to identify the groups that are most at risk and devote increased resources to obtaining good monitoring data for those groups. The computerization and standardization of individual health records mandated by Kennedy-Kassebaum may improve the value of these records for monitoring, provided that new legislation or a set of security standards established under the Act does not impose undue restric-

2. D. Weinberg, "A Survey of Program Dynamics for Addressing Welfare Reform," U.S. Bureau of the Census, October 28, 1996.
3. P. Kemper et al., "The Design of the Community Tracking Study: A Longitudinal Study of Health System Change and Its Effects on People," *Inquiry* 33 (Summer 1996): 195-206.

tions on such use of the data. At the same time, the Act's requirement for creating a national computerized database underscores and increases the urgency of the need for legislation governing the use of health care records in the private sector. Such legislation must ensure that the records in the system cannot be used to discriminate against individuals and that individuals are fully informed about and have a reasonable degree of control over the uses that will be made of information about them.

The people of the United States have expressed their dissatisfactions with the existing health care and welfare systems and their representatives have responded by embarking on a course of fundamental reforms. This is clearly a time for people who subscribe to human rights principles to pay close attention to the extent to which proposed reforms are being guided by those principles. We hope that our findings and conclusions will help them to do this.

Staff and Advisory Committee of the AAAS Project on Developing a National Health Information System Consistent with Human Rights Criteria

Staff

Audrey R. Chapman, Ph.D. Project Director, and Director, Science and Human Rights Program, American Association for the Advancement of Science

Advisory Committee

Sheri Alpert, M.A., M.P.A., and Ph.D. candidate at George Mason University. Privacy Policy Analyst, Washington, D.C.

Mary Ann Baily, Ph.D. Adjunct Associate Professor of Economics and Public Policy, George Washington University

Paula Bruening, J.D. Information Policy Consultant, formerly Senior Analyst, Office of Technology Assessment

Floyd J. Fowler, Jr., Ph.D. Senior Research Fellow, Center for Survey Research, University of Massachusetts Boston

B. Thomas Jabine, M.S. Statistical Consultant, Washington, D.C.

Barbara Kurtzig, M.A. Associate Director, National Association of Health Data Organizations (NAHDO)

Katie Maslow, M.S.W. Consultant, formerly Senior Associate, Office of Technology Assessment

Janet O'Keeffe, Dr.P.H. Senior Policy Analyst, American Association of Retired Persons, Public Policy Institute

Elsie Pamuk, Ph.D. Health Statistician, Office of Analysis and Epidemiology, National Center for Health Statistics, Centers for Disease Control and Prevention

Douglas A. Samuelson, D.Sc. President of InfoLogix Inc., a statistical and analytical consulting firm in Annandale, VA

Marian Gray Secundy, Ph.D. Professor, College of Medicine, Department of Community Health and Family Practice, Howard University, President's Health Reform Task Force

Ronald W. Wilson. Special Assistant, NCHS HIV Liaison, Office of Analysis, Epidemiology, and Health Promotion, The National Center for Health Statistics

Contributing Authors

R. Clifton Bailey, Ph.D., Statistician, McLean, VA.

Mary Ann Baily, Ph.D., Adjunct Associate Professor of Economics, Department of Economics, The George Washington University.

Bernd Beier, J.D., M.D., Adjunct Professor, Medical Computer Law, Faculty of Medicine, Goethe University.

Trude Bennett, M.S.W., Dr.P.H., Assistant Professor, Department of Maternal and Child Health, School of Public Health, The University of North Carolina at Chapel Hill.

Charlyn D. Black, M.D., Sc.D., Assistant Professor, Manitoba Centre for Health Policy and Evaluation, Department of Community Health Sciences, University of Manitoba, Winnipeg, Manitoba.

James F. Blanchard, M.D., M.Sc., Provincial Epidemiologist, Manitoba Health, and Assistant Professor, Department of Community Health Sciences, Faculty of Medicine, University of Manitoba.

Bogdan Bogdanovic, B.Comm., B.A., Programmer Analyst, Manitoba Centre for Health Policy and Evaluation, Department of Community Health Sciences, University of Manitoba, Winnipeg, Manitoba.

Vincent M. Brannigan, J.D., Professor, College of Engineering, University of Maryland at College Park.

Paula J. Bruening, J.D., Information Policy Consultant, formerly Senior Analyst, Office of Technology Assessment.

Charles A. Burchill, B.Sc., M.Sc., Programmer Analyst, Manitoba Centre for Health Policy and Evaluation, Department of Community Health Sciences, University of Manitoba, Winnipeg, Manitoba.

Keumhee C. Carriere, Ph.D., Associate Professor, Department of Mathematical Sciences, University of Alberta, Edmonton, Alberta.

Audrey R. Chapman, Ph.D., Program Director, Science and Human Rights Program, American Association for the Advancement of Science.

Marsha M. Cohen, M.D., FRCPC, Health Scholar, Clinical Epidemiology Unit, Sunnybrook Health Sciences Centre, North York, Ontario.

Kathleen Decker, MHSA, Researcher, Manitoba Centre for Health Policy and Evaluation, Department of Community Health Sciences, University of Manitoba, Winnipeg, Manitoba.

Carolyn DeCoster, RN, M.B.A., Researcher, Manitoba Centre for Health Policy and Evaluation, Department of Community Health Sciences, University of Manitoba, Winnipeg, Manitoba.

George T. Duncan, Ph.D., Professor of Statistics, H. John Heinz III School of Public Policy Management, Carnegie Mellon University.

David S. Fedson, M.D., Director, Medical Affairs, Pasteur Merieux MSD.

James Fisher, Ph.D., Assistant Professor, School of Medicine and Research Director, Enhanced Treatment Project, Wright State University.

Norman Frohlich, Ph.D., Professor, Faculty of Management, University of Manitoba, Winnipeg, Manitoba.

Floyd J. Fowler, Jr., Ph.D., Senior Research Fellow, Center for Survey Research, University of Massachusetts-Boston.

Martha Holliday, M.P.H., Project Director, Hanford Tribal Service Program, and former Project Director, Health Statistics Project, Northwest Portland Area Indian Health Board.

Thomas B. Jabine, M.S., Statistical Consultant, Washington, D.C.

Lawrence R. Jacobs, Ph.D., Associate Professor, Department of Political Science, University of Minnesota.

Barbara S. Kurtzig, M.A., Associate Director, National Association of Health Data Organizations (NAHDO).

Leonard MacWilliam, M.Sc., MRNM, Senior Programmer, Manitoba Centre for Health Policy and Evaluation, Department of Community Health Sciences, University of Manitoba, Winnipeg, Manitoba.

Cameron A. Mustard, Sc.D., Associate Professor, Manitoba Centre for Health Policy and Evaluation, Department of Community Health Sciences, University of Manitoba, Winnipeg, Manitoba.

Janice D. Roberts, M.B., Ph.D., Associate Professor, Department of Community Health Sciences, Faculty of Medicine, University of Manitoba.

Noralou P. Roos, Ph.D., Director, Professor, and Career Scientist, Manitoba Centre for Health Policy and Evaluation, Department of Community Health Sciences, University of Manitoba, Winnipeg, Manitoba, and Associate, Canadian Institute for Advanced Research.

Leslie L. Roos, Ph.D., Professor and Career Scientist, Manitoba Centre for Health Policy and Evaluation, Department of Community Health Sciences, Faculty of Medicine, University of Manitoba, and Associate, Canadian Institute for Advanced Research.

Andrew Ross, M.S., former Director, Hanford Tribal Service Program, and former Assistant, Health Statistics Project, Northwest Portland Area Indian Health Board.

Douglas A. Samuelson, D.Sc., President of InfoLogix Inc., a statistical and analytical consulting firm in Annandale, VA.

Fritz Scheuren, Ph.D., Visiting Professor, Department of Statistics, George Washington University.

Robert Ellis Smith, J.D., Publisher of *Privacy Journal,* and Attorney, Providence, Rhode Island.

Eleanor Singer, Ph.D., Research Scientist, Survey Research Center, Institute for Social Research, and Adjunct Professor, Sociology, University of Michigan at Ann Arbor.

Robert Y. Shapiro, Ph.D., Professor, Department of Political Science and Associate Director, Center for the Social Sciences, Columbia University.

Jonathan R. Sugarman, M.D., M.P.H., Medical Director, Health Care Quality Improvement, PRO-WEST, Seattle.

Douglas J. Tataryn, Ph.D., Researcher, Faculty of Nursing, University of Manitoba, Winnipeg, Manitoba.

Fred Toll, Researcher, Manitoba Centre for Health Policy and Evaluation, Department of Community Health Sciences, University of Manitoba, Winnipeg, Manitoba.

Joseph Wagner, M.P.H., Instructor, School of Medicine and Research Associate, Enhanced Treatment Project, Wright State University.

Jichuan Wang, Ph.D., Assistant Professor, School of Medicine, and Research Director, AIDS Intervention Project, Wright State University.

Doni Wilder, Executive Director, Northwest Portland Area Indian Health Board.

Index